ÁLVAR NÚÑEZ CABEZA DE VACA

ÁLVAR NÚÑEZ
CABEZA DE VACA
American Trailblazer

ROBIN VARNUM

University of Oklahoma Press : Norman

Library of Congress Cataloging-in-Publication Data

Varnum, Robin, 1950–

  Álvar Núñez Cabeza de Vaca : American trailblazer / by Robin
  Varnum.

    pages cm.
  Includes bibliographical references and index.
  ISBN 978-0-8061-4497-9 (hardcover) ISBN 978-0-8061-6899-9 (paper) 1.
Núñez Cabeza de Vaca, Álvar, active 16th century. 2. Explorers—America—
Biography. 3. Explorers—Spain—Biography. 4. America—Discovery and
exploration—Spanish. I. Title.
  E125.N9V37 2014

  970.1'6092—dc23
  [B]
                           2014007121

The paper in this book meets the guidelines for permanence and durability of the
Committee on Production Guidelines for Book Longevity of the Council on Library
Resources, Inc. ∞

For Juris,
el querido compañero de mi vida

Contents

Illustrations

⌒

FIGURES

MAPS

Preface

~

I cannot claim that recorded U.S. history begins with Álvar Núñez Cabeza de Vaca, but it very nearly does. In 1528, more than ninety years before the *Mayflower* Pilgrims disembarked at Plymouth Rock, Cabeza de Vaca landed on the Florida Peninsula and made his way around the rim of the Gulf of Mexico to Texas. Only a few other European explorers, beginning with Juan Ponce de León in 1513, had previously visited the land that would become the United States, and none had made more than brief forays into its interior. In 1523, Giovanni Verrazano penned the earliest written description of the land's native people.[1] But Cabeza de Vaca spent eight years within the present U.S. borders and wrote extensively about the native people he encountered.

The explorer's significance is not limited to North America. He went on to play an influential role in the European colonization of South America. From 1540 until 1545, he served as governor of the Spanish province of Río de la Plata in what is now Paraguay. He was a trailblazer because he opened roads and because he endeavored to set a moral course for others to follow. By the standards of his day, both his voyages to the Americas ended in failure. But in our own multicultural world, his successes at brokering agreements and accommodating people of different races and cultures seem exemplary.

Almost five hundred years have gone by since Cabeza de Vaca came to the New World, but anyone who follows in his footsteps today will see that he is honored on three continents. In Jerez de la Frontera, his birthplace in southwestern Spain, a bronze statue of Cabeza de Vaca stands at the center of an ornamental fountain immediately outside the defensive wall that once encircled the town. Dated 1991, the statue is signed by its artist—Eladio Gil Zambrana. It portrays Cabeza de Vaca as long-haired, bearded, and naked except for a helmet (see the photograph in chapter 6). He has a shield slung over one shoulder, and he carries a battle-ax and three ears of Indian corn. Behind the bronze statue is a more stylized, cast-concrete sculpture representing eight New World Indians. In Hermann Park in Houston, Texas, a bronze bust of Cabeza de Vaca that Pilar Cortella de Rubín sculpted and cast in 1986 is on display; it was presented to the city of Houston by King Juan Carlos of Spain. The bust represents the explorer as a curly-haired, bushy-browed conquistador in a morion helmet (see the photograph in chapter 3). In the Mexican state of Chihuahua, both a statue in Ciudad Juárez and a mural in Ojinaga show Cabeza de Vaca as a nearly naked man holding a cross. In Puerto Iguazú, Argentina, an eight-panel set of murals in polychrome plaster relief, completed in 2005 by Daniela Almeida and Hector Kura, memorializes key events in Cabeza de Vaca's life. Among the panels, one depicts Cabeza de Vaca pointing the way to the Iguazú Falls, and another shows him defending the Indians of South America against Spanish injustice (see the photographs in chapters 12 and 13).

Well before he journeyed to South America, Cabeza de Vaca had come to see the native people of the New World as human beings, not savages. He opposed enslaving Indians, and because he knew that under existing Spanish law Indians could be enslaved for practicing idolatry or human sacrifice, he swore that during all his years in North America, he had seen no instances of either abomination. He had the temerity to advise Emperor Charles V, who was both king of Spain and head of the Holy Roman Empire, that with respect to the Indians, "it is clearly seen that all these peoples, to be drawn to become Christians and to obedience to the Imperial Majesty, must be given good treatment."[2] As governor of Río de la Plata, Cabeza de Vaca supported the colonialist enterprise but strove to protect the indigenous people of his province. He had a vision of a colonial society in which Spaniards and Indians, while not equals, would support one another and work together cooperatively for their mutual benefit. He decreed that the Spaniards of his province were to pay the Indians for their labor, were not to treat them as slaves, and were not to take their property or their children or women by force. However, the governor was pulled in different directions. To help the Indians, he had to work with his countrymen and within the established Spanish power structure. His compatriots resented the restrictions he imposed, and sometimes Cabeza de Vaca had to make unpalatable compromises. Ultimately he lost control of his province, and many of his mandates concerning the just treatment of Indians were overturned.

Cabeza de Vaca wrote two major reports concerning his career in the Indies. The first was his *Relación* (or *Report*) on his experiences in North America, and the second was his *Relación general* on his tenure as governor of Río de la Plata. He published the *Relación* in Spain in 1542 and republished it in 1555. He never published the *Relación general*, but on 7 December 1545, he presented it to the *señores* of the Royal Council of the Indies.

Two other sixteenth-century historians played a major role in preserving Cabeza de Vaca's story. One of these, Pero Hernández, was Cabeza de Vaca's secretary in Río de la Plata. The other, Gonzalo Fernández de Oviedo y Valdés (known conventionally as Oviedo), was the royal historian of the Indies. In 1555, Hernandez published the *Comentarios* to memorialize Cabeza de Vaca's South American governorship. Hernández also wrote the *Relación de las cosas sucedidas en el Río de la Plata*, which he never published. Oviedo preserved accounts of Cabeza de Vaca's experiences in both North and South America and included them in books 35 and 23, respectively, of his mammoth *Historia general y natural de las Indias*. I have used English translations of these primary sources where they are available.[3] But I have necessarily read other primary sources in Spanish. All translations from Cabeza de Vaca's *Relación general*, from Hernández's *Relación de las cosas sucedidas en el Río de la Plata*, and from book 23 of Oviedo's *Historia general* are my own.

I am deeply indebted to Rolena Adorno and Patrick Charles Pautz for their three-volume study, *Álvar Núñez Cabeza de Vaca: His Account, His Life, and the Expedition of Pánfilo de Narváez* (1999), and for their translation of Cabeza de Vaca's *Relación*. I am indebted also to David Howard for his *Conquistador in Chains* (1997), a closely researched history of Cabeza de Vaca's years in Río de la Plata. In addition, I owe much to Morris Bishop for *The Odyssey of Cabeza de Vaca* (1933) and to Manuel Serrano y Sanz for his estimable 1906 edition of sixteenth-century documents by or concerning the explorer.

The sixteenth-century narratives I have used are groundbreaking historical texts, but reading them today can be frustrating. Cabeza de Vaca and other early chroniclers do not tell today's readers everything we want to know. Cabeza de Vaca often had difficulty communicating with the native people he encountered. He had only a vague idea of where he was as he moved across North America, so although he describes bays, rivers, and mountains, it is not clear which bays, rivers, and mountains he saw, and it is difficult to plot his peregrinations on a map. Modern readers cannot use earlier historic documents to clarify the information Cabeza de Vaca provides, because there are none. Readers can turn only to subsequent historic documents, such as those produced by the De Soto and Coronado expeditions, or to the archaeological record. Scholars face similar difficulties when they attempt to trace Cabeza de Vaca's movements in South America.

I have endeavored to write what anthropologist Charles Hudson calls a braided narrative.[4] I have woven strands of information from my sixteenth-century sources with strands from recent scholarship and from archaeological investigation. Sometimes I have attempted to look at events as they unfolded before Cabeza de Vaca's eyes. At other times I have looked through twenty-first-century lenses at those broader movements of history in which the explorer participated.

I have examined several interpretations, especially in my notes, of Cabeza de Vaca's route across North America.[5] I accept the conclusions of Donald E. Chipman, Alex D. Krieger, T. N. Campbell and T. J. Campbell, Andrés Reséndez, Rolena Adorno and Patrick Charles Pautz, and others who argue that a substantial portion of Cabeza de Vaca's overland journey from southern Texas to Sinaloa was on the Mexican side of the present international border.

As to proper names, I have generally used the forms most widely recognized in the United States today. I have referred to Álvar Núñez Cabeza de Vaca by his second surname rather than by Núñez. I use "Coronado" for Francisco Vázquez de Coronado y Luxán, and "Oviedo" for Gonzalo Fernández de Oviedo y Valdés. Following common American usage, I speak of Hernando de Soto as De Soto, and of Bartolomé de las Casas as Las Casas. I have used "Christopher Columbus" in place of either the Italian "Cristoforo Colombo" or the Spanish "Cristóbal Colón," though I have referred to the admiral's son as Diego Colón. I speak of King Ferdinand rather than Fernando el Católico, and I refer to the Aztec emperor as Montezuma rather than Moctezuma or Motecuhzoma. Geographic names that bear an accent in Spanish but appear commonly in English without them, such as "Rio Grande" and "Peru," appear in my text with no accent.

I have not hesitated to use the term "Indians," which is a direct translation of *indios*, the Spanish word Cabeza de Vaca employs. And like Cabeza de Vaca and his contemporaries, I sometimes refer to groups of Spaniards and their co-religionists as Christians. The term can handily refer to Portuguese, Italians, Flemings, and a Christian slave from Morocco as well as to Spaniards. In Cabeza de Vaca's lifetime, moreover, men from Castile and men from Aragón did not necessarily view one another as compatriots, but they found common ground as Christians.

Acknowledgments

This book would never have seen the light of day without the help of many people who generously shared their time and insights with me. I am grateful for the support and assistance of the staff at the University of Oklahoma Press. Acquisitions editor Alessandra Jacobi Tamulevich has been a stalwart advocate. I thank manuscript editor Steven Baker, freelance copy editor Rosemary Wetherold, and freelance cartographer Carol Zuber-Mallison. The book has benefited enormously from the detailed comments of the two reviewers, José B. Fernández of the University of Central Florida and John F. Schwaller of the State University of New York, who read the manuscript for the Press.

I owe special thanks to Professor Barry O'Connell of Amherst College, who—by proposing and organizing the Different People, Different Places Program in the 1990s for the Massachusetts Foundation for the Humanities—first introduced me to Cabeza de Vaca.

I also thank those of my colleagues and friends who read portions of the manuscript. Among my colleagues, I am especially grateful to Josette Henschel, Thomas Maulucci, John Rogers, Fred Sard, Julie Walsh, and Art Wilkins. Among my friends, I thank Robin Dizard, Peter Elbow, Christina Gibbons, Sherrill Harbison, Camilla Humphreys, Ruth Owen Jones, Tom Leamon, and Lion G. Miles. My colleagues Arthur Natella and David Douglas and my student Kathyria Beltrán Rosario helped me with the Spanish language. Lisa Edwards of the University of Massachusetts at Lowell helped me understand the *encomienda* system.

I am deeply indebted to President Vincent Maniaci and the Board of Trustees of American International College for granting me a sabbatical in 2010–11 in which to complete drafting the book. I thank my colleagues Bruce Johnson and Lori Paige for minding the store while I was away. I am grateful also to Dean Vickie Hess and to Interim Dean Susanne Swanker for help and encouragement. I thank the staff, past and present, of AIC's James J. Shea Memorial Library—especially Gilana Chelimsky, Devon McArdle, Katherine Richter, Amy Schack, and Heidi Spencer—for their invaluable assistance.

I cannot even begin to express my gratitude to my family for their unflagging love and support. To Juris, Sofija, Marija, Ryan, Charlie, Mother, Terry, Dad, Ratana, Jill, and Elizabeth Anne, I can only say I will forever kiss your hands and feet. I am especially grateful to my husband, Juris Zagarins, for traveling with me to Spain, Florida, Texas, and Paraguay, for cheerfully providing technological assistance, and for taking many of the photographs that grace this book.

ÁLVAR NÚÑEZ CABEZA DE VACA

ONE

Jerez de la Frontera

At the time of Cabeza de Vaca's birth, Spain had not yet come together as a nation, and the kingdoms of Castile and Aragón were culturally and politically distinct. Cabeza de Vaca's native Castile was larger than Aragón and had an Atlantic orientation. Its economy was based on herding and on warfare against Muslim infidels. Aragón, by contrast, had a Mediterranean orientation and a mercantile economy. Despite these disunities, the country that would become Spain was, in 1492, at the center of three world-shaping events. The first occurred on January 2, when the last Moorish king of Granada surrendered his kingdom to Isabel of Castile and Ferdinand of Aragón, thus concluding the Reconquista. Jubilant Christians raised a cross that morning and flew the banners of their king and queen from the highest tower in Granada's fabled Alhambra Palace. The second event occurred in March, when Isabel and Ferdinand signed an edict requiring all Jews in their jurisdiction either to accept baptism or to leave their realms. Then, on April 17, the queen and king listened favorably to the proposals of a Genoese explorer they previously had rebuffed. Their victory in Granada had freed up their resources and made it possible for them to invest in westward expansion. The Ottoman Turks in the eastern Mediterranean were blocking Christian access to Asia, so Christopher Columbus's idea of sailing westward to reach India, China, and Japan seemed attractive. Another factor that swayed the queen and king was that the rival kingdom of Portugal was aggressively exploring the African coast and establishing

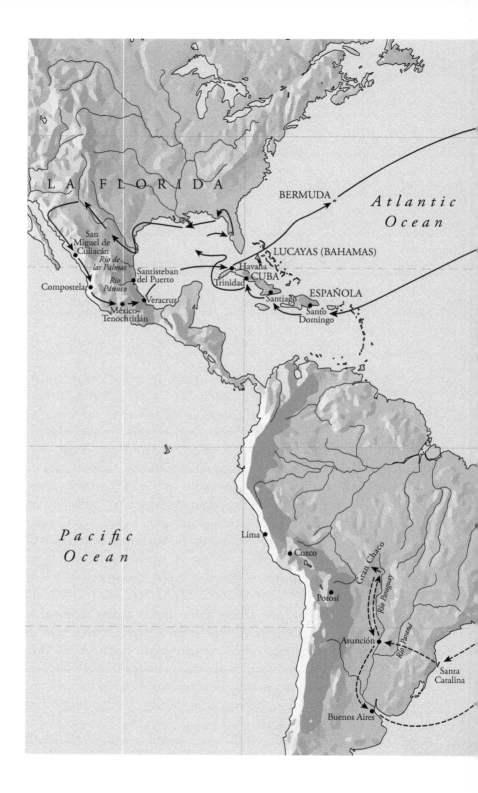

LA FLORIDA

San Miguel de Culiacán

Río de las Palmas

Santisteban del Puerto

Río Pánuco

Compostela

Veracruz

México-Tenochtitlán

BERMUDA

Atlantic Ocean

LUCAYAS (BAHAMAS)

Havana

CUBA

Trinidad

Santiago

ESPAÑOLA

Santo Domingo

Pacific Ocean

Lima

Cuzco

Gran Chaco

Río Paraguay

Potosí

Asunción

Río Paraná

Santa Catalina

Buenos Aires

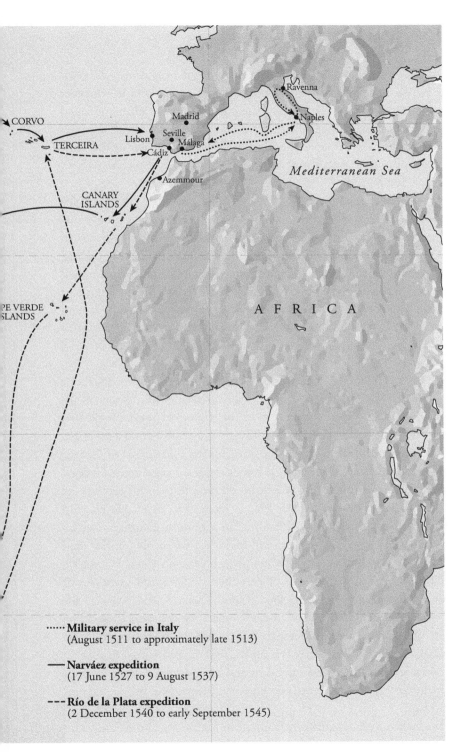

CORVO

TERCEIRA

Lisbon
Madrid
Seville
Cádiz
Málaga

Azemmour

CANARY
ISLANDS

PE VERDE
SLANDS

Ravenna
Naples

Mediterranean Sea

A F R I C A

······ **Military service in Italy**
(August 1511 to approximately late 1513)

——— **Narváez expedition**
(17 June 1527 to 9 August 1537)

- - - **Río de la Plata expedition**
(2 December 1540 to early September 1545)

Travels of Álvar Núñez Cabeza de Vaca, 1511–1545. Copyright © 2014 by the
University of Oklahoma Press.

trading monopolies there. Isabel and Ferdinand signed a contract with Columbus, both authorizing his voyage and staking a royal claim to whatever territory he might discover. Ironically, the day on which Columbus sailed off in search of China, 2 August 1492, was also the day on which the Jews were compelled to leave Spain. The third world-shaping event of that momentous year occurred on October 12, when Columbus made landfall on the island of San Salvador.[1]

For those Christians who took part in the Reconquista, the most glorious event of 1492 was their victory in what they viewed as a holy war against Islam. But for their sons and grandsons, the most significant of the year's events would prove to be the Columbus landfall. Men of Cabeza de Vaca's generation, fueled by the same crusading zeal that had sustained the Reconquista, would follow Columbus to the New World and claim it for Spain and for Christ. As the historian Francisco López de Gómara observed in 1552, "the conquests of the Indians commenced once that of the Moors was completed so that the Spaniards would always be warring against infidels."[2]

Álvar Núñez Cabeza de Vaca must have grown up hearing stories about how the Moors from Islamic North Africa had invaded his homeland in 711 and how, over the ensuing centuries, Christians had gradually pushed them back toward Africa. The boy's father and grandfather and a long line of his ancestors had participated in the Reconquista. No record of Cabeza de Vaca's birth has been discovered, but judging from statements on legal documents filed after the deaths of first his father and then his mother, he cannot have been born earlier than 1485 or later than 1492. He was old enough when his father died in 1506 not to require a guardian, but he was not yet twenty-five (the age of legal majority) when his mother died in 1509. At the very end of the *Relación* he published in 1542, Cabeza de Vaca identifies himself as the "son of Francisco de Vera and grandson of Pedro de Vera, the one who conquered [Gran] Canaria" and says that his mother "was named Doña Teresa Cabeza de Vaca." In the same context, he identifies himself as "a native of Jerez de la Frontera," a fortified town in the province of Andalusia. His father was an hidalgo, or gentleman belonging to the lowest level of the Spanish nobility, and his mother was the daughter of an hidalgo. Álvar Núñez Cabeza de Vaca was his parents' third child and their first son.[3]

The boy's name came exclusively from his mother's side of the family and was given in honor of her wealthy uncle and her great-grandfather, both of whom had also borne the name "Álvar Núñez Cabeza de Vaca." Of his two surnames, the future explorer favored "Cabeza de Vaca" over "Núñez." His favored surname was a distinguished one and appears in the chronicles of Castile from the thirteenth century onward. "Cabeza de Vaca" means "head of a cow," and the three words form a unit that should not be shortened or subdivided.[4]

In the thirteenth century, according to a legend that may be apocryphal, a shepherd named Martín Alhaja directed an army of Christians under King Alfonso VIII of Castile to a mountain pass in the Sierra Morena so that they might surprise an army of Moors on the other side. Alhaja marked the entrance to the pass with a cow's skull mounted on a stake. The Christians crossed the pass and, on 16 July 1212, won a decisive victory in the battle of Las Navas de Tolosa. Shortly thereafter, King Alfonso knighted Martín Alhaja and bestowed the honorific name of "Cabeza de Vaca" upon him. Most of the major cities of Andalusia fell to the Christians within the next few decades. Seville was liberated from the Moors in 1248, and Jerez de la Frontera was liberated in 1255. The name of Cabeza de Vaca's hometown derives, in part, from its strategic location on the frontier between Christian and Moorish territories.[5]

Jerez de la Frontera stands at the edge of an escarpment overlooking Spain's southern Atlantic coast. It is an ancient city and was colonized by the Phoenicians and by the Romans long before it came under the control of the Moors. The Phoenicians introduced viniculture and winemaking to the region, and Jerez has been known ever since for its wine. Today it is known particularly for its sherry. Cabeza de Vaca's hometown is roughly equidistant from the Atlantic seaports of Sanlúcar de Barrameda and Cádiz, and approximately fifty miles southwest of Seville. Jerez is also south of Andalusia's major river, the Guadalquivir, which runs through Córdoba and Seville and reaches the Atlantic at Sanlúcar de Barrameda. During the years the Moors controlled Jerez, they fortified it with a 2.5-mile encircling wall and an *alcázar*, or fortress. When Christians recaptured the town, they took over these fortifications and converted the existing mosques to churches. Jerez still boasts of its rich heritage of Mudéjar (or Moorish-style) churches.[6]

In 1477, when Queen Isabel and King Ferdinand made an official visit to Jerez de la Frontera, Cabeza de Vaca's father, Francisco de Vera, was one of the hidalgos given the honor of carrying the royal canopy. At the time of Cabeza de Vaca's birth, his father was serving on Jerez's municipal council.

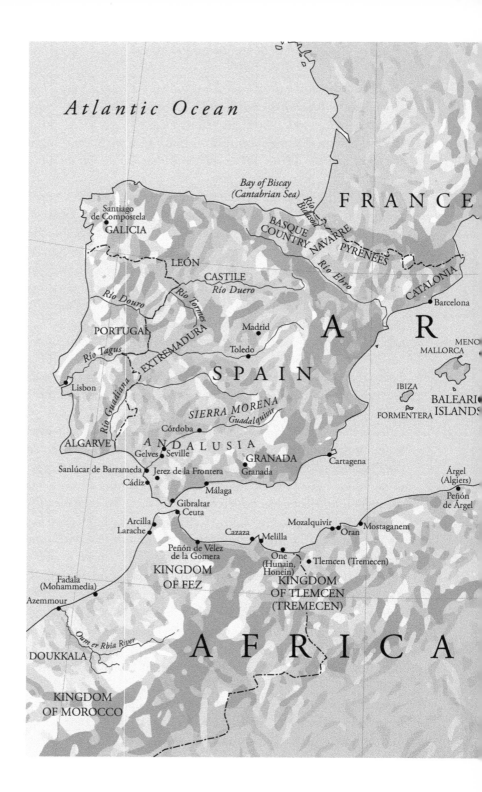

Atlantic Ocean

*Bay of Biscay
(Cantabrian Sea)*

FRANCE

Santiago
de Compostela
GALICIA

BASQUE
COUNTRY NAVARRE
Río Bidasoa
PYRENEES
Río Ebro
CATALONIA

LEÓN

CASTILE
Río Duero

Barcelona

Río Douro
Río Tormes

A   R

PORTUGAL

Madrid

MENO
MALLORCA

Río Tagus
EXTREMADURA

Toledo

SPAIN

IBIZA

BALEARI
FORMENTERA ISLANDS

Lisbon

Río Guadiana

SIERRA MORENA
Guadalquivir

ALGARVE

Córdoba

ANDALUSIA
Gelves Seville

GRANADA

Cartagena

Sanlúcar de Barrameda Jerez de la Frontera Granada
Cádiz

Árgel
(Algiers)

Málaga

Peñón
de Árgel

Gibraltar
Ceuta

Arcilla
Larache

Cazaza

Mozalquivir
Mostaganem
Oran

Melilla

Peñón de Vélez
de la Gomera

KINGDOM
OF FEZ

One
(Hunain,
Honein)

Tlemcen (Tremecen)

KINGDOM
OF TLEMCEN
(TREMECEN)

Fadala
(Mohammedia)

Azemmour

Oum er Rbia River

AFRICA

DOUKKALA

KINGDOM
OF MOROCCO

Milan

Venice

Pavia

LOMBARDY

Ferrara

Genoa

Bologna

Ravenna

Pisa

*Adriatic
Sea*

CORSICA

Rome

Gaeta

Naples

G

SARDINIA

O

N

*Mediterranean
Sea*

Messina

SICILY

La Goleta
(La Goulette)

Tunis

Gulf of Gabes

Djerba (Los Gelves)

Tripoli

CANARY ISLANDS

LANZAROTE

A PALMA

TENERIFE

GOMERA

FUERTEVENTURA

IERRO

GRAN
CANARIA

CAPE
OF
AGUER

AZORES

Atlantic Ocean

CANARY
ISLANDS

Madrid

Lisbon

Seville

Azemmour

AFRICA

Spain, Italy, and northern Africa. Copyright © 2014 by the University of Oklahoma Press.

Cabeza de Vaca was proud of his lineage, and many years later when he sailed for South America, he took a copy of his family genealogy with him. His grandfather Pedro de Vera was a purveyor of supplies to the royal army during the final phase of the Reconquista. At various times, Pedro de Vera served as *alcalde* (municipal judge) in the communities of Jimena, Arcos, and Cádiz. While in Jimena, Vera ran so short of wheat that he found it necessary to borrow some from the Muslim lord of Málaga. To secure the loan, he had to leave Francisco and another of his sons as hostages. Later, Vera led successful plundering raids on the North African cities of Fadala and Larache and brought booty and slaves back to Castile. Vera seems to have assumed, like most hidalgos of his generation, that victors were entitled to enslave the vanquished.[7]

By custom, Queen Isabel, acting either alone or in concert with her husband, signed contracts, or *capitulaciones*, with enterprising hidalgos like Pedro de Vera who undertook to lead military actions against infidels in Iberia and North Africa. Such contracts authorized the action and, in the event of victory, both guaranteed certain rewards to the commander and secured ultimate authority in the conquered territory to the royal crown. The *capitulaciones* provided Isabel with an orderly means of extending her power, and she subsequently made similar contracts with the men who undertook, in her name, to conquer the Canary Islands and the Americas. From a commander's point of view, the *capitulaciones* served as a reasonable guarantee that he would be compensated for his expenses, rewarded for his services, and granted title to the spoils of his victory.[8]

However, according to a testimonial filed by Álvar Núñez Cabeza de Vaca in 1537, his grandfather was disappointed in his expectations of compensation for the services he had performed for his queen. Pedro de Vera had contracted with the queen, not only to lead the raids on the North African cities, but also to conquer Gran Canaria, one of the major islands in the Canaries. According to his grandson, Vera conquered the island at his own expense, selling part of his land to finance the undertaking. He was subsequently appointed military governor of Gran Canaria, but he received no other compensation from his queen. When he died, Vera had relatively little to leave to his heirs.[9]

The Canary Islands were the first of many prizes taken by Castile in its expansion westward. Europeans had discovered the Canaries early in the fourteenth century, and for a time they were claimed by both Portugal and Castile. The islands were inhabited by the Guanches, an agricultural people who had been living there for thousands of years. Spanish Christians saw the Guanches as idolaters, and although fighting with idolaters who were ignorant of Christianity was different from fighting with Muslims who willfully rejected Christ, the Spaniards persuaded themselves that their war against the Guanches was no less just than their war against the Moors. The war in the Canaries was integral therefore to the evolution of Spanish thinking about what constituted a just war, and it would pave the way for later wars against the idolatrous Indians of the New World. The Canary Islands would also prove useful as a staging base for Spanish expeditions to the Americas.[10]

It took Pedro de Vera six years to subdue Gran Canaria. He built a fortress on the coast at Gáldar, but the Guanches retreated to the island's high peaks, which were inaccessible to the Spaniards' horses. Vera led his forces on foot into the mountains and, after killing the Guanche chief in hand-to-hand combat, succeeded in defeating the indigenous warriors. In reprisal for the deaths of Spaniards, Vera burned many captive Guanches at the stake and forced the others to accept Christianity. Then, although Queen Isabel had banned the enslaving of Christian converts, and although she wished to protect the Canary islanders, Vera sent 240 baptized Guanches to Spain to be sold as slaves. No doubt this was his way, in default of compensation from the queen, of financing his war of conquest. After his victory in Gran Canaria, Vera participated in the conquests of the neighboring islands of Tenerife and Gomera. In 1488, when the Guanches of Gomera killed their Spanish governor, Vera quelled the uprising, slaughtered all the indigenous males over the age of fifteen, and sold their women and children into slavery. For this, he incurred the censure of the Catholic Church, a substantial financial liability, and a recall to Castile. Vera defended his treatment of the Guanches on the grounds that they "were not Christian but the children of infidels and traitors who had murdered their lord." Slaves from the Canary Islands served in Vera's household in Jerez de la Frontera and perhaps in the household in which his grandson, Álvar Núñez Cabeza de Vaca, was growing up.[11]

Throughout his life, Cabeza de Vaca seems to have admired his grandfather very much. In 1541, when he took formal possession of a territory in what is now Brazil, Cabeza de Vaca named the area "the province of Vera" in his grandfather's honor. Judging from what little is now known about Pedro de Vera, it is hard to see what his grandson found to admire. And yet the older man clearly was brave and resourceful. He was described by his contemporaries as "expert in battles on sea as on land" and "very Christian." And even though he was recalled to Castile for overstepping his authority, Vera had won glory in Gran Canaria and captured a valuable territorial prize. There can be little question but that Cabeza de Vaca aspired to follow his grandfather's career path as a conquistador and a colonial governor.[12]

If, as is reasonable to assume, Cabeza de Vaca in his youth was much like other young Castilian men of his class and generation, he was jealous of his honor and motivated by ambition, the desire to get rich, and the hope of measuring up to his ancestors. He must have wished to serve God and his queen, and must have seen himself as the queen's vassal. In Castile's hierarchical social organization, Queen Isabel sat at the head, with a small number of titled nobles below her, and a larger number of *caballeros* (knights) and hidalgos below them. The peasants, who constituted some 80 percent of the Castilian population, rented the land they worked and paid seigneurial dues to their overlords. The titled nobles were vassals to the queen, owned 97 percent of the land in her kingdom, operated as regional warlords, and feuded among themselves. Hidalgos served as vassals to the titled nobles, performed military services for them, and strove to enrich themselves in the process with the spoils of conquest. During the long years of the Reconquista, they had repeatedly plundered their Muslim neighbors. In later years, those who sought their fortunes in the New World would primarily be hidalgos and the younger sons of titled noblemen.[13]

Spaniards first learned of the lands on the far side of the Atlantic in 1493, when Columbus returned to Spain, claiming to have discovered a westward route to the Indies. But as time would tell, he had actually visited the Bahamas, Cuba, and Hispaniola. On 31 March, Palm Sunday, Columbus made a triumphant entry into Seville. Bartolomé de las Casas, the future historian and champion of Indian rights, was in Seville and observed that Columbus brought seven captive Taíno Indians with him. According to Las Casas, Columbus also brought "many other things never before seen in Spain," including "beautiful green parrots," "masks made of precious stones and fishbone," and "sizeable samples of very fine gold." The royal court—which in that era had no fixed seat—was residing for the moment in Barcelona, so in April, Columbus met there with Isabel and Ferdinand.[14]

The king and queen immediately appealed to Pope Alexander VI for papal recognition of their claim to the lands Columbus had discovered. On 4 May 1493 the pope issued a bull giving Isabel, Ferdinand, and their heirs and successors sovereignty over "all islands and mainland found and to be found" west of a line running from pole to pole through a point one hundred leagues west of the Azores and the Cape Verde Islands. At the same time, Alexander VI assured Portugal of its sovereignty over all its newly discovered lands east of the line. Portugal was unhappy about the division, however, and contracted with Spain in the 1494 Treaty of Tordesillas to shift the line of demarcation 270 leagues westward. As a result of this treaty, Brazil would become a Portuguese possession. In making his 1493 donation, Alexander VI did not consider the territorial rights of the indigenous peoples of the newly discovered lands. He did, however, charge the king of Aragón and the queen of Castile with teaching the Indians to accept Christianity. The royal couple acknowledged the obligation and took it to heart.[15]

Alexander VI conferred an additional honor upon Isabel and Ferdinand and named them the Catholic Kings. From that time forward, the queen was known as Isabel the Catholic and the king as Ferdinand the Catholic. In many ways the reign of the Catholic Kings was an illustrious one, except for two black stains upon it. The first was their establishment, in 1478, of the Spanish Inquisition. The second was their expulsion of the Jews. Even the Italian political theorist Niccolò Machiavelli, who saw Ferdinand as "the most famous and most glorious of all the kings of Christendom," accused the king of "a pious cruelty, expropriating and expelling from his kingdom the Marranos [Jews]: an act without parallel and truly despicable."[16]

The purpose of the Inquisition was to root out heresy, for Ferdinand and Isabel saw doctrinal orthodoxy as an essential component of political unity. Under the Inquisition, suspected heretics could be imprisoned, interrogated, and tortured. Neighbor informed against neighbor and could do so in complete secrecy and safety. Even an accusation of heresy could ruin a suspect's reputation and that of his or her family. Condemned and unrepentant heretics were publicly burned. The lives of repentant heretics were spared, but their property was confiscated. The Inquisition bred a climate of mistrust and encouraged corruption, blackmail, and the settling of personal feuds. Isabel's secretary estimated that by 1490 two thousand men and women had been burned by the Inquisition in Spain. The especial targets were converted Muslims and Jews, the latter of whom were known as *conversos* or *marranos*. If suspected of practicing their former religion, or even simply lighting a menorah, *conversos* could be imprisoned.[17]

In 1494 Columbus embarked on his second voyage to the Indies. The admiral sailed with seventeen ships and some 1,200 men to Hispaniola, the island that houses the present nations of Haiti and the Dominican

Republic. There he established the first European colony on the western side of the Atlantic and began to reshape the island along Spanish lines. He took seeds and cuttings with him from Spain in order to cultivate wheat, grapes, chickpeas, onions, and sugarcane. He also brought horses, cattle, pigs, sheep, and goats, none of which had previously been seen in the Americas. Under pressure from his Spanish subordinates, Columbus also transplanted the *encomienda* system, whereby, in medieval Castile, kings had granted their vassals the temporary right to collect taxes and services from conquered peoples.[18]

Under his *encomienda* arrangement, Columbus granted his lieutenants temporary rights over the labor of groups of Indians. The recipient of such rights, known as an *encomendero*, was legally the steward or protector of his Indians rather than their owner. Although he could collect tribute from them and force them to work on his plantation or in his gold mine, he was obligated to feed, shelter, and protect them and to instruct them in the Christian religion. An *encomendero* could not sell his Indians, relocate them to a distant place, or bequeath them to his heirs in perpetuity. He paid taxes to the Spanish crown on his profits from their labor. The native Taínos of Hispaniola did not thrive under the *encomienda* system. Many of them died within two decades of the establishment of the Spanish colony there, succumbing to overwork, to maltreatment, or to European diseases against which they had no immunity. Bartolomé de las Casas, the great defender of Indian rights, abhorred the *encomienda* system and called it "a mortal pestilence."[19]

In Spain, the Catholic Kings also were troubled by the *encomienda* system, and Isabel asked: "By what authority does the Admiral give my vassals away?" The Indians were her subjects and vassals, she argued, not chattels. In 1495, when Columbus sent a consignment of Indians to Spain to be sold there as slaves, Isabel refused to permit the sale. But although she and Ferdinand styled themselves as champions of Christendom, they also needed the tax revenue supplied by the *encomenderos*. In 1500, Isabel and Ferdinand prohibited the enslavement of Indians, allowing exceptions only in cases where they had rebelled against Spanish rule or practiced such abominations as idolatry, cannibalism, or sodomy. In 1512–13, however, Ferdinand promulgated the Laws of Burgos, which compelled the Indians to spend nine months of each year laboring for their Spanish overlords. For the next half century, the question of how Spaniards should treat the Indians would continue to be a hot topic of debate, and royal policy concerning the subject people would seesaw in ways that made it easier at some times and more difficult at others for Spaniards to exploit or abuse them.[20]

In 1504 Isabel the Catholic died. She bequeathed her throne to her daughter Juana, who was married to Philip the Handsome, the heir of the House of Hapsburg. But when Philip died two years after Juana acceded to the throne of Castile, the young queen—who is known to history as Juana la Loca—proved unable to rule on her own. Ferdinand the Catholic continued as king of Aragón and, in view of his daughter's incapacity, administered Castile as well.[21]

Three other deaths following closely upon that of Isabel the Catholic must have affected Álvar Núñez Cabeza de Vaca more personally than the queen's. Both his father and his grandfather died in or around 1506, and his mother died in 1509. None of the three left more than a modest estate. Judging from the few records available, all three were buried in the thirteenth-century monastery of Santo Domingo in Jerez de la Frontera. Cabeza de Vaca's parents were probably interred there in the Vera family vault, but his grandfather was entombed in the monastery's royal chapel.[22]

When Teresa Cabeza de Vaca died in 1509, her seven children became orphans. Of the seven, Álvar was the oldest male. He had two older sisters, one younger sister, and three younger brothers. His younger siblings moved into the house of their mother's sister. Álvar himself had, in 1503, entered the service of Juan de Guzmán, third Duke of Medina Sidonia. One of Álvar's younger brothers and one of his cousins entered the duke's service as well.[23]

Álvar Núñez Cabeza de Vaca must have learned to ride at an early age. The society into which he was born was the most equestrian one in Europe at that time. Clearly, he also learned to read and write. Printing had been introduced to Spain in 1473, some twenty years after Johannes Gutenberg printed his first Bible. Cabeza de Vaca probably read *Amadís de Gaula*, a fabulous tale of romance and chivalry that, after its publication in 1508, became hugely popular with young Spaniards thirsting for adventure. He may also have read printed descriptions of Columbus's voyages and of the Americas. Cabeza de Vaca probably listened to the music of the lute, the dulcimer, the recorder, the rebec (an ancestor of the violin), and the vihuela (an early guitar with six courses of double strings) and enjoyed popular amusements like masquerades and bullfights. He must have attended mass regularly and, at some point in his childhood, made his first communion. No doubt he caroused during Carnival, fasted for Lent, and processed through the streets of Jerez de la Frontera with a cross or a candle during Holy Week. On various feast days, he may have helped carry the gorgeously robed statue of a saint.[24]

The rituals and festivals of the Catholic Church punctuated the calendar year. The patron saint of Jerez de la Frontera was San Dionisio, on whose feast day—9 October—the town had been liberated from the Moors. The feast day of Saint James, the patron saint of Spain, was celebrated on 25 July. Saint James was known throughout Spain as Santiago Matamoros—the slayer of Moors. Santiago is often depicted on horseback, wielding a spear or a sword and trampling a turbaned Moor underfoot. He was originally a Galilean fisherman and one of Christ's twelve disciples, but eight hundred years after his martyrdom in Jerusalem, Santiago miraculously appeared in Spain in the thick of the legendary battle of Clavijo and inspired the Christian forces to win a great victory over the Moors. For centuries thereafter, Spanish warriors shouted the name of Santiago as their battle cry.[25]

Life in sixteenth-century Castile could be brutal. Cabeza de Vaca probably witnessed public executions. The maggot-infested heads of outlaws were impaled on spikes over the gates of most cities. Travelers had to worry about bandits, and voyagers had to worry about pirates. Health care and sanitation were primitive. Approximately one hundred thousand people died in 1507 in a plague epidemic in southern Spain. Personal hygiene was minimal, and people rarely bathed. Many people had rotting or missing teeth.[26]

Dietary staples in Cabeza de Vaca's native region of Andalusia were wheat, olive oil, and wine, supplemented by fruits and vegetables, meat, fish, and shellfish. This diet was more varied than that in northern Europe at the time but did not yet include such New World foodstuffs as tomatoes, potatoes, maize (corn), or chocolate. The countryside surrounding Jerez de la Frontera was covered in vineyards and olive groves. Winters were mild, and the warm temperatures of summer were moderated by breezes from the Atlantic. In certain seasons, Cabeza de Vaca would have heard nightingales, seen storks nesting in the belfries of the churches, and watched swifts soar and tumble in the evening skies. In cultivated areas, he would have seen orange, pomegranate, and fig trees, date palms, roses, and geraniums. The Moors had introduced the oranges and pomegranates and also cotton, rice, eggplants, and such spices as saffron, pepper, cinnamon, and cumin. Andalusians bred horses, cattle, pigs, and sheep and managed profitable wool and leather industries. They caught tuna and other Atlantic fish and salted a portion of the catch for export to other parts of Europe. The duke of Medina Sidonia, Cabeza de Vaca's overlord, owned ships and engaged in both privateering and international trade.[27]

Cabeza de Vaca was between eleven and eighteen years old when he entered the service of the duke of Medina Sidonia. The future explorer was to work under four successive dukes and to serve the house of Medina Sidonia for twenty-four years. In the ducal accounts for 1503 he is listed among several "Cavalleros de Jerez" whom the duchy employed that year. In 1513 Cabeza de Vaca is listed as a page, and in 1519 as a *camarero*—or chamberlain—with the combined duties of a man-at-arms, an administrative assistant, and a gentleman-in-waiting. In a document dated 4 August 1524, Cabeza de Vaca describes himself as a *camarero* to "the illustrious and very magnificent lord the duke of Medina Sidonia." In June of 1525, Cabeza de Vaca was reimbursed for a length of black silk he had purchased for the duke.[28]

From 1511 to 1513, Cabeza de Vaca saw military action in Italy. Pope Julius II had appealed to Ferdinand the Catholic for aid against the French, and the king had seized the opportunity to expand the territory he already controlled in Naples, Sicily, and Sardinia. The weapons of the day included pikes, lances, crossbows, swords, harquebuses, and cannons. Soldiers wore morion helmets with peaked brims, and either metal cuirasses or chain mail to protect their torsos and loins. In 1511, when he was somewhere between nineteen and twenty-six years old, Cabeza de Vaca sailed from Spain to Naples to gain his first taste of warfare. On 4 February 1512 he took part in the battle of Bologna, which ended in the retreat of the Spanish and papal forces. On Easter Sunday, 11 April 1512, he participated in the battle of Ravenna, in which the Spanish were defeated by the French and twenty thousand men lost their lives. Cabeza de Vaca was, according to witnesses, "very battered." Subsequently, he was made *alférez* (royal standard-bearer) of Gaeta, a city near Naples.[29]

By 1513 he was back in Castile. The third duke of Medina Sidonia, Juan de Guzmán, had died in 1507, leaving three young sons who successively became the fourth, fifth, and sixth dukes. Each of the three was younger than Cabeza de Vaca. The fourth duke died in 1513 while still a minor. The fifth duke seems to have been mentally impaired, and in 1518 he was deposed by royal decree in favor of his younger brother, Juan Alonso de Guzmán. Juan Alonso succeeded not only to his brother's title but also ultimately to his wife, who was a granddaughter of Ferdinand and Isabel.

But before Juan Alonso could marry Ana of Aragón, her marriage to his older brother had to be annulled. Cabeza de Vaca assisted Juan Alonso by securing grounds for the annulment. A husband's impotence was a sufficient ground, so Cabeza de Vaca tempted the mentally impaired man with a series of prostitutes and then reported to Juan Alonso that none of them had succeeded in arousing the duke's older brother.[30]

The house of Medina Sidonia was one of the most powerful noble houses in Castile and had come to dominate the municipal government of Seville. In the course of his service to the duke, Cabeza de Vaca is known to have visited Seville. Although an inland city, it was Castile's foremost port and boasted a bustling dockyard and a vigorous commercial center. In 1503, Seville had secured a monopoly on trade with the Indies, and a Casa de Contratación, or House of Trade, was established in the city to administer trans-Atlantic commerce. Wine, wheat, olive oil, textiles, and other goods were shipped out of Seville to the Americas, and precious metals, pearls, sugar, and dyes from the New World came through Seville into Spain and Europe. Architecturally, although the city had been liberated from the Moors in 1248, the Seville that Cabeza de Vaca knew was still very much a Moorish city. Some of its principal edifices, including its Alcázar, Giralda, and Torre del Oro had been built by the Moors. The Alcázar, a fortified palace rivaling Granada's Alhambra, was the residence of Ferdinand the Catholic when he visited Seville. A Moorish aqueduct brought water into the Alcázar, and Moorish arches, patios, and fountains graced the palace. Once the minaret of a mosque, the Giralda was now the bell tower of Seville's Gothic cathedral, and the Torre del Oro, or Tower of Gold, was a polygonal fortress beside the Río Guadalquivir. The estimated population of Seville in 1500 was between sixty and seventy thousand, but as the city became increasingly prosperous, it attracted newcomers from northern Spain, Italy, and the Low Countries and became—after Paris and Naples—the third most populous city in Europe.[31]

In 1516, three years after Cabeza de Vaca returned from Italy, Ferdinand the Catholic died. Thereupon, his sixteen-year-old grandson, Charles of Hapsburg, became King Charles I of Spain. The new king was at least eight years younger than Cabeza de Vaca. The succession was not an easy one, for many Spaniards viewed Charles as a foreign king. He had been born and raised in Flanders, and in 1517, when he visited Spain for the first time, he could not speak the Castilian language. He was the son of Juana la Loca and Philip the Handsome, the grandson on his mother's side of Ferdinand

and Isabel, and the grandson on his father's side of Maximilian I, who headed both the House of Hapsburg and the Holy Roman Empire. From his father, who had died when Charles was six, the young king inherited Flanders, Holland, a claim to Burgundy, and the expectation of inheriting the Hapsburg possessions in Austria and Hungary. From his mother, who was legally the queen of Castile but incapable of ruling, Charles inherited Castile, Aragón, Sicily, Sardinia, Naples, and the Spanish possessions in the Americas. The young king brought a large entourage of Flemish courtiers with him to Spain and allowed them to allocate Spanish assets for use elsewhere in Europe. He ordered changes in the Spanish tax code and eliminated prerogatives previously enjoyed by the cities and by the hidalgos as a class. Spaniards resented the changes and disliked their new king's foreign ways, his foreign courtiers, and his appropriation of Spanish resources for expensive projects in Flanders and Holland.[32]

In 1519, Maximilian I died and left his imperial throne vacant. The nineteen-year-old Charles aspired to succeed his grandfather at the helm of the Holy Roman Empire. He lavished extravagant bribes upon the imperial electors, secured the election, and went to Germany to be crowned. As the fifth of his name to wear the imperial crown, he was known from that time forward as Emperor Charles V. In Spain he was known as Carlos Quinto, and his former title as Charles I of Spain was eclipsed.[33]

In the spring of 1520, just before he departed for Germany, Charles received a letter from Mexico, brought to him by supporters of an ambitious Spaniard named Hernán Cortés. Along with the letter, the ambassadors brought Charles the traditional *quinto real*, or royal fifth, of all the Mexican booty Cortés had managed thus far to acquire. Cortés was locked in a bitter struggle with the Spanish governor of Cuba and was desperate to secure Charles's favor. Most of the items Cortés sent to Charles had been presented to the conquistador by the Aztec emperor Montezuma. The items included a large gold wheel worked with a design of monsters and foliage and weighing 3,800 *pesos de oro*, a large silver wheel weighing forty-eight silver marks, two gold necklaces with carved stone pendants, a fan made from colored feathers and small gold rods, a headdress made from colored feathers and gold disks, a helmet of blue stone mosaic, a bracelet of blue jewels, sandals stitched with gold thread, a large golden alligator head with pendant ear ornaments, sixteen bucklers made of stone mosaic, a scepter made of red stone and mother-of-pearl, two jaguar skins, and two bark-paper codices inscribed with pictorial symbols. Cortés had not had

Charles's authorization to explore Mexico, but in the light of the conquistador's rich gifts, the emperor found this technicality easy to forgive.[34]

Charles was preoccupied, however, and had little attention to bestow upon Cortés. For the emperor, affairs in Europe almost always took precedence over those in the Americas. When he arrived in Germany in 1520, Charles had to deal with a rebellious German monk named Martin Luther, who in 1517 had nailed a list of ninety-five theses to the door of the Castle Church in Wittenberg. To Charles, any challenge to the Roman Catholic Church must have seemed like a challenge to his authority. As Holy Roman emperor, he was the right arm of the pope. Moreover, his position as king of Spain depended on the goodwill of the Spanish clergy and might be jeopardized if he appeared to tolerate heresy. Early in 1521, Charles convened an Imperial Diet in the city of Worms and summoned Martin Luther to testify. The emperor was barely twenty-one years old and almost seventeen years younger than Luther, but he stood against the German monk as the champion of traditional Christianity. Throughout his imperial reign, Charles would defend his Catholic faith against Protestantism in Germany, against Islam in North Africa and the Middle East, against pagan idolatry in the New World, and against heresy in all parts of his empire. He would ally himself with the Inquisition in Spain. He would defend his aunt, Catherine of Aragón, from divorce, and he would seek to prevent her husband, England's Henry VIII, from renouncing the Catholic Church.[35]

But in 1520, while Charles was busy in Germany, his government in Spain was faced with the revolt of the Comuneros. The insurgency began as a tax revolt but became a fight for a more representational type of government. It was fueled by widespread resentment of an emperor who seemed more Flemish than Spanish, drained the Spanish treasury, and spent little time in Spain. The Comuneros were a loose confederation of disgruntled hidalgos, civil and clerical administrators, and men of the wealthy commercial classes. Violence broke out in Medina del Campo, and much of the city was burned. A group of Comuneros seized both the city of Tordesillas and Charles's mother, Juana la Loca, who resided there. The rebels attempted to induce her to accede to their demands, but Queen Juana refused to sign any documents.[36]

Meanwhile, the working classes also became inflamed, and in Valencia a proletarian brotherhood of artisans and guild members took over the municipal government. Commoners on the island of Mallorca expelled the royal governor, and commoners elsewhere burned the palaces of nobles. As class warfare threatened to engulf Spain, most noblemen sided with the absent emperor and against the common people. Supporters of the emperor recaptured Valencia and Tordesillas and liberated Juana la Loca. On 23 April 1521 at Villalar, Charles's supporters dealt the Comuneros a crushing blow. But then Francis I of France sought to exploit the unrest by invading Navarra on the French and Spanish border. Many Spanish hidalgos rushed to Navarra to defend it against the French.[37]

Both Cabeza de Vaca and the duke of Medina Sidonia steadfastly supported Emperor Charles, and the future explorer took part in most of the major battles arising from the rebellion. On 16 September 1520 he supported his duke against a group of Comuneros who had seized the Alcázar in Seville and were seeking to oust *conversos* from Seville's municipal government. The duke swiftly recaptured the Alcázar, defended the *conversos*, and preserved his control of Sevillian municipal affairs. Cabeza de Vaca later testified that he "found himself with the other knights and servants of the duke of Medina Sidonia in its [the Alcázar's] loss and recapture." The duke put him in charge of defending the Puerta del Osario, one of several gates in Seville's encircling wall. On 5 December 1520, Cabeza de Vaca took part in liberating the city of Tordesillas. On 23 April 1521 he helped defeat the Comuneros at Villalar. When Francis I invaded Navarra, Cabeza de Vaca opposed the French in the battle of Puente de la Reina. In the course of these battles, the young Spaniard's loyalty to Charles V seems to have intensified. Throughout his remaining life, Cabeza de Vaca would demonstrate his devotion to the emperor's Sacred Caesarian Catholic Majesty and to the established order for which the emperor stood. During his years in South America, Cabeza de Vaca would express his disdain for the Comunero cause.[38]

Judging from a legal document his wife filed in 1520, Cabeza de Vaca was a married man when the revolt of the Comuneros broke out. His wife's name was María Marmolejo, and she belonged to a prominent Sevillian *converso* family. It seems likely that in opposing the Comuneros in Seville, Cabeza de Vaca was supporting not only his duke and his emperor but also his wife and *converso* in-laws. Marriages between wealthy *conversos* and respectable Christian hidalgos were not uncommon. Since being of Jewish ancestry could be dangerous, *conversos* sought to ally themselves with Christians in order to make themselves more secure. For Christian hidalgos like Cabeza de Vaca, money was often an incentive for marrying into a *converso* family. It is clear that María Marmolejo brought money into her marriage, because in his later life Cabeza de Vaca would assert that she had exhausted her resources in defending his good name. The future explorer may have been as old as thirty-five when he married, or he may have been considerably younger. There is no record that Cabeza de Vaca and his wife ever had children.[39]

Emperor Charles V returned to Spain in 1522. Although the revolt of the Comuneros had been quelled, it had spurred him to give Spain more attention, to adjust his policies, and to mend bridges. Charles rewarded his supporters with appointments and privileges, and he quickly replaced most of the foreigners in his government with Spaniards. He subjected officeholders to *visitas* and *residencias*, or reviews of their performance in office. He reorganized the government of Spain into six judicial councils, one of which—the Royal Council of the Indies—was created in 1524 to administer all Spanish affairs in the Americas. In 1526 Charles married his cousin Isabel of Portugal, and the following year she gave him an heir, the future Philip II. Charles V would continue to rule Spain as a largely absentee monarch (often leaving his queen as his regent), to divide his attention among many competing priorities, and to expend Spanish resources in the far corners of his empire, but his title to the Spanish throne was now firmly established. In the course of his reign, he would transform the medieval crowns of Castile and Aragón into the sovereign state of Spain.[40]

At the time of his marriage, Charles V was arguably already the most powerful leader in contemporary Christendom. To his Spanish subjects he had come to embody the sacred majesty of Christian authority. Charles's motto was *plus ultra* (or "more beyond"), and his personal emblems were the double-headed eagle and the Pillars of Hercules. The twin promontories known as the Pillars of Hercules stood on opposite sides of the Strait of Gibraltar and had once represented the end of the known world, the *non plus ultra* beyond which there was no more. *Plus ultra* was a repudiation of *non plus ultra*. To Charles, *plus ultra* probably meant something like "push beyond the limits." But to conquistadors who sailed under his banner, the motto must have meant "There's more out there beyond the European and Mediterranean world, and let's get it." Charles's power inspired these men and assured them of the righteousness of their project to extend his empire. Cabeza de Vaca would one day reproduce the emperor's coat of arms, with the Pillars of Hercules and the *plus ultra* motto, on the frontispiece of his 1542 *Relación* (see the photograph in chapter 11). The twin pillars and the *plus ultra* motto appear to this day on the Spanish national flag.[41]

At the time of Charles's accession to the Spanish throne, Spanish colonial settlements had been established on the four major Caribbean islands—Hispaniola, Cuba, Puerto Rico, and Jamaica—and on the Central American mainland in what is now Panama. These settlements served as bases for explorations of the smaller Caribbean islands and the adjacent mainland coasts. A demand among colonial *encomenderos* for Indian laborers was one of the forces driving these explorations. Slave hunters quickly depopulated the Bahamas, Curaçao, Aruba, and the Leeward Islands and may have conducted raids on the Florida Peninsula. At the same time, the Spanish governors of the larger Caribbean islands were racing one another to claim chunks of mainland territory. In 1519 the governor of Cuba sent Hernán Cortés to explore the Yucatán. The conquistador soon broke with the governor, however, and in August 1521 he toppled the Aztec empire. Cortés sent a letter to Charles V from Mexico—or New Spain, as he called it—suggesting that Charles might style himself "the emperor of this kingdom with no less glory than of Germany, which, by the Grace of God, Your Sacred Majesty already possesses."[42]

In Andalusia in the 1520s, Cabeza de Vaca would have had easy access to news of unfolding developments across the Atlantic. Two of the letters, or *cartas de relación*, that Cortés wrote to Charles V were published in Seville in 1522 and 1523 respectively, and a third was published in Toledo in 1525. Cabeza de Vaca must have known also that Ferdinand Magellan had sailed with five ships from Seville in 1519 and that although Magellan had perished, one of his ships had returned to Seville in 1522 after successfully circumnavigating the globe. It was only natural that Cabeza de Vaca, like many others of his generation, should turn his eyes toward the New World.[43]

Early in 1527, Cabeza de Vaca appeared before the royal court in Valladolid and, by royal warrant dated 15 February 1527, received an appointment to serve as royal treasurer to an expeditionary company that had recently been authorized to explore, conquer, and settle the portion of the North American mainland then known as La Florida. The commander of the expedition was to be Pánfilo de Narváez, a wealthy *encomendero* from Cuba with a grievance against Hernán Cortés. It is unclear why Cabeza de Vaca was made treasurer for the Narváez expedition, but it may have been because one of his relatives, Luis Cabeza de Vaca, was serving on the Royal Council of the Indies. Cabeza de Vaca's own service to King Ferdinand in Italy and to Emperor Charles V during the revolt of the Comuneros must also have elevated his candidacy for preferment. Cabeza de Vaca may have met Pánfilo de Narváez as early as 1525, when the latter came to Spain from Cuba, but the junior man's appointment as royal treasurer came directly from the emperor and not from Narváez. By appointing Cabeza de Vaca and two other royal officials to accompany Narváez, Charles V was placing checks on the expeditionary commander and increasing the likelihood that the royal interest would be served.[44]

Cabeza de Vaca was promised an annual salary of 130,000 *maravedíes* for the term of his appointment, but Narváez's compensation as captain general of the expedition and governor of La Florida was to be an annual salary of 250,000 *maravedíes* for the rest of his life. Before assuming his duties, Cabeza de Vaca had to guarantee his good conduct in office by depositing 2,000 ducats—the equivalent of 750,000 *maravedíes*, or his expected annual salary for more than five years—with the royal treasury in Seville. How he managed to amass the required sum is unknown. Perhaps he borrowed money at interest from bankers in Seville. Or perhaps the money came from his wife or from other relatives willing to invest in his enterprise.[45]

As royal treasurer, Cabeza de Vaca was to be the collector of royal revenues, including the *quinto real* of all income accruing from the expeditionary venture and from such acquisitions as gold, pearls, precious stones, and slaves. He was also to collect a 5 percent tax on any gold and silver that was melted down and on the income from any saltworks, and a 7.5 percent duty on imported goods. And he was to pay the royal officials of the expedition their salaries. One of his principal duties—and, as it happened, the one he was best able to fulfill—was to report to the emperor "extensively and particularly of every matter." Charles V was especially concerned about the Indians, and he instructed the treasurer to report meticulously on "how the natives are treated, our instructions observed, and other of the things respecting their liberties that we have commanded; especially the matters touching the service of our Lord and divine worship, [and] the teachings of the Indians in the Holy Faith."[46]

TWO

Pánfilo de Narváez

Narváez received his royal contract on 11 December 1526, two months before Cabeza de Vaca received his appointment as royal treasurer to the La Florida expedition. Narváez's *capitulaciones* authorized him to explore, conquer, and settle La Florida and to serve as governor of all the territory he might bring under Spanish control. He was to equip and lead his expedition at his own expense and would receive no funding from the crown. Gonzalo Fernández de Oviedo y Valdés, the historian who would preserve the earliest account of the Narváez expedition, noted wryly: "Their Majesties almost never put their property and money in these new discoveries: Just paper and good words, and they tell these captains: 'If you accomplish what you are promising to do, we shall do this or that, or give you a courtly title.' And they give him the title of *Adelantado* or Governor with license and authority to go wherever he may offer to go in his stipulation." As it happened, Narváez financed his expedition with money from his prosperous *encomienda* in Cuba. Additional money came from the men he recruited into his company, each of whom invested in the Florida enterprise.[1]

At the time he signed his contract, Narváez was in his mid-forties. He had been born in Valladolid around 1480 and so was five to ten years older than Cabeza de Vaca. The historians Bartolomé de las Casas, Bernal Díaz del Castillo, and Gonzalo Fernández de Oviedo y Valdés all knew Narváez personally. Las Casas described him as "tall, of fair complexion, which tended toward ruddy, honest, of good judgment, but not very prudent, of good conversation and manners, and also courageous in fighting against the Indians." Díaz described Narváez as "tall in stature and very muscular," adding that "he had a long face and a ruddy beard; his company and bearing were agreeable, and his voice boomed as though it emanated from a vault or cavern." Oviedo described Narváez as "virtuous and a man of genteel upbringing and of pure blood" and observed that "when necessary, he had demonstrated his courage in the military, showing himself no less a skillful soldier than later, a captain." Oviedo had met Narváez in 1525 in Spain and claimed to have advised him to give up his dream of conquering La Florida and instead to live peacefully on his *encomienda* in Cuba with his wife and children. According to Oviedo, Narváez did not "lack the age to need repose, having passed as many years (if not more) as had I and he appeared to me not a little worn." The historian added that Narváez was an hidalgo who had come to the New World "with a sword and cape in search of a living and found honor and a virtuous wife, daughter of an hidalgo, and God gave him children and enough wealth to get by on."[2]

By some accounts, Narváez had come to the New World with Columbus on his second voyage. Narváez subsequently took part in the conquests of Jamaica and Cuba, both of which were launched from Hispaniola. He led a company of thirty crossbowmen in Jamaica, and from 1509 to 1511 was second-in-command of that island. From 1511 through 1514 he was in Cuba, serving as field commander of the force of 330 Spaniards who conquered the island. Diego Velázquez, the commander in chief and later the governor of Cuba, rewarded Narváez by granting him a large *encomienda* with gold mines and a captive population of Taíno laborers.[3]

The indigenous Taíno people of Cuba, Hispaniola, and the neighboring islands were related to the Arawak people of South America and spoke an Arawakan language. Traditionally they fished, cultivated maize and cassava, and lived in small, multifamily communities. When Columbus made contact with them in 1492, two to three million Taínos lived throughout the Caribbean, but their population shrank within twenty-five years to a small fraction of its precontact size. Maltreatment, cultural disruption, and European diseases all took a heavy toll. Bartolomé de las Casas, who came to the New World in 1502, observed the decimation of the Taínos firsthand. In his *Short Account of the Destruction of the Indies*, Las Casas said of the Taínos: "They are without malice or guile, and are utterly faithful and obedient both to their own native lords and to the Spaniards in whose service they now find themselves." He also noted: "They are among the least robust of human beings: their delicate constitutions make them unable to withstand hard work or suffering and render them liable to succumb to almost any illness, no matter how mild."[4]

Las Casas, who entered the priesthood around 1510, became an indefatigable champion of Indian rights. He served as chaplain to the Spaniards who captured Cuba and was a horrified witness to atrocities committed against the Taínos by Diego Velázquez, Pánfilo de Narváez, and their followers. Las Casas reported, for example, that a Taíno leader named Hatuey was condemned to be burned at the stake and that a Franciscan friar attempted to persuade him to accept baptism first. The friar promised Hatuey that as a Christian he would enjoy eternal glory in heaven. Hatuey asked if there were Spaniards in heaven, and when the friar assured him there were, Hatuey refused bitterly to spend eternity in their company. Las Casas reported that on another occasion in a village near the Caonao River, Christians commanded by Pánfilo de Narváez "were suddenly inspired by the Devil and, without the slightest provocation, butchered, before my eyes, some three thousand souls—men, women and children—as they sat there in front of us." Narváez watched impassively and did nothing to curtail the slaughter. In the days that followed, Las Casas attempted to persuade Taíno survivors to come out of hiding and meet with Narváez, but when they did so, Narváez seized them and threatened to burn them. According to Las Casas, who pled successfully for their lives, Narváez justified his intended action on the grounds that, given time, the Taínos "were bound to do something that merited such punishment." Las Casas may have inflated the number of Taínos killed near the Caonao River, for in his report on the same incident, Diego Velázquez acknowledged only one hundred Taíno casualties.[5]

In addition to Narváez and Las Casas, a third individual who assisted Velázquez in conquering Cuba was Hernán Cortés. Although Cortés and Narváez later were rivals, Cortés claimed that during the conquest of Cuba they were friends.[6]

After prevailing in Cuba, Velázquez was anxious to secure a royal appointment to govern the island and a royal license to explore the mainland to the west. He therefore sent Narváez as his ambassador to the royal court in Spain. Velázquez did not wait for a license, however, to begin exploring westward. Each year from 1517 to 1519 he sent expeditions to the coast of the Yucatán Peninsula. The commanders of each of the first two expeditions duly returned to Cuba, bringing Velázquez useful information. The third expedition, which left Cuba on 18 November 1519, was commanded by Hernán Cortés. Velázquez still had no authorization from Charles V to explore the American mainland, and Cortés's only authorization came from Velázquez. But soon after he landed on the eastern Mexican coast, Cortés scuttled his ships, broke with Velázquez, and assumed independent leadership of his venture. In the meantime Narváez returned to Cuba from Spain, having obtained both Velázquez's appointment as governor of the island and his license to explore the nearby mainland. Velázquez sent Narváez in pursuit of Cortés with instructions to relieve him of his command. On 5 March 1520, Narváez sailed from Cuba in eighteen ships with eight hundred men and eighty horses. On 20 April he landed on the eastern Mexican coast.[7]

Cortés, meanwhile, was in Tenochtitlán, the Aztec capital, holding Aztec emperor Montezuma as his hostage. Messengers brought Cortés the unwelcome news that Narváez's armada had arrived on his eastern doorstep. Cortés hesitated to leave Tenochtitlán, for fear he would lose control of the city. According to Bernal Díaz del Castillo, who was with him in Tenochtitlán, Cortés learned that Narváez was not much liked by his captains and that their loyalty might be bought. Cortés therefore sent bribes to the leading men in the Narváez camp. At around the same time, Montezuma secretly sent his own ambassadors to Narváez with rich gifts for him. According to Díaz, Narváez was stingy and, instead of sharing the gifts with his men, kept everything for himself. Cortés, now fearing that some indigenous people might join forces with Narváez, went with a small number of men, including Díaz, to meet his Cuban challenger.[8]

A little after midnight on 27 May 1520, Cortés and his men entered Narváez's camp. As Narváez's sentries sounded the alarm, Cortés's fifers and drummers beat a charge. Narváez ordered his artillerymen to fire their cannons, but Cortés's men quickly seized the guns. They also used their pikes to unhorse six or seven of Narváez's cavalrymen. In the thick of the battle, Narváez suffered a pike thrust to the eye. Díaz recalls hearing Narváez cry: "Holy Mary protect me, they have killed me and destroyed my eye." Cortés ordered his men to bind Narváez with two pairs of fetters. The victorious commander then propitiated his rival's men with gifts and recruited them into his army. He also expropriated Narváez's horses, armaments, and supplies. As quickly as he could, Cortés returned to Tenochtitlán, leaving Narváez at the coast as his prisoner.[9]

In Tenochtitlán, Cortés found the Aztecs in rebellion. It took him more than a year to regain control of the city. Before Cortés's arrival, Tenochtitlán had a population of around two hundred thousand people and was three times the size of Seville. The Aztec capital was built on an island in Lake Texcoco, and although broad causeways linked it to the shore, it appeared to rise from the lake. Its Great Pyramid, surmounted by twin temples to the Aztec gods of war and of rain, stood sixty meters tall. Aqueducts brought water into Tenochtitlán, and the city also had a sewage system, an aviary, and a zoo. Bernal Díaz del Castillo reported the reaction of himself and his fellow Spaniards when they first saw the city: "We were amazed and said that it was like the enchantments they tell of in the legend of Amadis, on account of the great towers and cues and buildings rising from the water, and all built of masonry." He subsequently reported: "Of all these wonders that I then beheld today all is overthrown and lost, nothing left standing."[10]

Pánfilo de Narváez inadvertently helped Cortés conquer Tenochtitlán by introducing a European disease—probably smallpox—into the Mexican environment. The disease had broken out in Hispaniola in the winter of 1518–19 and traveled from there to the neighboring islands. A smallpox epidemic was raging in Cuba when Narváez left there in pursuit of Cortés. According to Bernal Díaz del Castillo, a black man "covered with smallpox" came from Cuba with Narváez, "and a very black affair it was for New Spain, for it was owing to him that the whole country was stricken and filled with it, from which there was great mortality, for according to what the Indians said they had never had such a disease." The pestilence spread quickly from Narváez's camp on the Mexican coast to Tenochtitlán. Aztec eyewitnesses reported that "sores erupted on our faces, our breasts, our bellies" and that "a great many died from this plague." Meanwhile, Cortés allied himself with the indigenous enemies of the Aztecs, and with their help, in August of 1521, he overwhelmed the disease-ravaged Aztec capital. After its fall, Tenochtitlán—known as México by the Spaniards—became the capital of the Spanish province of New Spain.[11]

Narváez remained Cortés's prisoner until 1524. During the first two years, he was held under tight security on the Gulf coast of New Spain, but he was then transferred to México/Tenochtitlán. While in the city, he must have reflected bitterly on the circumstances that had put it into Cortés's hands rather than his own, and he must have dreamed that he might someday capture a similar prize. No doubt he pondered the strategies Cortés had used to control his Spanish troops and to defeat the Aztecs. Narváez seems to have noted, for example, that Cortés had scuttled his ships in order to force his men to follow him into the unknown Mexican interior and that he had made a hostage of Montezuma. Narváez would employ these strategies in La Florida.[12]

Meanwhile, Narváez's wife wrote repeatedly to Cortés, begging him to set Narváez free. To ransom her husband, she hoarded the profits from the *encomienda* she was managing for him in Cuba. She managed so shrewdly that even after paying the ransom, she was able to present Narváez with 13,000 to 14,000 *pesos de oro* from mining operations carried out on their *encomienda* by Indian laborers. Narváez likely used some of these gold pesos later in Spain to buy friends at court.[13]

In 1525, not long after he regained his freedom, Narváez journeyed from Cuba to Spain to seek redress for the treatment he had received from Cortés. He met in Toledo with Charles V and the royal court. Oviedo, who was in Toledo at the time, reported that Narváez accused Cortés of being "treacherous, tyrannical, and ungrateful to his king and to Diego Velázquez, who had sent him to New Spain at his own expense." The royal court, already nervous about Cortés's power, responded by stripping a bit of contested territory from him.[14]

Meanwhile, Narváez had additional business to attend to. He had not ceased to dream that somewhere in North America he might discover a second Tenochtitlán. He petitioned Charles V for permission to lead an expedition into the unexplored territory north of New Spain, asking specifically for authorization to "discover the islands of *tierra firme* that there are from the Río de las Palmas to *Florida*, and all of the said *Florida* to the north and south." The Río de las Palmas of his petition was the present Río Soto la Marina, which parallels the Rio Grande and flows into the Gulf from the present Mexican state of Tamaulipas. The Florida of his petition included not only the Florida Peninsula but the entire Gulf coast of what is now the United States. In December of 1526, Charles V authorized Narváez to "discover and conquer and populate the lands from the Río de las Palmas to the island of *Florida*, as well as *Florida* itself and all the coast from one sea to the other."[15]

The two seas were the two oceans, for at that time the Atlantic was known as the North Sea and the Pacific as the South Sea. Officials at the Spanish royal court underestimated the distance from the one sea to the other at the latitude of the Río de las Palmas. They authorized Narváez to take control of as much of what is now the United States as he could seize, including the whole Gulf coast from the Río de las Palmas through the present states of Texas, Louisiana, Mississippi, and Alabama to Florida, and all the land north of New Spain—from the Atlantic to the Pacific.[16]

The notion that the Florida Peninsula was an island was the result of misinformation transmitted by Juan Ponce de León, the first European known to have sighted it. He did so during Holy Week in 1513, and he named it Florida in honor of Easter—known in Spain as Pascua Florida, or Feast of Flowers. Ponce de León thought he had discovered an island, and his error was perpetuated on several subsequent maps. The explorer had set out in three ships on 4 March 1513 from Puerto Rico. He made a brief landfall somewhere on Florida's mid-Atlantic coast, then sailed southward and rounded the Florida Cape. On 3 June he landed somewhere on Florida's southern Gulf coast to gather wood, water, and information, but he and his men were attacked twice by Florida natives and withdrew to Puerto Rico. In 1521 Ponce de León returned to the Florida Peninsula, intending to establish a settlement there, but he was wounded in yet another skirmish with Indians and retreated to Cuba, where he died of his injuries.[17]

Although neither Charles V nor Narváez had a clear idea in 1526 of the vastness of the territory the one was authorizing the other to explore and conquer, they did know that a continuous land mass encircled most of the Gulf of Mexico. They had two maps. The first of these had been sent to the Spanish royal court in 1519 and was drawn earlier that year by explorers sailing for the governor of Jamaica. This map has been attributed to Alonso Álvarez de Pineda, and although the attribution is contested, it is known as the Pineda map. The second map that Narváez and court officials must have consulted had been sent to Charles V in 1522 by Hernán Cortés. Both of these maps show a continuous coast from the Yucatán to the Florida Peninsula.[18]

The Pineda map shows few details, but among them are a Río Pánuco emptying into the Gulf of Mexico from the west and a Río del Espíritu Santo coming in from the north. The map also shows two unnamed harbors on the west coast of the Florida Peninsula. The explorers who collected the information for the map are the only group of Europeans known to have coasted the northern rim of the Gulf of Mexico before Narváez did so. These explorers sailed north from Jamaica through the Yucatán Channel and continued around the Gulf in a clockwise direction until they reached the tip of the Florida Peninsula. They then reversed their course, sailing back around the Gulf in the counterclockwise direction.

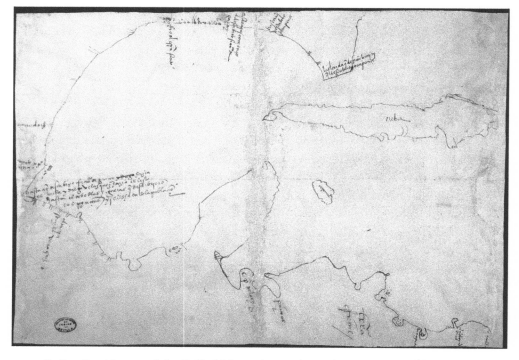

Earliest Spanish map of the Gulf of Mexico (ca. 1519), attributed to Alonso Álvarez de Pineda. Courtesy of España. Ministerio de Educación, Cultura y Deporte. Archivo General de Indias.

On the Feast Day of the Holy Spirit, 2 June 1519, they sighted what must have been the Mississippi River and, following the Spanish custom of naming geographic entities for religious holidays, named it Río del Espíritu Santo. Later they anchored at the mouth of the Río Pánuco, near the site of present-day Tampico in northeastern Mexico. They estimated the northern coast of the Gulf to have a length of about three hundred leagues, or nine hundred miles.[19]

The map Cortés sent to Charles V in 1522 includes the Río del Espíritu Santo, or Mississippi, and seems to have incorporated the information collected for the Pineda map. It may also have incorporated information Cortés received from Montezuma. The map's greatest concentration of detail is in the area between the Yucatán and the Río Pánuco, an area Cortés and his followers knew at first hand. The Río de las Palmas, or southwestern boundary of the territory Narváez was authorized to explore, appears on the Cortés map to the north of the Río Pánuco.[20]

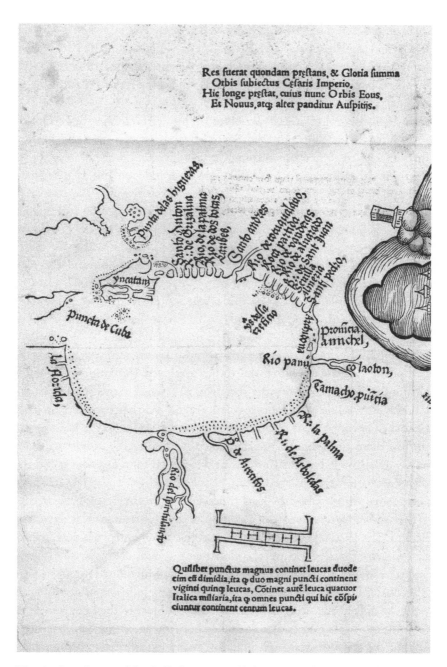

Res fuerat quondam prestans, & Gloria summa
Orbis subiectus Cesaris Imperio,
Hic longe prestat, cuius nunc Orbis Eous,
Et Nouus, atq; alter panditur Auspitijs.

Quilibet punctus magnus continet leucas duode
cim eu dimidia,ita q; duo magni puncti continent
viginti quinq; leucas, Cotinet aute leuca quatuor
Italica milaria,ita q; omnes puncti qui hic cospi
ciuntur continent centum leucas.

Hernán Cortés's map of the Gulf of Mexico, published in *Praeclara Ferdinandi Cortesii de Nova Maris Oceani Hyspanica Narratio* in Nuremberg in 1542. Courtesy of The Hispanic Society of America, New York.

In actual fact, the outlet of Narváez's Río de las Palmas (today's Río Soto la Marina) is ninety nautical miles north of the outlet of the Río Pánuco. In 1523 Cortés founded the settlement of Santisteban del Puerto on the southern bank of the Río Pánuco, near where the city of Tampico now stands.[21]

In 1525, a year before Narváez obtained his *capitulaciones* for La Florida, royal officials in Spain removed Santisteban del Puerto and the territory surrounding the Río Pánuco from Cortés's jurisdiction. They reorganized the territory as the province of Pánuco, made it independent of New Spain, and appointed Nuño Beltrán de Guzmán as its governor. The Río de las Palmas was the northern limit of the province of Pánuco and of Spanish power on the North American mainland, and Santisteban del Puerto was the northernmost Spanish settlement on the Gulf coast. The Río de las Palmas seems to have been Narváez's primary destination and the place at which he hoped to establish his base camp. No other Spaniard had yet secured a foothold on the river, but it was not far from an area Spaniards already controlled. Thus, if Narváez set up a base there, he could count on easy access to supplies and, if necessary, military aid.[22]

In November of 1526, a month before Narváez received his *capitulaciones*, the Royal Council of the Indies approved legislation designed to ensure that the conquest of the Americas proceeded according to just and Christian principles. The new legislation required that two clergymen accompany all expeditions of conquest, preach the gospel to the Indians, and protect them from abuse. The clergymen were to testify in writing that if any war was waged against Indians, it was waged for a just cause, and that if any Indians were enslaved, they were enslaved for a just reason and in accordance with established legal procedure. If, in the opinion of the clergymen, a war or enslavement was unjust, the commander was to lose his license. The 1526 legislation also obliged the commander of an expedition of conquest to carry a copy of a document known as the Requerimiento and to read it to any Indian or group of Indians who offered him resistance. This document had been drawn up in 1513 for the purpose of notifying the native people of the Americas that they were subject to the pope and to the Spanish crown. It gave Indians a choice between accepting Spanish rule or risking slavery and death. In practice, many expeditionary commanders read the Requerimiento in Spanish, a language most Indians could not understand, and—as often as not—read it out of their earshot. Bartolomé de las Casas, the champion of Indian rights, said commanders often read it in the dead of night when the Indians were asleep. The specific version of the Requerimiento issued to Narváez informed Indians of the consequences for them if they did not submit to the pope, to Queen Juana of Castile, and to Emperor Charles V:

> I [Narváez] will enter by force, making war upon you from all directions and in every manner that I may be able, when I will subject you to obedience to the Church and the yoke of Their Majesties; and I will take the persons of yourselves, your wives and your children to make slaves, sell and dispose of you, as Their Majesties shall think fit; and I will take your goods, doing you all the evil and injury that I may be able, as to vassals who do not obey but reject their master, resist and deny him: and I declare to you that the deaths and damages that arise therefrom, will be your fault and not that of His Majesty, nor mine, nor of those cavaliers who come with me.

If, after hearing the Requerimiento, the Indians continued to resist Spanish rule and the gospel, Narváez was entitled to make good on his threats. Today the logic of the Requerimiento seems twisted, but the Royal Council of the Indies was endeavoring—by ordering commanders to read it under the supervision of clergymen—to put procedural checks on the rapacious instincts of conquistadors.[23]

Narváez complied with the new legislation and agreed to include several clergymen in his expeditionary company. In fact, five Franciscans were appointed by the Royal Council of the Indies to accompany him and ensure that he dealt justly with Indians. The chief of the five, Fray Juan Suárez, was a commissary, or provincial governor, in the Order of Saint Francis. The title of commissary was a religious one, and Suárez was assured by Charles V that if the pope approved, the Franciscan would become bishop of the Río de las Palmas and La Florida. Suárez already had experience in the Americas, having gone to New Spain in 1524 as one of the first twelve Franciscans sent there.[24]

All the highest-ranking officials of the Narváez expedition were appointed to their positions by the crown. These royal appointees included, in addition to the five Franciscans, three officers of the royal treasury. Most expeditions of conquest were overseen by four royal officials who were responsible for looking after the emperor's interests—a *tesorero* (treasurer), a *contador* (comptroller or accountant), a *factor* (quartermaster), and a *veedor* (inspector of mines). Only three royal officials were assigned to the Narváez expedition, however. Cabeza de Vaca, as treasurer, was the foremost of these and was to be the chief representative of Charles V in La Florida. Alonso Enríquez was to serve as *contador*, and Diego de Solís as both *factor* and *veedor*. All three were to receive salaries from the crown.[25]

Narváez himself must have recruited most of the approximately six hundred men who would sail with him from Spain. Most of these men would go as *compañeros*, or investors in his expeditionary company. In lieu of a salary, each would have expected to receive a share of the profits of their enterprise. Each may have had to pay Narváez in advance for the transatlantic passage and rations. Each would also have supplied his own armor and weapons and, if he could afford one, his horse. Thus no uniformity of quality or appearance would be found in the company's equipment. A disproportionate number of the *compañeros* would be men-at-arms, and Narváez's company was to prove short of skilled craftsmen. Only one *compañero*, for example, was a carpenter. Most of the men were hidalgos, who were in a better position than craftsmen or peasants to invest in a colonial venture. The names of some of the lower-ranking officers of Narváez's company are known, but it is not always clear whether a particular individual joined the expedition in Spain or later in the Caribbean. Jerónimo de Alaniz, the *escribano* (scribe and notary), joined at Cuba. Juan Pantoja, serving as a maritime and military captain, also seems to have joined at Cuba. Both Pantoja and Alaniz had fought with Narváez in Mexico in 1520 during the action in which Narváez lost an eye. Others who commanded ships for Narváez were Captains Caravallo and Álvaro de la Cerda, but Cerda almost certainly joined the expedition at Cuba. Military officers included Alonso del Castillo Maldonado, Andrés Dorantes, and Captains Valenzuela, Téllez, and Peñalosa. Captains Castillo and Dorantes are known to have joined the expedition in Spain.[26]

Most of those who went with Narváez were Castilian, although some were Greek or Portuguese. Not all who went were members of the expeditionary company. Ten married women and at least two African slaves went along. Accompanying Fray Juan Suárez were six natives of New Spain who had come to Spain with Suárez and were now returning to the New World. One of the six was a high-ranking lord from the Mexican city of Texcoco who had fought with Cortés against Tenochtitlán. This man's original name is variously reported to have been Ixtlilxochitl or Tetlahuehuetzquititzin, but his baptismal name was Pedro.[27]

A stipulation in his contract required Narváez to depart from Spain before the end of 1527. His expedition actually set sail in June of that year, just six months after the commander signed his *capitulaciones*. Narváez must have spent that time purchasing and fitting out his ships, recruiting personnel, and gathering equipment, provisions, and trade goods, and he took care of most of this business in Seville. Narváez purchased five caravels, which were light, swift ships with slim hulls, shallow keels, and two or three masts each. Caravels traditionally were rigged with lateen (or triangular) sails, but for an Atlantic crossing, most were rerigged with square sails. It is possible that none of Narváez's caravels measured more than fifty feet in length. Or they may have been around the size of Columbus's *Niña*, which is estimated to have measured sixty-seven by twenty-one feet, with a draft of seven feet and a burden of sixty tons. Caravels were easy to maneuver both at sea and in shallow water. They had no problem navigating the stretch of the Río Guadalquivir between Seville and the river's Atlantic outlet. Because a 1496 Spanish law required caravels to carry at least ten *bombardas* on a journey to the Indies, each of Narváez's ships must have had ten or more of the long, breech-loading cannons mounted on its deck. The ships may also have had swivel guns mounted on their gunwales. Narváez found pilots to guide him across the Atlantic, but he was unable to find any pilot in Spain with knowledge of the Gulf of Mexico. Not until he reached the Caribbean would he find a pilot who could take him to his ultimate destination.[28]

The navigational equipment of the day included an astrolabe and a quadrant for measuring latitude, a magnetic compass, a chip log, a sandglass, and a sounding lead. Columbus used a quadrant, but both the astrolabe and the quadrant were difficult to use at sea. During the age of discovery, such instruments were employed chiefly on land in order to determine the latitude of an unfamiliar territory. The only method available in the sixteenth century for measuring longitude involved timing an eclipse, and no other method would be developed until the eighteenth century. Columbus and those who followed in his wake relied more upon dead reckoning than on celestial navigation to find their way across the Atlantic. Navigation by dead reckoning involved plotting one's compass course and estimating one's speed. The magnetic compass had been in use in the Mediterranean at least since the eleventh century, and a commander like Narváez would have provided at least two of the instruments and several spare needles for each of his ships. Speed could be estimated by means of a chip log, which was attached to a long, knotted line and weighted so as to float without moving in the water. A mariner would toss a chip log overboard and then count the number of knots on its line that passed through his fingers in the space of half a minute, which explains why nautical speed even today is measured in knots. A small sandglass, in addition to a chip log, was necessary for estimating a ship's speed, and both half-minute and half-hour glasses were used at sea. By means of a half-hour glass, the daily watches were divided into equal intervals. A ship's boy generally was assigned to watch the half-hour glass and to turn it promptly when all the sand had run through. The final item of navigational equipment, the sounding lead, was not necessary in the open ocean but was indispensable in shallow water or when approaching land.[29]

Narváez probably laid in such stores as wheat, flour, sea biscuit, olive oil, wine, garlic, chickpeas, cheese, salt pork, and fresh water, which are what the caravel *Niña* is known to have carried in 1498 on Columbus's third voyage to the New World. Such provisions could be cooked at sea over a wood fire in a firebox lined with sand. Most Spanish ships at that time also carried live animals to provide meat for the officers. But if Narváez's fleet carried any live animals other than horses, there is no record of it. In addition to food stores and firewood, Narváez must have purchased ammunition and gunpowder. He and the members of his company equipped themselves well with crossbows and other weapons, but they would later find themselves short of tools, nails, rope, and other more mundane items. Narváez had the foresight to stock up on beads and bells, and probably scissors, knives, and other items he could trade with the Indians he encountered. During the spring of 1527, two expeditionary commanders were in Seville preparing to cross the Atlantic. The second was Francisco de Montejo, who was aiming to conquer and settle Cozumel and the Yucatán. Narváez and Montejo must have competed in recruiting personnel and procuring equipment and supplies.[30]

Cabeza de Vaca must have gone to Seville soon after he received his royal appointment as treasurer to the Narváez expedition. There he would have visited the Casa de Contratación to obtain instructions and what little information was available about the geography of La Florida and the Gulf of Mexico. He must also have deposited his 2,000-ducat bond with the royal treasury. He would have purchased whatever he needed in the way of personal armor, weapons, equipment, clothing, and horseflesh. Captain Alonso del Castillo Maldonado, who became Cabeza de Vaca's close associate, is known to have purchased armaments, horses, and supplies in his native Salamanca. To finance these purchases and his participation in the Narváez expedition, Castillo sold a part of his estate.[31]

One of the ten married women sailing with the expedition took the precaution of consulting a fortune teller. The seer, a Moorish woman from Hornachos, warned her client that all or almost all of those who followed Narváez into the North American interior would die. The seer hinted, however, that God might spare one man and work great miracles through him. The woman who had consulted the seer was frightened by this prophecy and lost no time in apprising her husband and other members of Narváez's company of the prediction. Apparently none of the men took it seriously.[32]

Late in the spring of 1527, Narváez mustered his expeditionary company and sailed down the Río Guadalquivir from Seville to the port of Sanlúcar de Barrameda at the river's mouth. Sanlúcar was only fourteen miles from Jerez de la Frontera, so Cabeza de Vaca probably took the opportunity to bid farewell to his relatives there. It is not known whether his wife was in Jerez or in Seville at the time, or whether she would stay with her husband's family or with hers during his absence. Before leaving his birthplace, Cabeza de Vaca probably visited the tombs of his grandfather and his parents in Jerez's monastery of Santo Domingo. No doubt, as any prudent Christian would have done before undertaking a perilous Atlantic voyage, the royal treasurer confessed his sins, received absolution, and partook of the sacrament of the Eucharist. In 1527, Cabeza de Vaca was between thirty-five and forty-two years old. Only thirty-five years had elapsed since Columbus made his historic first voyage to the New World.[33]

On 17 June 1527, Narváez's five caravels and six hundred men set sail from Sanlúcar de Barrameda for the New World. Cabeza de Vaca's cousin, Pedro Estopiñán Cabeza de Vaca, witnessed the departure. As was customary, the high-ranking members of Narváez's company probably hung their shields outboard along the gunwales of the ships. Narváez likely flew not only his personal ensign but also the imperial standard of Charles V, with its double-headed eagle, Pillars of Hercules, and *plus ultra* motto. The four ships Francisco de Montejo was taking to Cozumel and Yucatán probably left Sanlúcar at the same time. For better protection against pirates, the two expeditionary commanders would have desired to sail in tandem. As they weighed anchor and the wind filled their sails, Narváez and Montejo probably were saluted with a trumpet fanfare and the discharge of artillery, as was Hernando de Soto when his expedition sailed from Sanlúcar eleven years later.[34]

THREE

The Caribbean

Neither of the two important primary sources concerning the Narváez expedition specifies how long the expedition's Atlantic crossing took. One of those sources is Cabeza de Vaca's *Relación*, published in 1542 in Spain. The other is the account that Gonzalo Fernández de Oviedo y Valdés, the royal historian of the Indies, included in his *Historia general y natural de las Indias*. Oviedo's account is shorter and less detailed than Cabeza de Vaca's, but it supplements, generally corroborates, and occasionally differs from the *Relación*. Oviedo's account begins with the sojourn of the Narváez expedition on the island of Cuba, while Cabeza de Vaca's commences with the expedition's departure from Spain.[1]

Cabeza de Vaca wrote the *Relación* as an official report for Charles V and therefore omitted details, such as the duration of the ocean crossing, he thought were too routine to concern his sovereign. The details of the 1527 voyage can be reconstructed, however, from what is known of other voyages at the same period. Typically, a Spanish ship crossing the Atlantic would have touched briefly at the Canary Islands and would have reached the Caribbean some thirty-five to forty days after leaving Spain.[2]

The quarters aboard Narváez's five caravels must have been cramped for the six hundred people who sailed with the expedition. Most of these people would have had no assigned sleeping space, but as a high-ranking royal official, Cabeza de Vaca may have had or shared a berth in an officer's cabin. Toilet facilities would have included night buckets and perhaps a seat hung over the rail at the back of each ship. Whatever washing was done must have been done in salt water, and shaving would have been all but impossible. Vermin surely ran rampant, and the ships must have reeked with the stench of the bilges and the aroma, at mealtimes, of garlic frying in olive oil. Cabeza de Vaca's experience at sea would have been colored also by the pitch and roll of his ship, the creak of the windlasses, the groan of the masts, the whistle of the wind in the rigging, and the chanteys of the sailors as they hoisted the sails.[3]

Life at sea was punctuated by regular formalities. Watches were relieved and observations were made in a prescribed manner. On Columbus's first voyage, for example, a ship's boy turned the sandglass every half hour, and as he did so, he sang a hymn appropriate to that half hour. His song signaled the captain of the watch to check the compass bearing and the speed of the ship. Every evening before one watch relieved the other, Columbus called all hands on deck for prayers. While at sea, sailors went barefoot. The only distinctive garments Spanish sailors wore at that period were a hooded smock and a red woolen stocking cap. In the summer of 1527 the two expeditionary commanders sailing across the Atlantic in tandem, Narváez and Montejo, must have employed some system of signals for keeping their fleets together. If they used the standard system devised by the Portuguese, each vessel hung a brazier over its stern in which to make fire by night or smoke by day.[4]

The first Caribbean port of call for both the Narváez and the Montejo expeditions was Santo Domingo on the island of Hispaniola. The city, founded in 1496, served during the first quarter of the sixteenth century as the principal Spanish port in the Caribbean and the regional center of Spanish authority. It was the seat of the Audiencia of Santo Domingo, the Spanish administrative court that had jurisdiction over La Florida and the northern rim of the Gulf of Mexico. Narváez was accountable to the Audiencia and must have had to meet with its officials before proceeding onward. Santo Domingo was also home to Oviedo, the royal historian of the Indies, who would later play a role in preserving the story of the Narváez expedition.[5]

In the fall of 1527, when Narváez and Cabeza de Vaca visited Santo Domingo, the city already boasted many stone and masonry structures. Cabeza de Vaca probably entered the walled city through its Water Gate, erected in 1500. A large plaza occupied the center of the city, and a two-story palace had been built by Diego Colón, the son of Christopher Columbus. The construction of the Cathedral of Santo Domingo had begun in 1523.[6]

In addition to Santo Domingo, at least sixteen other Spanish settlements had been established in Hispaniola, and the island supported mining, cowhide, and sugar industries. The Narváez expedition spent forty five days in Santo Domingo stocking up on necessities. Among other things, Narváez purchased a sixth ship there. Supplies in Hispaniola were limited, however, and he must have had to compete with Montejo for whatever he bought.[7]

Narváez was especially anxious to acquire horses, but he was not able to purchase enough in Santo Domingo to fill his needs. He had personal experience of the valuable role horses had played in the conquests of Cuba and New Spain. The Taíno Indians were terrified of horses, which they had never seen before Columbus began importing the animals in 1493. Bartolomé de las Casas, who witnessed the conquest of the Taínos of Cuba, reported that "the horse is the deadliest weapon imaginable against these people." When Cortés first brought horses to the kingdom of Montezuma, Aztecs who saw the beasts compared them to stags: "These 'stags,' these 'horses,' snort and bellow. . . . They make a loud noise when they run; they make a great din, as if stones were raining on the earth. Then the ground is pitted and scarred where they set down their hooves." It is not clear how many horses Narváez brought with him from Spain, but some of them probably died en route. An ocean crossing was difficult for horses because they were hoisted aboard ship with a winch and then, to prevent their legs from breaking in rough seas, they were hobbled and suspended in slings for the duration of the voyage. The Atlantic tropics, where horses frequently died and had to be thrown overboard, came to be known as the "horse latitudes." The breeding of horses in Hispaniola had become a profitable business, but the animals reproduced slowly. They were in such short supply in the Caribbean islands that in 1526 the governors of both Hispaniola and Cuba banned their exportation. Narváez had had to request special dispensation from Charles V to export livestock from the islands.[8]

The economy in Hispaniola was somewhat better than that on the neighboring islands, but it had depended on the labor of Taíno workers, and many Taínos had already succumbed to exploitation and European diseases. Because of the decline in the Taíno population, the Spanish colonists in Hispaniola and the other islands found it difficult to operate their gold mines, sugar plantations, and cattle ranches. Many Spaniards, discouraged by conditions on the islands and lured by stories of Montezuma's wealth, migrated to New Spain. Other Spaniards remained on the islands and began importing African slaves. In the northwestern part of Hispaniola, a group of Taínos was waging a guerrilla war against the Spanish colonists. In an effort to bolster the Spanish presence on the island, the colonists endeavored to persuade Spanish newcomers, including the men who came with Narváez, to settle in Hispaniola. While Narváez was on the island, more than 140 men deserted from his ranks.[9]

Some of the deserters may have been frightened away from the Narváez expedition by news of the recent death of Lucas Vázquez de Ayllón, who had unsuccessfully attempted to establish a Spanish settlement on the North American mainland. This news would have concerned Narváez because he, like Ayllón, was aiming to establish a Spanish colony in North America. Ayllón had been a judge in the Audiencia of Santo Domingo, and in 1521 he had sent a slaving expedition up North America's Atlantic seaboard. The captain of this expedition sailed as far north as a region known to its natives as Chicora, probably in what is now South Carolina, and then returned to Hispaniola with a quantity of pearls and around sixty Chicoran natives, whom he had lured aboard his ship and then held captive. Most of the sixty soon died, but one of them became Ayllón's personal slave. Ayllón named this man Francisco Chicorano, taught him Spanish, and took him to Spain. Chicorano, whose chief concern seems to have been to get home again, told Ayllón many details about the riches of his homeland and about such wonders as men with tails. Ayllón used these details to persuade Charles V to authorize him to establish a colonial settlement in Chicora.[10]

In July of 1526, Ayllón left Hispaniola with Francisco Chicorano and six hundred prospective colonists and sailed northward in six ships along the Atlantic coast of North America. At Chicora, Ayllón's flagship ran aground and was lost along with most of the expedition's supplies. Soon afterward, Francisco Chicorano seized an opportunity to escape into the woods, and Ayllón never saw him again. Ayllón and his followers moved southward to a more suitable location, probably in present-day Georgia, and constructed a few buildings at a place they called San Miguel de Gualdape. San Miguel is on record as the first European colonial settlement in what is now the United States, but it was short-lived. (Not until 1565 would a permanent European colony—Saint Augustine in Florida—be established within the present U.S. borders.) Most of San Miguel's colonists quickly succumbed to hunger, disease, or hostile natives. Ayllón himself died on 18 October 1526. His surviving followers abandoned the colony, but only some 150 of them made it back to Hispaniola. Narváez and Cabeza de Vaca likely spoke with some of the survivors.[11]

After forty-five days in Hispaniola, Narváez and his armada crossed the Windward Passage to Cuba, 52 miles away. Since 1511, Narváez had made Cuba his primary home, and he must have known the island and its resources well. Gold mining and livestock production were its chief industries. Narváez's objective in Cuba was to secure additional horses and replacements for the men he had lost in Hispaniola. He also planned to visit his wife and children. His fleet anchored initially at Santiago de Cuba, on the island's southeastern coast.[12]

Santiago was the commercial center of Cuba. Narváez's friend Governor Diego Velázquez (who had died in 1524) had founded the town in 1514 and made it his capital. On its main square, Velázquez had built himself a great house of masonry and tile. In 1527, when Narváez and Cabeza de Vaca visited Santiago, the town already boasted a cathedral and a smelting works. The size of Santiago in 1527 can only be estimated, but when Hernando de Soto visited the town eleven years later, it had a Franciscan monastery and "about eighty large and well-apportioned houses."[13]

De Soto left Spain on 7 April 1538 and anchored at Santiago de Cuba two months later. His itinerary—from Spain to Cuba and then Florida—paralleled that of Narváez. Although the eleven-year interval between the two expeditions is not insignificant, it is often possible—when Cabeza de Vaca's *Relación* fails to tell us everything we want to know—to supplement the royal treasurer's observations with those made by the chroniclers of the De Soto expedition. One of these chroniclers noted, for example, that in Santiago de Cuba most of the houses had "wooden walls and roofs of hay," but some were built "of stone and lime" and were "roofed with tiles."[14]

Surrounding Santiago was Cuba's tallest mountain range, the Sierra Maestra, which shelters the town from much of the rainfall that makes the rest of the island a lush paradise. The relatively dry landscape around Santiago supports an abundance of cacti, New World plants that must have seemed exotic to Cabeza de Vaca. During the months he spent in Cuba, Cabeza de Vaca must have marveled at the many plants, birds, and other animals that were entirely new to his experience. He must also have encountered living things with which he was comfortably familiar because they had been introduced from Spain. In the latter category were oranges and figs, as well as horses, cattle, and pigs. Indigenous to Cuba were palm trees, calabash trees, mangroves, flamingos, iguanas, and manatees, all of which Columbus had reported seeing. Although New World palms were similar to palm trees in Africa, no European reptiles were as big as the iguana. One of the chroniclers of the De Soto expedition saw alligators in Cuba and snakes "as thick as a man's thigh." This same chronicler also documented the presence of pineapples, guavas, plantains, and sweet potatoes and reported that most of the island was "covered with a very lofty and dense forest."[15]

In Cuba, as in Hispaniola, Cabeza de Vaca encountered Taínos. The native people cultivated beans, squashes, peppers, gourds, and yucca in addition to maize and cassava. They wove cotton and made pottery, baskets, and stone tools. For weapons, they carried spears barbed with fish teeth. The Taínos were skilled fishermen, and they also harvested oysters, conches, and crayfish. They had a method for catching sea turtles that involved using a remora, or sucking fish, attached to a long line. The fisherman would cast the remora into the sea, wait for it to attach to a turtle, haul it and the turtle in, gaff the turtle, and then reward the remora with a few bits of turtle flesh. In both Cuba and Hispaniola, Cabeza de Vaca would have seen people smoking tobacco. The word "tobacco" is of Taíno origin, and the Taínos rolled the leaves into cigars, which they smoked by inserting one end into a nostril, lighting the other end, and inhaling. Many Spanish colonists on both islands had acquired the smoking habit from the Taínos.[16]

While in Santiago, Narváez met with Jerónimo de Alaniz, a licensed notary public who had been with him in Mexico in 1520. The captain general persuaded Alaniz to join his North American expedition as its *escribano*. Alaniz's duties were to record and notarize all the expedition's legal proceedings, especially those involving the taking of land and those that might engender either reward or blame. Narváez also recruited Alonso de Sotomayor to be his *maestre de campo*, or chief of staff.[17]

Narváez arranged with Vasco Porcallo de Figueroa, Sotomayor's brother, for the purchase of necessary supplies. Porcallo was one of the wealthiest *encomenderos* in Cuba and one of the island's most ruthless men where Indians were concerned. Narváez probably heard from Porcallo about recent Taíno uprisings in Cuba. Porcallo personally had punished three Taínos by castrating them, forcing them to eat their genitals, and then burning the men at the stake. On another occasion, when Porcallo's overworked Taíno laborers were threatening to hang themselves en masse, the *encomendero* sent his overseer to dissuade them. The overseer met the Taínos with a rope in his hands and warned them that he would hang himself along with them so that he might continue to persecute them in the afterlife. The Taínos were so horrified by this prospect that they gave up their plans for mass suicide.[18]

Porcallo lived in Trinidad, on the southern coast of Cuba and in the heart of its gold-mining region. The town was situated about one hundred leagues, or three hundred miles, west of Santiago. Not far from Santiago on the way to Trinidad was the Spanish settlement of San Salvador de Bayamo, where Narváez owned property and held a seat on the municipal council. Soon after contracting with Porcallo, Narváez took his fleet westward and anchored in the Gulf of Guacanayabo. He stationed four ships there and perhaps took the opportunity to visit San Salvador de Bayamo. Meanwhile, he ordered two of his officers, Juan Pantoja and Cabeza de Vaca, to take two ships to Trinidad to fetch the supplies Porcallo had agreed to sell. Ninety men and twenty horses went with Pantoja and Cabeza de Vaca. Their course wound through an archipelago whose hundreds of tiny islets Columbus had collectively named Los Jardines de la Reina, or the Queen's Gardens. Pantoja, Cabeza de Vaca, and their pilots must have taken frequent soundings in order to avoid running aground.[19]

The Spanish colonial settlement at Trinidad was located a league, or three miles, from the port that served it. The town was beautifully situated on a fertile plain between mountains to the north and the sea to the south, and it already had two churches. But the facilities at the port of Trinidad must have been minimal, and the harbor was made treacherous by outlying reefs. After anchoring there, Cabeza de Vaca remained offshore with the ships while Pantoja and a few men went into town. Soon after their departure, the weather took an ominous turn. The pilots on the ships grew concerned and warned Cabeza de Vaca that the port of Trinidad was unsafe.[20]

By the following morning, a Saturday, the wind and seas had grown still rougher, and rain was pouring down. Oarsmen in a dugout canoe rowed out to the ships and brought Cabeza de Vaca a letter beseeching him to come ashore to assist Pantoja with securing the supplies. Feeling responsible for the ships, Cabeza de Vaca was reluctant to leave them. The pilots, however, urged him to go and to return quickly with Pantoja so that they could depart from the unsafe harbor. Before complying, Cabeza de Vaca instructed the pilots that if the weather became truly threatening, they were to beach the ships and to land all the remaining men and horses. He entreated several men to go with him to the town, but most chose to remain on the ships in relatively dry quarters.[21]

When Cabeza de Vaca reached the town, he found the weather no better there than at the port. The wind blew now from the north and grew so strong during the night that it flattened both churches, most other buildings, and many trees and stripped the leaves from those trees that remained standing. People feared to take shelter under anything that might come crashing down around their ears. Cabeza de Vaca and seven or eight other men linked arms to resist being blown away, but they endured a hellish night of wind, torrential rain, and uninterrupted danger. At the height of the storm, Cabeza de Vaca heard voices, flutes, bells, and tambourines and worried that the local Taínos were rising against the Spaniards. These fears proved groundless, but the citizens of Trinidad lost many of their cattle and most of their stored provisions. No doubt Porcallo lost whatever he had planned to sell to Narváez. Cabeza de Vaca probably learned the Taíno word—"hurricane"—for a violent wind and rain storm. His *Relación* would contain the first description in Western literature of a Caribbean hurricane.[22]

On Monday morning, Cabeza de Vaca returned to the port with a group of men to see what had become of Narváez's two ships. Both had disappeared, and only their buoys remained. A quarter of a league away, the search party found a rowboat from one of the ships lodged at the top of a tree. At a distance of ten leagues, or thirty miles, they found some wreckage and the disfigured bodies of two men from Narváez's company. All sixty men and twenty horses that had remained aboard the ships were lost. Because he had been among the last to leave the ships, it probably seemed to Cabeza de Vaca that God had chosen him for survival. He took measures to clear himself of any appearance of negligence and sent an official report of the incident to Emperor Charles V in Spain.[23]

Narváez's four other ships in the Gulf of Guacanayabo successfully weathered the hurricane. The men aboard them were so unnerved by the experience, however, that they begged their captain general to postpone departing for the Río de las Palmas and La Florida until spring. Early in November, Narváez sailed to Trinidad and retrieved Cabeza de Vaca, Pantoja, and the approximately thirty men with them. Narváez then put Cabeza de Vaca in charge of his four remaining ships and directed him to anchor them for the winter at the Bay of Jagua. This bay, now called Cienfuegos, was west of Trinidad on the southern coast of Cuba, and it afforded a fine harbor. Cabeza de Vaca noted that Jagua was twelve leagues from Trinidad.[24]

For purposes of estimation, a league is the distance a person can walk in an hour—roughly three miles. But technically, a league is a unit of measure that has had different values at different times and in different places. Sixteenth-century Spaniards employed two kinds of leagues, and it can be difficult for modern readers to determine in a given context which kind is meant. The *legua legal* (4.19 kilometers, or 2.59 miles) was used for measuring the extent of a property. The *legua común* (5.57 kilometers, or 3.46 miles) was used for measuring the length of a journey. Most of the distances Cabeza de Vaca gives in his *Relación* are estimates, but when he wrote that Jagua was twelve leagues from Trinidad, he was probably reporting a reasonably precise figure he had learned from other Spaniards in Cuba. The distance between the two anchorages, therefore, provides a key for determining the length of Cabeza de Vaca's league. Since, in modern terms, the distance between the port of Trinidad and the entrance to the Bay of Cienfuegos is 61.5 kilometers, Cabeza de Vaca's league is equivalent to 5.13 kilometers, or 3.18 miles.[25]

Narváez probably spent the winter with his wife and family. Most of his expeditionary personnel wintered at the Bay of Jagua. Perhaps they passed the time cleaning and caulking the ships or mending ropes and sails. The entire Spanish community in Cuba that winter must have worried about continuing trouble with the Taínos. In the course of that winter, Taínos killed a number of Spaniards, burned their houses, and slaughtered their cattle.[26]

While at Jagua, Cabeza de Vaca learned some words in the Arawakan language of the Taínos. Arawakan words that have entered European lexicons, in addition to "hurricane" and "tobacco," include "maize," "cassava," "hammock," "potato," "tomato," and "canoe." In his *Relación*, Cabeza de Vaca uses most of these words, plus *areito, buhío, cacique,* and *tuna.* The word "maize," or *maíz* in the original Spanish of the *Relación*, refers to a grain known more commonly in the United States today as corn. The grain did not reach Europe until after 1492, so although it would become a staple of his diet, Cabeza de Vaca probably never tasted it before he came to the New World. The word *cacique* signified a native leader or chief, *areito* meant "festival" or "ceremony," *tuna* was the fruit of the prickly-pear cactus, and *buhío* meant "house." Oarsmen bearing a letter in a "canoe" had summoned Cabeza de Vaca to Trinidad before the hurricane. Some Taíno canoes, made from the hollowed boles of large trees, could carry more than a hundred people. Most of the Taíno *buhíos* Cabeza de Vaca saw in Cuba during the winter of 1527–28 were probably small circular structures made of wooden posts and palm thatch. *Buhíos* were furnished with wooden stools carved in the shapes of animals and with hammocks of woven cotton or grass. The house of a *cacique* might have been larger than others, rectangular, and made of wattle and daub. Cabeza de Vaca does not indicate in his *Relación* whether he witnessed any Taíno *areitos*, but other Spaniards who saw them report that they included singing and dancing. The flutes and tambourines Cabeza de Vaca heard on the night of the hurricane were probably played at *areitos*. The Taínos are known to have venerated supernatural spirits called Zemis, whose presence they represented with figurines of stone, pottery, shell, bone, or wood. Zemi figurines typically depict skeletally thin males in the squatting position with raised knees, large sunken eyes, and wide-open grimacing mouths. Among ritual and ceremonial items found in twentieth-century excavations of a Taíno site in present-day Haiti are Zemi figurines, tobacco pipes, and tubes for ingesting snuff or hallucinogens. Such items were used in Taíno *areitos* in Cuba as well.[27]

In fulfillment of his duty to keep the emperor informed of all that concerned the Narváez expedition, Cabeza de Vaca sent a letter from Jagua on 15 February 1528 to Charles V in Spain. But Cabeza de Vaca reckoned dates by the old-style Julian calendar, which had been inaugurated by Julius Caesar and was used in Spain until 1582. Over the centuries this calendar had wandered from the solar year, and so Cabeza de Vaca's dates run about ten days earlier than they should. When he says he wrote to the emperor on 15 February 1528, for example, we must add ten days and understand 25 February. Although the letter has not survived, Cabeza de Vaca's sending of it is noteworthy because it is the first event that Oviedo, as the royal historian of the Indies, recorded in his account of the Narváez expedition.[28]

At around the time Cabeza de Vaca sent his letter to the emperor, Narváez arrived at Jagua aboard a brigantine, a small, broad-beamed vessel especially suitable for navigating rivers and shallow water. Brigantines generally had one or two masts and were rigged with lateen sails and fitted with benches for oarsmen. Narváez had purchased his brigantine in Trinidad to replace one of the two ships he lost there. He had purchased another ship as well and placed it under the command of Álvaro de la Cerda, but Cerda and this ship were at Havana, on the north coast of Cuba. With Cerda's ship and the brigantine, plus the four ships Narváez had placed at Jagua in Cabeza de Vaca's charge, the governor again had six ships in his fleet.[29]

Along with him to Jagua, Narváez brought a pilot named Miruelo, whom he had recruited to guide his expedition to its destination in La Florida. Cabeza de Vaca states that Narváez hired Miruelo because he "said that he knew and had been in the Río de las Palmas and was a very good pilot of the entire north coast." The Río de las Palmas, as the southern boundary of the lands that had been granted to Narváez in La Florida, seems—judging from Cabeza de Vaca's statement—to have been Narváez's primary destination. The river's outlet into the Gulf of Mexico from present-day Tamaulipas is between the outlets of the Río Pánuco to the south and of the Rio Grande to the north, and Miruelo probably had visited at least the two more southern of the three rivers. The pilot's identity and curriculum vitae are now a matter of dispute, but it is possible that he took part in the 1519 voyage whose cartographer produced the Pineda map. It is also possible that Miruelo took part in a 1523 voyage known to have touched at the Río de las Palmas. In his discussions with Narváez, Miruelo may have claimed to know more about the Gulf coast than he actually did, and his subsequent behavior indicates that he was more familiar with its western (or Mexican) part than with its eastern part. But since the foremost qualification Narváez seems to have been seeking in a pilot was that he be able to locate the Río de las Palmas, the governor may not have concerned himself overly much with Miruelo's knowledge of the eastern Gulf.[30]

Narváez's immediate goal was to take his fleet from Jagua, on Cuba's southern coast, to Havana, on the northern coast. He intended to connect there with Álvaro de la Cerda and the ship he had placed under Cerda's command. From Havana, Narváez planned to set sail with all six of his ships for the North American mainland.

Late in February, 1528, two days after he and Miruelo arrived in Jagua, Narváez departed with his fleet of five ships for Havana. Miruelo was now the chief pilot. The composition of the expedition leaving Jagua differed from what it had been when the expedition left Spain the previous June. Of the five caravels that set out from Spain, two had been lost. Of the original six hundred men, 140 had deserted and sixty others had drowned. Narváez left Jagua with four hundred men, ten women, and eighty horses. Thus, his 1528 expedition was much smaller than the expedition of eighteen ships and eight hundred men he had taken to Mexico in 1520. Horses are the only recorded livestock that Narváez took with him from Jagua.[31]

More than likely, Narváez was unable to make all the preparations he had planned before proceeding to La Florida. He probably intended to take on livestock and provisions in Havana. Or he may have planned to sail to the Río de las Palmas, establish his base camp there, and then send back to Cuba for whatever livestock and supplies he needed. What is clear is that after leaving Cuba, Narváez and his men were very soon in want of food.[32]

The expedition ran into trouble almost immediately after leaving Jagua. In shoals off the southern coast of Cuba in what now is known as the Gulf of Batabanó, Miruelo ran the fleet aground. In this same area on his second voyage, Columbus had had to kedge the *Niña* through the shallow water by sending men in a boat to plant an anchor ahead and then pulling the ship up to the anchor. The Narváez expedition was stalled in the Gulf of Batabanó for fifteen days, its men staring at a marshy and mangrove-covered Cuban shore until the high waters of a storm finally freed the ships. The fleet then encountered another storm that delayed it for three days in the vicinity of Cabo Corrientes. Once the fleet had rounded not only that cape but also Cabo de San Antón, the westernmost point of Cuba, it proceeded eastward against the wind toward Havana.[33]

Before reaching Havana, however, and before Narváez could link up with Álvaro de la Cerda and his sixth ship or procure additional supplies, the fleet was swept away from Cuba by yet another storm and blown out into the open waters of the Gulf of Mexico. Cabeza de Vaca does not record the date on which he and his shipmates lost sight of Cuba, but it must have been in March of 1528, and they must have endured several days of bad weather and high seas before they again saw land. They surely spent at least as much time at sea as would normally be required for a voyage from Cuba to New Spain. The powerful Gulf Stream, which enters the Gulf of Mexico through the Yucatán Channel and exits through the Florida Straits, may have affected their course more than they knew.[34]

FOUR

Florida

Cabeza de Vaca reports that he and his shipmates first sighted the North American mainland on 12 April 1528, the Tuesday of Holy Week. However, his date, which he recorded eight years after the event, cannot be correct. In 1528, April 12 was actually Easter Sunday. La Florida, the region that Narváez had been authorized to explore and settle, was far vaster than the governor and his pilots seemed to realize. Miruelo seems to have thought that the fleet had arrived roughly where Narváez had hoped to arrive—somewhere near the Río de las Palmas and north of New Spain, or, in today's terms, off the northeastern coast of Mexico. But Cabeza de Vaca says that Miruelo "had already miscalculated, and he did not know where we were nor where the port was." In fact, Narváez and his men were more than nine hundred miles from the Río de las Palmas and on the opposite side of the Gulf. They were somewhere off the Florida Peninsula, probably a little north of Tampa Bay and almost due north of Havana. Why Miruelo thought they had sailed to the western side of the Gulf rather than the eastern side is hard to understand. Although he and his associate pilots had no means of determining longitude, they must have had a compass. And even if they endured bad weather for a protracted period, they must eventually have regained sight of the sun and the stars. During the time they spent at sea, the pilots seem to have grown completely disoriented. Miruelo's confusion seems especially reprehensible, since he had claimed to have prior knowledge of the Gulf coast.[1]

By 1528, only the western portion of the Gulf of Mexico coastline, from the Yucatán to the Río Pánuco, had been well mapped by Europeans, and the only available map of the eastern portion was the Pineda map. The northernmost Spanish settlement on the Gulf coast was Santisteban del Puerto, near the mouth of the Río Pánuco. In the poorly charted region north and east of Santisteban, Narváez and his pilots had only three distinct points of reference. The first was the Río de las Palmas, ninety nautical miles north of the Río Pánuco and the southwestern boundary of the lands granted to Narváez. The second was Cape Sable, at the tip of the Florida Peninsula. The third was the Río del Espíritu Santo (apparently the Mississippi), somewhere between the Río de las Palmas and Cape Sable.[2]

From a European point of view, the Florida Peninsula in 1528 was terra incognita. Only fifteen years had passed since Juan Ponce de León, in 1513, became the first European to sight and name the peninsula. Hernández de Córdoba set sail from Cuba in 1517 and coasted both the Yucatán and Florida before returning to his island base. In 1519 the maritime explorers who made the Pineda map sailed around the entire Gulf coast, reconnoitering the west coast of the Florida Peninsula in the process. Ponce de León visited Florida again in 1521 and died in the attempt to establish a colony there. And in both 1521 and 1526, Lucas Vázquez de Ayllón sent ships up Florida's Atlantic coast. But if any other Europeans visited the peninsula before 1528, they must have done so in the course of either an illegal slaving operation or a shipwreck and, in either case, left no records or maps. The Narváez expedition would make the first *entrada*, or armed entry, into the Florida interior, and Cabeza de Vaca would write the first detailed description of Florida and its native people.[3]

Cabeza de Vaca says that after sighting land, the Narváez expedition sailed along the Gulf coast for two days in the direction of Florida. He apparently meant they sailed toward Cape Sable, their eastern point of reference. In this and other contexts, Cabeza de Vaca indicates the expedition's direction of travel by speaking alternatively of "la vía de la Florida" or "la vía de Pánuco." On those occasions when Narváez and his men went in the direction of Pánuco, they were heading toward their western point of reference, the Río Pánuco in present-day Mexico.[4]

During the two days they sailed in the direction of Florida, Narváez and his pilots were probably seeking a suitable anchorage. The pilots must frequently have lowered a lead line to take depth soundings. On Maundy Thursday, two days after they first sighted land, they anchored in a coastal

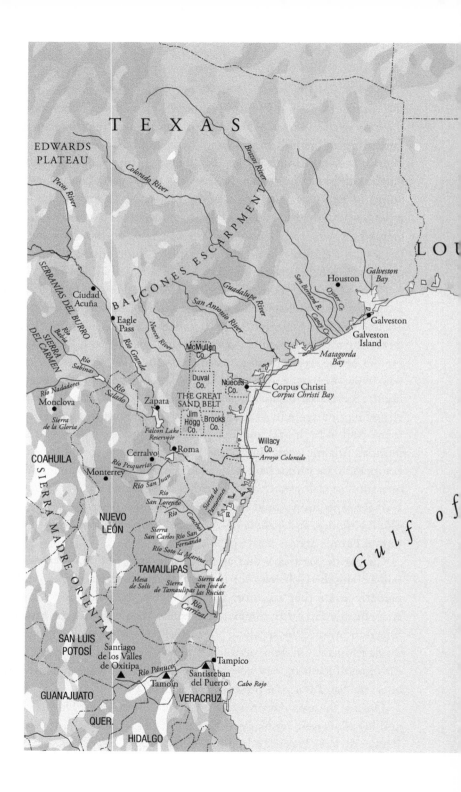

TEXAS

EDWARDS
PLATEAU

Pecos River

Colorado River

Brazos River

SERRANÍAS DEL BURRO

Ciudad
Acuña

Río
Bravia

SIERRA
DEL CARMEN

Río
Sabinas

Río Grande

Río Nadadores

Monclova

Río
Salado

Sierra
de la Gloria

BALCONES ESCARPMENT

Guadalupe River

San Antonio River

Nueces River

Eagle
Pass

Zapata

Falcon Lake
Reservoir

McMullen
Co.

THE GREAT
SAND BELT

Duval
Co.

Jim
Hogg
Co.

Brooks
Co.

Nueces
Co.

San Bernard R.

Caney Cr.

Houston

Galveston
Bay

Oyster Cr.

Galveston

Galveston
Island

Matagorda
Bay

Corpus Christi
Corpus Christi Bay

Willacy
Co.

Arroyo Colorado

LOU

COAHUILA

Cerralvo!

Río Pesquerías

Monterrey

Roma

Río San Juan

Río
San Lorenzo

Río
Conchos

Sierra de
Pamorones

Río San
Fernando

NUEVO
LEÓN

Sierra
San Carlos

Río Soto la Marina

SIERRA MADRE ORIENTAL

TAMAULIPAS

Mesa
de Solís

Sierra
de Tamaulipas

Sierra de
San José de
las Rucias

Río
Carrizal

SAN LUIS
POTOSÍ

Santiago
de los Valles
de Oxitipa

Río Pánuco

Tamoín

Tampico

Santisteban
del Puerto

Cabo Rojo

GUANAJUATO

VERACRUZ

QUER.

HIDALGO

Gulf of

Florida Peninsula, eastern Texas, and northeastern Mexico. Copyright © 2014 by the
University of Oklahoma Press.

lagoon within sight of an Indian village on the mainland shore. Cabeza de Vaca describes the houses in the village as *buhíos*. By using this Taíno term, he implies that the houses were made of wood and thatch like the houses of the indigenous people of Cuba. The royal comptroller, Alonso Enríquez, made his way in a small boat to an island in the lagoon. He was joined there by Indians who gave him fish and pieces of venison, probably in exchange for beads and other European trinkets. The meeting between Enríquez and these Indians was almost certainly a first-contact encounter.[5]

On Good Friday, the day after they anchored the ships, Narváez and most of his men disembarked by means of the ships' boats and reassembled on shore near the Indian village. Their precise landing site is not known, but Cabeza de Vaca notes that "five leagues below where we had disembarked," or approximately fifteen miles to the south, some of Narváez's men later discovered a large bay that extended seven to eight leagues into the Florida interior and could accommodate many ships. Cabeza de Vaca says that "[the bay] lies one hundred leagues from Havana, which is a settlement of Christians in Cuba, and it lies in a line north to south with this town."[6]

The men who reconnoitered the large bay were unable to communicate their discovery to Narváez, and Cabeza de Vaca did not learn of it until years afterward. Various modern researchers have proposed that the bay may have been Charlotte Harbor, Sarasota Bay, Tampa Bay, Apalachee Bay, or Pensacola Bay. Charlotte Harbor, the southernmost alternative, is only 253 miles north of Havana. Apalachee Bay and Pensacola Bay, the two northernmost alternatives, are too far from Havana to answer Cabeza de Vaca's description. The mouth of Tampa Bay, however, is some 307 miles north of Havana, or almost exactly the one hundred leagues Cabeza de Vaca's shipmates estimated. Archaeological evidence also supports the correlation of Tampa Bay with the Narváez landing site. Few European artifacts from the first half of the sixteenth century have been retrieved from sites south of Tampa Bay—that is, in the areas of Charlotte Harbor or Sarasota Bay. However, such artifacts, including glass beads and fragments of armor, have been found at several sites near or north of Tampa Bay. These artifacts probably were introduced either by the Narváez expedition in 1528 or by the De Soto expedition in 1539. Although it is not possible to distinguish Narváez's archaeological footprint from De Soto's, both expeditions seem likely to have landed somewhere in the vicinity of Tampa Bay.[7]

If Cabeza de Vaca's large bay was in fact Tampa Bay, and if the royal treasurer was correct in locating the Narváez landfall five leagues above its mouth, then Narváez must have landed somewhere on the western side of Pinellas Peninsula, in what is now Pinellas County, Florida. Tampa Bay is a large estuary with two arms. The eastern arm is known today as Hillsborough Bay, and the western as Old Tampa Bay. Pinellas Peninsula shelters the entire estuary and separates Old Tampa Bay on the east from the Gulf of Mexico on the west. A chain of sandy barrier islands lies off the outer coast of Pinellas Peninsula, and tidal passes between these islands would have allowed Narváez to access the quiet waters of any of several lagoons. Today the large lagoon that lies north of what might be described as the knuckle of Pinellas Peninsula is known as Clearwater Bay. The large lagoon south of the knuckle is known as Boca Ciega Bay. Although the configuration of islands and lagoons along Florida's Gulf coast has undoubtedly changed in the almost five hundred years since Narváez anchored there, both Clearwater Bay and Boca Ciega Bay have been proposed as the site of the Narváez anchorage.[8]

Before the arrival of the first Europeans, the Tampa Bay region supported a large population of Native Americans. Evidence of human habitation in what is now the state of Florida dates back more than ten thousand years. In 1513, when Ponce de León first visited Florida, its native population is estimated to have numbered some 350,000. During the next two centuries, however, the indigenous population of Florida would decline sharply. Many shell middens and other Native American assemblages once dotted the landscape around Tampa Bay, but most of them have by now been paved over or otherwise obliterated.[9]

One site that does remain, the Narváez/Anderson Site, can be accessed from Park Street in St. Petersburg. Its name honors Harold and Frances Anderson, who in the 1940s purchased the three-acre property in Pinellas County on which it is located. The Anderson property is on the mainland shore of Boca Ciega Bay, immediately south of Jungle Prada, a defunct 1920s shopping center. Efforts have been made to associate the Anderson property with the Narváez landfall, and a large sign, visible from Park Street, identifies the property as *the* Narváez landing site. The Anderson property features a shell mound that may have had a ceremonial function, and a large shell midden. A nearby Native American burial ground lies under the Jungle Prada complex. When I visited the Narváez/Anderson Site in 2005, I saw that someone had used a ribbon to suspend an egret feather from an oak tree overarching the shell mound. I assumed that the feather had been hung there in honor of the Native Americans who once inhabited the site, and not in honor of Narváez.

The Anderson property has been excavated twice. The first time was in the mid-1960s by Frank Bushnell, who measured the shell midden as nine hundred feet long by three hundred feet wide. Bushnell dug a test pit and found pot sherds in the indigenous Pinellas Plain style, fish and animal bones, shell tools, and—near the top—Spanish olive jar sherds. The Anderson property was excavated for the second time between 1994 and 1998 by the Central Gulf Coast Archaeological Society. Carbon 14 evidence obtained by the CGCAS suggests that the site flourished between A.D. 1300 and 1500. The shell mound may date from after A.D. 1550, however, because historic European artifacts were found at its lowest levels. Artifacts that the CGCAS recovered from the Anderson property include ceramics of both indigenous and European manufacture, bone hairpins, stone and shell tools, European glass beads, and metal fragments. Bones found at the site indicate that its aboriginal inhabitants ate fresh- and saltwater fish and shellfish, deer, turtles, and birds.[10]

Although the Native American village that once stood on the Anderson property cannot be correlated definitively with the Narváez expedition, it must have been similar to villages Narváez visited. Archaeologists have classified the Narváez/Anderson Site as one of more than a hundred Safety Harbor sites that once clustered around Tampa Bay. The archaeological nomenclature derives from the town of Safety Harbor in Pinellas County, near which several aboriginal sites have been excavated. The Safety Harbor culture flourished from approximately A.D. 900 through the period of first European contact. Safety Harbor people lived primarily as hunters and gatherers, with fish, shellfish, and wild plants as their dietary staples. Safety Harbor villages typically included a central plaza and one or more raised earthwork mounds.[11]

In 1528, soon after Narváez and his men disembarked, they visited the Indian village they had seen when they came to anchor. They found that its inhabitants had deserted the village during the night. The Spaniards explored the village, and although it consisted mostly of small huts, they discovered one structure large enough to accommodate three hundred people. They also found many fishing nets and a rattle that Cabeza de Vaca says was made of gold. The rattle must have raised their hopes of finding more such treasures.[12]

Narváez and his men set up camp in the deserted village. On Holy Saturday, their first full day ashore, Narváez ceremoniously raised the Castilian flag and—in the names of Queen Juana of Castile and her son Charles V—took possession of the land the emperor had authorized him to explore, conquer, and settle. No Indians seem to have been present, but Narváez probably read the Requerimiento, thereby giving notice to the native people that they were now subject to the pope and to the Spanish crown and faced slavery if they resisted Spanish authority. In accordance with standard protocol, Narváez presented his royal charter to the three officers of the royal treasury—Cabeza de Vaca, Alonso Enríquez, and Diego de Solís—and they in turn presented their royal commissions to him. The officers and men acknowledged Narváez as their governor and captain general, and he recognized the three royal officers as representatives of the crown. Jerónimo de Alaniz, as the expedition's *escribano*, must have recorded all these actions and certified that they occurred in the officially prescribed manner.[13]

In his first official act as governor, Narváez commanded his men to offload the horses. This was a cumbersome business that probably involved winching the animals up from the holds of the ships and swimming them to shore. Only forty-two of the eighty horses Narváez had brought from Cuba survived the journey, and they were emaciated and feeble after their long confinement in the ships.[14]

On Easter Sunday, some of the Indians from the village Narváez had occupied returned and made threatening gestures. Cabeza de Vaca reports, "It seemed to us that they were telling us to leave the land, and with this they parted from us without producing any confrontation." On Monday, Narváez decided to explore the surrounding countryside. With him, he took Cabeza de Vaca, two other officers, six horses, and forty men. Narváez, as befit his status as captain general, rode one of the horses. He and his men proceeded in a northeasterly direction, probably using preestablished Indian trails, and arrived in the evening at the inner shore of a large bay they named La Bahía de la Cruz, or the Bay of the Cross. Given that they recognized that it was a bay and not a lake, they had probably crossed Pinellas Peninsula and arrived at the western shore of Old Tampa Bay.[15]

The following day, Narváez and the men of his exploring party returned to where they had left their ships. Narváez commanded Miruelo, his chief pilot, to take the brigantine, sail along the coast in the direction of Cape Sable, and "look for the port" he "had said he knew." The pilot was apparently to look for the mouth of the Río de las Palmas, which both he and

Narváez believed was nearby. Neither man seems to have imagined that the company was anywhere near Cape Sable, at the tip of the Florida Peninsula. Nevertheless, Narváez instructed Miruelo that if he came to Cape Sable before finding the Río de las Palmas, he should proceed to Havana to fetch Álvaro de la Cerda, who was waiting there with Narváez's sixth ship. Miruelo was then to return with the captain, his ship, and additional supplies to where Narváez and the majority of his men were encamped. Miruelo set off southward in the brigantine and soon discovered the mouth of a large bay. On some subsequent sixteenth-century maps, beginning with a map drawn in 1536 but now lost, a large bay on the Gulf coast of Florida is labeled "Miruelo Bay," indicating that Miruelo recorded his discovery. Continuing southward from the bay, Miruelo must very shortly have come to Cape Sable. At that point, he must have understood how greatly he had erred in thinking Narváez was near the Río de las Palmas. Instead of returning to Narváez to apprise him of his actual location, however, Miruelo did as instructed and proceeded to Cuba to fetch Álvaro de la Cerda and the sixth ship.[16]

After sending Miruelo away, Narváez named the comptroller, Alonso Enríquez, as his lieutenant governor and turned the command of the camp and the remaining ships over to him. It is not clear whether Enríquez assumed command of three ships or of four. The expedition had left Cuba with four ships and a brigantine, and Miruelo had taken the brigantine. Then, either before or after Miruelo departed, one of the four larger ships was disabled. What most concerned Narváez on the day in question, however, was the shortage of edible provisions. Because of the many difficulties the expedition had encountered since leaving Jagua, its stores were running low, and Narváez needed to find a local source of food. He took Cabeza de Vaca, the Franciscan commissary Fray Juan Suárez, and some forty other men and returned via the overland route he had already reconnoitered to the inland shore of the Bay of the Cross. The exploring party marched four leagues along the shore of the bay and captured four Indians. Narváez had brought along some ears of maize from Cuba, and he showed these to the Indians. They indicated they knew where more could be found, and they led Narváez and his men to a village. There, the Spaniards found a small quantity of unripe maize—the first they had seen since their arrival on the North American mainland.[17]

Their discovery of maize provides another clue that the area Narváez reconnoitered was somewhere west or northwest of Old Tampa Bay. Forty years later, in 1567, Pedro Menéndez de Avilés found maize on the western side of Old Tampa Bay, but that was the only place in the greater Tampa Bay region where he found it. Archaeological evidence indicates that maize was not significant in the diet of most Safety Harbor people.[18]

In addition to maize, Narváez and his men found a number of wooden chests that were apparently of Spanish manufacture. They opened the chests, and inside each one was a decomposed human corpse covered with a painted deer hide. In the chests, they also found woven cloth, shoes, and iron that seemed to have come from Spain, and feathers and gold that seemed to have come from New Spain. Narváez and his men inferred that the local Indians had salvaged these items from a wrecked Spanish ship. The governor was interested chiefly in the gold, and when he showed it to the Indians, they indicated through gestures that more of the yellow metal could be found far to the north in a community or region they called Apalachee. The Indians indicated that there was a great deal of maize also in Apalachee.[19]

Cabeza de Vaca observed that whenever Narváez expressed an interest in some item, the Indians assured him that Apalachee held great quantities of that item. The Indians may have been trying to direct Narváez away from their home territory and into the territory of unfriendly neighbors. The chroniclers of the De Soto expedition, the next expedition to visit Florida after that of Narváez, recorded several instances when Indians lied to De Soto, telling him in effect that great riches lay on the other side of a distant hill or across a distant river, in the lands of their enemies. Similarly, Bartolomé de las Casas reported that when Columbus showed samples of gold to a group of Indians, they indicated that it was plentiful, and "whatever they saw that he showed them, they assented to it only in order to please him, for they had never seen nor known nor heard about any of the things about which he asked them." Narváez apparently heard what he wanted to hear in the reports of his Indian informants. Apalachee, he seems to have imagined, might prove as rich a prize as Tenochtitlán, the golden city of the Aztecs.[20]

Meanwhile, even though the decomposed bodies seemed to be those of Christians, Fray Juan Suárez objected to the idolatrous manner in which they had been encased in the funereal chests, and he burned both the chests and bodies inside. The governor and his men then left the village, taking their Indian captives as guides. The Indians led them to a second village, ten to twelve leagues away. The occupants of that village had fled, so Narváez and his men camped there two days. They found a large plot of ripe maize and a store of dried grain.[21]

Cabeza de Vaca says little about either of the villages Narváez and his exploring party visited, but the anonymous Gentleman of Elvas, who visited the Tampa Bay area with De Soto in 1539, describes a village he saw there that consisted of seven or eight houses made "of wood" and "covered with palm leaves." The Gentleman reports that "the chief's house stood near the beach on a very high hill which had been artificially built as a fortress," adding that "at the other side of the town was the temple and on top of it a wooden bird with its eyes gilded."[22]

On 1 May 1528, shortly after Narváez and his exploring party had returned to their base camp, the governor called a meeting to which he summoned Fray Juan Suárez, the three royal officers—Cabeza de Vaca, Alonso Enríquez, and Diego de Solís—and a mariner named Bartolomé Fernández, who was probably a pilot. The *escribano*, Jerónimo de Alaniz, took notes and made a legal record of the proceedings.

Narváez informed his officers that he had decided to make an *entrada* into the Florida interior. He wished to find the Río de las Palmas, where he hoped to establish his base camp. He needed provisions, and because one of his ships had apparently already been lost, he needed a more secure harbor. No doubt he also wished to visit Apalachee, the wealthy city or region his Indian captives had told him about. He may have been thinking, additionally, of how Cortés had scuttled his ships before leading his men into the Mexican interior. Narváez said he would take three hundred men and march in the direction of his western point of reference, the Río Pánuco. Meanwhile, the remaining one hundred men and ten women would sail along the coastline on a course parallel to that of the overland party but opposite to that Miruelo had taken a few days earlier. Whereas the maritime party would be sailing toward the Río Pánuco near present-day Tampico, Miruelo had sailed toward the tip of the Florida Peninsula.[23]

A pilot (probably Bartolomé Fernández) assured Narváez that his present position could not be more than ten to fifteen leagues from the Río de las Palmas. In the absence of Miruelo, the junior pilots seem to have reversed their opinion about the direction in which the Río de las Palmas was to be found. Or perhaps they wished to please their governor by favoring the direction he wished to take.

Cabeza de Vaca objected strenuously to Narváez's proposal to divide the expedition into overland and maritime parties. Everyone's security would be jeopardized, he argued, if they all did not stick together, and he pointed out that the pilots did not agree on their present location. Miruelo had sailed down the coast in search of the Río de las Palmas, but other pilots were encouraging Narváez to move up the coast in search of the same river. Cabeza de Vaca insisted that Narváez and his men ought to remain where they were until Miruelo returned. Not only was Miruelo the chief pilot, and the only one with firsthand knowledge of the Río de las Palmas, but he also was fetching Álvaro de la Cerda with his ship and much-needed supplies from Cuba.[24]

Narváez countered that his present location did not have "adequate foodstuffs" to support "a settlement or a port for the ships," and he noted that his current anchorage was a poor one. If he continued to moor his ships there, he risked losing them.[25]

Cabeza de Vaca suggested: "We should set sail and go seek a port and a land better for settling." If they were to move, he maintained, the entire company should move together to a more suitable port and base of operations. An overland party could then leave this base with reasonable confidence of returning there later. If the present base were abandoned before another was established, Cabeza de Vaca warned, the men of the overland party might lose track of the ships. Moreover, these men would be taking a grave risk, because they had no information about the country they would be entering, and they were all but unable to communicate with their Indian guides.[26]

Jerónimo de Alaniz agreed with Cabeza de Vaca about the importance of establishing a secure base. However, Fray Suárez said he preferred to travel overland rather than by ship, because the expedition already had suffered many storms and other hardships at sea. He accepted the opinion of the pilots that the Río de las Palmas could not be more than ten to fifteen leagues away. Suárez suggested that both an overland party and the ships might safely leave their present base, for if both moved in the same direction and hugged the coast, both would soon discover the river they were seeking. He proposed that whichever party discovered the river first should establish a base there and wait for the other to arrive. The inspector, Diego de Solís, agreed with the friar, and so Narváez decided to do as Suárez and Solís advocated and as he himself wished.[27]

Cabeza de Vaca repeated his objections to Narváez's plan and asked Alaniz to enter them into the official record of the expedition. At least this is what Cabeza de Vaca reports in his *Relación* that he did. But he wrote the *Relación* nine to ten years after his 1528 dispute with Narváez, and when he wrote it, he knew that Alaniz's records had not survived. He also knew that Narváez would never challenge his account of the argument. It is impossible to know whether Cabeza de Vaca objected to Narváez's plan as vehemently as he says he did, or whether with benefit of hindsight he merely wished he had. Perhaps, since he wrote the *Relación* for Charles V, he wished the emperor to think he had opposed Narváez's plan. Judging from Cabeza de Vaca's subsequent behavior, however, it seems likely his confrontation with Narváez occurred much as he says it did. On at least two other occasions, Cabeza de Vaca would argue eloquently in favor of keeping the men of Narváez's expeditionary company together.[28]

Oviedo's account of the Narváez expedition, moreover, confirms what Cabeza de Vaca relates about the dispute. Oviedo's narrative is based on the now lost *Joint Report* that Cabeza de Vaca and two other survivors of the Narváez expedition prepared in 1536 in New Spain. Part of the historical significance of Oviedo's narrative is that it is based on information that two other witnesses, and not just Cabeza de Vaca, swore to be true. Regarding the instance of the confrontation that occurred on 1 May 1528 between Narváez and Cabeza de Vaca, Oviedo states that "the Treasurer, Cabeza de Vaca, said that he thought the ships should not be abandoned, but that they should be left in port at the settlement."[29]

In his *Relación*, Cabeza de Vaca reports that after he asked Alaniz to record his objections to Narváez's plan, the governor countered by asking the *escribano* to record and certify his own reasons for splitting his force into land and sea parties. Narváez then suggested that if Cabeza de Vaca were so fearful of losing track of the ships, he should travel with them. The governor intended to take command of the overland party, and he proposed to put Cabeza de Vaca in charge of the maritime contingent. Recoiling from the imputation of cowardice, Cabeza de Vaca replied hotly:

> I refused to take that responsibility because I was certain and knew that he would not see the ships again nor the ships him, and that I understood this on seeing how unprepared they were to go inland, and that I was more willing than he and the others to expose myself to danger and endure whatever he and the others were to endure than to take charge of the ships and give occasion that it be said, as I had opposed the overland expedition, that I remained out of fear, for which my honor would be under attack, and that I preferred risking my life to placing my honor in jeopardy.

Narváez, seeing that Cabeza de Vaca was adamant, gave command of the ships to Captain Caravallo, a magistrate from Cuenca de Huete. Narváez informed Cabeza de Vaca that he was welcome to march with the overland party, but relations between the governor and the royal treasurer were now strained.[30]

Meanwhile, the news of Narváez's decision to march with three hundred men into the unknown interior of La Florida spread quickly through the camp. The men who were to accompany the governor began readying their weapons and gear. Narváez directed that two pounds of ship biscuit and half a pound of salt pork be issued to each member of his overland party, but these meager rations were not sufficient to sustain the men for more than a few days. Upon learning that her husband was to march with Narváez, one of the ten married women associated with the expeditionary company became very agitated. This was the woman who, before leaving Spain, had consulted the seer of Hornachos. She confronted Narváez, told him of the seer's prophecy, and admonished him not to go inland. She warned that if he did, "neither he nor any one of those who went with him would escape from the land, and that if one of them were to come out, God would perform great miracles through him." She believed, however, that few or none would survive. Narváez replied that although some of the men undoubtedly would die, those who survived and succeeded in conquering La Florida would become rich. The woman then turned to the other nine wives and advised them henceforth to consider themselves widows and to waste no time finding new husbands.[31]

Narváez instructed Captain Caravallo to take the ships, the women, and the remaining one hundred men and sail northward in the direction of the Río Pánuco. When they came to a good harbor, they should stop there and wait for the overland party. The governor then set off northward at the head of a company of 40 horsemen and 260 foot soldiers.[32]

Cabeza de Vaca says that in addition to their ship biscuit and salt pork, the men took along beads and bells to trade with the Indians. He notes that some of the men carried crossbows and arrows. Other men probably carried harquebuses, swords, shields, lances, and halberds. A harquebus was a matchlock gun and was difficult to fire and reload. A lance was a long wooden shaft with a steel point at the end. A halberd was similar to a spear, but its head combined a spear point, an ax blade, and a hook.[33]

Narváez's men must have worn helmets and body armor. Most of their helmets probably were of the morion type, with a peaked crest and a short brim rising to a peak in both front and back. Some of the cavalrymen may

Bronze bust, sculpted by Pilar Cortella de Rubín, representing Álvar Núñez Cabeza de Vaca. The bust, presented to the city of Houston in 1986 by King Juan Carlos of Spain, stands in Hermann Park in Houston, Texas. Photograph by Juris Zagarins.

have worn plate armor, consisting of a metal cuirass to protect the body trunk, and metal coverings for the outsides of the arms and thighs. Other men may have worn chain mail. Plate armor was very heavy, and even a shirt of chain mail could weigh between fifteen and thirty pounds. A lighter alternative was brigandine armor, made by riveting small overlapping steel plates to a leather or canvas doublet. Such a brigandine doublet might weigh around twenty pounds and afforded more freedom of movement than plate armor. An even lighter option was the kind of quilted cotton armor that Cortés's men had adapted from the Aztecs. The cotton armor was more comfortable than metal in a hot climate, but still afforded good protection against Indian arrows. Some of De Soto's men are known to have worn quilted cotton armor when they visited Florida. A suit of plate armor now in New York City's Metropolitan Museum of Art—consisting of a helmet, a cuirass, cuisses for the thighs, plates for the upper and lower arms, gauntlets, and elbow and knee cops—weighs seventy-seven pounds. At the same museum, another suit of armor—which features a brigandine doublet, a helmet, pauldrons for the shoulders, elbow and knee cops, gauntlets, cuisses, greaves for the lower legs, and sabatons for the feet—weighs forty-one pounds.[34]

Among the members of the overland company, in addition to Governor Narváez and Cabeza de Vaca, were the other two officials of the royal treasury and the five Franciscans. Narváez led his men on a course parallel to the coast but several miles inland from it. The coastline was convoluted and lined with salt marshes, mudflats, and swamps. A few miles inland, however, the ground was higher and less marshy. Narváez's exact route is not known, but it corresponded roughly to the present U.S. Route 19. The governor probably made use of existing Indian trails.[35]

Narváez and his three hundred men marched northward for fifteen days without encountering any major natural obstacles. This fact provides further evidence that they began their trek from a point north of Tampa Bay. If they had begun from a more southerly point such as Charlotte Harbor or Sarasota Bay, they would have to have marched around Tampa Bay and crossed the Manatee River, but Cabeza de Vaca does not mention either skirting the one or crossing the other. During these first fifteen days, Narváez and his men saw no Indians or native settlements, but they were aware of their vulnerability to Indian attack. The land, Cabeza de Vaca observed, was "flat" and "composed of hard, firm sand."[36]

The men passed many small lagoons and saw many deer. Although they were short of food, they do not seem to have hunted the deer or fished. The land was forested with longleaf and loblolly pines, southern magnolias, sweet gums, white oaks, and beeches. Many of the trees were festooned with Spanish moss. Cabeza de Vaca saw palmetto palms, which reminded him of similar palms that grew in his Andalusian homeland. He and his companions ate the large leaf buds of the palmettos, and during the early stages of their journey, this seems to have been the only food they found to supplement their ship biscuit and salt pork. They did not lack for water, though. Florida has many springs, fed by a porous limestone aquifer that extends into parts of Mississippi, Alabama, Georgia, and South Carolina and contains more water than all the Great Lakes combined.[37]

After fifteen days, Narváez and his men came to a river with a swift current, which they spent a day in crossing. It probably was the Withlacoochee. Some of the men swam across it; others built rafts. On the opposite side, they were confronted by a party of two hundred Indians, who had probably been watching the Spaniards for several days and chose to meet them at the spot where they would be most vulnerable. Narváez attempted through signs to communicate with the Indians, but they answered with hostile gestures, and both sides quickly resorted to blows.[38]

It may be no coincidence that near the Withlacoochee, at the Tatham Mound site in present-day Citrus County, archaeologists excavating native burials have unearthed a human arm bone and a human shoulder bone displaying cuts from edged metal weapons. Because early sixteenth-century European beads were found at the same site, it seems likely that the men of either the Narváez or the De Soto expedition inflicted the cuts to these bones. Also at Tatham Mound, archaeologists have uncovered the bones of at least seventy-seven individuals in a mass grave. A plausible explanation is that these individuals all died within a short space of time, perhaps of a disease introduced into Florida by either Narváez or De Soto.[39]

Cabeza de Vaca reports that in the course of their struggle near the swift river, Narváez's men succeeded in capturing five or six Indians before the others withdrew. Narváez and his men forced their captives to lead them to a village half a league away, where the hungry Spaniards found a great quantity of maize. They remained in the village several days, feasting on the maize.

Three days after their arrival at the village, Cabeza de Vaca, the other two officers of the royal treasury, and Fray Suárez approached Narváez and begged him to allow them to search westward for the sea and their ships. They had learned from their Indian captives that the sea was not far away, and they probably hoped that the swift river they recently had crossed would prove to be either the Río de las Palmas or the Río Pánuco. Narváez replied that the sea and the ships were not a major concern. For the governor, the priority clearly was gold, and finding Apalachee was more important than finding the Río de las Palmas. But when Cabeza de Vaca persisted with his entreaties, Narváez conceded that he might take a party of men downriver on a scouting expedition. The governor would not permit him to take any horses, however. Narváez said the terrain was too difficult for horses, and he was reluctant to risk losing any on what he considered an unnecessary venture.[40]

Cabeza de Vaca took forty men on his reconnaissance mission. One of them was Captain Alonso del Castillo Maldonado, whose name appears at this point for the first time in Cabeza de Vaca's *Relación* and reappears many times thereafter. Cabeza de Vaca and his party marched westward for half a day until they came to a large swampy area. In the sixteenth century, much of the area around the Withlacoochee River was forested wetland with lofty stands of cypress trees. In addition to trees, Cabeza de Vaca and his men probably encountered thorny bamboo and poison ivy. They probably saw egrets and other herons, white ibis, wood storks, and wild turkeys. There must have been many birds. And many bugs. It was late May, and probably hot, and the men probably were wearing armor. They waded through the swamp for a league and a half, or about five miles. The water in many places was up to their knees, and they cut their feet repeatedly on oyster shells. They must have been wearing boots, so they probably damaged their boots as well. After their painful struggle across the swamp, they again encountered the river they had crossed four days previously. Having no means to cross it again, they returned through the swamp to the village where Narváez was encamped.[41]

The following day, the governor sent out a larger exploring party consisting of six horsemen and sixty foot soldiers under the command of Captain Valenzuela. Narváez instructed Valenzuela to cross the river where the entire expedition had crossed it and then to follow its course to the sea. Valenzuela returned after two days, saying that although he had reached the mouth of the river, the water there was barely knee-deep and afforded no harbor. He had found only salt marsh and mudflat and had seen no sign of Narváez's ships. No ships could anchor there, and the river clearly was neither the Río de las Palmas nor the Río Pánuco. Valenzuela had only seen five or six canoes manned by Indians bedecked in large plume feathers.[42]

After receiving Valenzuela's report, Narváez ordered his men to pack up their gear and whatever maize remained in the village they were occupying. The company then set off again with their captive Indian guides, in search of Apalachee and the riches Narváez hoped to find there. The men marched northward for several weeks without meeting any Indians. They were aware of Indians around them, watching them, but none came forward either to greet them or to obstruct their progress. The Spaniards were marching on empty stomachs. They were subsisting primarily on maize they seized from Indian farms and villages, but they often went four or five days without finding any grain to seize.[43]

On 17 June 1528, some seven weeks after Narváez had parted with his ships, a native chief came out in procession with many of his people to meet the Spanish governor and his men. Indians playing reed flutes marched at the head of the procession. The chief, who was called Dulchanchellin, wore a painted deer-hide cloak and was carried on the shoulders of other Indians. Narváez presented Dulchanchellin with beads and bells he had brought from Spain.[44]

Dulchanchellin is the only Florida native whom Cabeza de Vaca identifies in his *Relación* by name, but the royal treasurer fails to identify either the chief's village or his cultural community. Dulchanchellin and his people probably spoke a Timucuan language. From Spanish accounts dating from later in the sixteenth century, Timucuan speakers are known to have occupied most of northern peninsular Florida from the Atlantic seaboard in the east to the Aucilla River in the west. From the chronicles of the De Soto expedition, which passed through the Timucuan homeland in 1539, it is clear that at least some Timucuans were inimical to their neighbors the Apalachees, who lived west of the Aucilla. The honor accorded to Dulchanchellin by his people suggests they had a hierarchical social organization. The meeting between Narváez and Dulchanchellin was almost certainly a first-contact encounter.[45]

A painting made later in the sixteenth century by the French artist Jacques le Moyne de Morgues can give us an idea of Dulchanchellin's appearance. Le Moyne came to Florida in 1564 with a group of French Huguenots who were chased out of the area a year later by the Spanish. During his year in Florida, Le Moyne made several paintings of the Timucuan Indians, and although engraved copies of these can still be viewed, only one of his originals has survived. It shows a Timucuan chief with his arm around the shoulder of a Frenchman, while a nearby group of Timucuan people venerates a stone column erected by the French. The chief is significantly taller than the Frenchman he embraces. The Timucuans have decorated the stone column with flowers and have arranged a bow and arrows and baskets of corn, squash, and beans in a cleared space before it. Le Moyne represents the Timucuans as wearing breechclouts and earrings. In a narrative commentary, the artist observes that, among Timucuans, both "men and women have their ears pierced, and fix in them little inflated fish-bladders, shining like pearls, colored and looking like wet carbuncles." In the painting, the Timucuan men wear their hair roped around the crowns of their heads and then gathered into a topknot. The chief is heavily tattooed, he wears bracelets and anklets, and his breechclout is fringed with shell or copper beads. He has draped three strands of beads over one shoulder, and he has inserted a plume feather into his topknot.[46]

At the meeting between Dulchanchellin and Narváez, the chief received the beads and bells the governor gave him, and he presented the Spaniard with the deer-hide cloak he was wearing. Having no common language and no interpreter, the two leaders conferred by means of gestures and may not have understood one another well. The one word they had in common was "Apalachee." Narváez indicated he was searching for a city or region of that name, and he understood from Dulchanchellin's response that the

LAUDONNIERVS ET REX ATHORE ANTE COLVMNAM A PRÆFECTO PRIMA NAVIGATIONE LOCATAM QVAMQVE VENERANTVR FLORIDENSES.
deerbin de Moyne de tuus de Morgues ad vinom pinxit

Gouache by Jacques le Moyne de Morgues, showing French explorer René de Laudonnière and Timucuan chief Athore, 1564. Print Collection, Miriam and Ira D. Wallach Division of Art, Prints and Photographs, The New York Public Library, Astor, Lenox and Tilden Foundations.

chief and his people were on unfriendly terms with the city or region he was seeking. Narváez understood also that Dulchanchellin would aid him in a military action against Apalachee, and he welcomed the chief's offer of aid. Dulchanchellin's familiarity with Apalachee must have reassured Narváez that he was not chasing a will-o'-the-wisp.[47]

When the conference was at an end, Dulchanchellin and his people withdrew, and Narváez and his men followed slowly after them. At nightfall the Spaniards came to a river that was too wide, deep, and swift for them to cross on rafts. The river was the second to confront them since they parted from their ships, and it was larger than the one they had crossed three to four weeks earlier. This second river probably was the Suwannee. One of the horsemen, Juan Velázquez, rode foolhardily into the river, and his comrades watched in horror as he and his horse were swept away by the current and drowned. The remaining men had no choice but to camp where they were for the night. Velázquez was the first of their company to die in La Florida, and as they sat around their campfires that evening, they must have remembered the prophecy of the woman who foretold the deaths of all who followed Narváez into the Florida interior. In the morning the men somehow constructed a canoe and began the laborious process of crossing the river. It took them an entire day to cross it, and they worried the whole time about the danger of Indian attack. As it happened, Indians from Dulchanchellin's village gave them some assistance in crossing and also helped them retrieve the bodies of Juan Velázquez and his horse. Cabeza de Vaca was averse to eating horseflesh, but many of his companions dined that evening upon Velázquez's horse.[48]

The following day, Narváez and his men arrived at the village of Dulchanchellin. The chief sent Narváez a gift of maize, but when a group of Spaniards went to get water, Dulchanchellin's people shot arrows at them. None of the Spaniards were hurt, but their relations with the Indians soured. When they awoke the next morning, the Spaniards discovered that Dulchanchellin and his people had fled. Narváez and his men soon pulled up stakes too, probably after first helping themselves to more maize. During the ensuing days, they occasionally were confronted by Indians who threatened but did not molest them. Narváez captured three or four of these Indians and forced them to serve as guides. The captives probably led Narváez toward Apalachee territory, but it is not clear whether their line of march was northward or paralleled the coast, which gradually turns westward beyond the Suwannee.[49]

Cabeza de Vaca observed that, beyond the Suwannee, "[the country became] very difficult to maneuver and glorious to see, because in it there are very great forests, and the trees wonderfully tall, and there are so many that are fallen upon the ground that they hindered our progress, so that we could not pass without making many detours." Many of these trees, Cabeza de Vaca noted, "were split from top to bottom by lightning bolts that strike in that land where there are always great storms and tempests." In the sultry June weather of north central Florida, several of the Spaniards developed sores on their backs and shoulders from the chafing of their armor and heavy weapons.[50]

FIVE

Apalachee

On 25 June 1528, the day after the Feast of Saint John the Baptist and eight days after their meeting with Dulchanchellin, Narváez and his men caught sight of the largest native settlement they had yet beheld. The village of forty houses probably lay somewhere between the Aucilla and the Apalachicola Rivers. Narváez and his men had marched for forty-nine days since parting with their ships at the Bay of the Cross, and they believed they had reached Apalachee. The Spaniards gave thanks to God for putting foodstuffs and much gold within their reach and for bringing their hardships to an end. As it happened, their prayers of thanksgiving were premature.[1]

Narváez ordered Cabeza de Vaca and Diego de Solís, the royal quartermaster, to take nine horsemen and fifty foot soldiers and attack the village. Cabeza de Vaca seems to have complied without hesitation. And since the five Franciscans were supposed to rule on the justice of any action against Indians, they must have given Narváez their blessing. When Cabeza de Vaca and Solís entered the village, they found no adult males in residence. They rounded up the women and children and searched the houses. The two royal officers found maize, both dried and ready to be harvested. They also found mortars for grinding maize, many deer hides, and some woven blankets of the type the village women were wearing as cloaks. The Spaniards found no gold. Cabeza de Vaca observed that the village's "forty small houses" were "built low to the ground and in protected places, out of fear of the great tempests that commonly occur with great frequency in that land." After a short time, the men to whom the village was home attempted to regain it from the Spanish intruders. The native men succeeded in killing Solís's horse but then retreated. Narváez and the main body of Spaniards must have occupied the village soon afterward.[2]

Our current knowledge of the Apalachee people and their culture derives partly from European accounts, beginning with Cabeza de Vaca's, and partly from archaeological investigation. The Apalachees had developed the most complex pre-Columbian society in what is now the state of Florida, and archaeologists can trace their ancestors back to approximately A.D. 1100. At the time Narváez encountered them, the Apalachees were living in several villages in the area bordered by the Aucilla River on the east, the Gulf of Mexico on the south, the Ochlockonee River on the west, and roughly the present Florida-Georgia border on the north. The St. Marks River and its tributary, the Wakulla, flow through the center of this area. The present Florida state capital, Tallahassee, lies within what once was Apalachee territory. And although the range does not extend into Florida, the Apalachee name became associated through some historical fluke with the Appalachian Mountains, which stretch along the Atlantic seaboard of the United States from Maine to Georgia. Cabeza de Vaca's narrative indicates that, in 1528, Florida natives from as far away as Tampa Bay recognized the Apalachees as a distinct and powerful people. Chief Dulchanchellin, whom Narváez and Cabeza de Vaca encountered in the region of the Suwannee, identified himself as an enemy of the Apalachees.[3]

Two days after Narváez occupied the village of forty houses, its chief and a delegation of his men met with the Spanish governor to negotiate. The native men asked the governor to release their wives and children. Narváez complied, but he kept the chief as his hostage. The governor clearly was imitating the action of Cortés, who, soon after entering Tenochtitlán, had made a hostage of the Aztec emperor Montezuma. The relations between Narváez and the people of the village he was occupying took an immediate turn for the worse. The following day, in an attempt to liberate their chief, two hundred Indians attacked the village and set fire to several houses. Narváez and his men killed one of them and repulsed the others, but the Indians hid in the nearby lagoons and in the cornfields and continued to harass the Spaniards. Since Narváez hoped to conserve the cornfields, he refrained from engaging the Indians there. When the Spaniards went to get water, Indians appeared seemingly from nowhere and shot arrows at

them. The Indians wounded several men and horses, and they killed one of
the six natives of New Spain who had joined the Narváez expedition along
with Fray Juan Suárez. The slain man, whom Cabeza de Vaca knew as don
Pedro, had been a lord of Texcoco and had fought with Cortés against the
Aztecs. Don Pedro's death must have further unnerved Narváez's already
nervous men.[4]

The Apalachee chief whom Narváez was holding hostage told the Spanish governor he was occupying the largest and richest village of the region,
or so Narváez understood. But either the chief lied to Narváez or the two
men failed to understand one another. Perhaps the chief wished to dissuade Narváez from exploring, and thus from discovering a richer town
nearby. He warned Narváez that much of the land surrounding his village
was densely wooded and difficult to traverse. Narváez spent twenty-five
or twenty-six days in the village, and during this time he and his men
made three forays into the nearby countryside. In the area immediately
surrounding the village, Cabeza de Vaca saw outlying houses and many
fields of maize. At a further distance, however, the country seemed poor
and sparsely populated. Narváez must have been bitterly disappointed. His
dreams of finding gold and another treasure city like Tenochtitlán must
quickly have evaporated. The local Indians continued to harass him, and
their hostility seems to have drained Narváez of his desire to emulate his
erstwhile rival, Hernán Cortés.[5]

In his assessment of the poverty of the Apalachee region, however,
Narváez clearly was mistaken. Perhaps he was too fixated on gold and not
sufficiently cognizant of the region's fertile soils and agricultural richness.
Eleven years after Narváez visited the Apalachee region, the De Soto expedition spent five months there. De Soto visited at least one Apalachee
village that was larger and more prosperous than the one Cabeza de Vaca
describes. Luys Hernández de Biedma, one of the De Soto chroniclers,
reports that "[in the] province of Apalache there are many towns, and it
is a land of plentiful food." Another De Soto chronicler, the anonymous
Gentleman of Elvas, lists the kinds of available foods, noting that, in addition to maize, there were "pumpkins, beans, and dried plums native to the
land, which are better than those of Spain and grow wild in the fields without being planted." The Gentleman of Elvas identifies the town of Anhaica
Apalache as the largest one in the region and says that several smaller towns
were under its jurisdiction. A third De Soto chronicler, El Inca Garcilaso,
says that the principal town "consisted of 250 large and substantial houses."

Garcilaso's report of 250 large houses is significantly at variance with Cabeza de Vaca's report of "forty small houses, built low to the ground." It seems likely that De Soto visited the principal town and several satellite villages of what is known to ethnographers today as the Apalachee chiefdom. Narváez and Cabeza de Vaca seem merely to have visited one of the satellite villages.[6]

Narváez and Cabeza de Vaca retain the distinction, however, of having brought the Apalachee chiefdom its first contact with the European world. A chiefdom is a type of social structure in which several kinship groups or clans live and work together cooperatively under a chief or hierarchical series of chiefs. Such a social structure can evolve only among people who practice agriculture and live in fixed villages. While the majority of individuals in a chiefdom work to produce food, some are able to specialize in such activities as canoe building or the making of pottery or of bows and arrows. The Apalachee chiefdom was the largest and most complex native society the Narváez expedition would encounter in what is now the state of Florida. Neither the hunting-and-gathering people Narváez met in the region of Tampa Bay nor the Timucuans he met near the Suwannee River had developed a chiefdom.[7]

Apalachee villages typically boasted a plaza and one or more large, flat-topped earthen mounds that served as bases for temples and chiefly residences and as burial sites. Although Cabeza de Vaca does not mention mounds, the De Soto chroniclers saw several of them in the Apalachee region. El Inca Garcilaso, in the first written account of Indian laborers constructing a mound, says: "Amassing a very large quantity of earth, they pack it down by treading on it, raising it up in the form of a hill two or three pike-lengths in height." The most significant Apalachee mound center is located in present-day Tallahassee at the Lake Jackson Mounds Archaeological State Park and seems to have flourished from approximately A.D. 1100 to 1500. A pre-Columbian copper plate found at this site bears an image in hammered relief of an Apalachee falcon dancer. The dancer wears a ceremonial feathered cape and an elaborate beaked headdress. No European artifacts, however, have been found at the site. For reasons that are not now clear, the Apalachees abandoned the Lake Jackson mound center around A.D. 1500, just decades before Narváez and Cabeza de Vaca visited the area.[8]

Cabeza de Vaca observes that the Apalachees cultivated maize. They also are known to have cultivated squash and beans and to have periodically burned their fields to clear them for planting. In addition to farming, the Apalachees hunted, fished, and gathered shellfish, wild fruits, and nuts. They used canoes to get from place to place and to transport goods. They used stone, wood, bone, and shell tools, and they manufactured pottery. They spoke a Muskogean language, and they played an elaborate and often brutal ball game.[9]

During the time that Narváez and his men spent in the Apalachee village of forty houses, Cabeza de Vaca marveled at northern Florida's primordial forest and its numerous lakes and springs. He saw "very thick woods and great groves and many lagoons where there are many and very large fallen trees that form obstructions and make it impossible to traverse the land without great difficulty and danger." In the forest, he came across "walnut trees, and laurels and others that are called liquidambars, cedars, savins and evergreen oaks and pines and oaks, [and] palmettos of the type commonly found in Castile." He encountered many kinds of birds, including "geese in great numbers, ducks, mallards, royal-ducks, fly-catchers and night-herons and herons, [and] partridges," as well as "many falcons, gyrfalcons, sparrow hawks, merlins, and many other birds." He also documents "deer of three types, rabbits and hares, bears and lions, and other wild beasts, among which we saw an animal that carries its young in a pouch in its belly, and all the while the offspring are small, they carry them there until they know how to forage for food, and if by chance they are searching for food and human beings come upon them, the mother does not flee until she has gathered them up in her pouch." This last animal, clearly an opossum, was new to Cabeza de Vaca—since there were no marsupials in Europe—and he was the first writer ever to describe it. The "lions" he refers to must have been Florida panthers. Cabeza de Vaca fails to mention other plants and animals he is likely to have seen. He does not mention alligators or the green-and-yellow Carolina parakeets that, although plentiful in the sixteenth century, are now extinct. He makes no reference to hummingbirds, even though they are native exclusively to the Americas.[10]

Meanwhile, Narváez was growing increasingly discouraged by the apparent poverty of the land and by the constant harassment from Indians. The Apalachee chief he was holding hostage told Narváez that if he marched southward for nine days, he would find the sea. Near the sea, the chief said, was the village of Aute, which had abundant resources of maize, beans, squash, and fish. The chief seems to have been trying to persuade Narváez to go south.[11]

Narváez and his men withdrew from the chief's village without incident on or about 19 July 1528. Narváez took the chief along as a guide, but the hostage seems to have led the Spaniards through difficult terrain where they would be vulnerable to attack. On the second day of their march, Narváez and his men came to the shores of a lagoon they could not easily cross. The water came up to a man's chest, and in it were many submerged trees. When the Spaniards were in the midst of this swamp, they were attacked by Indians—apparently Apalachees—who had been hiding in the forest. In short order, the Indians wounded many Spaniards and their horses and liberated the hostage chief. The Spaniards managed to free themselves from the swamp, but the Indians pursued them, and the Spaniards quickly became demoralized. They marveled at the power of the Indians' bows, which Cabeza de Vaca says were made of wood "as thick as an arm [and] eleven or twelve spans long so that they can shoot arrows at two hundred paces with such great skill that they never miss their target." Some Spaniards swore they had seen an oak as thick as the calf of a man's leg pierced through by an arrow. Cabeza de Vaca saw a poplar tree that an arrow had penetrated to a depth equivalent to the distance between a man's thumb and his outstretched forefinger. The Indians seemed to Cabeza de Vaca to be giants, and he reports they were "wonderfully well built, very lean and of great strength and agility."[12]

No doubt the Indians used paint to enhance the ferocity of their appearance. In 1700 a Spanish missionary wrote of the Apalachees that "in order to give battle they dress themselves elaborately, after their usage, painted all over with red ochre and with their heads full of multicolored feathers." Cabeza de Vaca says nothing about scalping, but the chroniclers of the De Soto expedition later testified that Apalachee warriors scalped their fallen enemies.[13]

A league from the lagoon where the Indians attacked them, the Spaniards came to an even more daunting body of water that was half a league long. The Spaniards feared to cross it, but when they did so, the Indians inexplicably left them alone.

At a third lagoon the Spaniards came to on the following day, Cabeza de Vaca, in the advance guard, spotted footprints and alerted Narváez in the rear. The Indians attacked the Spaniards shortly thereafter but did them little harm because the Spaniards were expecting the attack. After the Spaniards cleared the lagoon, the Indians continued to stalk them, so the Spaniards set an ambush and killed two of the stalkers. In return, the Indians wounded Cabeza de Vaca and two or three other Spaniards, but apparently not seriously. The Indians retreated to the woods and, although they followed after the Spaniards, offered no further provocation for eight days. Meanwhile, the Spaniards were cheered by their discovery of a river that they named the Río de la Magdalena. The likely date of their discovery was 22 July, the Feast of Saint Mary Magdalene.[14]

The Spaniards were one league from Aute when Indians again attacked them. A boy in the rear guard shouted the alarm, and an hidalgo named Avellaneda responded. But as soon as he turned to the rear, an Indian arrow caught him through the neck, killing him. Avellaneda was at least the third of Narváez's men to die in La Florida.

The Spaniards arrived in Aute nine days after leaving the Apalachee village of forty houses. Their journey had taken exactly as long as the hostage chief had said it would, but the chief seems to have sent the Spaniards to Aute by the worst possible route, through one swamp after another. We do not now know the exact locations of either the Apalachee village Narváez occupied or of Aute, but nine days is more time than Narváez should have needed to travel from one to the other. The distance between the two villages cannot have been much more than forty miles.[15]

The residents of Aute had clearly anticipated the Spaniards' arrival, and Narváez and his men found the village abandoned and its houses and cornfields burned. The Spaniards were pleased to discover, however, that the retreating Indians had failed to destroy all their maize. Nor had they destroyed the squash and beans they had been on the point of harvesting. Narváez and his men rested at Aute for two days.[16]

Whether Aute was a part of the Apalachee chiefdom is uncertain. It is only clear that the village was on the Río de la Magdalena and grew maize, beans, and squash. Cabeza de Vaca testifies that maize was cultivated throughout those parts of the present state of Florida he visited. His meticulousness in reporting where he and his companions found maize may reflect the hunger he experienced while traveling in Florida, but it also demonstrates his awareness that information on the availability of maize would be invaluable to any future explorer attempting to follow in Narváez's footsteps. Hernando de Soto, as it happened, would appreciate the information.[17]

On their third day at Aute, Narváez ordered Cabeza de Vaca to go in search of the sea, which the Apalachee hostage chief had said was nearby. Narváez seems finally to have perceived the danger in remaining indefinitely out of contact with his ships. He had given up on discovering a second Tenochtitlán, and survival had become his paramount concern. Cabeza de Vaca complied with the governor's orders and recruited three of his fellow officers, seven horsemen, and fifty foot soldiers to follow him down the Río de la Magdalena. The three other officers were Fray Juan Suárez, Captain Alonso del Castillo Maldonado, and Captain Andrés Dorantes. Captain Dorantes, like Captain Castillo, was destined to become important to Cabeza de Vaca, and his name appears at this point for the first time in the royal treasurer's *Relación*. Cabeza de Vaca set off with his sixty men, and in the evening they reached the mouth of the river. They found many oysters and feasted on shellfish that night. The following morning, Cabeza de Vaca sent twenty men out to explore the coastline. The men floundered across the mudflats and through the salt marshes lining what must have been Apalachee Bay and returned to Cabeza de Vaca on the evening of the following day. They reported that the coast was convoluted with coves and bays, which made it difficult to pursue a straight course. They had not managed to catch sight of the open sea. This news dashed Cabeza de Vaca's hopes of reconnecting easily with Narváez's ships. The royal treasurer and his companions returned to Aute to deliver their discouraging news.[18]

When they arrived at Narváez's camp, they found that the governor and many of his men had fallen ill. The other two royal officials, Alonso Enríquez and Diego de Solís, were among the sick. Indians had attacked the camp the previous night and killed a horse. This was the third of the horses, by Cabeza de Vaca's account, to die in La Florida. However, the Spaniards are likely by this point in their ordeal to have lost more than three of the forty-two horses they had brought ashore in the spring. A shortage of horses was clearly one of the problems now confronting them.[19]

On the day after Cabeza de Vaca and his exploring party returned to Aute, the entire company of Spaniards took what maize they could and evacuated the village. Narváez seems to have grown desperate to escape the Indians who were tormenting him. Because it was nearer the sea, he decided to move his company to the camp Cabeza de Vaca had established at the mouth of the Río de la Magdalena. The distance between Aute and the camp was not great, but the move was difficult because there were not enough horses to carry Narváez and all the men who were ill. The coastal terrain was marshy and overgrown with brambles. When the governor and his men finally reached their objective, they had little idea what to do next. The identity of the Río de la Magdalena and the location of Cabeza de Vaca's camp are not now known, but the river was probably either the Aucilla, the St. Marks, or the Ochlockonee—all of which drain into Apalachee Bay. Narváez and his men soon came to know the bay as La Bahía de Caballos, or the Bay of Horses.[20]

Since separating from their ships near the Bay of the Cross, Narváez and his men had spent approximately fifty-nine days in traveling to the Bay of Horses—or in modern terms, traveling from the Tampa Bay region to the Apalachee Bay region. Those days were actual travel days, not days the men spent encamped at such places as the Apalachee village of forty houses or Aute. Cabeza de Vaca estimated that the distance from the Bay of the Cross to the Bay of Horses was about 280 leagues. His estimate must have reflected the hardship of the journey, because it is three times greater than the actual distance from Tampa Bay to Apalachee Bay. Narváez and his men cannot have marched much more than 280 miles.[21]

The Spaniards found little at the Bay of Horses to sustain them and little hope of escape. Narváez remained ill. A third of his men were ill also with a disease that was both contagious and rapidly spreading. It is not clear whether the Spaniards had brought this disease with them from Europe, whether they picked it up in the Spanish communities of the Caribbean, or whether they contracted it in Florida. Perhaps one man carried the pathogen for several weeks without showing symptoms until, weakened by hunger and exertion, he suddenly fell sick. If the illness was imported from Spain or the Caribbean, it would have posed an even greater danger to the Florida Indians than to Narváez's men, for the Indians had little immunity to such diseases.[22]

In view of the gravity of their situation, some of the more able-bodied of Narváez's men began to talk secretly of abandoning their ailing comrades in order to save themselves. When word of the scheme reached Cabeza de Vaca's ears, he and the other royal officials managed to dissuade the plotters from putting it into effect. The royal treasurer warned them that deserting Narváez would be an act of treason against His Majesty Charles V. Cabeza de Vaca also argued, just as he had done in May when he opposed Narváez's plan to part with his ships, that the security of each member of the expeditionary company depended upon everyone's sticking together. The plotters agreed in the end to stand by their governor and share his fate.[23]

From his sickbed, Narváez conducted a series of meetings with his officers in order to assess his options. If he and his men remained where they were, they would likely all die. Without their ships, they had no hope of returning to Cuba. With some luck, however, Narváez and his officers thought they might reach the Spanish outpost of Santisteban del Puerto on the Río Pánuco. They seem never to have comprehended the actual distance between their location in present-day Florida and the Río Pánuco in present-day Mexico. Ever since the day in April when they first spotted the North American mainland, they had persisted in thinking they were somewhere near both the Río de las Palmas and the Río Pánuco. Narváez and his officers considered building boats, but they had few tools and little knowledge of how to make them. They had no forge, and they lacked such other necessities as nails, ropes, canvas, pitch, and oakum—and able-bodied men to carry out the work. Above all, they lacked food with which to sustain the company during the time it would take to complete the project.[24]

At length, a member of the company came forward with a plan for building boats. In all likelihood, the man was Álvaro Fernández, a Portuguese who was the only carpenter known to have accompanied Narváez into the Florida interior. The shipwright, whether Fernández or someone else, commenced his boatbuilding project by making tubes of hollowed wood. Cabeza de Vaca does not indicate how he made these tubes, but perhaps he split straight saplings lengthwise into four equal parts, cut away the core of each section, and then glued the outer shells back together. From these tubes and some deerskins, the shipwright was able to make a bellows. Apparently he then made a forge. He collected and melted down whatever iron objects were to be had, including stirrups, bridles, spurs, and crossbows. Whether he collected or melted any armor is unclear. From the molten metal, the shipwright made or supervised the making of hammers, nails, saws, axes, and other tools. It is hard to imagine how he worked the metal without tongs or an anvil. Although the axes he produced must have been brittle and dull, and his saws must have been inflexible and thick, he and his companions were driven by desperation to make do with what he could create. The shipwright sent men out to gather the palmettos that grew abundantly in the area. He used the palmetto fiber both for ropes and for caulking material. Meanwhile, a Greek named Doroteo Teodoro made a kind of pitch from pine resin. Early in August, the first of five crude boats or barges (*barcas* in Spanish) began to take shape.[25]

Cabeza de Vaca provides few details concerning the barges. But he notes that he steered his barge with a tiller, so it must have had a rudder. The barges had raised sides, but they may have been flat-bottomed like rafts. Each one was twenty-two cubits long, or approximately thirty-three feet.

If they were square like rafts, they may have measured thirty-three feet to a side and had a surface area of approximately a thousand square feet. To make them watertight, the men caulked the barges with palmetto oakum and tarred them with Teodoro's pine pitch. The crude vessels could be propelled either by sails or by oars. Narváez's men gave up their shirts to make sails, and they made oars from the wood of evergreen trees. They gathered rocks to use for anchors and for ballast, but had difficulty finding rocks in the sandy Florida terrain. Their need for ballast suggests that the barges were not flat-bottomed.[26]

To sustain the company, Narváez sent groups of armed horsemen back to Aute to seize maize and other foodstuffs. Despite resistance from Indians, the raiding parties succeeded in seizing 400 *fanegas* (about 640 bushels) of maize. Some of Narváez's men tried to supplement their diet with fish and shellfish, but Indians killed ten Spaniards while they were gathering shellfish within sight of the Spanish camp. Forty other Spaniards died of disease or malnutrition at the Bay of Horses. In the extremity of their circumstances, Narváez and his officers decided to begin slaughtering the horses. They knew there would be no room for horses on the barges, and so every third day they slaughtered a horse and distributed its meat. It was for this reason that they came to know the bay where they were encamped as the "Bay of Horses." In Spain, eating a horse was viewed as a "sin against the Holy Ghost." Cabeza de Vaca claims he refused to eat horseflesh, but his companions put aside their scruples. The men let no part of a horse go to waste. They fashioned water containers from the hides of the animals and made ropes from the manes and tails. On 22 September they ate the last of the horses.[27]

On that same day, 22 September 1528, they launched their five barges and quitted their camp. About one-fifth of the three hundred men who had followed Narváez into the Florida interior the previous May had died, and by Cabeza de Vaca's account, only 242 remained. These 242 men were divided more or less evenly among the five barges, but with their weight and that of their equipment, the rude boats rode dangerously low in the water. Cabeza de Vaca observed: "So greatly can necessity prevail that it made us risk going in this manner and placing ourselves in a sea so treacherous, and without any one of us who went having any knowledge of the art of navigation." The royal treasurer can have taken little pleasure in remembering he had warned Narváez in May that the men of the overland party risked losing contact with the company's ships.[28]

Meanwhile, Captain Caravallo and the people of his maritime party had not forgotten Narváez and the men of the overland party. Narváez's wife, María de Valenzuela, did not forget her husband either, and she funded searches for him from Cuba at least until 1530. After parting from Narváez in May of 1528, Caravallo did as the governor had instructed and sailed northward, on a course parallel with that of the overland party, in search of the Río de las Palmas and the Río Pánuco. After a reasonable time, however, when Caravallo still had not found either a suitable port or any sign of the overland party, he reversed course and returned to the place where he and Narváez had separated. He sailed on southward, and within about five leagues, he discovered the mouth of a great bay that extended for seven to eight leagues into the land. Years later, when Cabeza de Vaca heard of Caravallo's great bay, he equated it with the Bay of the Cross, whose inland shore he and Narváez had reconnoitered on foot. In all likelihood, the great bay that Narváez, Caravallo, and also the pilot Miruelo each discovered independently was Tampa Bay. At some point, Caravallo and the people aboard his three ships reconnected with Miruelo and with Captain Álvaro de la Cerda. Miruelo had done as Narváez directed: sailed to Cuba, collected Cerda and the ship Narváez had inadvertently left at Havana, purchased additional supplies, and then returned to peninsular Florida. The two captains and the pilot searched for Narváez up and down the Gulf coast for almost a year. We may imagine that the women whose husbands were lost in the Florida interior were among the last to give up hope of finding them. But when the searchers failed utterly to find Narváez and his three hundred men, they abandoned their efforts, withdrew to New Spain, and went their separate ways.[29]

When they gave up searching for Narváez, Miruelo and the two captains unintentionally left another member of their company stranded in the Florida interior. The man they left behind, Juan Ortiz, was rescued eleven years later, in 1539, by Hernando de Soto. All four of the De Soto chroniclers mention Ortiz, but only the Gentleman of Elvas and El Inca Garcilaso include accounts of his captivity. Of the two, the account by the Gentleman of Elvas is the more credible.[30]

The Gentleman reports that a small group of De Soto's horsemen encountered Ortiz among ten or eleven Indians. They mistook him at first for an Indian because he was naked, sunburned, and tattooed. Ortiz called to them in halting Spanish, pleading, "Sirs, I am a Christian; do not kill me. Do not kill these Indians, for they have given me my life." Ortiz was

then brought to De Soto's camp, where, although he had difficulty recall-
ing his native language, he answered questions about his experiences. He
had come to Florida with Narváez, but then gone back to Cuba, apparently with Miruelo. Ortiz returned to Florida in a brigantine, which also
suggests he was with Miruelo. At some point along Florida's Gulf coast,
Ortiz and his shipmates spotted a stake posted upright in the ground, with
a letter wedged in its split top. Thinking the letter had been left there by
Narváez, Ortiz and a shipmate went ashore to retrieve it. The two were
ambushed by Indians, Ortiz was captured, and his companion was killed.
Their shipmates gave both men up for dead. Ortiz spent the next eleven
years uneasily among his Indian captors, who repeatedly threatened to kill
him. Ultimately, he became a translator for De Soto.[31]

El Inca Garcilaso tells a more lurid story. According to Garcilaso, soon
after Ortiz returned to Florida, he became the captive of a native chief
named Hirrihigua. The chief hated all Spaniards, and most particularly
Pánfilo de Narváez, because the one-eyed commander had ordered his men
to cut off Hirrihigua's nose and to throw his mother to their war dogs.
In retaliation, Hirrihigua roasted Ortiz over a slow fire. When Ortiz was
very nearly done for, the chief's daughter stepped forward to plead for his
life. Much as the seventeenth-century Pocahontas protected John Smith,
Hirrihigua's daughter protected Ortiz and eventually helped him flee to a
neighboring village.[32]

The Gentleman of Elvas confirms Garcilaso's account of the roasting of
Juan Ortiz and the intervention of the chief's daughter, but he says nothing
about the chief's hatred of Narváez. The Gentleman took part in the De
Soto expedition and interviewed Ortiz. Garcilaso, however, was not born
until 1539 (the very year De Soto began his Florida *entrada*), and he never
visited North America. He was the child of an Inca mother and a Spanish
father, and he wrote from a mestizo point of view. Garcilaso based his account of the De Soto expedition upon previously published accounts and
upon interviews with the expedition's survivors. His story of Narváez and
Hirrihigua is fascinating, but it is not verified by the Gentleman of Elvas,
Cabeza de Vaca, Oviedo, or any other chronicler. De Soto brought Spanish
war dogs to Florida, but no evidence, beyond what Garcilaso says, suggests that Narváez did so. Narváez is known to have committed atrocities
against Indians during the conquest of Cuba, but neither Cabeza de Vaca
nor Oviedo indicates that he abused Indians in Florida. It is possible that
Cabeza de Vaca kept quiet about such abuse, but it seems unlikely that

the royal treasurer would hesitate to accuse Narváez of maltreating Indians when he did not scruple to accuse the governor of selfishness, greed, and poor judgment.[33]

In addition to finding Ortiz, De Soto and his men found other relics of the Narváez expedition in Florida. In the spring of 1539, De Soto made his Florida landfall near Tampa Bay in approximately the area where Narváez had landed eleven years earlier. Subsequently, De Soto crossed his predecessor's footsteps more than once. In the winter of 1539, he and his men camped somewhere within the territory of the Apalachee chiefdom and found the remains of the camp at which Narváez and his men had built their barges. All four chroniclers of the De Soto expedition report this. The Gentleman of Elvas says that on the Gulf coast, eight to nine leagues from the large native settlement of Anhaica Apalachee, one of De Soto's captains found a camp where a large tree had been cut down and made into troughs to serve as mangers for horses. The captain also found the skulls of horses and, because the natives did not possess such animals, took this as a sign that Europeans had been there. Luys Hernández de Biedma says De Soto's men found the remains of the forge Narváez's men had constructed and the bones of many horses. Indians living nearby explained to the Spaniards via sign language that other men like themselves had constructed boats at the site. Rodrigo Rangel reports that in addition to the forge, the mangers, and the horse skulls, De Soto's men found mortars that Narváez's men had used to grind corn, and crosses they had carved on trees. El Inca Garcilaso simply repeats the information given by the Gentleman of Elvas. Unfortunately, even though De Soto's men discovered Narváez's camp at the Bay of Horses, the knowledge of its location died with them.[34]

Twentieth-century archaeological evidence suggests that Narváez's camp may have been located south of Tallahassee, at or near a site excavated in the 1930s in the St. Marks National Wildlife Refuge. This site was used by aboriginal peoples as a burial place, but metal and glass artifacts of early sixteenth-century European origin have been discovered there in connection with native burials. Among these artifacts were glass beads and small brass bells of the kind Cabeza de Vaca says Narváez gave as gifts to Indians. The glass beads, especially those of an oblong type not found in the New World after 1550, indicate an early sixteenth-century European presence in the area of the St. Marks River. If the early sixteenth-century dating is correct, the beads and bells must have been introduced either by Narváez in 1528 or by De Soto in 1539. Two other archaeological sites in north central

Florida seem also to have been associated with either Narváez or De Soto. One is the Work Place site, near the junction of the Wakulla and the St. Marks rivers, and the other is the Martin site, discovered in 1987 near the Florida state capitol in Tallahassee. Iron tools and glass beads have been found at the Work Place site, and it has tentatively been identified as the native settlement of Aute. The Martin site has tentatively been identified as the location of De Soto's 1539–40 winter camp. A crossbow point, iron nails, fragments of chain mail, and five copper coins are among the European artifacts unearthed at the Martin site. Two of these coins are Spanish *maravedíes* minted between 1505 and 1517. The other three appear to be badly corroded Portuguese coins from the sixteenth century or earlier.[35]

Both Narváez and De Soto helped set changes in motion that led ultimately to the collapse of the aboriginal cultures of Florida. The village of Aute likely did not recover quickly from Narváez's theft of 640 bushels of maize. And the impact upon Aute may have been even more terrible if Narváez and his men infected its people with the disease that felled many of the Spaniards while they were camping there. Between 1539 and 1543, when De Soto traveled through the North American southeast, he and his men found abandoned villages whose people had apparently succumbed to epidemic disease. The Narváez expedition may have introduced pathogens that wiped out some of these villages. No doubt, De Soto introduced additional pathogens, because mass burials of native men, women, and children have been discovered at a number of sixteenth- and seventeenth-century sites across the southeastern United States. Across this same region, native populations in general were smaller in the seventeenth century than in the sixteenth. The Apalachees, for example, are known to have experienced devastating epidemics in the seventeenth century. The sixteenth-century Apalachees were powerful enough militarily to drive Narváez away, but they were not able to resist European incursion indefinitely. Their culture was dealt a death blow in 1704, when English settlers from the Carolinas destroyed thirty-two Apalachee villages and at least five missions that Spanish friars had built in their territory. Survivors of the 1704 raids were absorbed into such coalescent societies as the Creeks and the Seminoles, which formed in the eighteenth century from the remnant populations of older, shattered societies. None of the native societies Narváez and Cabeza de Vaca encountered in Florida in 1528 exists today in any recognizable form.[36]

SIX

Castaways

When they left their camp at the Bay of Horses on 22 September, the 242 surviving men of Narváez's overland party set off westward in the direction, they hoped, of the Spanish outpost of Santisteban del Puerto on the Río Pánuco. Each barge carried between 47 and 49 men. Governor Narváez commanded the first barge with the assistance of Juan Pantoja, the captain with whom Cabeza de Vaca had weathered the hurricane in Cuba. Cabeza de Vaca observes that Narváez and Pantoja chose the strongest and healthiest of the men for their barge. The second of the crude boats was commanded by the royal comptroller, Alonso Enríquez, and the Franciscan commissary, Fray Juan Suárez. The third and fourth barges were commanded respectively by Captains Alonso del Castillo and Andrés Dorantes, and by Captains Téllez and Peñalosa. The fifth and final barge was commanded by Cabeza de Vaca and the royal quartermaster, Diego de Solís. All five barges were furnished with drinking water in the horsehide containers the men had made and with a share of the maize they had commandeered at Aute. The men also brought along what remained of their clothing, weapons, and the beads and bells they used for barter with the Indians. Cabeza de Vaca notes that when his barge was loaded, he and his men "were so crowded that we could not even move."[1]

The flotilla spent seven days poking through the tidal salt marshes, shallow inlets, and barrier islands of Apalachee Bay without ever catching sight of the open sea. The water was little more than waist deep. At the end of the week, the barge commanded by Cabeza de Vaca and Solís was in the lead, and the men aboard it spotted an island in what seemed to be open water. The other barges followed them to the island, and there the Spaniards commandeered five Indian canoes and a supply of mullet and dried roe. They did this on 29 September, the feast day of St. Michael the Archangel. Even though six months had elapsed since they left Cuba, the Spaniards seem still to have retained a firm grasp of dates and holy days.[2]

That night, Narváez and his men camped on the mainland, and using the wood from the five stolen canoes, they built up the sideboards of their barges so that they stood higher above water. They then continued their westward journey, hugging the coast of the Florida panhandle and frequently crossing shallow inlets and bays. They had no clear idea where they were, and their various stopping places cannot be identified with precision.[3]

During most of October the only Indians Narváez and his men encountered were fishermen whom Cabeza de Vaca describes as "poor and wretched." By this time, the Spaniards were experiencing hunger and thirst. The water in their makeshift water bags had gone bad because they had tanned the horsehide improperly, and their supply of maize was running low. Although Cabeza de Vaca did not know it then, seven years would pass by before he again saw maize under cultivation. Near the end of October he and his companions landed on a small island, hoping to find water, but they found none. While on the island, they were surprised by a powerful storm that forced them to remain where they were for six days. Apparently the storm brought no potable water, for Cabeza de Vaca says he and his companions were so thirsty, they drank salt water. Five men drank it in such quantity that they died.[4]

At this point in his *Relación*, Cabeza de Vaca says: "I do not think there is need to tell in detail the miseries and hardships in which we found ourselves, since considering the place where we were and the little hope we had of survival, each one can imagine a great deal of what would happen there." The men were floundering in a vast and unmapped wilderness. They were trapped on their flimsy barges between a hostile and threatening sea, and a forest inhabited by Indians who seemed equally hostile and threatening. The Spaniards had given up their shirts in order to make sails, so no man is likely to have had more than a ragged doublet and pair of breeches with which to fend off the cold and wet. The men's boots must have shown severe wear and tear. They had no water and very little maize.[5]

Unless it is properly processed or is eaten with complimentary foods like beans, maize is difficult for humans to digest. Maize lacks two of the essential amino acids the human body needs to produce proteins and niacin. Beans possess the amino acids that maize lacks, so eating maize together with beans—as the Indians did—solves the problem. Another way to render maize more digestible is to turn it into hominy by soaking dried corn kernels in a lye solution made from wood ashes. The Apalachee Indians of Florida processed their maize in this way. But the Spaniards did not know enough about maize to process it correctly. They were probably beginning to suffer from pellagra, caused by niacin deficiency. Many of them, moreover, were likely still suffering from the disease that had killed forty of their comrades at the Bay of Horses. We can only wonder whether any of the five Franciscans was well enough to perform such priestly functions as celebrating mass, hearing confessions, tending the sick, administering extreme unction, and presiding at burials.[6]

On their sixth day without water, the men decided to launch their barges in heavy seas rather than die of thirst on the island. Although several of the barges came near to sinking, all five eventually rounded a point on the mainland shore and came into calmer waters. Cabeza de Vaca gave thanks to God whom, he reflected, "at the time of greatest need customarily shows his favor."[7]

Many unarmed Indians came out in canoes to hail the Spaniards and lead them to their village, where they had set out pots of water and an array of cooked fish. Their chief invited the hungry and thirsty Spaniards to partake of this bounty. Narváez, Cabeza de Vaca, and several other officers went with the chief into his residence, where they were given all the fish they desired. In return, Narváez gave the chief some of the maize he had commandeered at Aute, and the chief ate it with great relish. Narváez also gave him some beads and bells. In the middle of the night, however, while Narváez and Cabeza de Vaca were still in the chief's house, the Indians suddenly attacked their guests. Three Spaniards who were lying ill on the shore were killed, and Narváez was struck in the face by a rock. The Spaniards seized the village chief, intending to hold him hostage, but he gave them a cloak made of marten skins in exchange for his liberty. Cabeza de Vaca described the skins as "the finest to be found anywhere in the world," adding that "they have a scent that resembles nothing other than ambergris and musk, and it is so strong that it can be detected at a great distance."[8]

Cabeza de Vaca and his fellow officers helped the wounded Narváez back onto his barge, and they ordered all the other sick and wounded men of their company to return to the barges as well. Cabeza de Vaca and some fifty able-bodied Spaniards, including Captains Dorantes, Peñalosa, and Téllez, remained onshore to defend the barges. The Indians attacked the defenders three times during the night, and each time forced them to give ground. Most of the defenders suffered injury, including Cabeza de Vaca, who was wounded in the face. The Indians were poorly supplied with arrows, however, so the damage they were able to inflict was relatively light. During the third assault, Captains Dorantes, Peñalosa, and Téllez took fifteen men and ambushed the Indians from their rear. The Indians scattered in confusion and gave the Spaniards no further trouble.

In the morning, the Spaniards found themselves in possession of the village. The weather was cold and stormy, and Cabeza de Vaca decided to remain where he was rather than expose the barges to the wind and sea. He and his men broke up thirty Indian canoes and burned the wood, both to keep themselves warm and to prevent the Indians from ever pursuing them. When the Spaniards finally resumed their journey, they took water with them in some earthen containers they had found at the village.[9]

They didn't take enough water, however, and within three days they had exhausted their supply. On the third or fourth day, with the Narváez and Pantoja barge in the lead, the flotilla entered an estuary. Someone spotted Indians in a canoe, and Narváez hailed them and asked them for water. The Indians offered to bring some if he provided a container. Doroteo Teodoro, the Greek who had made pitch for the barges at the Bay of Horses, volunteered to take what containers they had and go with the Indians for water. Narváez protested, but Teodoro insisted, and the governor finally contented himself with requiring the Indians to leave two of their men with him as hostages. Teodoro, accompanied by his black slave, stepped into an Indian canoe and disappeared into the unknown.[10]

In the evening, the Indians returned to where Narváez was waiting. With them, they had Narváez's containers, but no water and no Teodoro or his slave. The two Indians who had remained with Narváez as hostages tried to rejoin their friends, but the Spaniards restrained them.[11]

The following morning, many canoes approached the barges. Five or six of the Indians aboard appeared to be chiefs—they had long flowing hair and were robed in cloaks of marten skins similar to the one the Spaniards had previously acquired. The chiefs asked for the return of the two Indian hostages, but Narváez refused to release them unless in exchange for Teodoro and his slave. The chiefs invited Narváez and his men to their village, where they said Teodoro and the slave were waiting. They promised to give Narváez water and food, but the governor mistrusted the situation. He observed that more and more canoes were gathering, and that they seemed bent on blocking the mouth of the estuary. Narváez finally ordered his five barges to break through the blockade and put out to sea. The Indians, using slings, threw stones at them and shot a few arrows but seem not to have had many of the deadlier projectiles. They dogged the flotilla until noon, but then a breeze arose, the barges set sail, and the Indians gave up their pursuit. Cabeza de Vaca does not say what became of the Indian hostages.[12]

Eleven or twelve years later, two of the chroniclers of the De Soto expedition heard conflicting reports concerning the fates of Teodoro and his slave. The first, Luys Hernández de Biedma, says that near a large river, "we had news of how the boats of Narváez had arrived in need of water, and that here among these Indians remained a Christian who was called Don Teodoro, and a black man with him." Indians showed Biedma a dagger that had belonged to Teodoro. The second chronicler, Rodrigo Rangel, heard that Indians "had killed Don Teodoro, and a black man, who came forth from the boats of Pánfilo de Narváez."[13]

A few days after the loss of Teodoro, Cabeza de Vaca and Solís—whose barge was in the lead—rounded a point of land and caught sight of a very large river that must have been the Mississippi. The two officers brought their barge to anchor on an island and found that, due to the powerful discharge of the river, the water surrounding the island was fresh and potable. Meanwhile, Narváez and the other barge captains chose not to follow them to the island and anchored instead on the nearby mainland. Cabeza de Vaca and Solís attempted to join them but were unable to do so because of the strong current and a northerly headwind.[14]

Cabeza de Vaca and Solís quickly found themselves half a league out to sea and in deep water. They tried to take a sounding but were unable to touch bottom. They continued westward all that night and for the next two days. Late in the afternoon of the second day, they spotted many columns of smoke rising from the mainland shore. They were now in only three *brazas* (roughly three fathoms, or 16.5 feet) of water, but they feared to land because of the smoke signals they had seen and because night was coming on. They tried to anchor in the relatively shallow water, but they had only stones for anchors, and during the night a current dragged them far from land. At sunrise, they found themselves alone on a wide and empty sea. Cabeza de Vaca and Solís took another sounding and determined they were in thirty *brazas* (165 feet) of water.[15]

After several hours they finally, to their great relief, sighted two other barges. They approached the nearer of the two and found it was the one commanded by Narváez and Pantoja. Narváez hailed Cabeza de Vaca and asked what he thought they should do. The royal treasurer said they should pursue the third barge so that all three might travel together. Narváez protested that the third barge was far out to sea. Cabeza de Vaca argued, as he had done six months previously when Narváez chose to divide his force into land and sea parties, that security depended upon everyone's sticking together. Narváez insisted upon rowing toward land, however, and he told Cabeza de Vaca to put his men to their oars. Pantoja added that if they did not reach land soon, they might never reach it and would likely die of hunger and thirst.[16]

Cabeza de Vaca took up an oar, but he and all his able-bodied men were unable to keep up with the other barge. The royal treasurer finally called to Narváez and asked to tie his barge to the governor's with a rope. Narváez replied that his men lacked the strength to row one barge and tow another. No doubt with heavy sarcasm, Cabeza de Vaca asked the governor to tell him what to do. Narváez answered that he was no longer in a position to command anyone and that the treasurer might do as he liked. The time had come, the governor said, for every man to look to himself and "do whatever seemed best to him in order to save his own life." As it happened, these were the last words Cabeza de Vaca would ever hear from Pánfilo de Narváez.[17]

Seeing little hope of following the governor, Cabeza de Vaca decided to make instead for the third barge, which remained visible far out at sea. This barge proved to be the one commanded by Captains Téllez and Peñalosa. When the captains perceived Cabeza de Vaca trying to reach them, they waited for him. The two barges then continued in tandem for four days. All anyone aboard either barge had to eat was half a handful of dry uncooked maize. The weather, according to Cabeza de Vaca, was very cold.[18]

On the fourth day, a storm arose. The two barges were driven apart and lost sight of one another. Cabeza de Vaca expected at any moment to capsize. Most of his men lay upon the deck, drenching wet and "so close to death that few were conscious." Cabeza de Vaca and his helmsman took turns at the tiller. Early in the evening the helmsman said he had exhausted his strength, but shortly after midnight he resumed his post. Cabeza de

Vaca lay upon the deck but was unable to rest. Toward dawn he and the helmsman began to hear the pounding of surf. The two men took a sounding and touched bottom at seven *brazas*, or about 38 feet. They feared to come ashore before daybreak, so Cabeza de Vaca took an oar and succeeded in turning the barge away from the land. But then a huge wave caught them and hurled them onto a beach, startling the half-dead men into consciousness. They crawled up onto the beach and to the base of some bluffs. There they built a fire and cooked a little of their remaining maize. They also found rainwater to drink, and with that, the maize, and the warmth of the fire, they began to revive. The date, Cabeza de Vaca believed, was 6 November 1528. He had no idea where he and his men were, but they must have been somewhere along the coast of the present state of Texas. At least nine days had passed since they sighted the Mississippi River, and if Cabeza de Vaca's dating is correct, six and a half weeks had passed since they left the Bay of Horses.[19]

After sunrise, Cabeza de Vaca ordered Lope de Oviedo, who was among the strongest of the men, to climb a tree and survey the surrounding area. Oviedo reported that he and his companions had come ashore on an island. The Spaniards soon would name it Isla de Malhado, or Isle of Evil Fate.[20]

From up in the tree, Oviedo could see trails or pathways that he thought had been made by cattle. Since only Spaniards possessed cattle, Oviedo concluded that he and his companions were near the Spanish outpost of Santisteban del Puerto on the Río Pánuco. With all the enthusiasm of wishful thinking, he set off to explore one of the trails and followed it for half a league until he came to some Indian dwellings. Seeing no Indians, he helped himself to a pot, a small dog, and some fish, and he started back with these treasures to where his companions were waiting. Meanwhile, because Oviedo had been gone a long time, Cabeza de Vaca sent two other men out to find him. These two found not only Oviedo but also three naked Indians, armed with bows and arrows, who were following him and calling to him. Although their languages were mutually unintelligible, Oviedo was calling and gesturing to the Indians in return. Oviedo and the other two Spaniards inched their way backward to the beach, followed every step of the way by the Indians. When the three Spaniards reached the shore and reconnected with their companions, the Indians took up a position on a nearby bluff and waited. Within half an hour, they were joined by a hundred additional archers.[21]

The situation must have been tense. The Indians had never before seen men with beards and white skin, nor men dressed in doublets, breeches, and boots. And to Cabeza de Vaca and his exhausted crew, who were outnumbered two to one, the native archers seemed like giants. All were males, tall, and well formed, and all were completely naked. Many had pierced their ears, their lower lips, and one or both nipples and had inserted lengths of cane through the piercings. The canes through their nipples were up to two and a half *palmos* (about twenty inches) long and as big around as two fingers. The canes in their lower lips were much smaller in diameter. Although Cabeza de Vaca and Solís knew that the Indians could easily kill them, they approached the archers and attempted to negotiate with them. They gave the Indians beads and bells, and each archer gave Cabeza de Vaca an arrow in return. The royal treasurer cannot have understood this at the time, but he later reported that the giving of arrows was "a sign of friendship." By means of gestures, the Indians endeavored to assure him and Solís they would return the next morning with food.[22]

The following day, at sunrise, the Indians returned with fish and some roots that tasted like nuts or truffles. Cabeza de Vaca soon learned the roots had been dug with difficulty from under water. They may have been cattail roots, which are common on the Texas coast and high in carbohydrates, though fibrous. The Indians again withdrew but returned in the afternoon with more fish and roots, and with their women and children. Some of the women wore skirts made of Spanish moss or of deerskin. The Spaniards gave the Indians more beads and bells, and the Indians brought them more fish and roots the following day. The regular supply of food revived the Spaniards and inspired them to attempt to relaunch their barge.[23]

They dug the barge out of the sand and provisioned it with fresh water. After stripping off their clothes to keep them dry, the men stowed them aboard the flimsy vessel. They then waded into the water, pushed the barge out to sea, clambered aboard, and took up their oars. But when they were two crossbow shots from the shore, a huge wave drenched them and dragged the oars from their hands. Distances measured in crossbow shots are problematic because they might indicate either the maximum distance an arrow can reach (about 390 yards) or the distance at which an archer can consistently hit a target (65–70 yards). Thus, when the wave struck, the barge may have been anywhere from 130 to 780 yards offshore. A second wave overturned the barge and sank it, taking three men down with it, including the royal quartermaster, Diego de Solís. The other men swam

Bronze statue, sculpted by Eladio Gil Zambrana, representing Álvar
Núñez Cabeza de Vaca. The statue, dated 1991, stands in Jerez de la
Frontera, Spain. Photograph by Juris Zagarins.

back to the island from which they had tried to escape. They had lost not
only the three men and their barge, but also whatever had remained of their
clothing, their weapons, their trade goods, and their maize. As meager as
these possessions had been, the men regretted their loss bitterly. They were
now castaways, and they sat naked, wet, and shivering in the chill November air. Cabeza de Vaca says that he and most of the men were "so thin that
with little difficulty our bones could be counted."[24]

An icy north wind arose that seemed cold enough to freeze the fish in the
sea. Cabeza de Vaca and his men poked through the ashes of their campfire
and rekindled it with a still smoldering brand. They begged God to forgive
them for their sins and to have mercy upon them. Many of the men wept,

each sorrowing, as Cabeza de Vaca observed, "not only for himself but for all the others whom they saw in the same state." As the ranking officer, Cabeza de Vaca must have felt the full weight of his responsibility for the lives of his men. He had little hope of saving any of them, and he could no longer call upon his co-commander, Diego de Solís, to share in the burdens of leadership.[25]

At sunset, the Indians who had previously brought fish and roots returned with more food to the Spanish camp. They were probably expecting to exchange the food for more beads and bells, but when they reached the Spaniards and found them naked, the Indians became alarmed and turned back toward their village. They were naked themselves, or nearly so, but they must have perceived the Spaniards as radically different without their doublets and breeches. Perhaps they were alarmed by the white skin, hairy chests, and hairy legs of the castaways. Cabeza de Vaca ran after the Indians, and using gestures, tried to indicate that he and his men had lost their barge and three members of their company. The Indians must have understood something of what he was trying to communicate, because they sat down among the Spaniards and for half an hour made a great show of weeping and commiserating with them. Cabeza de Vaca was moved to fresh tears because, he says, seeing that "these men, so lacking in reason and so crude in the manner of brutes, grieved so much for us, increased in me and in others of our company even more the magnitude of our suffering and the estimation of our misfortune."[26]

Cabeza de Vaca proposed to ask the Indians for shelter, but several of his men objected. Some had participated in the conquest of the Aztec empire and knew at firsthand about the Aztec practice of human sacrifice. They feared that if they put themselves in the hands of these unknown Indians, their hosts would offer them to pagan gods. But since remaining on the beach would mean certain death, Cabeza de Vaca saw moving to the Indian village as their only option. He would later report that, in all his travels in North America, he found no evidence of human sacrifice.[27]

By means of gestures, Cabeza de Vaca begged the Indians to take him and his men to their village. Thirty of the Indians went ahead to prepare the way. The remaining Indians waited until evening and then escorted the castaways, urging them to walk rapidly in order to keep themselves warm. At four or five intervals along the way, they came upon large bonfires that the men of the advance party had kindled. The castaways and their escorts stopped at each bonfire and warmed themselves before moving onward.[28]

At the village, which proved to be a nomadic camp rather than a fixed settlement, the thirty men of the advance group had prepared more bonfires and a special house for their strange guests. The house was probably little more than a windbreak. It must have been similar to all the houses in the camp, which had frames made of long flexible poles, sharpened at one end and driven into the ground in a circle, then tied together at the top. The house probably was covered on the windward side with mats made from woven reeds, and it probably had a fire pit at the center. As Cabeza de Vaca would soon learn, such houses could be dismantled easily. Everyone at the camp seemed excited by the arrival of the strangers. The Indians began immediately to dance and sing, and they continued these festivities all night. The Spaniards, however, were fearful and despite their exhaustion could not rest. They expected at any moment to feel the blows of war clubs or sacrificial knives, and they did not begin to relax until the next morning, when the Indians again gave them fish and roots.[29]

During that next day, Cabeza de Vaca noticed that one of the Indians was wearing an item of European manufacture that did not originate from his barge. He asked the man, through gestures, where he had obtained the item. The Indian replied that he had obtained it from other men like Cabeza de Vaca who had come to the far end of the island. Cabeza de Vaca began to hope that another of the Narváez barges had beached on Malhado, and he sent two of his men with Indian guides to ascertain whether other Spaniards were nearby. The scouting party soon met with Captains Andrés Dorantes and Alonso del Castillo, who were likewise seeking to verify rumors that other Spaniards were on the island.

Dorantes and Castillo followed Cabeza de Vaca's scouts back to the camp where the royal treasurer was waiting. The captains expressed consternation upon finding that Cabeza de Vaca and his men were naked. Dorantes and Castillo were still wearing their doublets, breeches, and boots, and although they had little additional clothing to share with their more destitute comrades, they shared what they had. The captains explained that on the fifth of November, their barge had come ashore at the north end of the island on which Cabeza de Vaca and his men had landed the following day. To Castillo and Dorantes, therefore, belongs the honor of being the first Europeans—and to Estevanico (the slave of Dorantes), that of being the first African—to visit Texas.[30]

Malhado was probably one of the barrier islands protecting either Galveston Bay or the mainland shore immediately to its southwest. Cabeza de Vaca estimated that Malhado was half a league wide by five leagues long, or, in modern terms, a mile and a half by fifteen miles. Some students of Cabeza de Vaca's route have proposed that Malhado was today's Galveston Island, but the latter is three times as long as Cabeza de Vaca estimated Malhado to be. Other route interpreters have suggested that Malhado was a combination of San Luis Island and the spit of land variously known in the early twentieth century as San Luis Peninsula, Oyster Bay Peninsula, or Velasco Peninsula. However, the shape and configuration of the land masses outlining the Texas coast shift with the actions of hurricanes and tides, and the former San Luis Peninsula is currently again an island. Known as Follet's Island, it is in the Brazosport area and roughly answers Cabeza de Vaca's description of his sixteenth-century Malhado.[31]

Castillo, Dorantes, and their men—like Cabeza de Vaca and his—had taken refuge with Indians, but their hosts belonged to a different cultural community. The two bands of Indians in Malhado were the Capoques and the Hans. Cabeza de Vaca is not always as clear as a reader would like, and he does not say which band was sheltering which group of castaways. He does say that the language of the Capoques was different from that of the Hans and that the two peoples were of different lineage. Castillo and Dorantes reported that their barge was badly damaged, but all their possessions were intact. Cabeza de Vaca and the two captains quickly formulated a plan for repairing the barge, but it was so heavily infested with shipworm that in attempting to launch it, they sank it.[32]

The surviving Spaniards now had little choice but to remain in Malhado with their Indian benefactors for the winter. The castaways clung to the belief that they were near the Spanish frontier settlement of Santisteban del Puerto on the Río Pánuco, but in actuality they were some six hundred miles from there. The only means they now had of reaching the Spanish outpost was to make their way on foot. Most of the castaways were in no condition for such a trek, the weather was too cold, and they had no food. There were about eighty castaways in Malhado, and as royal treasurer, Cabeza de Vaca was their ranking officer. He and Captains Castillo and Dorantes discussed their options, but the only action they could think to take was to select four of their fittest men and send them southward to Santisteban del Puerto. The officers knew that the men they sent might have to swim across rivers and tidal channels, so they were careful to select men who could swim. Cabeza de Vaca was able to swim, but he elected to remain at Malhado with the majority of his men. The four swimmers the officers chose to send down the coast were Álvaro Fernández of Portugal, Figueroa of Toledo, Estudillo of Zafra, and Méndez. Álvaro Fernández was a carpenter and may have been the man who directed the building of the barges at the Bay of Horses. Cabeza de Vaca told the chosen four that if they succeeded in reaching Santisteban del Puerto, they were to send Spaniards from the outpost back to Malhado to rescue the remaining survivors of the two Narváez barges. An Indian guide accompanied the four swimmers when they set off on their impossible mission.[33]

The castaways remaining at Malhado separated into their preestablished groups, one to live under the protection of the Capoques and the other under that of the Hans. Castillo, Dorantes, and their men returned with their Indian protectors to the northeastern part of the island while Cabeza de Vaca remained with his men in the southwest. The Spaniards performed heavy labor for the Indians who supported them. They received little food in return, and they feared that at any moment the Indians might turn upon them. No doubt the castaways cheered themselves with the hope that either the four swimmers or one or more of the other Narváez barges would succeed in reaching the Río Pánuco and organizing a rescue expedition.[34]

A few days after the four swimmers departed, the weather again turned brutally cold. Cabeza de Vaca described it as "the harshest weather ever seen in the world." The royal treasurer found little protection from the cold, since, like the Indians he was living among, he went naked. But unlike some of the more fortunate Indians, he probably did not have an animal skin in which to wrap himself at night. His Indian benefactors could no longer harvest the roots they previously had shared with the Spaniards, nor could they fish. They found it difficult to provide for the castaways and so divided them amongst themselves, with each household or foraging group accepting one or more dependents. Cabeza de Vaca lived in the household of a man in whose possession he says he was placed. The man seems to have had some authority in the native community and may have been a shaman, for, according to Cabeza de Vaca, there were no chiefs other than shamans in Malhado. Cabeza de Vaca observed that shamans were much respected and that a shaman could have more than one wife. The chronicler does not actually use the word *shaman*, however, as it is of Mongolian origin. Nor does he use the words *curandero* or *saludadore*, although the latter occurs in Oviedo's account and both are common Spanish terms for herbal healers. Instead, Cabeza de Vaca uses the words *médico*, meaning "doctor," and *físico*, meaning "physician."[35]

Soon after the cold weather set in, the already weakened castaways began to die of hunger, disease, and exposure. It was at around this time that they gave the name "Isla de Malhado" (Isle of Evil Fate) to the island on which they were stranded. During the coldest part of the winter, five Spaniards who mistrusted the Indians and had camped apart from them resorted to cannibalism. After each man died, his surviving comrades ate his flesh until only one was left, and he died alone. When the Indians discovered the grisly remains, they became very upset and threatened to kill the remaining Spaniards. Cabeza de Vaca says the incident caused "a great scandal" among the Indians and badly frightened the Spaniards. At the same time, some deadly stomach ailment began to take a toll on both communities. Half the Indians of Malhado died of this ailment during the winter of 1528–29, and many Spaniards died as well. Some Indians, apparently fearing sorcery, blamed the Spaniards for bringing illness among them and clamored again to kill them. Sorcery aside, it seems likely that the Spaniards had indeed introduced the disease. Perhaps it was the same illness that had killed forty of their comrades at the Bay of Horses.[36]

Fortunately for the surviving Spaniards, the Indian in whose household Cabeza de Vaca was living succeeded in preventing his kinsmen from killing them. This man, who seems to have been a shaman, reasoned that if the Spaniards had the power to cause the deaths of so many Indians, they would have the power also to preserve their own lives. Cabeza de Vaca breathed a prayer of thanksgiving and later wrote: "Our Lord God granted that the others followed this advice and opinion, and thus they were diverted from their intention."[37]

Soon afterward, either Cabeza de Vaca's benefactor or some other shaman asked the Spaniard to make himself useful by curing the sick. Cabeza de Vaca protested that he did not know how. The shaman forced his compliance, however, by withholding food. When the shaman next was called to attend a patient, Cabeza de Vaca accompanied him and observed his practice. The shaman began by blowing upon his patient and pressing on his body to expel the disease. The shaman made incisions around the site of the patient's pain and sucked fluids from the incisions. As best he could, the shaman explained to Cabeza de Vaca that many natural objects, such as stones, possessed power. He demonstrated by heating a stone and placing it on the patient's abdomen. After a time the patient reported he was free of pain. He was so grateful, he gave the shaman everything he possessed and urged his relatives to give him presents as well. On another occasion,

Cabeza de Vaca watched the shaman use fire to cauterize a patient's wound. Again the patient rewarded the shaman with gifts.

The shaman continued to insist that Cabeza de Vaca also perform cures, and although the castaway could imagine what might happen to him if he failed, he had little choice but to comply. What he did was to make the sign of the cross over a patient and blow on his body. He recited such Latin prayers as the Pater Noster and the Ave Maria. He implored God, no doubt with great earnestness, both to restore the patient's health and to move the Indians to treat the Spaniards well. Since none of Cabeza de Vaca's patients could understand Latin or Spanish, they were impressed by their physician's command of apparently otherworldly languages. They may have thought that because of his beard, pale skin, and exotic appearance, he possessed magical powers. It seemed to Cabeza de Vaca that God blessed his medical practice with success, because his patients not only recovered from their illnesses but also told others they were cured. His patients gave him food, animal skins, and other commodities that made his life more comfortable. Soon after he began to enjoy a reputation as a healer, Cabeza de Vaca became so bold as to heat stones, as his mentoring shaman had showed him to do, and place them upon the afflicted parts of his patients' bodies.[38]

It is difficult, however, to reconcile what Cabeza de Vaca says about his success as a healer with what he says about his status in Malhado, the misery of his life there, and the harsh treatment he received from the Indians. In his perception, the Indians he lived among forced him to toil like a slave. As an hidalgo, he had never before had to perform such heavy labor as he now performed. He spent long days wading barefoot and naked through clumps of reeds in cold, marshy water, with no other tool than a digging stick, grubbing for submerged roots. He cut his fingers and his feet on the splintery reeds, and his body became scratched and bloodied in many places. Sometimes he gathered large bundles of firewood and carried them to camp on his bare back. On days when the Indians moved their camp, he carried their belongings to the new location. The work he was doing, digging for reeds and bearing burdens, was women's work, and Cabeza de Vaca observed that the Indian women worked very hard. Perhaps, had he been more skilled, he could have joined the men in hunting, fishing, and other traditionally male activities.[39]

Although Cabeza de Vaca thought he was treated like a slave, the Indians he lived among probably saw him more as an unskilled dependent who would have to earn his keep. Since food was scarce, they may have withheld it from those Spaniards who couldn't or wouldn't work. Cabeza de Vaca says that during the brutal winter of 1528–29, he sometimes went three days without eating. But he also says that his Indian hosts suffered from food shortage and cold the same as he and shared with him what little they had.[40]

If Cabeza de Vaca practiced cures in Malhado as he says he did, he cannot have enjoyed more than a brief success as a healer. Otherwise, his status among the Indians would have been higher. He does not mention performing cures again until 1533, so it must have taken him several years to figure out how to capitalize on the particular assets he had. Another possibility is that his chronology in the *Relación* is faulty. The explorer was not able to write of his experiences until long after he left Texas, and judging from the way he sometimes lumps his observations together, he was less than scrupulous about sticking to chronological order. Perhaps he first witnessed cures in Malhado but did not begin to practice healing until after he had become more familiar with Indian languages and customs.[41]

With regard to chronology and other perplexing details, Oviedo's account of the Narváez expedition provides a helpful counterpoise to Cabeza de Vaca's *Relación*. According to Oviedo, Cabeza de Vaca did not begin practicing medicine until 1535.[42]

During the remainder of the winter of 1528–29, the castaways and their Indian benefactors subsisted on the roots Cabeza de Vaca participated in gathering. The Indians were constantly on the move, for when they had exhausted the food resources of one area, as they did every three of four days, they shifted their camp. They had no maize and cultivated no crops of any kind. However, as the castaways had discovered soon after their arrival at Malhado, the Indians had pottery and kept domesticated dogs. During the time he spent in Malhado, Cabeza de Vaca learned many other things about the nomadic hunting-and-gathering people who were supporting him.[43]

Their community, he notes, was organized along kinship lines. All those of the same lineage operated as an extended family and assisted one another. Since the Capoques and the Hans were of different lineages and did not speak the same language, they did not live or forage together. The size of a band of hunters and gatherers tends to be small, but the one supporting Cabeza de Vaca may have included as many as four to five hundred people. Like all hunting-and-gathering communities, it had a simple and relatively egalitarian social structure because everyone had to spend all his or her time seeking food. Cabeza de Vaca says his Malhado band had no chief. During the previous summer in Florida when he came into contact with the Apalachees, the explorer had had the opportunity to observe a more complex Native American society with a hierarchical organization and economic specialization. The Apalachees had had both chiefs and skilled individuals who specialized in such activities as canoe building and pottery making. And yet, because he did not speak their language or live for an extended period among them, Cabeza de Vaca recorded relatively little about them beyond what the women wore and how skilled the men were at archery. The ethnographic observations he made while living among simpler people in Texas are much richer and more detailed. Cabeza de Vaca would spend more time in Texas than in Florida, and while in Texas, he would learn several indigenous languages. No doubt he quickly picked up the language of his Malhado hosts.[44]

During the winter of 1528–29, when half the Indian population of Malhado died of the stomach ailment the Spaniards had probably introduced, Cabeza de Vaca was able to observe their funeral customs. When an Indian died, the explorer noted, his or her relatives would dust themselves with ashes and the entire community would weep with a great show of sorrow and respect. Each morning before sunrise and again at noon, the grieving family would begin a weeping ceremony in which their neighbors would join. They would continue these weeping rituals, as Cabeza de Vaca would learn, for a full year. At the end of the year, they cleansed their bodies of the ashes of mourning and performed another ceremony honoring the deceased. Mourning for a child was especially poignant. It seemed to Cabeza de Vaca that the Malhado Indians "love their children more and treat them better than any other people in the world." When a child died, the bereaved parents and siblings would abstain for three months from gathering food. Their relatives would bring them food, but since few families were untouched by death in the winter of 1528–29, many families went hungry. And although all members of the community shared food freely with one another, the burden of finding food for those who were in mourning must have fallen upon an ever-shrinking number of people.[45]

When an elderly person died, Cabeza de Vaca observed, there was no weeping. The elderly were said to be unproductive and to have lived past their time, depriving their children of their proper share of food. The bodies of most of those who died were buried. But when a shaman died, his remains were burned and pulverized, and everyone in the community joined in ritual dancing. After a year had passed, the people lacerated themselves, paid homage to the pulverized ashes, mixed them with water, and gave the mixture to the shaman's relatives to drink.

Most of the Indian men were married to a single wife. A shaman was an exception, and Cabeza de Vaca noted that the co-wives dwelt together in friendship and harmony. The castaway observed that after a man married, he avoided his wife's parents. He would not enter the house of his in-laws, nor would they enter his house. If the son-in-law should happen to catch sight of his father- or mother-in-law, he would lower his head and eyes and make a large detour in order to avoid meeting or speaking with them. A daughter, however, remained free after her marriage to meet and speak with her parents, and she carried presents and messages between them and her husband. At the end of each day, when the husband brought home his catch of fish or game, the wife would carry all of it to her parents. They would take what they wanted and send the remainder back with their daughter for her husband. Cabeza de Vaca says these marriage customs were common to all the Indians who lived within a fifty-league radius of Malhado.[46]

Cabeza de Vaca witnessed hospitality rituals in Malhado that he would later see elsewhere in Texas. When a person came to the home of a friend or relative after some period of separation, neither person would say anything and both would weep for at least half an hour. Finally the host would rise and give the guest everything he possessed. The guest would then carry everything away, sometimes without exchanging words with the host. This ritualized weeping and gift-giving must have reminded Cabeza de Vaca both of the show of weeping the Indians had made on the beach when he and his men lost their barge and of the arrows the Indians had given him. Ritualized gift-giving was a custom Cabeza de Vaca would later turn to his advantage.[47]

By approximately the end of February in 1529, although Cabeza de Vaca had begun to lose track of calendar time, the roots upon which he and his Indian hosts had been subsisting began to sprout and became inedible. He and his hosts, therefore, loaded their possessions into canoes, quitted Malhado Island, and crossed over to the Texas mainland. Cabeza de Vaca estimated that where the water was widest, the distance from the island to the mainland was about two leagues, or six miles. For the next two to three months, he and his hosts lived upon oysters they gathered from salt marshes and tidal flats along the mainland shore. But the only water they found to drink was brackish, they found little firewood, and they were tormented by mosquitoes. The Indians camped on beds of oyster shells where their ancestors before them had camped, eaten oysters, and discarded shells. At some point that spring, Cabeza de Vaca became so ill, he expected to die.[48]

Meanwhile, Captains Castillo and Dorantes had moved with their Indian hosts to a different part of the mainland, where they too gathered oysters. Hoping to resume their journey (now perforce overland) to the Spanish outpost of Santisteban del Puerto on the Río Pánuco, the captains began mustering those castaways they could locate. The men had dispersed, and while some had remained at Malhado, others had moved to nearby islands or to the mainland. The captains gathered them from the mainland and Malhado, and they retrieved a cleric and an African slave from an island farther to the northeast. Castillo and Dorantes found that few of the eighty castaways who had taken refuge in Malhado the previous November had survived the winter. They could account for only thirteen or fourteen men, besides themselves, and of these, only ten were fit to travel.[49]

Two Spaniards at Malhado, Jerónimo de Alaniz and Lope de Oviedo, were too ill to leave the island. Cabeza de Vaca, on the mainland, was also very ill. Castillo and Dorantes heard of still another man who had traveled far inland with his Indian benefactors, but the captains were unable to locate him. In exchange for taking them and the ten other able-bodied castaways back to the mainland, the captains gave the marten-skin cloak they had acquired the previous autumn to an Indian with a canoe. When they reached the mainland, they attempted to find Cabeza de Vaca, but Indians told them he was dead. They therefore set off southward for the Río Pánuco without him. The ten castaways who accompanied the captains in the spring of 1529 included Diego Dorantes, Pedro de Valdivieso, Diego de Huelva, Estevanico, and a cleric from Asturias in northern Spain. Diego Dorantes and Pedro de Valdivieso were both cousins to Andrés Dorantes, and Estevanico, of course, was the captain's slave. Cabeza de Vaca heard they had gone, but he was too weak to follow them.[50]

SEVEN

Texas

When they went southward, Castillo and Dorantes abandoned not only Cabeza de Vaca but also Jerónimo de Alaniz and Lope de Oviedo. Alaniz was the *escribano* who, at the Bay of the Cross the previous May, had recorded Cabeza de Vaca's objections to Narváez's decision to part with his ships. Oviedo was the man who had climbed a tree in November and discovered that Malhado was an island. After a time, Alaniz died, but both Oviedo and Cabeza de Vaca recovered from the illnesses that had kept them from joining Castillo and Dorantes. Cabeza de Vaca now had little choice but to remain with the Indians who had supported him ever since he came to Malhado. He would spend more than a year with these Indians and observe the full annual cycle of their foraging activities.[1]

At the end of April 1529, he and his hosts moved to a new area of the mainland coast, where they gathered blackberries. Blackberry season proved to be a time of great merrymaking among the Indians, and they celebrated several festivals that Cabeza de Vaca, using the language of the Taíno Indians of Cuba, describes as *areitos*. During times of plenty, large groups of people could sustain themselves collectively in one place, so during blackberry season each spring, the Indians congregated to perform ritual dances, barter for goods, exchange news and gossip, and no doubt arrange marriages. Sensitive to the resources of their environment, the Indians modified their lifestyle according to the seasonal availability of food. Their diet, though unbalanced at any one time, was balanced over the course of a year.

Cabeza de Vaca reports that his hosts lived on Malhado from October to February, subsisting on fish and roots. For the following three months they gathered oysters on the mainland, and then for a month they ate blackberries. For part of the year, they subsisted on snakes, lizards, rats, and spiders, but occasionally they killed and feasted upon a deer. Cabeza de Vaca observes that their only weapons were bows and arrows, and it seemed to him they were highly skilled archers. They used bows and arrows when fishing, but they may also have used fish traps. The Indians crafted dugout canoes, but they employed these mainly in the sheltered waters behind Texas's barrier islands and did not venture into the open Gulf. Shells and fish bones found at archaeological sites along the central Texas coast and its islands indicate that the area's aboriginal people ate oysters, scallops, quahogs, black drum, redfish, speckled sea trout, Atlantic croaker, sea catfish, perch, and mullet. During the time of year when his hosts subsisted on reptiles, rats, and spiders, Cabeza de Vaca must have remembered ruefully that at the Bay of Horses he had refused to eat horseflesh. He returned to Malhado in the fall of 1529 and endured a second winter there, but his hosts treated him harshly and made it clear he had outstayed his welcome.[2]

Sometime in the spring of 1530, probably during blackberry season when many bands of people gathered together, Cabeza de Vaca parted ways with the Indians who had been supporting him and took up instead with a band he identifies as the Charrucos. Unlike his previous hosts, who moved back and forth seasonally between Malhado and the mainland, the Charrucos lived on the mainland year-round. Cabeza de Vaca seems to have had no trouble communicating with them, and it is likely they shared a language with the people (either the Capoques or the Hans) he had previously lived among.[3]

His life was easier with the Charrucos than it had formerly been, for they allowed him to transform himself into a traveling merchant. The Charrucos were unable to move beyond their foraging territory or to trade with their neighbors because they were continuously at war with most of them. But Cabeza de Vaca was an outsider, and with his exotic beard and pale skin, he was able to mediate and to carry goods and messages between inimical groups. He transported his wares inland to some distance and southward for forty to fifty leagues, or probably as far as Matagorda Bay. He carried shells, shell tools, shell beads, and other coastal products to Indians who lived inland. He brought animal skins, tassels made from dyed deer hairs, flints for arrowheads, reeds for arrow shafts, paste, red ocher for use as face and body paint and as hair dye, and other inland products back to the coast. He says that his occupation as a merchant served him well: "Practicing it, I had the freedom to go wherever I wanted, and I was not constrained in any way nor enslaved, and wherever I went they treated me well and gave me food out of want for my wares, and most importantly because doing that, I was able to seek out the way by which I would go forward." In other words, he reconnoitered the section of the Texas coast he knew he would have to traverse if he was ever to reach Santisteban del Puerto on the Río Pánuco, and he made contacts and learned skills that would enable him to negotiate his way through many future difficulties. Cabeza de Vaca says of his relationship with his trading customers: "I was very well known; when they saw me and I brought them the things they needed, they were greatly pleased." Among his customers were the Deaguanes, a coastal people who lived in the region of Texas's lower Colorado River.[4]

A chain of sandy barrier islands protects the whole length of the Texas coast. Behind the islands is a series of shallow lagoons and estuarine bays, and tidal passes between the islands allow the water of the Gulf of Mexico to flow in and out of the lagoons. The mainland shore is a majestically flat patchwork of alternating prairie, saltwater and freshwater marshes, and woodland, carved by several rivers and bayous. Trees grow abundantly in the river valleys, the most common being live oaks, hackberries, elms, and pecans. The coastal plain provides a fertile habitat for fish, shellfish, and insects and lies on North America's central flyway for migrating birds. Pelicans and other shorebirds, herons, ibises, ducks, and quail are plentiful, and snow geese and sandhill cranes visit the Texas shore every winter. Common small mammals include javelinas, skunks, raccoons, opossums, and armadillos. Among the region's more dangerous creatures are the eastern cottonmouth, the rattlesnake, and the American alligator. The northern part of the coast receives more rainfall than the southern part. Summers are hot and humid, and hurricanes may hit in August or September. Winters, although generally mild, are punctuated by occasional northers—arctic cold fronts like the one Cabeza de Vaca experienced soon after his arrival at Malhado.[5]

Connecting the Indian groups Cabeza de Vaca encountered in Texas with those known either from subsequent historical accounts or through archaeological investigation is difficult. Some researchers have attempted to link the explorer's sixteenth-century Capoques, Hans, Charrucos, and Deaguanes with the Karankawa people, who are known to have inhabited the central Texas coast in the eighteenth century. However, a 150-year hiatus occurred between Cabeza de Vaca's sojourn on the Texas coast and the arrival in 1685 of the next European to visit the area—René-Robert Cavelier, Sieur de la Salle. The term "Karankawa" does not enter the historical record until the late seventeenth century, and Cabeza de Vaca never uses it. The five separate Karankawa bands of the eighteenth century shared a common language and culture. The northernmost band lived in the region of Texas's lower Colorado River, with the Brazos River as its northern limit. Cabeza de Vaca's sixteenth-century Capoques and Hans seem to have lived north of the Brazos, but his Deaguanes lived near the lower Colorado and may have been ancestors to the eighteenth-century Karankawas. One distinction Cabeza de Vaca insisted upon was that between coastal and inland peoples. His Capoques, Hans, Charrucos, and Deaguanes were all coastal people, and all except the Charrucos spent part of the year on the offshore islands. The later Karankawas were also coastal people.[6]

Archaeological research indicates that the historical Karankawa culture had prehistoric antecedents extending back over the course of several centuries. Its late-prehistoric ancestral form, the Rockport Focus, flourished from roughly 1200 until Cabeza de Vaca's era. This prehistoric culture is identified by an artifact assemblage that includes small arrowheads and a distinctive style of pottery decorated or coated with asphaltum, a tar that washes up on Gulf coastal beaches. Unfortunately, Cabeza de Vaca rarely mentions pottery, so correlating Rockport Focus artifacts with any particular band of people he encountered is no easier than correlating such a band with the historical Karankawas. One thing that, tragically, the Capoques, Hans, Charrucos, Deaguanes, and Karankawas have in common is that their cultures are now extinct. Some of Cabeza de Vaca's sixteenth-century bands may have evolved into the eighteenth-century Karankawas, but Texas ranchers killed the last known Karankawas in 1858.[7]

Cabeza de Vaca lived as a merchant for about three years. Since winters could bring harsh weather, he did not travel or engage in trade during that season. Instead, he accepted what shelter his Charruco hosts could provide and endured the hunger and hardships of the season with them. The only other Spaniard with whom he came in contact was Lope de Oviedo, who was still at Malhado. As the man's senior officer, Cabeza de Vaca felt responsible for Oviedo, and he visited Malhado once a year to implore Oviedo to go southward with him to the Río Pánuco. Oviedo was reluctant to go, partly because he could not swim. But something additional—perhaps

PL. VIII.

Carancahueses

Watercolor of a Karankawa couple (ca. 1834–1838) by Lino Sánchez y Tapia, from "Indigenes Du Mexique Voyage De J. Luis Berlandier," Plate 8 "Carancahueses" 4016.336.13. © Gilcrease Museum, Tulsa, Oklahoma.

newly acquired skills that increased his status in Malhado, or perhaps a wife and children—seems to have held him to the island. Possibly, both Oviedo and Cabeza de Vaca had formed liaisons with native women. But even if so, Cabeza de Vaca never wavered in his determination to return to the Spanish-speaking world, and he never let go of his Christian identity. He had a wife in Castile, and he had an emperor in whose royal service he was bound. He owed it to his emperor and to the families of the lost men of the Narváez expedition to bring news of their fate back to Spain.[8]

Finally, in the spring of 1533, four and a half years after the two men had washed ashore on Malhado and four years after Castillo and Dorantes had abandoned them, Cabeza de Vaca succeeded in persuading Oviedo to accompany him southward. The two men were guided part of their way by a group of Deaguanes with whom Cabeza de Vaca had become friendly during his years as a trader. The castaways crossed four large and swift rivers—almost certainly Oyster Creek, the Brazos River, the San Bernard River, and Caney Creek. Cabeza de Vaca says he swam across all four with Oviedo clinging to his back. The castaways seem to have followed Texas's outer coastline down the long sandbar of Matagorda Peninsula, but they were confronted finally by a tidal channel that Cabeza de Vaca estimated to be a league wide and very deep. The channel was probably Pass Cavallo, which separates Matagorda Peninsula from Matagorda Island. The castaways managed to cross the barrier with the help of the Deaguanes, but whether they crossed to Matagorda Island or back to the mainland is unclear.[9]

Cabeza de Vaca and Oviedo camped with the Deaguanes on the opposite side of the channel, but around midnight a band of enemy people ambushed them. Three of the Deaguanes were killed and many others wounded. In their panic, the Deaguanes and both castaways abandoned their camp and fled into the surrounding woods. They hid quietly until their attackers, the Quevenes, had taken what they wanted and quitted the area. The Deaguanes then gathered up the arrows the Quevenes had expended and followed after them. They attacked the Quevenes at dawn, killed five of them, frightened the others away, and looted their camp. Later that morning, several Quevenes women approached the Deaguanes and negotiated a truce. Among Texas coastal natives, Cabeza de Vaca observed, women were more likely than men to mediate in cases of intertribal conflict.[10]

Apparently, the skirmish between the Deaguanes and the Quevenes took place near the boundary between their respective foraging territories. The Quevenes lived in the vicinity of Matagorda Bay, south of the Deaguanes, and probably spent part of each year on Matagorda Island. Cabeza de Vaca seized the opportunity to establish relations with the Quevenes, because he knew that to reach his objective on the Río Pánuco, he would have to pass through their territory. He drew on the negotiation skills he had acquired during his years as a trader and presented himself as neutral in the conflict between them and the Deaguanes. He seems to have had no trouble communicating with either of the bands, so they probably shared a common language.[11]

Cabeza de Vaca obtained a great deal of information from the Quevenes. They told him that the land to the south was sparsely populated and afforded little to eat. Moreover, they had neighbors in the south who had killed other bearded men like him and Oviedo. Three bearded men were living nearby, however, among people who abused them and forced them to work incessantly. One of the bearded men was living with the Mariames, and the other two with the Yguases. Suspecting that the three were survivors of the group of twelve castaways who had set off from Malhado in the spring of 1529, Cabeza de Vaca asked what had become of the other nine. The Quevenes said that some of the men had died of hunger and exposure, and others had been killed by Indians who kicked and cudgeled them or shot them with arrows. To demonstrate the harsh treatment the men had received, the Quevenes slapped Cabeza de Vaca and Oviedo, threw mud balls at them, and fitted arrows to their bows as if to shoot them. The Quevenes boasted that they themselves had killed some of the men Cabeza de Vaca was asking about. Oviedo, already on edge from the previous night's ambush, was overwhelmed by the rough treatment. Although Cabeza de Vaca implored him to stay, he turned back northward with the Deaguanes toward Malhado, choosing to live humbly among familiar and moderately friendly Indians rather than to risk his life among Indians he did not know.[12]

Cabeza de Vaca opted to remain with the Quevenes and seek the company of the three bearded men they said were nearby. In a few days, the Quevenes told him, the Mariames, Yguases, and many other bands of people would converge on the banks of a river where they would gather nuts. The Quevenes must have led Cabeza de Vaca to the river, which was probably the Guadalupe below its confluence with the San Antonio. The Mariames, Yguases, and other bands lived primarily upon nuts for two months, and Cabeza de Vaca observed that the nut trees were large and numerous. They probably were pecans, a New World species common in Texas. The nuts reminded Cabeza de Vaca of the walnuts that grew in the province of Galicia in northwestern Spain, but he noted that the meats were difficult to extract.[13]

Shortly after Cabeza de Vaca arrived in the nut groves, an Indian told him that the Mariames and their bearded dependent had arrived there as well. The Indian spoke a language different from that of the Quevenes, but he indicated that he had business with the Mariames, and he offered to lead Cabeza de Vaca to their camp. The Spaniard was instinctively cautious but accepted the offer. When he and his guide arrived at the Mariames camp, Captain Andrés Dorantes came forward to greet his superior officer. Dorantes expressed astonishment because, four years earlier, he had given Cabeza de Vaca up for dead. Their reunion during the nut harvest of 1533 seemed to the two Spaniards to be almost miraculous, and they gave thanks to God for bringing them together again after their long separation. Both men, Cabeza de Vaca reports, felt that "this day was one of the days of greatest pleasure that we have had in our lives."[14]

No doubt each man looked savage to the other. Their hair and beards had grown long, and they were naked, work-hardened, and sun-browned. Dorantes informed Cabeza de Vaca that Captain Alonso del Castillo and Estevanico, the African slave whom Dorantes had brought to the New World, were the only other survivors of the group of twelve men who, in the spring of 1529, had marched southward from Malhado. The two were now living with the Yguases, who were camping nearby. Dorantes led Cabeza de Vaca to the Yguases camp and presented him to the astonished Castillo and Estevanico. The gladness Cabeza de Vaca felt at finding other survivors of the Narváez expedition must have been even greater than what he had felt in the winter of 1528 when he learned that the barge commanded by Dorantes and Castillo had beached on Malhado not far from where his own barge had washed up. Memories concerning Dorantes and Castillo undoubtedly came flooding into his mind. He probably recalled the day he and Castillo had cut their feet on oyster shells near the Withlacoochee River in peninsular Florida, and the time that the three of them had explored the Río de la Magdalena and established a camp at the Bay of Horses. He must also have remembered the time during their barge journey when he and Dorantes had defended Narváez at the village of the chief with the marten-skin cloak.[15]

Both the captains were unmarried men, younger than Cabeza de Vaca. Andrés Dorantes had joined the Narváez expedition as a captain of infantry. An hidalgo, he was born in the province of Extremadura but had later established residence in Andalusia. Like Cabeza de Vaca, Dorantes had fought for the crown in 1520–21 during the revolt of the Comuneros. In the course of that rebellion, he had received a face wound that left him scarred.[16]

Alonso del Castillo Maldonado was a native of Salamanca, the site of the oldest university in Spain. As a member of the *caballero* class, he ranked higher on the social scale than Cabeza de Vaca or Dorantes. His father was a physician, and two of his uncles were judges. These facts suggest that Captain Castillo and his family were *conversos* because medicine was a profession often associated with Jews and Jewish converts, and judges were often of Jewish ancestry. Many *converso* families took a new surname as a sign of their conversion, and "del Castillo"—which literally means "of the castle"—was a popular choice because it implied that its bearers were loyal Castilians. All these indications of Captain Castillo's religious heritage are circumstantial, but if he was in fact a *converso*, the threat of persecution by the Inquisition would have given him a strong reason for joining the Narváez expedition. Officially, it was illegal for *conversos* to emigrate to the New World, but the Americas became a haven for them, and some 5 to 8 percent of the Spaniards who fought with Cortés against the Aztecs were probably of Jewish ancestry.[17]

Estevanico was a native of Azemmour, a large and populous city under Portuguese control on the Atlantic coast of present-day Morocco. He was a black man who spoke both Arabic and Spanish. Whether he had been a longtime member of Dorantes's household or had been purchased by Dorantes expressly for the expedition to the New World is unclear. Like the three Spanish castaways, Estevanico was Christian. The three Spaniards did not see him as their equal, but the Indians saw him—perhaps because of his beard, body hair, and exotic origin—as more similar to his Spanish companions than to themselves. The Quevenes, for example, had told Cabeza de Vaca that three men like himself were traveling with the Mariames and the Yguases.[18]

The four castaways were the first men of the Old World to live for a period of years within the borders of the present United States. It is noteworthy that three were Europeans, one was possibly of Jewish ancestry, and one was African. In some ways, the four men and their Native American benefactors prefigured the great amalgam of cultures that was to become emblematic of the United States.[19]

Cabeza de Vaca was the natural leader of the castaways because he was the oldest man among them and the ranking officer. Dorantes and Castillo informed him of what had happened to them during the four years since they last had seen him. They also told him what they knew about the fates of other men of the Narváez expedition. Except for the men of the Téllez-Peñalosa barge, which they couldn't account for, Dorantes and Castillo knew that most of the three hundred men who had marched with Narváez in 1528 into the Florida interior were now dead. Most of them had died during the harsh winter of 1528–29. Those who had had the help of Indians survived longer than those who had tried to live on their own.

Of the two early accounts of the Narváez expedition—Cabeza de Vaca's and Oviedo's—the latter is more detailed with regard to what happened to Dorantes, Castillo, and Estevanico during the four years between their departure from Malhado in 1529 and their reunion with Cabeza de Vaca in 1533. Oviedo's source was the now-lost *Joint Report* that Cabeza de Vaca, Dorantes, and Castillo prepared collectively after they emerged from the

North American wilderness. Oviedo, the royal historian of the Indies, should not be confused with the Lope de Oviedo who returned to Malhado in 1533 after his rough encounter with the Quevenes.[20]

Both Oviedo (the historian) and Cabeza de Vaca give confusing accounts of the journey Dorantes, Castillo, and Estevanico made down the Texas coast in 1529. Dorantes and Castillo did not know precisely where they were at any given time, and so when they reported on their travels first to Cabeza de Vaca and later to the viceroy of New Spain, they had no clear way of referring to the various islands they had visited or to the various rivers and tidal channels they had crossed. They seem to have hopscotched from islands to mainland and back again, but they hugged the shore, hoping thereby to reach the Río Pánuco. As they moved southward, they passed through the territories of several bands of Indians. Oviedo does not identify any of these bands, but Cabeza de Vaca identifies twenty-three. He says that the Capoques, Hans, Deaguanes, and Quevenes spent at least part of each year on the offshore islands. Facing the islands, the Charrucos, Mendicas, Mariames, and Yguases lived on the mainland shore, with the Charrucos being the northernmost of these mainland bands and the Yguases the southernmost.[21]

After they left Malhado in the spring of 1529, Dorantes, Castillo, Estevanico, and the nine other men of their group crossed the four rivers that Cabeza de Vaca and Lope de Oviedo would cross in 1533. The rivers, which were swift and swelled by spring rains, were probably Oyster Creek, the Brazos, the San Bernard, and Caney Creek. The castaways built rafts to cross the first and second rivers. However, the strong current of the second (certainly the Brazos) carried one raft a league out to sea, where two (according to Oviedo, the historian) or four (according to Cabeza de Vaca) of the men drowned. Two other men on this raft swam to safety, and a third man used his body as a sail so that the wind pushed him back to shore. Somewhere near the mouth of the third river, probably the San Bernard, the surviving castaways came across the hulk of a Narváez expedition barge. They recognized it as the one commanded by Alonso Enríquez and Fray Juan Suárez, but they could only guess at what had happened to its commanders and crew. Castillo and Dorantes now knew that three of the expedition's five barges had failed to reach the Río Pánuco.[22]

Meanwhile, the number of men in their party was dwindling. In addition to the two or four men who drowned while crossing the second river, two others died of starvation. The only things the castaways had to eat were raw crayfish and briny kelp. Most of the men were bloated, either from the kelp or from starvation. They seem not to have had the help of Indians in obtaining food, but Indians helped them cross the last of the four rivers. Four days later, the castaways came to a tidal channel that was a league wide. They crossed it in a broken canoe that they had salvaged. On a point of land on the opposite shore, they saw large white sand dunes, which they thought must be visible from far out at sea. Twelve to fifteen leagues south of the first channel, they came to a second.[23]

The first tidal channel must have been the one Cabeza de Vaca and Oviedo would later cross with the help of the Deaguanes—probably Pass Cavallo, between Matagorda Peninsula and Matagorda Island. The second tidal channel was probably Cedar Bayou, which separates Matagorda Island from St. Joseph Island. At the second channel, Dorantes, Castillo, and their companions found Indians who were eating blackberries. The Indians fled in their canoes, leaving the Spaniards stranded at, apparently, the southern tip of Matagorda Island.[24]

After a time, one of the Indians returned, bringing another Spaniard with him. The accounts are not clear, but the Indian and his Spanish companion seem to have swum across the channel. The new Spaniard proved to be Figueroa, the sole survivor of the group of four swimmers who had left Malhado in November of 1528. An hidalgo from Toledo, Figueroa had been living for several months in the Matagorda Bay region, apparently with the Quevenes. He was able to tell Dorantes and Castillo what had happened not only to him and the other three swimmers but also to the men of two of the three Narváez expedition barges whose fates the captains did not know. It was around April of 1529 when Dorantes and Castillo met up with Figueroa.[25]

Figueroa said that soon after he and the other three swimmers had set off down the coast, two of them died of hunger and exposure. He and Méndez, his remaining companion, were taken in by Indians. Méndez later fled from these Indians, but another group of native people killed him. At some point after the death of Méndez but before his encounter with Dorantes and Castillo, Figueroa met Hernando de Esquivel, another survivor of the Narváez expedition. Esquivel had traveled on the barge commanded by Alonso Enríquez and Fray Juan Suárez. This barge had capsized in November of 1528, at around the time the barges commanded by Dorantes and

Castillo and by Cabeza de Vaca had beached on Malhado. Dorantes and Castillo had seen the hulk of the Enríquez-Suárez barge near the mouth of what probably was the San Bernard River.[26]

At this point the narrative becomes especially confusing because Dorantes and Castillo were telling Cabeza de Vaca what Figueroa told them he had learned from Esquivel. Thus we have a story within a story within a story. When Figueroa met him, Esquivel was walking northward up the Texas coast in search of Santisteban del Puerto on the Río Pánuco. Figueroa was dumbfounded because he had come southward from Malhado in search of the same Spanish outpost. Esquivel said that Fray Suárez had convinced him that the Río Pánuco lay to the north, and he added that the Franciscan was now dead. Esquivel was the sole survivor of the men who had traveled on the Enríquez-Suárez barge.[27]

Esquivel gave a great deal of information to Figueroa, including what had happened to Narváez and the men of his barge. Esquivel said that after the Enríquez-Suárez barge capsized, its crew abandoned it and began walking southward down the coast. As they walked, they were spotted by Narváez and the crew of his barge. Narváez at this time was thin, ill, and consumed by some leprous skin disease. He landed most of his men, probably somewhere between the San Bernard River and the tip of Matagorda Peninsula, so that they might walk with Enríquez, Suárez, and their men. The governor and a skeleton crew remained on their barge but hugged the coastline and kept within sight of the men on shore, who may have numbered as many as eighty souls. At the tidal channel near the large white sand dunes, which apparently was Pass Cavallo, Narváez used his barge to ferry all the men, in several trips, from what probably was Matagorda Peninsula to Matagorda Island.[28]

Tensions were so high between Narváez and his officers that the governor relieved Alonso Enríquez of his position as lieutenant governor, a position the royal comptroller had held since the previous spring in Florida. Narváez then elevated Captain Juan Pantoja to the lieutenant governorship. Pantoja had fought with Narváez in Mexico and served as deputy commander of the governor's barge. He was also the man with whom Cabeza de Vaca had weathered the hurricane in Cuba. Enríquez had been the first man of Narváez's company to venture ashore on Florida and to encounter Indians there. The co-commander of his barge, Fray Suárez, was the officer who—at an Indian village near the Bay of the Cross—had insisted on burning the chests containing corpses. Subsequently, Suárez had backed Narváez in his decision to part with his ships and enter the Florida interior.[29]

After ferrying his men across the tidal channel, Narváez spent the night on his barge, refusing to sleep on land with his men. With him, he had only a helmsman and a page. The page was sick, and the three men had no water or food, nor any anchor except a rock. During the night, the north wind carried them out to sea, and no one on land perceived it. Narváez and his two companions were never heard from again.[30]

Now having no barge, the surviving castaways continued to walk southward down the length of what probably was Matagorda Island. At the southern tip of the island, they built rafts to traverse a tidal channel, crossing probably to St. Joseph Island, or perhaps to Blackjack Peninsula on the mainland. On the far side of the channel, they frightened some Indians, who fled from them. At this point in the late autumn of 1528, as Cabeza de Vaca knew from his own experience at Malhado, the weather turned brutally cold.[31]

The men of the Narváez and Enríquez-Suárez barges decided to spend the winter where they were, but although they found water, firewood, and some crayfish and shellfish, they did not know how to use most of the resources of their environment, and they began to die. Unlike Cabeza de Vaca and the castaways at Malhado, these unfortunate men did not have the help of Indians. In the extremity of their situation, the starving Spaniards bickered over the direction in which the Río Pánuco lay. Fray Suárez insisted, incorrectly, that the way they had been marching—southward—was the wrong way. Meanwhile Captain Pantoja, who acted as governor in the absence of Narváez, treated his men abusively. Alonso de Sotomayor, Narváez's *maestre de campo*, became so exasperated that he killed Pantoja with a powerful blow. Meanwhile the starving castaways continued to die, and the dead were eaten by the survivors. The penultimate man to die was Sotomayor, and Esquivel "made jerky of him."[32]

Esquivel sustained himself on jerked flesh until around the first of March in 1529. Then the Indians who had fled from the castaways the previous autumn either captured or adopted him. It was while he was living with these Indians that Esquivel met Figueroa. The latter tried to persuade him to go southward to the Río Pánuco, but Esquivel persisted in believing that the Spanish frontier lay to the north. Since the two men could not agree upon a direction, they parted ways. Apparently, Figueroa remained with the

Quevenes on the coastal islands, and Esquivel crossed over to the mainland and lived with the Mariames. When Dorantes and Castillo met Figueroa in April 1529, he told them that Esquivel was living somewhere nearby on the mainland. However, Dorantes and Castillo later discovered that Esquivel had tried to flee from the Mariames, and the Indians had killed him. He had survived just long enough to inform Figueroa of the fates of the men of the Narváez and Enríquez-Suárez barges. If Esquivel had not met Figueroa, and if Figueroa had not then met Dorantes and Castillo, that information would have been lost to history.[33]

Dorantes and Castillo were not able to spend much time with Figueroa, because his Indian companion was impatient to return to where his people were camped. The Indian urged all the castaways to accompany him, promising that his people would give them fish. The three of the men who could swim—Figueroa, the Asturian cleric, and a youth—swam across the tidal channel with the Indian, promising to bring fish back to where the nonswimmers were stranded. The following morning, the Spanish youth rejoined Dorantes, Castillo, and their companions, bringing them a small quantity of fish. Figueroa and the Asturian, he said, had gone with the Indians to a place where the native people could harvest a leaf they used for brewing a tea.[34]

The next day, the men of the Dorantes-Castillo party were confronted by a new group of Indians who had come to the island to eat blackberries. These Indians seized whatever material goods the Spaniards still possessed and stripped them of their clothes, but then the Indians gave them fish and transported them in canoes across the tidal channel they had been unable to cross. The Spaniards camped with the Indians on the opposite side but did not succeed in reconnecting with Figueroa or the Asturian. The Indians quickly grew tired of feeding the Spaniards and threw several of them out, suggesting contemptuously that they find other benefactors to sponge off.[35]

The ejected men—including Alonso del Castillo, Pedro de Valdivieso, Diego de Huelva, and the youthful swimmer—moved farther down the coast. Andrés Dorantes, Diego Dorantes, and Estevanico remained where they were, carrying wood and water for their Indian benefactors, but after a time the Indians threw them out as well. The three now-naked men moved southward, and at some point they stumbled upon the bodies of two of their fellow castaways. These two, one of whom apparently was the young swimmer, had died of starvation. Andrés Dorantes succeeded in attaching himself to a new band of Indians, and perhaps Estevanico did too, but Diego Dorantes continued onward to the southern tip of the island and found Castillo and Huelva there, confronting yet another tidal channel. This third channel was likely Aransas Pass, between St. Joseph and Mustang Islands. Valdivieso had already crossed over to what probably was Mustang Island.[36]

As mentioned earlier, both Valdivieso and Diego Dorantes were cousins to Andrés Dorantes. Let us assume for the sake of narrative simplicity that Valdivieso was indeed on Mustang Island and Diego Dorantes was on St. Joseph Island. When Valdivieso heard that Diego Dorantes was searching for him, he returned to St. Joseph Island and told Dorantes that he had briefly encountered Figueroa and the Asturian cleric. The two castaways had been beaten and robbed by Indians, and the Asturian had suffered an arrow wound, but since both men could swim, they urged one another to press onward to the Spanish outpost on the Río Pánuco, vowing to reach it or die in the attempt. Probably because he could not swim, Valdivieso took no part in their undertaking. Later, he saw the Asturian's clothing, breviary, and book of hours in the possession of Indians. Two days after he spoke with Diego Dorantes, Valdivieso attempted to return to what probably was Mustang Island, but Indians killed him because they thought he was trying to run from them. At around the same time, Indians killed Diego de Huelva because he tried to move from one house to another.[37]

After the deaths of Valdivieso and Huelva, no more than five of the men who left Malhado in the spring of 1529 can have remained alive: Andrés Dorantes, Diego Dorantes, Alonso del Castillo, Estevanico, and possibly the Asturian cleric. Except for the Asturian, who had fled southward with Figueroa, the castaways saw no way to escape from their situation. They were trapped on an island in the midst of a vast and bewildering maze of islands and salt marshes, and they could not swim. They must have been somewhere in the region of Copano and Corpus Christi Bays, probably on St. Joseph Island.[38]

Andrés Dorantes remained on the island for more than a year, serving a group of Indians. He thought of himself as their slave, and because of what had happened to Valdivieso and Huelva, he feared that at any moment his masters would kill him. He and the other surviving castaways were made to carry heavy burdens on their bare backs and, in the sticky heat of a Texas summer, to pull canoes through the marshes. They suffered both from hunger and from thirst, for the water near the coast was brackish, and finding and hauling sweet water was another of their principal tasks. All the Indians, but especially the children, delighted in scratching the castaways, throwing stones at them, and pulling their hair and beards. Dorantes said he accepted these mortifications as a kind of penance for his sins.[39]

Around August of 1530, Andrés Dorantes escaped from his island-dwelling masters. He left them at noon, walking boldly as if nothing were unusual and somehow managed to cross over to the mainland. Castillo and Estevanico did not accompany him, but Diego Dorantes may have, and one or both cousins took up with a group of mainland Indians. Three months later, perhaps in November, Estevanico followed Andrés and maybe Diego Dorantes to the mainland, but although the African and Andrés Dorantes occasionally saw one another, they were never together for any length of time. Castillo remained on the island for an additional year and a half, and then he too found an opportunity to escape to the mainland. He joined the Yguases, with whom Estevanico was then living, but by that time Andrés Dorantes was living among the Mariames, and Diego Dorantes was dead. Diego had lived for two years among a group of mainland Indians, serving them faithfully all the while, but then they killed him. Cabeza de Vaca suggests that Indians killed Diego Dorantes, Pedro de Valdivieso, and Diego de Huelva "for their own amusement."[40]

In moving to the Mariames, Andrés Dorantes backtracked twenty leagues northward, away from the Río Pánuco. Why he backtracked is uncertain, but he may have wished to distance himself from the Indians who killed his cousin Diego. The foraging territory of the Mariames was north of that of the Yguases and centered for at least part of the year in the region of the pecan groves at the confluence of the Guadalupe and San Antonio Rivers. Apparently, it was the Mariames who had killed Esquivel, for they showed Andrés Dorantes a sword that had belonged to his late compatriot. The Mariames may have killed Méndez as well. According to Oviedo's account, they killed Esquivel because he tried to run from them. According to Cabeza de Vaca's, they killed him because an Indian woman had seen in a dream that Esquivel would kill her son. Dorantes said the Mariames and their neighbors often acted on the promptings of dreams. Sometimes, acting upon a dream, they even killed their own sons. During the four years between his departure from Malhado in 1529 and his reunion with Cabeza de Vaca in 1533, Dorantes had seen eleven or twelve Indian boys killed or buried alive because of things their elders saw in dreams. Although

Dorantes had never seen an Indian girl treated in this manner, infant girls were sometimes fed to the dogs.[41]

During his time with the Mariames, Dorantes said he labored like a beast and expected death at any moment. The murders of his two cousins—and the killing of Esquivel by the very Indians upon whom he now depended—must have preyed on Dorantes's mind. Whenever an Indian approached him, he flinched, and the Mariames delighted in frightening him. A favorite game they played was to scowl fiercely, fit an arrow to a bow, aim at Dorantes's breast, draw back the bowstring, pause threateningly, then laugh and ask, "Were you afraid?" Another good game was to send an arrow whizzing past the castaway's ear.[42]

Dorantes moved with the Mariames as they made their seasonal migratory circuit. They spent nine months of each year in the region of the pecan groves. Then, every summer, they traveled thirty to forty leagues southward to a region where they could harvest the fruits of the prickly-pear cactus. This region was probably southwest of the lower Nueces River, in the present Duval and Jim Wells Counties. The migratory range of the Yguases, with whom Castillo and Estevanico were living, overlapped that of the Mariames, for the Yguases joined in both the pecan and prickly-pear harvests. Other Indian bands joined in these harvests as well, but prickly-pear season was the most bountiful time for all of them. Dorantes was the first of the castaways to take part in the prickly-pear harvest, perhaps as early as 1530. Estevanico may have participated in 1531, and he, Dorantes, and Castillo are all known to have taken part in 1532, because when the cactus was ripe that year, they attempted unsuccessfully to flee from their Indian masters. When they failed, they agreed to try again the following year. Cactus season and pecan season were the two times of each year when the castaways could count on seeing one another.[43]

As it happened, during the pecan harvest of 1533, Dorantes, Castillo, and Estevanico were reunited with Cabeza de Vaca. When they finished reporting to him on everything that had happened to them since they had last seen him, Dorantes and Castillo asked their superior officer what he intended to do next. He said he intended to press onward to the Spanish outpost on the Río Pánuco. Dorantes said Pánuco was his goal as well, but every time he proposed it to Castillo and Estevanico, they protested they were unable to swim or to cross the rivers, tidal channels, and bays that barred their way. Cabeza de Vaca turned to Castillo and Estevanico and argued that God had preserved their lives for a purpose and had brought them together again for a purpose. God must want them to go forward to bring news to their emperor and to the Spanish world of what had happened to the Narváez expedition. It was their obligation as Christians, he added, to escape from the savage life they were leading and return to the world of Christians.[44]

Castillo and Estevanico agreed to move on toward the Río Pánuco, but they implored Cabeza de Vaca not to reveal their plans to any Indians. They reminded him that Indians had killed Esquivel, Méndez, Valdivieso, Huelva, and Diego Dorantes for attempting to escape from the miserable situation in which they were trapped. Castillo and Dorantes advised Cabeza de Vaca that the time of the cactus harvest afforded their best opportunity for escape. They could count on seeing one another at the harvest, and in the cactus thickets they would be thirty to forty leagues closer to the Pánuco than they now were. Since many different bands of Indians converged in the cactus region, the four Christians would find a way to leave the Mariames and Yguases and join some other band whose migratory path would take them in the direction they wished to go.[45]

Meanwhile, Cabeza de Vaca was to live with Dorantes and the Mariames, and Castillo and Estevanico would continue to live with the Yguases. By separating, the Christians would reduce both the burden on their hosts and the risk of incurring their hostility. Cabeza de Vaca put himself in the service of the Mariames Indian whom Dorantes was serving. This man was blind in one eye, as were his wife and son. Cabeza de Vaca believed he was indenturing himself as a slave to the one-eyed man, and although the concept of slavery may have been more present in the Spaniard's mind than in that of his master, the murders of Esquivel, Valdivieso, and some of the others indicate that the Christians were not free to move about as they liked. Cabeza de Vaca had reason to be cautious, and the fact that he had survived among Indians for as long as he had is a testament to his circumspection. He was aware he had few skills of value to the Mariames and was fit only for the most menial work. Moreover, he was middle-aged—somewhere between forty-one and forty-eight years old. He was a man with a goal, however, and as such he accepted the necessity of serving his one-eyed master until the next cactus harvest.[46]

During the time he spent among the Mariames, Cabeza de Vaca observed them closely. And because he was later able to report on their lifeways, they are the best-described group of indigenous people in sixteenth-century Texas. Their population at the time Cabeza de Vaca lived among them consisted of approximately two hundred persons. The males were archers, but although they were well built, they were not as tall as the Capoques and the Hans of Malhado Island. As at Malhado, each adult male had his lower lip and one nipple pierced. Adult males were the most privileged members of the Mariames community. Its least valued members were the old people. To Cabeza de Vaca, the Mariames did not seem to love their children as much as the Indians of Malhado did.[47]

Among the Mariames, the men carried no burdens. Instead, the women, the old people, and no doubt Cabeza de Vaca and Dorantes carried whatever was to be carried. The Mariames lived in portable shelters made of woven mats fastened to bent poles. Every two or three days, when they had exhausted the local food supply, they dismantled their houses and moved their camp. The women worked very hard and averaged only six hours of sleep per day. They retired late and rose early to fetch wood and water, dig for roots, bake them, and care for their children.[48]

Since Dorantes had told him the Mariames sometimes killed their infant daughters, Cabeza de Vaca asked his Mariames master to explain why they did so, and recorded the response:

> [He said that] all the people of the land are their enemies, and with them they have continual war, and that if by chance they should marry off their daughters, their enemies would multiply so much that they would be captured and enslaved by them, and for this reason they preferred rather to kill them, than that there be born of them those who would be their enemies. We asked them why they did not marry them themselves and also among one another. They said it was an ugly thing to marry them to their relatives, and that it was much better to kill them than to give them either to a relative or to an enemy.

As nomadic hunter-gatherers, the Mariames must have found it difficult to sustain themselves and provide for all the children born to them. From what the one-eyed man told Cabeza de Vaca, it is clear the Mariames were exogamous. No one married within his or her kinship group, and the women moved away upon marriage. The Mariames bought their wives from their enemies, no doubt at those times when many different bands of people came together, such as at the cactus harvest. The price for a bride was either a bow and two arrows or a net one *braza* long on each side. Marriages, which lasted only so long as both parties were content with the arrangement, could be dissolved for the slightest reason. Couples with children, however, were likely to stay together. If a couple separated, each partner was free to remarry as he or she pleased.[49]

Cabeza de Vaca says the Mariames were "great thieves." Although they freely shared what they had with one another, they stole from each other whenever they could. Cabeza de Vaca also accuses the Mariames of lying and drunkenness. He observed that two men might live together as if married, which he describes as a "sin against nature." Or a man might dress as a woman, behave in an effeminate manner, and perform tasks traditionally assigned to women. Such a man would carry heavy loads like a woman, heavier in fact than a woman could carry, but would not participate in hunting or other male activities.[50]

The mainstay of the Mariames diet was roots of two or three kinds, but these roots were hard to find and to dig up. Roasting them took two days, and even so, they tasted bitter and caused bloating. The Mariames did not practice agriculture, and their only domesticated animals were dogs. In April and May, when the rivers were in flood, the Mariames were able to catch many fish, but most of them spoiled because, Cabeza de Vaca says, the Indians had no salt with which to preserve them. Cabeza de Vaca claims that occasionally while he was living among the Mariames, he tasted buffalo meat, and he reports that the Indians made robes, shoes, and shields from buffalo hides. At that time, buffalo ranged as far south as what is now the Mexican state of Coahuila.[51]

The Mariames had several methods for capturing deer. One method was to fire the savannahs in order to flush out the animals. Another method was for many hunters to march together in a long line, moving toward the sea and driving the deer before them into the water, where they drowned. In this manner, Dorantes told Cabeza de Vaca he had seen sixty Indians kill two or three hundred deer over the course of eight days. A third method for capturing deer was to chase after them, apparently in relays, until the animals were exhausted. The Mariames were great runners and could run from dawn until dusk without tiring.[52]

In the absence of other foods, Cabeza de Vaca says the Mariames ate "spiders and ant eggs and worms and lizards and salamanders and snakes and vipers that kill men when they strike," as well as "rats, crickets, cicadas, frogs, and all insects." He also mentioned that "they eat earth and wood and everything they can find and deer excrement and other things that I refrain from mentioning." The Indians pulverized the bones of fish and snakes and consumed the resulting powder, which obviously was high in calcium. Often while Cabeza de Vaca was living with the Mariames, everyone went three or four days without eating. At such times, the Indians consoled one another and their Spanish dependents by saying that soon there would be plenty of prickly pears for everyone.[53]

Late in the summer of 1533, Cabeza de Vaca and Dorantes traveled thirty to forty leagues with the Mariames to the part of their foraging territory where prickly pears grew in abundance. This area was somewhat inland, in a region where water was scarce. Cabeza de Vaca observed that the prickly-pear fruits were vermilion and black, the size of an egg, and "of very good flavor." Of the several varieties, some were tastier than others, but in his hunger, Cabeza de Vaca was never choosy. The Indians lived upon the pears for two to three months of each year, and during this time their only other food was snails. They squeezed the juice from the cactus pears and dried the fleshy remainder, storing it in baskets to eat later. They stored the juice in a specially prepared hole in the ground that they must have lined with some nonporous material. Apparently, the Indians allowed the juice to ferment, for it reminded Cabeza de Vaca of the fermenting must of wine grapes in his native Jerez de la Frontera.[54]

During cactus season, the Mariames and their Spanish dependents were tormented by mosquitoes. Cabeza de Vaca says people were so badly stung that, like Saint Lazarus, they seemed to have contracted leprosy. The Mariames built smudge fires to drive the insects away, but the smoke caused people to cough and weep and made sleeping difficult. Apparently, Cabeza de Vaca and Dorantes were responsible for keeping the smudge fires burning, because if they dozed and allowed the fires to smolder, their master would pummel them awake and force them to attend to their duties.[55]

The harvest season for prickly pears was the only time when the Mariames had plenty to eat and, therefore, the time when they made most merry, holding feasts and ceremonial dances and no doubt enjoying their fermented cactus juice. And because many different bands of Indians came together for the cactus harvest, they took advantage of the opportunity to trade with one another. The Mariames traded with the Avavares, in particular, for bows that the latter brought to the harvest. Dorantes, Castillo, and Estevanico had made acquaintance with the Avavares in 1532, and it was to the Avavares that they hoped to escape. The cactus thickets were at the northern limit of the band's territorial range and at the southern limit of the ranges of the Mariames and the Yguases. So if they escaped to the

Avavares, the Christians could move southward with them and closer to the Spanish outpost on the Río Pánuco.[56]

During the prickly-pear harvest of 1533, however, the Christians were unable to put their plan into effect. Before they could flee to the Avavares, several Indian men began brawling over a woman. The men struck and bloodied one another until mediators separated them. The brawlers and their kinsmen withdrew, took apart their campsites, and cleared out of the cactus thickets, each group going in a different direction to cool off. The Christians were forced to part company and follow their established masters. They knew they would have to wait an entire year before they would again have an opportunity to escape from the Indians they grudgingly were serving.[57]

That next year was a difficult one for Cabeza de Vaca as he suffered both hunger and harsh treatment from the Mariames. Three times he ran away from them, and each time, they endeavored to find him and kill him. He does not explain how he escaped death nor whether he returned to the Mariames each time. He simply says that "God our Lord in his mercy chose to preserve and protect me."[58]

EIGHT

The Children of the Sun

Late in the summer of 1534, Cabeza de Vaca again traveled to the region of the prickly pears. Dorantes, Castillo, and Estevanico made their way there as well, and the four men met briefly and agreed to flee from their Indian masters at the time of the next new moon. Perhaps they chose that phase of the moon because it would give them a cover of darkness, or perhaps they were awaiting the arrival of the Avavares, to whom they hoped to escape. On the very day of the new moon, however, the Mariames and the Yguases chose to depart from the cactus thickets, taking their bearded dependents with them. Cabeza de Vaca had just time enough to tell his fellow Christians that he intended to carry through with their plans and would wait for them in the thickets until the moon was full. If they did not join him by then, he would press on to the Río Pánuco by himself.[1]

Cabeza de Vaca's movements over the next few days are not clear, but he managed to take up with a band of Indians he does not identify. Meanwhile, Dorantes slipped away from the Mariames and took up with their enemies, the Eanagados. Castillo and Estevanico escaped from the Yguases and joined Dorantes. The three men saw smoke at a distance and guessed it came from the campfire of the Indians who were sheltering Cabeza de Vaca. Leaving Castillo with the Eanagados in pledge of their return, Dorantes and Estevanico set off in the direction of the smoke. They walked a long way, but when the moon was one day short of full, they reconnected with Cabeza de Vaca. The unnamed Indians who were sheltering him moved their camp the next day and reestablished it near the camp of the Eanagados—and Castillo. Thus, on the day of the full moon, sometime in late September or early October of 1534, the four Christians succeeded in reuniting.[2]

From the unnamed Indians with whom he was camping, Cabeza de Vaca obtained information about what had happened six years earlier to a group of bearded men like himself. He deduced that the information related to the men of the Peñalosa and Téllez barge, the only one of the five Narváez expedition barges whose fate he did not know. Cabeza de Vaca remembered that in November of 1528 his barge and that of Captains Peñalosa and Téllez had sailed in tandem for four days until a storm separated them and drove his barge onto Malhado. Peñalosa and Téllez must have held their course, but, Cabeza de Vaca's Indian informants said, their barge ultimately came ashore in the territory of the Camones. Peñalosa, Téllez, and their emaciated men were unable to defend themselves, and the Camones killed them all and stripped them of their clothes and weapons. Upon receiving this grim news, Cabeza de Vaca knew that he, Dorantes, Castillo, and Estevanico were probably the only survivors of the three hundred men who in 1528 had followed Pánfilo de Narváez into the Florida interior. Cabeza de Vaca gave up all hope that any of Narváez's men, except perhaps Figueroa or the Asturian cleric, had succeeded in reaching Santisteban del Puerto on the Río Pánuco. No rescuers would be coming from that Spanish outpost to find the royal treasurer and his three fellow castaways.[3]

The four men spent two additional days with the Eanagados and Cabeza de Vaca's unnamed hosts before they seized an opportunity to flee. The prickly-pear season was almost at an end, and the fugitives were nervous about finding food. They feared also that their erstwhile hosts would pursue them. The four men seem to have been looking for the Avavares, with whom they had hoped to rendezvous during the cactus harvest. Late in the afternoon, they saw columns of smoke on the horizon. They made their way toward the smoke, but although they soon caught sight of an Indian, he ran from them. The three Spaniards sent Estevanico after him, and when the Indian saw that only one man was chasing him, rather than four, he stopped and waited for the African. The people who were making the smoke, the Indian said, were the Avavares. He guided the Christians for a distance and then ran ahead to notify the Avavares of their approach.[4]

At sunset, four Indians came out from the camp to welcome the travelers. The Christians addressed them in the language of the Mariames, and the Avavares understood them, but they spoke a different language amongst themselves. They lodged Dorantes and Estevanico in the household of a shaman, and Cabeza de Vaca and Castillo in another household. The Avavares had become acquainted with Dorantes, Castillo, and Estevanico during the cactus harvest of 1532, and they somehow knew of Cabeza de Vaca's reputation as a healer. They offered their four guests many prickly pears to eat and celebrated their arrival with three days of feasting and dancing.[5]

Cabeza de Vaca says the Avavares "already had news of us and about how we were curing and about the wonders that our Lord was working through us." This is surprising because prior to his meeting with the Avavares in the autumn of 1534, the only cures Cabeza de Vaca enumerates in his *Relación* are the ones he says he performed during the winter of 1528–29 at Malhado Island and one he obliquely mentions performing in the pecan groves at the time of his reunion in 1533 with Dorantes, Castillo, and Estevanico. The apparently sporadic nature of Cabeza de Vaca's medical practice is hard to understand. Why, after he had begun curing, would he ever have put his practice aside? And why, once he had begun to acquire a reputation as a healer, would such Indians as the Quevenes and the Mariames have treated him as harshly and contemptuously as he says they did?[6]

Another puzzle concerning the sequence of the cures is that Oviedo's chronology differs from Cabeza de Vaca's. Oviedo's account gives no indication either that Cabeza de Vaca performed cures at Malhado or that any of the Narváez survivors did any curing among the Avavares in 1534. The first cures Oviedo describes occurred after the four men left the Avavares in 1535.[7]

Nevertheless, the fact that the Avavares lodged Dorantes and Estevanico in the household of a shaman is suggestive. Perhaps this shaman was the one who taught Cabeza de Vaca the healing arts and not, as he reports, a shaman in Malhado. The castaway might have learned from the Avavares, and not at Malhado, to make incisions at the site of a patient's pain, to suck the evil from the incisions, and to perform cauterizations. And perhaps he was among the Avavares when he began making the sign of the cross over his patients and reciting Latin prayers. Cabeza de Vaca says that the reputation he and his fellow Christians enjoyed as healers opened "roads for us through a land so deserted, bringing us people where many times there were none, and liberating us from so many dangers and not permitting us to be killed, and sustaining us through so much hunger, and inspiring these people to treat us well." Clearly, from the time of their arrival at the camp of the Avavares, the four Christians were treated with more respect.[8]

Of the four, Castillo initially was the one most sought after as a healer. The son of a doctor, he may have learned something about Castilian medical practice from his father. Cabeza de Vaca says that on the night he and his companions arrived in the Avavares camp, some Indians came to Castillo, complained of headaches, and begged him to cure them. Castillo made the sign of the cross over his patients and recited prayers in their behalf. The patients soon reported that all pain had left them, and in gratitude, they rewarded Castillo with prickly pears and a slab of venison. News of the cures spread like wildfire, and many other Indians beseeched Castillo for medical attention. Each supplicant brought him a piece of venison, and the supplicants were so numerous that Castillo and his Christian companions did not know what to do with all the meat. They thanked God for his many blessings.[9]

In moving to the Avavares, the Christians must have traveled not only southward but also away from the coast. Cabeza de Vaca says that a coastal band, the Quitoles, lived between the Avavares and the shore and blocked their access to the sea. The route the Christians followed is important because the better we understand where they were at any given time, the better we can interpret the ethnographic and biological observations they were able to record. The Avavares seem to have spent most of each year in the vicinity of the lower Nueces River, northwest of Corpus Christi Bay. Because they could not easily obtain fish or other marine products, their lifeways differed considerably from those of the coastal people with whom the Christians had lived previously. The Avavares depended on such inland products as prickly pears and mesquite beans. They also had access to a kind of wood they used for making bows, and they were known to the Mariames and other coastal people for the excellence of their bows. Cabeza de Vaca says that to drive away mosquitoes, the Avavares did not build smudge fires the way the Mariames did. Rather, they burned large swaths of grassland, thereby driving out not only insects but also lizards, rodents, and other small creatures they could catch and eat. Cabeza de Vaca describes the Avavares in more detail than he gives for any other inland people in southern Texas.[10]

The Christians wished to press on toward the Río Pánuco, but first they needed deer hides for protecting themselves from the elements. They asked the Avavares about the land to the south and about its inhabitants and resources. The Avavares said that although the land was rich in prickly pears and supported many bands of people when the cactus fruits were in season, it was now sparsely populated because the season was finished. They also said the region afforded few hides and was cold in the winter. Because the cold season was fast approaching, the Avavares encouraged the Christians to remain with them until spring.[11]

A few days after the Christians joined them, the Avavares broke camp and led their guests toward another region where they said ripe prickly pears could still be found. In the course of the journey, everyone went hungry because there were no prickly pears along the way. After five days of walking on empty stomachs, the Avavares arrived at a river, where they again established camp.

From this camp, Cabeza de Vaca set off with a foraging party to look for the seeds of a tree that may have been either a Texas ebony or a mesquite. He wandered too far from his companions and inadvertently became separated from them. With no trail, and with night coming on, Cabeza de Vaca had no idea how to get back to camp. In the chill darkness, he spotted a light he took to be a campfire. It proved to be a tree that, perhaps due to lightning, was blazing like a torch in the wilderness. He huddled near the fire for the remainder of the night, thanking God for its warmth. In the morning, he seized two burning brands, gathered a load of firewood, and set off to look for the Avavares and his three Christian companions. He searched all day but was unable to find them, and so as a second night approached, he used his burning brands to kindle a fire. He continued in this way for four days, camping each night in a brushy river bottom and each day securing a firebrand and a load of wood before resuming his search. He always chose a campsite before sunset, dug a shallow trench for a bed, and lit four fires: one each at his head, feet, and right and left sides. For additional warmth, he covered himself with dry grass. He wakened often during the night to tend his fires, but one night as he was sleeping, a spark ignited the dry grass of his nest. He woke with a start and scrambled out of his burning bed, singeing his hair in the process. Throughout his ordeal he found nothing to eat, and he scraped and bloodied his bare feet.[12]

On the fifth day, Cabeza de Vaca succeeded in finding the Avavares camp. His Christian companions had given him up for dead and were delighted to see him again. They told him they had been too hungry to search for him, but they gave him some prickly pears they had hoarded. The following day, the Avavares again moved their camp and reestablished it at a place with many ripe prickly pears. This was the more southern of the two prickly-pear regions the Avavares frequented, and since it was never visited by the Mariames and the Yguases, it was new to the Christians.[13]

Cabeza de Vaca observed that the country in which he now found himself was flat and semiarid. Although the Avavares often resorted to drinking standing water from rain pools, there were rivers in the region, and Cabeza de Vaca imagined a future in which Spanish colonists would channel them for irrigation. He dreamed of returning someday to Spain and persuading Emperor Charles V to invest resources and personnel in those parts of North America that he and the other survivors of the Narváez expedition had reconnoitered. The land where he had been living for the last six years, Cabeza de Vaca planned to argue, was fertile and would afford good grazing for cattle. It would be very productive, he would add, "if it were worked and inhabited by men of reason."[14]

Although Cabeza de Vaca did not think of the Avavares and other Texas Indians as "men of reason," he had come to appreciate their special skills and their adaptation to their environment. He would later report: "All these people did not know how to calculate the seasons either by the sun or the moon, nor do they have reckoning of the months and years, but they understand and know the differences between the times when the fruit comes to mature and when the fish die and the stars appear, in the observance of which they are very skilled and well practiced."[15]

Soon after the Avavares arrived in the second prickly-pear region, an unidentified group of Indians visited their camp, bringing five sick or lame people with them. They were seeking Castillo because of his reputation as a healer, and each of the sick Indians offered him a bow and several arrows. Castillo accepted the presents and observed a vigil until sunset. Then he made the sign of the cross over each of his patients and entreated God to restore him or her to health. Cabeza de Vaca, Dorantes, and Estevanico prayed also, because they understood that the goodwill of the Indians depended on Castillo's success. They prayed through the night, and in the morning all five of Castillo's patients arose with renewed health and vigor. They departed from the Avavares camp as if they had never been ill, and this was a source of wonderment to everyone. The four Christians expressed their gratitude to God, and Cabeza de Vaca says he was certain that God "would deliver us and take us to where we could serve him," adding, "And for myself I can say that I always had complete faith in his mercy that he would deliver me from that captivity."[16]

Many bands of Indians were encamped in this second prickly-pear region. Cabeza de Vaca identifies them as Cuthalchuches, Maliacones, Coayos, Susolas, and Atayos. The Susolas and the Atayos were engaged in a long-standing war and shot arrows at one another at every opportunity. Nevertheless, the chief topic of conversation among all the Indians was the cures that Castillo was performing. A delegation of Susolas entreated Castillo to come to their camp to cure a wounded man and others who were ill with a kind of "sleeping sickness."

According to Cabeza de Vaca, Castillo was a timid physician and feared that his sins would prevent him from effecting more cures. He was unwilling to minister to the Susolas, but they remembered Cabeza de Vaca had cured someone in the pecan groves the previous year, so they turned to him instead. He readily agreed to help them, and Dorantes and Estevanico accompanied him to their camp. When they arrived there, however, they saw that the dwelling of the wounded man had been taken apart, a sign that he had died. Mourners had gathered, and a mat had been placed over the man's body. Cabeza de Vaca removed it and found that the man had no pulse and his eyes were rolled back in his head. Dorantes said the man was dead, but Cabeza de Vaca made the sign of the cross over him, blew reverently upon him, and entreated God to restore him to life and health. The man's relatives presented Cabeza de Vaca with their kinsman's bow and a basket of prickly pears. Cabeza de Vaca then attended to those Susolas suffering from the "sleeping sickness," and they gave him two additional baskets of prickly pears. He returned to the camp of the Avavares and shared all his rewards with them. Later, Indians brought him the news that his seemingly dead patient had arisen, walked about, eaten food, and spoken with his friends. The sleeping-sickness patients had recovered as well.[17]

Cabeza de Vaca gave God the credit for his success as a healer. His perception that he had raised a man from the dead must have caused him to do some serious soul-searching. In the span of roughly six years, he had metamorphosed from a somewhat arrogant hidalgo to a wretched castaway, then a trader, and now a shaman. Along the way, his Christian faith seems to have intensified.

News of Cabeza de Vaca's cures inspired awe in everyone who heard it. People came from far and wide to ask him and Castillo to heal them and to bless their children. The demand was so great that Dorantes and Estevanico also began ministering to the sick, but Cabeza de Vaca says he was the boldest physician of the four. Indians began referring to all four healers as *hijos del sol*, or Children of the Sun, but what the Indians understood by the term or whether they all understood it in the same way is unclear. As Cabeza de Vaca later acknowledged, some of the Indians may have been spreading tall tales about the four healers in order to take advantage of other Indians. He says that "we never cured anyone who did not say that he was better, and they had so much confidence that they would be cured if we performed the cures, that they believed that as long as we were there, none of them would die." When it came time for one group of Indians, the Cuthalchuches, to depart from the southern cactus thickets, they presented the Children of the Sun with all the prickly pears they had set aside for their journey, not keeping any for themselves. They also gave the four men a number of flints that were useful for cutting and scraping. Cabeza de Vaca observed that the flints and the stored prickly pears represented the best things the Cuthalchuches possessed. In return for these gifts, the Cuthalchuches asked only that the Children of the Sun remember them in their prayers and ask God to keep them in good health.[18]

The Avavares saw the Children of the Sun as assets, treated them well, and gave them the liberty to do as they wished. The four men had to work as hard as the Avavares did, digging up roots and carrying heavy loads of water and firewood, but they no longer thought of themselves as slaves. At night they wrapped themselves in deerskins they had procured from the Avavares, but by day they went as naked as the Indians. Cabeza de Vaca says that because of his nakedness, he suffered from exposure to the sun and wind and shed his skin twice a year like a snake. The heavy loads he and his companions carried caused sores to appear on their backs and chests, and the ropes with which they secured these loads cut into their arms. While foraging or gathering firewood, Cabeza de Vaca was so badly scratched by thorny cactus and brambles that his only consolation was "to think about the Passion of our Redeemer Jesus Christ and the blood he shed for me, and to consider how much greater had been the torment that he suffered from the thorns, than that which I had to endure." The Christians also endured longer periods of hunger while living with the Avavares than at any prior time during their sojourn in Texas. Among the Avavares, prickly-pear season was the only season of plenty. Their children were bloated from malnutrition and, according to the Christians, looked "like toads."[19]

Cabeza de Vaca and his companions were able to trade with the Avavares for the deerskins they needed and for chunks of meat. The four men were averse to eating the meat raw, but they knew that if they tried to cook it, the first hungry Indian who happened by would snatch it. To acquire the things they wanted, they manufactured objects for the Avavares, such as combs, nets, and mats. Although the Avavares knew how to make these items, they were reluctant to occupy their time with anything other than gathering food. Cabeza de Vaca and his companions sometimes scraped and softened deer hides, and they welcomed such work because they were able to eat the bits of flesh they scraped from the hides.[20]

The Avavares gave Cabeza de Vaca and his companions the only additional information they ever received about Figueroa and the Asturian cleric. Dorantes, Castillo, and Estevanico had last seen these two in the spring of 1529, somewhere in the vicinity of Matagorda Island. Later in 1529, Dorantes heard that Figueroa and the Asturian had vowed to reach the Río Pánuco or die in the attempt. The Avavares said they had seen the two Spaniards with a band of coastal Indians whom they identified as the "People of the Figs." The two castaways may have got as far south as Padre Island, but they never reached the Río Pánuco.[21]

The Avavares also told Cabeza de Vaca about an evil being—or Mala Cosa in Spanish—who had visited them some fifteen or sixteen years previously. This Mala Cosa was small in stature and had appeared in the doorway of a dwelling place, holding a flaming torch. No one was able to see his face clearly, but he was bearded like Cabeza de Vaca and his companions. All those who saw the Mala Cosa began to tremble, and their hair stood on end. He entered the house and seized a man who was sitting inside. Then, using a long, sharp flint, the Mala Cosa cut three incisions in his victim's sides and plunged his hand into one of the incisions, pulling out the victim's entrails. Next, he cut off a short length of intestine and threw it into the fire. He also made three cuts in his victim's arm and dislocated the arm. But later he set the arm back in its proper place and passed his hands over his victim's wounds, causing them to heal quickly. Afterward, the Mala Cosa appeared several times when the Avavares were performing their sacred dances. Sometimes he was dressed as a man, and sometimes as a woman. He demonstrated that he could pick up a house, raise it high in the air, and drop it with a loud crash. The Avavares offered the Mala Cosa food, but he never ate anything. When they questioned him about where he came from, the Mala Cosa showed them a cleft in the ground and said he had come out of the cleft.[22]

Cabeza de Vaca expressed skepticism about the tale, but several of the Avavares showed him scars they bore from the Mala Cosa's surgeries. Cabeza de Vaca assured them that so long as he and the other Children of the Sun were with them, they need fear nothing, and he endeavored to inform them about the Christian God, who, he said, would protect them from evil. The Avavares seemed to be comforted by his words. But although Cabeza de Vaca understood the Mala Cosa to be some kind of devil, the Avavares may have seen him as both good and evil, male and female, creator and destroyer. Their Mala Cosa embodies many of the characteristics of the traditional trickster figure who appears in many Native American tales. Additionally, since the Mala Cosa was a bearded healer and similar in some respects to Cabeza de Vaca, it is possible that in telling him about the supernatural being, the Avavares were expressing their ambivalence toward their bearded guest.[23]

According to Oviedo's account of the Narváez expedition, its four survivors were with the Avavares from October of 1534 until August of the following year, or more than ten calendar months. Cabeza de Vaca says that he spent eight lunar months with the Avavares and left them at midsummer, and that during six of those eight months, he was hungry. But whether in June or August of 1535, when the Avavares began preparing to return to their northern prickly-pear grounds, Cabeza de Vaca and his companions decided to leave them and to push on southward toward the Río Pánuco. The four men had spent six and a half years in what is now Texas.[24]

They found an opportunity to slip away from the Avavares and take up with the Maliacones, who were encamped a day's journey away. Shortly thereafter they set out with the Maliacones in search of trees—probably mesquites—that bore a kind of bean that would be a mainstay of their diet until the prickly pears ripened. In the bean-harvesting area, they met the Arbadaos, who seemed unusually sickly, malnourished, and bloated. But as their camp was south of that of the Maliacones, the Christians decided to take up with the Arbadaos. The Maliacones expressed sorrow at this decision but did not prevent their guests from doing as they chose. The Christians spent the next eight days with the Arbadaos, and during this time the only things they had to eat were cactus pads and unripe mesquite beans. To assuage their hunger, they traded some nets and a deerskin for two dogs, which they ate.[25]

At around the point in his *Relación* where Cabeza de Vaca reports on his sojourn with the Arbadaos, he interrupts his narrative to list the twenty-three groups of Indians he had thus far encountered in Texas and to generalize about their customs. He divides these groups into three categories: those who spent at least a part of each year on the offshore islands, those who lived on the adjacent mainland shore, and those who lived farther inland. Among the island dwellers were the Capoques and Hans of Malhado, and—in north-to-south order—the Deaguanes, Quevenes, Guaycones, Camoles (or Camones), and People of the Figs. The southernmost of these groups, the People of the Figs, probably lived on Padre Island. The shoreline groups included the Charrucos, Mendicas, Mariames, Yguases, and Quitoles. The northernmost of these, the Charrucos, lived in the Galveston Bay area. The Mendicas lived south of the Charrucos, opposite the island-dwelling Deaguanes. The Mariames lived opposite the island-dwelling Quevenes, and the Yguases opposite the Guaycones. In the third category, the Avavares lived inland from the shoreline-dwelling Quitoles. Other inland groups included the Atayos, Acubadaos, Eanagados, Cuthalchuches, Maliacones, Coayos, Susolas, Arbadaos, Cuchendados, and Comos. Linguistic differences existed among various groups, but Cabeza de Vaca notes only that the Capoques spoke a different language from the Hans, and the Avavares spoke a different language from the Mariames.[26]

Cabeza de Vaca says that, in all twenty-three groups, a man refrained from sleeping with his wife from the time he discovered her to be pregnant until two years after she had given birth. The spacing of children was important among these nomadic people because a woman could not tote more than one small child at a time. Mothers suckled their children until they reached the age—approximately twelve years—when they could find food on their own. This practice ensured that even when a mother had nothing to eat, her children received some nourishment. During times of migration, parents carried their sick children on their backs, but people would sometimes abandon a sick child who was not a blood relative. No one would eat food gathered by a woman who was menstruating, and so during the time of her period, a woman foraged only for herself.[27]

When disputes arose between members of a kinship group, the parties would strike one another with fists or clubs, but they would not use bows and arrows. They would fight until exhausted or until onlookers, usually women, separated them. Both parties might withdraw until they had cooled off, and then they were likely to behave toward one another as if they had never quarreled. A bachelor involved in a dispute might withdraw indefinitely and take up with some other band. But if he later chose to return to his home community, his adoptive community was likely to send him home loaded with presents.

The various bands of Texas coastal Indians often warred with their neighbors, ambushed their camps at night, and inflicted cruelties upon captives. Therefore, when establishing a new camp, each band took care to provide for its defense. When possible, they chose to camp within the protection of a wooded or brushy area, and with sufficient vegetation, they might prepare a second, more hidden camp in which the women and children would sleep. The warriors might dig a long trench and sleep in it fully armed, after first covering and camouflaging themselves with grasses and brush. In such cases, they would light decoy fires in their ostensible camp, and if enemies attacked during the night, the home team would leap from their hiding place and surprise them. Sometimes, even when they were encamped on an open plain where hiding the women and children was impossible, the men would prepare camouflaged sleeping trenches for themselves around the camp's perimeter. Shifts of warriors would keep watch while the others slept. At the slightest sign of danger, a sentry would alert his sleeping friends, and all would stand guard together with arrows fitted to their bows. During a battle, warriors would crouch low to the ground and leap about so as not to present an easy target. Cabeza de Vaca guessed that Spanish harquebuses and crossbows would be ineffectual against this type of warfare. By contrast, he guessed that horses, which were unknown to the Indians, would terrify them.

Cabeza de Vaca observed that if the attacking warriors expended all their arrows during an intertribal battle, they would withdraw, even when they outnumbered the defenders. He witnessed cases in which warriors who had received multiple arrow wounds recovered quickly. They were not likely to die unless shot through the heart or the abdomen. All the Indians were capable of enduring great hunger and cold, and, according to Cabeza de Vaca, their eyesight and hearing were unusually acute.[28]

The explorer says the Texas coastal Indians used two kinds of intoxicants. The first was a substance they smoked, but he does not give enough detail to indicate whether it was tobacco or peyote. The second was a purgative tea made from the leaves of a shrub that resembled an oak and was probably the yaupon bush (*Ilex vomitoria*). Only the men drank this tea, which they prepared by toasting the leaves in a special vessel, adding water, and bringing the mixture to a boil twice. They poured the finished tea, which was yellow and frothy, into a drinking gourd and drank it when it was almost too hot to tolerate. The tea caused them to vomit, and each man drank it continuously for three days, consuming the equivalent of thirty-seven pints per day and ingesting nothing else the whole time. Such a drastic regimen must have produced a powerfully altered state of consciousness. Cabeza de Vaca says that as soon as the men had brewed the tea, they would begin to shout, "Who wants to drink?" If a woman heard these shouts, she had to freeze in her tracks, even if she was carrying a heavy burden. If she happened to move, the men would beat her and violate her sexually, and they would pour out their tea in disgust. They would even discard their tea if a woman happened to pass by while they were brewing it. If they were to drink tea polluted by a woman, the men explained, they would die.[29]

Cabeza de Vaca concludes his generalizations about the Indians and their lifeways by noting: "This I have wanted to tell because, beyond the fact that all men desire to know the customs and practices of others, the ones who sometime might come to confront them should be informed about their customs and stratagems." The explorer's own interest in the customs of the Indians is clear, but he was also anticipating that other Spaniards might visit the areas he had reconnoitered. He had learned much from the Indians of Texas that would prove useful during his struggle to return to Spanish civilization. He had witnessed ritual acts of hospitality at Malhado in which a weeping host bestowed all his possessions upon a valued guest. He had seen that women and exotic strangers like himself could pass as neutrals and mediate between warring groups of men. He had learned to perform cures, and he had discovered that shamans were respected and rewarded.[30]

When Cabeza de Vaca resumes his narrative, he reports that after he and his companions ate the dogs they had purchased from the Arbadaos, they felt ready to resume their journey. The Arbadaos, although sorry to see them go, guided them to the camp of a neighboring people. In his *Relación*, Cabeza de Vaca does not identify these new people or any other group of native North Americans he subsequently encountered. From this point forward, he was to move rapidly from one group of Indians to another, and the quality of his ethnographic observations would diminish. His richest observations date from the six and a half years he spent in Texas living a more or less settled life among Indians he came to know well. He had spent more than a year in Malhado among either the Capoques or the Hans and three years on the mainland shore, living primarily among the Charrucos but moving back and forth as a merchant among different Indian bands. Then he had spent a year and a half with the Mariames and eight months with the Avavares. During all this time, he and his Christian companions had learned six Indian languages, but soon after leaving the Arbadaos, they moved beyond the area where any of those languages was spoken.[31]

In moving from the Avavares to the Maliacones, and from the latter to the Arbadaos, Cabeza de Vaca and his companions seem to have been traveling southward on a course parallel to the coast. Their goal ever since they built the barges at the Bay of Horses had been to reach the Spanish frontier outpost on the Río Pánuco. They knew that the Pánuco emptied into the Gulf of Mexico and that the best way to find the river would be to follow the shoreline southward. They preferred to walk a few leagues inland, however, because the coast was marshy and interrupted by rivers, tidal channels and bays that would have presented obstacles to the three nonswimmers among them. Shortly after they left the Arbadaos, the four men spent at least a day walking southward without native guides, and since they had no knowledge of the terrain, they lost their way. It was raining, and they had to wade through water and mud. They camped in a wooded area, gathered the thorny pads of a prickly-pear cactus, roasted them overnight, and ate them in the morning. After breakfast, they succeeded in finding a path, which they followed until they surprised some Indians who ran from them in evident fear. Cabeza de Vaca and his companions hailed the Indians, and although the native people said they had nothing to eat, they offered to guide the travelers to an encampment where they would find food.[32]

The encampment consisted of fifty houses and, according to Oviedo's account of the Narváez expedition, was the place where the Christians first began to practice cures Oviedo says:

[The Indians] began to fear and have reverence for these few Christians and to hold them in high regard, and they would come near them and would rub themselves, telling the Christians with signs to rub and cure them. They brought them some sick people to be cured, and the Christians would do it, although they were more accustomed to working than to performing miracles. But in virtue of the confidence given them by God they would bless and blow on them like those who are called healers in Castile did. The Indians would feel better immediately and would give them of what they had to eat.

The Spanish term Oviedo uses for healers is *saludadores*. Why the Indians feared their guests and solicited them for cures is hard to understand— unless the four men's reputation as the Children of the Sun had preceded them. Perhaps the men's beards and exotic appearance were enough to inspire awe.[33]

The people of the encampment went without food in order to feed their guests. Cabeza de Vaca and his companions spent fifteen days with these people and were given the honor, which they had never previously received, of resting from manual labor the whole time. At the end of the fifteen days, the cactus fruits were beginning to ripen, and a new group of Indians set up camp nearby to the south. The four healers decided to join them, and the people of the fifty-house encampment wept bitterly at their departure.[34]

The people at the more southerly camp welcomed the healers, gave them mesquite flour, and went out hunting to obtain meat for them. A New World plant, the mesquite was unfamiliar to Cabeza de Vaca, and he likened it to the Mediterranean carob but complained of the bitter taste of its beans. His hosts prepared mesquite beans for consumption by mixing them with dirt, thereby—in their opinion—improving the flavor. They dug a hole in the ground, poured mesquite beans into the hole, and pounded them to a mash with a log the size of a man's leg. The person in charge of the pounding tasted the mash periodically and, when it met his satisfaction, transferred it from the hole to a two-handled basket. Several people then gathered around the basket, picked through the mash, and removed large particles and fragments of pod for further pounding. The Indians prepared a large quantity of mesquite mash in this manner and celebrated the arrival of their four guests with feasting and dancing. Everyone who ate the bean mash, however, ended up with a heavy belly.[35]

At night the mesquite-eaters posted six warriors to stand guard outside the shelter in which Cabeza de Vaca and his companions were sleeping. After a few days, some women arrived from a more southerly camp with gifts for the four healers. The gender of the ambassadors suggests that the people of the more southerly camp were not on friendly terms with the mesquite-eaters, for, as Cabeza de Vaca observes, women often were employed to mediate between hostile communities. The Christians wished to set off immediately for the more southerly camp, but the women said that it was far away and that no trails led in its direction. The women were exhausted from their journey and begged the healers to wait until they had rested and could guide them southward, but the impatient Christians refused to wait. They walked four leagues and, not surprisingly, got lost. They stumbled at last upon a water hole, and there they met the women who had been too tired to guide them earlier, as well as other women from the mesquite-eaters' camp. The women led the four men southward to a river that was as broad, Cabeza de Vaca reports, as the Río Guadalquivir in

Seville. The river was probably the Rio Grande, and although its current was swift and its water came up to a man's chest, the Christians and their guides crossed it.[36]

If the river was indeed the Rio Grande, then they crossed the present international border between Texas and Mexico. But not all interpreters of their route agree that the broad river was the Rio Grande. Two major theories have developed about the route the survivors of the Narváez expedition followed after they left the Avavares in 1535. The first is the trans-Texas theory, which proposes that after leaving the Avavares, the four men pursued a westerly course, moving away from the Gulf coast into the interior of what is now the Lone Star State. The second and more plausible theory is that in the early stages of their journey, the four men walked southward on a course that paralleled the coast and took them from southeastern Texas across the lower Rio Grande into northeastern Mexico. This second theory relies partly on the fact that for more than six and a half years the men had been seeking the Río Pánuco and the Spanish outpost of Santisteban del Puerto, and partly on descriptions of landforms, rivers, flora, and fauna in the narratives of Cabeza de Vaca and Oviedo. Route theorists have considered, for example, where prickly pears and mesquite trees grow and how far southward buffalo have historically ranged. In a 1987 survey of studies of Cabeza de Vaca's route, University of North Texas historian Donald E. Chipman argued that the trans-Texas theory "defies logic in that the overall goal of the Narváez expedition from the time it left Florida was to reach Pánuco" and "defies documentation in that it is frequently at variance with evidence in the two original accounts on which all route interpretations must ultimately rest."[37]

After they crossed the broad river, Cabeza de Vaca and his companions came to a large encampment of a hundred houses. The people of this encampment greeted the four healers enthusiastically, crowding around them to touch them and very nearly crushing them and poking out their eyes in the process. All the while, the Indians were shouting, slapping their thighs, and rattling dried gourds filled with pebbles. The Indians venerated these rattles, and when Cabeza de Vaca asked about their origin, he was told the gourds did not grow locally but came "from the sky," borne on the waters of the river he had crossed earlier in the afternoon.[38]

The Indians settled their guests in shelters prepared especially for them, but once inside, the four men refused to venture out again. Their hosts danced all night, celebrating the arrival of the Children of the Sun. To thank the women from the mesquite-eaters' camp for bringing the healers, the people of the hundred houses gave them arrows. In the morning, Cabeza de Vaca and his companions began the process of touching and making the sign of the cross over all the people of the encampment. They did this ceremoniously, almost as if they were celebrating mass. On the following day, they pressed on southward, guided by the people of the hundred houses. The travelers accepted the guidance gratefully, having learned the hard way that they were likely to lose their way if they attempted to move forward on their own.

The guides led the travelers to a smaller encampment of seventy to eighty houses. But when it came time for them to turn the Children of the Sun over to their new hosts, the people of the larger camp took bows and arrows, shoes, beads, and other things from the people of the smaller camp. As they were taking these items, the thieves told their victims about the miraculous cures the Children of the Sun had performed and urged them to come forward to be healed. The people came forward enthusiastically, and the four healers received each supplicant, laid hands upon him or her, made the sign of the cross, and intoned a Latin prayer. Each patient told his friends either that he had been cured or that he expected to feel better soon. The people of the hundred houses returned with all their booty to their own camp. Long before the days of traveling medicine shows, the native people of the Rio Grande area seem to have known how to sell snake oil.[39]

That shoes were among the items seized by the erstwhile guides raises the question of whether Cabeza de Vaca and his companions had acquired anything by this time to wear on their feet. They might have had shoes made of deer or buffalo hide or woven from grasses or fibers.

Their new hosts in the camp of the seventy to eighty houses gave the Children of the Sun a freshly killed deer and twenty-eight cakes made from mesquite flour. When the healers decided to move on, their hosts guided them to a camp that was still farther southward. There the travelers watched in dismay as their guides ransacked the houses of their new hosts and seized their possessions. The four men feared the bad behavior of their former hosts would cause their new hosts to treat them harshly, but their new hosts said they were contented with the situation. In the first place, they desired the ministrations of the Children of the Sun. In the second place, they would recover their losses from whichever of their neighbors the four healers might choose to visit next. The four men seem to have become catalysts for intertribal exchange.[40]

A day or two later, their current hosts led the travelers six leagues onward to a camp where the majority of people were suffering from a disease that caused a film to cloud over one or both eyes. In keeping with the pattern that was beginning to develop, the escorting group robbed the receiving group. Meanwhile, Cabeza de Vaca and his companions were exhausted by the people who constantly crowded around them, wanting to touch them and be healed. The four men spent as many as three hours per day touching and blessing the sick. They dreamed of fleeing from their hosts, but they dared not forgo the sustenance and guidance the Indians provided.[41]

According to Oviedo, the four Narváez expedition survivors succeeded in restoring the sight of their blind and half-blind hosts. But Cabeza de Vaca makes no such claim. He merely says that despite their eye problems, his hosts were well proportioned and of a fairer complexion than most of the Indians he had encountered previously.[42]

A little before arriving at the camp of the people with the eye disease, Cabeza de Vaca and his companions had begun to see mountains. The *sierras*, as Cabeza de Vaca termed them, were the first he had seen in North America, and they seemed to run "in a chain from toward the North Sea" (or Gulf of Mexico). Oviedo indicates that a *cordillera*, or mountain range, "traversed the land directly to the north." The sea, as Cabeza de Vaca learned from his blind and half-blind hosts, was some fifteen leagues to the east. The four Christians had traveled at least seven and a half leagues toward the Río Pánuco since crossing the broad river that probably was the Rio Grande.[43]

That Cabeza de Vaca and his companions saw mountains at a distance of fifteen leagues, or forty-five miles, from the Gulf of Mexico must be taken into account by anyone attempting to determine their route. The distance between the broad river and the sighting of the first mountains is also significant. Southern Texas is more or less flat, so proponents of a trans-Texas route have had to claim that the Narváez expedition survivors received faulty information or were mistaken in their judgment of distances. Two mountain ranges in northeastern Mexico, however, are approximately the requisite distance from the Gulf. The first of these, the Sierra de Pamoranes, is only about 1,000 feet high. But the second, the Sierra de Cerralvo, has a maximum elevation of 4,800 feet and can be seen from a distance of thirty to forty miles. This second range links to the Sierra de Santa Clara and the Sierra de la Iguana in a 160-mile chain that runs parallel to the Rio Grande.[44]

The people with the eye disease took Cabeza de Vaca and his companions five leagues onward to a camp that belonged to their kinsmen and was located on a river at the foot of the mountains. The blind and half-blind guides preferred to give their kinsmen, rather than an enemy group, the opportunity to host the Children of the Sun. Even so, the guides ransacked their kinsmen's camp, thereby recovering the equivalent of what they had lost when the Children of the Sun were brought to them. The kinsmen seem to have expected this outrage and had taken the precaution of hiding some of their most valuable possessions, including beads, red ocher, and small bags of silver. They presented these valuables to the Children of the Sun with great ceremony and expressions of pleasure, but the four healers refused to keep the gifts and turned them over to their former hosts. Cabeza de Vaca says that he and his companions made it a practice never to keep anything and that they took pains to see that both their former and new hosts were happy. Property could breed ill will, and any appearance of acquisitiveness might put the healers' lives at risk. Meanwhile, their new hosts sent for friends and relatives living nearer the coast, and those who answered the summons brought beads or bows or other presents for the Children of the Sun. The healers declined to keep the gifts and redistributed the items among their hosts in the river camp.[45]

The next morning, the Children of the Sun expressed their desire to move on, but they disagreed with their hosts about the route they should take. They could either cross the mountains that lay ahead or skirt them on the east or west. The hosts proposed to take their guests eastward to the camp of a friendly people living closer to the sea "at the near end of the sierras." They undoubtedly were thinking of the loot they might seize, for they said that the camp contained many houses, and its people were rich and able to give the Children of the Sun many things. The four healers were reluctant, however, either to climb into the mountains or to venture nearer to the coast. Cabeza de Vaca says they preferred to travel "through the plain near the mountains." According to Oviedo, the four men wished to go westward "in the direction of the sunset." Their hosts said that no one was living to the west and that nothing to eat lay in that direction. After long negotiation, the hosts sent two scouts to search westward for people and an encampment their guests could visit.[46]

Why Cabeza de Vaca and his companions wanted to turn westward at this point is hard to understand. Their goal for six and a half years had been to reach the Spanish outpost on the Río Pánuco, which they knew was near the coast. They cannot have known it, but they were probably only about three hundred miles from the outpost when they turned west. They cannot have known, either, that the turn would add some 2,500 miles to their journey. They must have thought they were making only a small detour around the mountains and not abandoning either their search for Pánuco or the more or less coastal route they had followed since leaving Malhado. Cabeza de Vaca gives three reasons for the decision to turn west:

> All the people of the coast are very bad, and we considered it preferable to go through the land because the people further inland are of a better disposition and they treated us better, and we considered it certain that we would find the land more populated and with better means of sustenance. Finally, we did this because, by crossing through the land, we would see many of its particularities, because if God our Lord were served by taking some one of us out of there and bringing him to the land of Christians, he could give an account and description of it.

Cabeza de Vaca knew that Spanish maritime explorers had already scouted the coast of the Gulf of Mexico. But no Spaniard had previously explored the coastal interior where he and his companions now found themselves. The hope that they might return one day to the "land of Christians" made him want to gather information that Emperor Charles V would value. Why Cabeza de Vaca expected to find more food by traveling away from the coast is unclear, but in expressing his opinion about the bad nature of the coastal Indians, he was probably thinking of the harsh treatment he and other men of the Narváez expedition had received from the Quevenes, the Mariames, and the Yguases. He was probably thinking also of the coastal Camones, who had slaughtered the men of the Peñalosa and Téllez barge. Additionally, since Cabeza de Vaca was now fairly close to the Spanish frontier, he may have begun to meet Indians who had seen or heard about Spaniards and already regarded them as enemies.[47]

NINE

The Overland Journey

On the day after the scouts departed, Cabeza de Vaca and his companions followed after them, heading inland and upriver with a large escort from the riverside encampment where they had sojourned. The day was hot, and the women in the escorting group carried food and water. However, the authority of the Children of the Sun was so great that no Indian dared to drink without their permission. Within two leagues the group met their scouts, who said they had found no people in the region they had reconnoitered. This report caused the escorts to beg the Children of the Sun not to continue westward but to go instead to the camp of a friendly people in the mountains. The four healers refused to accept this alternative and parted ways with their guides. Although the Indians had hoped to recover the losses they had incurred when the Children of the Sun were brought to them, they dropped whatever food and supplies they were carrying and returned sadly to their camp downriver.[1]

The four Christians continued upriver, but this was the last time they would travel without guides. They soon met two women who were walking downstream with heavy burdens of what Cabeza de Vaca describes as maize flour. He and his companions had not tasted maize since they beached at Malhado. Oviedo's account of the meeting with the women contains no mention of maize, but if the women had some, their having it provides retrospective justification for the men's decision to turn westward. The women, who had probably acquired their flour through trade, shared some with the men and told them that farther upstream they would come to a small camp, where they would find prickly pears and more maize. Cabeza de Vaca and his companions arrived at the camp around sunset and were greeted by people who were weeping in anticipation of losing their possessions. They had already heard of the Children of the Sun and knew that whenever the healers were handed by one group of people to another, the receiving group was sure to be robbed. When the people saw that the four men were alone, however, they ceased to fear them. They grudgingly offered the men prickly pears, but nothing else. Cabeza de Vaca, who had expected maize too, was disappointed. The incident must have shown him that he needed an escort, not only for guidance, but also for ensuring a favorable reception at his destination.[2]

At dawn the next morning, the people from downriver who had previously hosted the Children of the Sun attacked the small camp in which they were sleeping. The attackers were determined to recover what they had lost when the healers were brought to them, and they had followed the four men to their current place of shelter. They caught the people of the small camp off guard and seized all their valuables. The thieves then consoled their victims by telling them, Cabeza de Vaca says, that their guests had "the power to cure the sick and to kill them and other lies even greater than these, since they know how best to do it when they feel that it suits them." He adds, "They told them to lead us onward with great respect and to be careful not to anger us in anything, and to give us everything they had, and to try to take us where there were many people, and that wherever we arrived, to steal and loot what the others had, because such was the custom." The people of the small camp took this lesson to heart. They began to treat their guests with more respect and led them on a three-day journey to a place where many people were encamped. When they were near this place, the escorting group sent messengers ahead to announce the impending arrival of the Children of the Sun and to tell tall tales about the cures they had performed. This was a prudent measure, since the escorts were outnumbered by the people of the camp they were approaching, and the larger group could easily have repelled them. But because of the advance notice, the people of the large encampment came out with pleasure to greet their guests, and a pair of shamans presented them with two gourd rattles. The rattles were similar to the ones Cabeza de Vaca had seen soon after he and his companions crossed the broad river that probably was the Rio Grande. And because the Indians venerated such rattles, he recognized they would enhance his status as a healer, and he accepted them reverently. From then on, he and his companions employed the rattles in their curing ceremonies, shaking them over their patients' bodies as they had seen Indian shamans do. Meanwhile, the people of their escorting group looted the encampment, but as it was large and they were few, the looters had to leave many things behind.[3]

From this large encampment, Cabeza de Vaca reports, he and his companions traveled inland more than fifty leagues, going through the foothills of the mountains. Oviedo says the four men "advanced eighty leagues more or less, skirting the mountain range going inland, due north." Neither Cabeza de Vaca nor Oviedo explains why the men traveled so far out of their way, but they were probably funneled northwestward by the lay of the land. They must have skirted the northwest-trending Sierra Madre Oriental and traveled up the drainage basin of the Rio Grande, moving from the present Mexican state of Tamaulipas through Nuevo León and into Coahuila. As they moved farther from the Gulf coast and found that mountains always prevented them from resuming their southward course, they must gradually have given up the goal of reaching the Río Pánuco and begun to consider alternate objectives.[4]

When they were many leagues from the coast, Cabeza de Vaca and his companions came to an encampment of forty houses inhabited by people whose language was different from any they had heard previously. There they were given cotton cloaks, and Andrés Dorantes was given a cast copper bell. Cabeza de Vaca asked about the origins of these obviously valuable gifts and was told that the objects had come from the north. According to Oviedo, they came from a region 150 leagues away in the direction of the "South Sea," or Pacific Ocean. Cabeza de Vaca saw the cotton cloaks as evidence of agriculture and weaving, and he saw the bell as evidence of mining and metalworking. The civilization that produced these items, he recognized, was more advanced than any he had encountered since that of the Apalachees. And although copper was a relatively modest metal, he planned to mention it in the report he hoped to present one day to Charles V in Spain.[5]

Soon after they received the cloaks and the bell, Cabeza de Vaca and his companions crossed a range of mountains that was seven leagues wide and composed largely of iron slag. On the far side of these mountains, they came to a large encampment beside a beautiful river. The encampment was probably somewhere near the present city of Monclova in Coahuila,

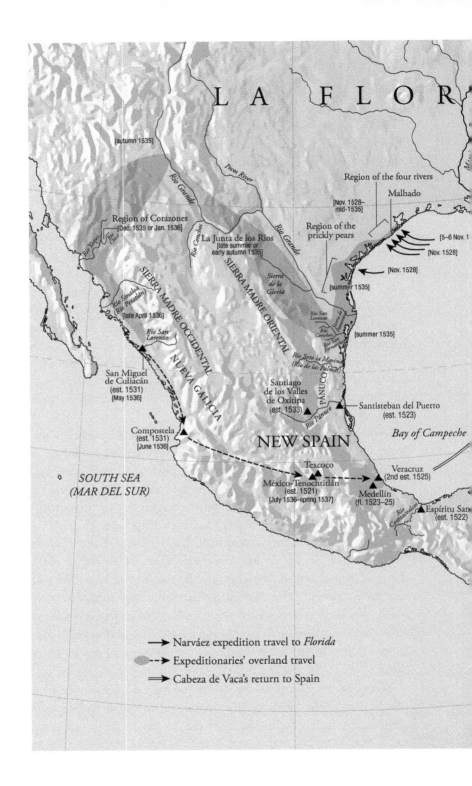

LA FLOR

[autumn 1535]

Pecos River

Rio Grande

Region of the four rivers

Malhado

[Nov. 1528–
mid-1535]

Region of Corazones
[Dec. 1535 or Jan. 1536]

Rio Chico

Rio Yaqui

Rio Conchos

La Junta de los Ríos
[late summer or
early autumn 1535]

Rio Grande

Region of the
prickly pears

[5–6 Nov. 1]

[Nov. 1528]

SIERRA MADRE ORIENTAL

SIERRA MADRE OCCIDENTAL

Sierra
de la
Gloria

[Nov. 1528]

[summer 1535]

Rio Sinaloa
Rio Petatlán

Rio San
Lorenzo

[late April 1536]

Rio San
Lorenzo

Rio San
Lorenzo

Rio
Conchos

Rio San
Fernando

[summer 1535]

NUEVA GALICIA

San Miguel
de Culiacán
(est. 1531)
[May 1536]

Rio Soto la Marina
(Rio de las Palmas)

PÁNUCO

Santiago
de los Valles
de Oxitipa
(est. 1533)

Santisteban del Puerto
(est. 1523)

Compostela
(est. 1531)
[June 1536]

Rio Pánuco

NEW SPAIN

Bay of Campeche

SOUTH SEA
(MAR DEL SUR)

Texcoco

México-Tenochtitlán
(est. 1521)
[July 1536–spring 1537]

Veracruz
(2nd est. 1525)

Medellín
(fl. 1523–25)

Rio Coatzacoalcos

Espíritu San
(est. 1522)

⟶ Narváez expedition travel to *Florida*

⤏ Expeditionaries' overland travel

⟹ Cabeza de Vaca's return to Spain

152

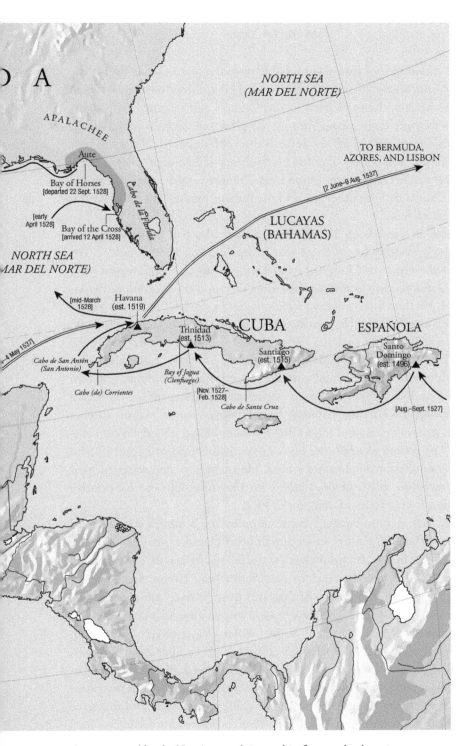

ᗞ A

NORTH SEA
(MAR DEL NORTE)

APALACHEE

Aute

Bay of Horses
[departed 22 Sept. 1528]

[early
April 1528]
Bay of the Cross
[arrived 12 April 1528]

Cabo de la Florida

TO BERMUDA,
AZORES, AND LISBON

[2 June–9 Aug. 1537]

LUCAYAS
(BAHAMAS)

NORTH SEA
(MAR DEL NORTE)

[mid-March
1528]
Havana
(est. 1519)

Trinidad
(est. 1513)

CUBA

ESPAÑOLA

Santo
Domingo
(est. 1496)

[–4 May 1537]

Cabo de San Antón
(San Antonio)

Santiago
(est. 1515)

Cabo (de) Corrientes

Bay of Jagua
(Cienfuegos)

[Nov. 1527–
Feb. 1528]

Cabo de Santa Cruz

[Aug.–Sept. 1527]

Areas traversed by the Narváez expedition and its four overland survivors,
1527–1536. Copyright © 2014 by the University of Oklahoma Press.

153

and the mountains of iron slag probably were the Sierra de la Gloria. The people of the encampment came out with their children on their backs to greet the healers, then ran back to their houses and returned with many presents to greet them again. Among the gifts were buffalo hides, beads, powdered antimony (which the Indians used as face paint), and small bags of crystallized iron pyrites. For dinner, the hosts offered their guests prickly pears and a mash made from piñon nuts. Piñon trees were plentiful in the region, Cabeza de Vaca observed, and the Indians mashed the nuts without hulling them first.[6]

Cabeza de Vaca's hosts brought him a man who had been wounded a long time previously by an arrow that had pierced his right shoulder. The point of the arrow had lodged just above his heart and caused him great pain. Cabeza de Vaca examined the man and found the location of the arrowhead. He then used his knife, which no doubt was of flint, to cut deeply into his patient's chest. He extracted the arrowhead, which was very long, and presented it to his patient's relatives, who showed it to everyone in the camp. Then although his patient was bleeding profusely, Cabeza de Vaca used a thin strip of leather and a needle made from deer bone to give him two stitches. Everyone in the camp celebrated the success of the operation with dancing and feasting. Two days later, the surgeon removed the stitches from his patient's chest and found that his incision had healed almost completely. His patient assured him he was experiencing no pain, and Cabeza de Vaca's reputation for healing soared. He must have had some surgical skill in addition to his obvious talent for showmanship, the cooperative participation of his patient, and lots of luck.

While they were sojourning in the camp by the beautiful river, Cabeza de Vaca and his companions showed their hosts Dorantes's copper bell. The hosts said that in the area from which the bell had come, which was vaguely northwestward in the direction of the "South Sea," copper was plentiful and highly valued. The people of that area lived in fixed settlements. Cabeza de Vaca took note of this new evidence of an advanced civilization to the northwest. The only Indians he had so far encountered who lived in fixed settlements were the Apalachees. If he and his companions continued on their northwestward course, they might visit the Indians who lived in fixed villages and knew how to work copper. Meanwhile, the four men were getting more to eat than they had on the Gulf coastal plain, and that gave them another incentive for holding to their northwestward course. They may already have given up their goal of reaching the Río Pánuco and begun aiming for the South Sea instead. However, they can have had no clear idea how far they were from the South Sea.[7]

Cabeza de Vaca says that after they left the camp by the beautiful river, he and his companions went through a series of valleys and encountered "so many types of people and such diverse languages that memory is insufficient to be able to recount them." The four men crossed a "great river that flowed from the north" and then crossed a high plateau. The great river was probably either the Río Sabinas or one of its tributaries, and the plateau was probably in Coahuila, south or southeast of the Big Bend in the Rio Grande. The pattern continued in which the four men were escorted from one camp to another by large groups of Indians who expected substantial compensation at the end of their journey. Oviedo says that the escort group never consisted of fewer than two thousand people, and Cabeza de Vaca says that often it numbered as many as three to four thousand. But camps of potential new hosts were few and far between.[8]

As Cabeza de Vaca and his companions moved westward, the men in their escort groups hunted. Some of them brought their bows and arrows and spread out into the mountains to hunt deer, quail, and other game. Others carried clubs and moved forward in a line, driving out rabbits and rodents. They brought the carcasses to the Children of the Sun, and by the end of the day each of the healers staggered under a heavy load of small game. The women, meanwhile, carried mats and other household accouterments, plus their infants and small children. Despite these burdens, the women also managed to gather prickly pears, spiders, crickets, and worms. Even the children foraged for food. In the evening, if they had not come to a camp of prospective new hosts, the women set up camp along the trail, erecting shelters for their families and for each of the four healers. The hunters brought their trophies to the Children of the Sun to be blessed, and the women and children brought their small hordes of spiders and worms. The four healers directed the Indians to build fires and cook the day's catch. The four received the choicest portions of meat, but when they had taken what they wanted, they directed the headmen among their escorts to redistribute the rest. No Indian dared to do or eat anything without the blessing of the Children of the Sun, and so the healers were kept busy making the sign of the cross over handfuls of spiders and hundreds of portions of rabbit stew.[9]

Cabeza de Vaca's mention of headmen suggests that he and his Christian companions were not solely in charge of their escort groups. His account is not always clear about who was manipulating whom for whose purposes, but both the Christians and the Indians must have had to maneuver delicately. Cabeza de Vaca's indication that he and the other Christians each slept in a separate shelter suggests that each may have had an Indian sleeping companion. Understandably, the explorer says nothing in the *Relación* he wrote for his emperor about sexual liaisons with Indians, but he and the other Christians may have left mixed-race children behind them.[10]

Since the healers were traveling with large numbers of Indians, they necessarily moved slowly. They and their guides developed the practice of sending out scouts to locate an appropriate new group of hosts and prepare them to receive the Children of the Sun. When the scouts had accomplished their mission, they led the prospective hosts back—sometimes a distance as great as fifteen to twenty leagues—to meet the healers halfway. The prospective hosts brought presents for the Children of the Sun and their escorts because the scouts had warned them in advance not to hold anything back. The scouts said that the Children of the Sun would detect and punish any transgression, and they instilled such fear in the prospective hosts that when they met at last with the four healers, they dared neither to speak nor to raise their eyes. With lowered eyes, they would spread out all their possessions as offerings to the healers, or they would erect a house for each one and place the presents inside. Cabeza de Vaca and his companions would receive the offerings graciously and then turn everything over to the headmen in their escort group for distribution to the escorting people. By giving their goods away, the new hosts avoided being robbed, but they put themselves in a position where their only hope of recovering their losses was to conduct the healers onward and turn them over to yet another host group.[11]

One group of Indians guided the four healers for more than fifty leagues through dry and uninhabited mountains. Along the way, they found little game or food of any kind. Finally, when everyone had begun to suffer desperately from hunger, they came to a deep river and crossed it with difficulty. The river may have been the Rio Grande, and if so, Cabeza de Vaca and his companions were crossing it for at least the second time and were now back in Texas.[12]

Around the time of the river crossing, many of the Indian escorts began to fall ill. The origin of the disease is impossible to determine, but since Cabeza de Vaca and his companions had already spent seven years in North America, they are unlikely to have introduced it. European diseases seem to have spread across the American landscape at a faster rate than the Europeans themselves, and this one may have come northward from colonial New

Spain. Cabeza de Vaca and his companions were hard-pressed to minister to all the sick. Despite their ill health, the Indians led the four men onward to a large encampment on a plateau, where many people had gathered in anticipation of their arrival. These people offered presents and a great quantity of piñon nuts to the Children of the Sun. The four men turned everything over to their previous hosts, but there was too much for the sick people to carry, and they had to leave many things behind. The healers invited their new hosts to reclaim the things the sick people had abandoned, but the piñon-eaters refused, saying it was not their custom to reclaim anything they had given away.[13]

The healers told their new hosts that they "wanted to go to where the sun set." The piñon-eaters protested that the only people living to the west were far away and were their enemies. Cabeza de Vaca directed the piñon-eaters to send messengers to these people to inform them of the immanent arrival of the Children of the Sun. The piñon-eaters were reluctant to do this but did not dare to refuse. They selected two women to serve as messengers, one of whom was a member of their own community and the other a captive from the enemy people in the west. Like other Indians whom Cabeza de Vaca had encountered, the piñon-eaters relied on women to mediate for them with hostile people. The two women departed, and the four healers followed slowly after them with the main body of piñon-eaters until they reached a place where they had prearranged to wait. They waited for five days, and as they waited, the piñon-eaters grumbled that the messengers must have failed to perform their mission. Cabeza de Vaca and his companions became exasperated with the grumbling and told the piñon-eaters that if they couldn't go westward, they would go northward. But the piñon-eaters declined to go either northward or westward, because they were at war with all their neighbors. The Indians also claimed that the country to the north held no food or water. Cabeza de Vaca finally became so angry with them that, he says, "I went one night to sleep in the countryside, apart from them, but later they went to where I was. And they were there the entire night without sleeping and with very great fear and speaking to me and telling me how terrified they were, begging us to not be angry anymore, and that even though they knew they would die on the road, they would take us wherever we wanted to go." Although he eventually returned to the main camp, Cabeza de Vaca pretended that he was still angry. In Oviedo's account, it was Andrés Dorantes rather than Cabeza de Vaca who made a strategic display of anger and warned the piñon-eaters they would die if they did not cooperate. And then, as if the four healers were exercising supernatural powers, three hundred of the Indians fell ill and eight of them died. No doubt they had contracted the disease that had afflicted the healers' previous hosts. The piñon-eaters begged the Children of the Sun not to harm any more of their people. Cabeza de Vaca and his companions worried that all the Indians might die or that so many would sicken, the others would flee. The four healers ministered to the sick and beseeched God to spare the lives of the people upon whom their own lives depended. At last, after an interval of great anxiety, the sick began to recover.[14]

The relatives of the people who had died refused to express their grief. They did not even bury the dead until the Children of the Sun directed them to do so. No one spoke or laughed, and even the small children did not cry. When one girl did cry, her people took her far from the camp and, using the jawbone and sharp teeth of a rat, scratched her from her shoulders to her feet. Cabeza de Vaca was angered by this cruelty and asked the Indians why they had done it. They said they had punished the girl for crying in front of him.[15]

After a five-day absence, the two female messengers returned with the news that most of the people they had been seeking had gone northward to hunt buffalo, as they did every summer. Despite this discouraging report, Castillo and Estevanico set off with the women to visit the area the latter had reconnoitered. The other two Christians remained with the piñon-eaters, perhaps as hostages. The woman who was a captive led Castillo and Estevanico to her father's village, which was near "a river that flowed between some mountains." The village proved to be a permanent settlement, the first Castillo and Estevanico had seen since their visit to Apalachee territory. Leaving Estevanico to follow more slowly behind him, Castillo took five or six Indians and hastened back to Cabeza de Vaca and Dorantes. He told them that the people of the village he had seen were farmers who cultivated beans, squash, and even a little maize. Although the four survivors of the Narváez expedition had tasted maize at an early stage of their overland journey, they had seen no sign of agriculture since leaving the Apalachees. Cabeza de Vaca reports that "[Castillo's news] was the thing that gladdened us more than anything else in the world, and for this we gave infinite thanks to our Lord."[16]

Cabeza de Vaca and Castillo regarded farming as a more advanced way to make a living than hunting and gathering, and they saw fixed settlements as superior to nomadic camps. In these views, they differed little from present-day anthropologists who see agriculture as prerequisite to the development of a complex, economically specialized society. Hunters and gatherers move about in small bands of relative equals, but farmers can produce enough food to sustain large groups of people, including some individuals who take no part in farming but serve as chiefs, priests, specialized crafts workers, and merchants. And because farmers live in fixed settlements near their fields, they accumulate more property than hunters and gatherers, who must carry their belongings with them.[17]

Cabeza de Vaca, Dorantes, and Castillo hurried toward the village with a small group of piñon-eaters, and within a league and a half they met Estevanico and a large group of village dwellers. The villagers had brought squash and beans, dried gourds for carrying water, buffalo robes, deer skins, and bows and arrows as presents for the Children of the Sun. The four healers turned the gifts over to the piñon-eaters and took leave of them before proceeding to the village. They arrived there after dark and were welcomed with a great celebration. The next day, they moved on to another permanent village, where they were given many buffalo robes. The region was quite populous, and Cabeza de Vaca referred to its inhabitants as the "people of the cows." He used the Spanish word for "cow," *vaca*, because he had no other word to describe buffalo.[18]

The cow people hunted buffalo in the summer and prized them for their meat and hides. Cabeza de Vaca, who authored the first written description of the American bison, observes that the animals were about the size of cows in Castile, adding, "[They] have small horns like Moorish cows, and their fur is very long. Some are brown and others black, and in my opinion they have better meat and more of it than those from here [Castile]. From [the skins] of the young ones the Indians make robes to cover themselves, and from [the hides of] the mature animals they make shoes and shields." The explorer says he saw and ate buffalo three times during his years in North America. The first instance occurred while he was living among the Mariames on the Texas coast, but the circumstances of the other two occasions are not clear. Cabeza de Vaca learned that large herds of buffalo came every year from the north, migrating through the valleys and spreading out across a territory that extended for more than four hundred leagues. The cow people must have killed buffalo without the aid of horses, but Cabeza de Vaca does not explain how they did so.[19]

Cabeza de Vaca and his companions arrived in the region of the cow people in the late summer or early autumn of 1535. We can infer this because summer was buffalo-hunting season, and most of the villagers were away at the hunt when the four men arrived. The permanent villages must have been located near La Junta de los Ríos, where the Rio Grande and Río Conchos come together and where the present-day communities of Presidio, Texas, and Ojinaga, Chihuahua, are located. Although neither Cabeza de Vaca's account nor Oviedo's mentions this confluence, we know that in 1582, nearly fifty years after the survivors of the Narváez expedition met the cow people, Antonio de Espejo led an expedition from Nueva Vizcaya through Chihuahua down the Río Conchos to its confluence with the Rio Grande and found five large permanent pueblos there. Espejo reported that he met Indians in these pueblos who remembered the Narváez men. He identified these Indians as Jumanos and said, "[They] told us and gave us to understand through interpreters that three Christians and a black had passed through there, and by the indications they gave they appeared to have been Alonso [sic] Núñez Cabeza de Vaca, Dorantes Castillo Maldonado [sic], and a black, who had all escaped from the fleet with which Pánfilo de Narváez entered Florida."[20]

Cabeza de Vaca reports that the manner in which the people of the second permanent village received him and his companions was new to his experience. The villagers prepared four houses, one for each of the healers, and then withdrew to their own homes to await their guests' arrival. The healers found them seated in their houses with their faces turned to the wall, their heads bowed, and their hair hanging over their eyes. Each family had piled all their possessions near their door for the Children of the Sun to take. Cabeza de Vaca perceived the cow people as "the people with the most well formed bodies we saw and of the greatest vitality and capacity and who best understood us and responded to what we asked them." The young men went naked, but the women and old men clothed themselves in deerskins.[21]

According to Cabeza de Vaca, the cow people had no pottery. The explorer's information conflicts, however, with archaeological evidence demonstrating the presence of pottery in the area of La Junta de los Ríos from the thirteenth century onward. Cabeza de Vaca says that, lacking pottery, the cow people employed an unusual method for cooking their food, and he describes it, explaining that he does so in order that "the extraordinary ingenuity and industry of humankind might be seen and known in all its diversity." When a woman wished to cook something, she filled a dried gourd half full with water and began heating rocks in a fire. When a rock was sufficiently heated, she grasped it with wooden tongs and dropped it into the water in the gourd. As soon as the water came to a boil, she added whatever it was she wished to cook. Once a rock had cooled, she removed it from the pot, placed it back in the fire, and replaced it with a hotter rock.[22]

The cow people grew their own squash and beans, but they told their guests that their maize had come "from where the sun set." When Cabeza de Vaca asked them why they did not cultivate maize, the people replied that they usually did, but they had not had sufficient rain during the previous two years and had lost whatever maize they had sown. They begged the Children of the Sun to use their magical powers to bring rain. After promising to pray for rain, the four healers expressed their desire to move westward to the place where the maize originated. Their hosts, however, preferred to take them northward to their buffalo-hunting grounds. The hosts had enemies in the west, and they said that anyone who went west would find nothing to eat for seventeen days except a nearly inedible kind of fruit. This fruit, even when ground between rocks, was dry and woody. To demonstrate the truth of what they said, they offered some of the fruit to their guests, and Cabeza de Vaca and his companions could not stomach it.[23]

The cow people said that if the Children of the Sun wished to go west, they should first go upstream along the nearby river. Then, if the four men went west and could endure seventeen days of hunger, they would meet people who could give them buffalo hides, robes of woven cotton, and—eventually—maize. Cabeza de Vaca reports: "We decided to go in search of the maize. And we did not want to follow the road of the cows [bison] because it is toward the north, and this was for us a very great detour, because we always held it for certain that going the route of the setting sun we would find what we desired." The new information about agricultural people to the west, together with what they had heard earlier about copper mining and cotton weaving in that direction, must have drawn the four travelers toward the sunset. They knew that if they went far enough westward, they would come to the Pacific Ocean, and by this point in their journey they must have known that their best hope of finding other Spaniards was to continue on to the Pacific. But Cabeza de Vaca is oversimplifying when he says he and his companions had always intended to follow "the route of the setting sun." He wrote his *Relación* retrospectively, rather than as events were unfolding, and his comments about his route make it seem as though he had planned to go where in fact he went.[24]

Early in the fall of 1535, the four travelers left the villages of the cow people and made their way upstream along what probably was the Rio Grande but may have been the Río Conchos. For seventeen days, they were hungry—just as the cow people had predicted. They refused to eat the dry, woody fruit and instead ate deer fat, which they carried on their backs and had probably acquired from the cow people. New people they met along their way gave them buffalo robes. At the end of seventeen days, the four men crossed a river that probably was the Rio Grande. If so, they must have crossed it somewhere south of the present El Paso, Texas, leaving Texas for the final time and entering the present Mexican state of Chihuahua.[25]

After crossing the river, the men walked westward for another seventeen days, traversing a high plateau and threading through passes and river valleys around some formidable mountains, probably the Sierra Madre Occidental. They traveled through this region in the autumn, and all that its people could give them to eat were jackrabbits and a kind of herb they ground to a powder. At the end of this second seventeen-day period, the travelers again encountered permanent villages. The people of these villages, which probably were situated along either the Río Casas Grandes in northwestern Chihuahua or the Río Bavispe in northeastern Sonora, cultivated maize and possessed large stores of it. The houses in the villages had flat roofs, and some were made of adobe and others of woven reed mats. The villagers gave maize, squash, beans, and cotton cloaks to the Children of the Sun. As was their practice, the healers turned the presents over to their escorts and sent them home again. Cabeza de Vaca notes, "We gave many thanks to God our Lord for having brought us there where we had found so much sustenance."[26]

The explorer doesn't mention seeing the ruins of Casas Grandes, but that spectacular archaeological site is in northwestern Chihuahua, in the Río Casas Grandes valley at the foot of the Sierra Madre Occidental. Covering ninety acres, the site includes a terraced, multistory adobe pueblo with hundreds of contiguous rooms. It flourished during A.D. 1200–1425 and at its height was the center of a cultural sphere that extended over much of present-day Chihuahua and New Mexico, into Sonora and Arizona, and as far eastward as La Junta de los Ríos. The pueblo had almost certainly been abandoned before Cabeza de Vaca and his companions passed through Chihuahua, because the Francisco de Ibarra expedition, which visited Casas Grandes in the mid-1560s and produced the first documents concerning the site, found it ruined and deserted. And yet some traces of the advanced Casas Grandes culture may have persisted, for in 1535 Cabeza de Vaca and his companions encountered maize cultivation and permanent villages along the proximate one hundred leagues of their route.[27]

As the travelers walked westward from present-day Chihuahua into Sonora, they are likely to have followed the course of one or more rivers, possibly the Río Casas Grandes and probably the Río Bavispe and the Río Yaqui. The people of these valleys had, from approximately A.D. 1300 through Cabeza de Vaca's period, developed what archaeologists today know as the Sonora River culture. Sonora River artifacts include dwellings with stone foundations and adobe walls, pottery, and elaborately decorated earthenware weights used in spinning cotton. Items made from copper, turquoise, and shell found at Sonora River sites, but originating elsewhere, indicate that the Sonora River people engaged in long-distance trade. The descendants of these people have been known since the seventeenth century as the Opatas.[28]

According to Cabeza de Vaca, the people of the maize villages had plenty to eat, including venison and large stores of maize and beans. They gave the Children of the Sun beads made of turquoise and coral, and woven cotton robes that Cabeza de Vaca says were "better than those of New Spain." The explorer was familiar with an Old World cotton species (*Gossypium herbaceum*) that had originally been domesticated in Africa. The cotton he encountered in the New World (*Gossypium hirsutum*) had been domesticated in Mesoamerica, but its cultivation and the arts of spinning and weaving had subsequently spread northward as far as what is now the southwestern United States. Although the men of the maize villages went naked, Cabeza de Vaca says the women were "the most decently clad women we had ever seen in any part of the Indies." They wore cotton shifts under floor-length leather garments that were open in front but laced with thongs. The women also wore shoes. They kept their garments clean by rubbing them with some sort of root.[29]

Cabeza de Vaca and his companions were escorted through the maize villages by groups of at least a thousand and sometimes as many as three thousand people. Some of these people never left them, even though their home communities were far away. The four healers walked for two or three days between villages and then spent a day or two resting at each. After their long months on the trail, the four men were in excellent physical condition and were able to walk long distances through rugged terrain with little or no food. They generally hiked all day without eating, and ate only when they stopped for the night. "We never felt tired," Cabeza de Vaca reports, "and in truth we were so hardened to the task that we did not even notice it." The healers were nearly overwhelmed, however, by their escorts' demands for cures and blessings. Whether healthy or sick, the people of the maize villages clamored to be touched, fearing that if they failed to receive a blessing, they would die. Sick people were brought to the Children of the Sun from places ten to twelve leagues distant. People who were at war with one another patched up their differences in order to receive blessings. Many times, Cabeza de Vaca says, a woman in the escort groups would give birth along the trail and then bring her newborn to the Children of the Sun, believing that a blessing would give her child lifelong immunity from suffering. The people of the maize villages said the Children of the Sun had come from the sky, but Cabeza de Vaca noticed that they said much the same about anything whose origin they did not know.[30]

According to Cabeza de Vaca, he and his companions enjoyed a great deal of authority among the people who escorted them. The healers attempted at least twice to teach their escorts about the Christian religion. Using signs, they explained that a God in heaven had created the earth and bestowed his blessings upon humanity. The Christians served this God, who was their Lord, and obeyed his commandments. If the Indians did the same, all would go well for them. Cabeza de Vaca later reported that if he and his fellow Christians had been better able to communicate with the Indians, they might have converted them all to Christianity: "We found such great readiness in them, that if we had had an interpreter through whom we could have understood each other perfectly, we would have left all of them Christians. This we gave them to understand as best we could. And henceforth when the sun rose, with very great shouting they opened their joined hands to the sky and afterward passed them over their entire bodies. And they did the same when the sun set. They are a people of good disposition and diligent [and] well equipped to follow any course."[31]

Cabeza de Vaca notes that in the course of their overland journey he and his companions "passed through a great number and diversity of languages," but they communicated with their escorts by means of signs and a trading language known as Primahaitu, which was used and understood for more than four hundred leagues. When groups of Indians from different communities did not speak the same language, they nevertheless could transact business in Primahaitu. Cabeza de Vaca became the first writer to document the use of a trading language among North American Indians.[32]

Apparently, Estevanico was the most gifted linguist among the four survivors of the Narváez expedition. The African could speak Castilian Spanish and several Indian languages in addition to his native Arabic. He must have been skilled at communicating in both signs and Primahaitu, for he devoted much of his time to conferring with Indians and gathering information that would be useful to him and his three Spanish companions. The three Spaniards generally kept a dignified distance from the Indians and, in order to demonstrate their lordliness, employed Estevanico as their go-between. But by virtue of his communication skills and his darker skin, Estevanico possibly enjoyed a special status among the Indians. To them, all the Children of the Sun must have seemed exotic, but three of them resembled each other, and only Estevanico was unique.[33]

Around Christmastime in 1535 the four travelers came out of the mountains onto the Sonoran coastal plain. They seem to have been following the course of a south-flowing river. The weather, Cabeza de Vaca says, was hot. They came to a permanent settlement consisting of three small villages where they met people who gave Dorantes more than six hundred deer hearts that had been split open and dried. Because of the gift, the captain and his companions referred to the settlement as Corazones, which means "hearts."[34]

Cabeza de Vaca observes that three kinds of deer could be found in the vicinity of Corazones. The adult males of one type were as large as young bulls in Castile. The men of Corazones hunted deer with poisoned arrows and said they obtained the poison from the fruit and sap of trees that resembled apple trees. Even the leaves of these trees were so poisonous that if hunters simply scattered them in a pool of water, any animal that drank from it would bloat and die. Several years later, two of the chroniclers of the Coronado expedition would also report on the use of poison in the region of Corazones.[35]

In addition to the six hundred deer hearts, the people of Corazones gave Dorantes what Cabeza de Vaca describes as "emeralds made into arrowheads." These arrowheads seemed to Cabeza de Vaca to be "very fine," but what he took for emerald was probably some copper alloy such as malachite or turquoise. The people of Corazones used the emerald arrowheads in their ceremonial dances and said they had obtained them in exchange for parrot feathers and bird plumes from people who lived in large villages in a mountainous region to the north. These northern villages possessed much food and cotton and were a source of turquoise. Cabeza de Vaca noted this new evidence of long-distance trading networks and later became the first European to describe such networks. The people in the north who had produced the "emerald" arrowheads were probably the pueblo Indians of what are now Arizona and New Mexico, and the parrot feathers probably originated in Mesoamerica. Present-day archaeologists have found evidence of a major indigenous trade route running from Mesoamerica along the western side of the Sierra Madre Occidental into what is now the south-western United States. Trade items included cotton cloth, cured animal hides, polychrome ceramics, copper, turquoise, coral, shells, salt, feathers, and such brightly colored birds as the military macaw, the scarlet macaw, and the thick-billed parrot.[36]

The people of Corazones cultivated maize and beans and raised three cycles of crops per year. They explained to their guests via signs that some twelve to fifteen leagues beyond their community was the sea. The four travelers thought they had come nearly to the South Sea, or the Pacific. They had no idea that the Gulf of California and the peninsula now known as Baja California lay between them and the ocean. In 1528, when they had last had contact with the Spanish-speaking world, no European had yet discovered either the Gulf of California or its sheltering peninsula.[37]

Cabeza de Vaca would later describe Corazones as "the entrance to many provinces that lie toward the South Sea." He knew Corazones was the gateway to the maize villages he had visited to its east. But he must have meant also that it was the gateway to the prosperous region in the north where, he had heard, there were turquoises, emeralds, and copper. He had not visited this prosperous region, but he had been told that it was vaguely near the South Sea. He speculated that to the north of Corazones "there are more than a thousand leagues of populated land." He would soon learn that the coastal plain south of Corazones was a barren region where he and his companions would find no maize.[38]

The four travelers spent three days at Corazones. Then, although it was raining, they resumed their journey and in one day covered a distance of five leagues. In the evening they came to a village, but a nearby river was so swollen with rain that it barred their further progress. They had probably walked downstream along the Río Yaqui and arrived at the elbow where the south-flowing Yaqui turns westward toward the Gulf of California. The rains continued for fifteen days, and during the whole of that time the travelers were unable to cross the river.[39]

The diet of the Indians the explorers encountered after leaving Corazones consisted of herbs and grasses and of fish they took from the Gulf of

California. The people fished from rafts because they had no canoes. Their houses were made of straw mats rather than adobe, and the people slept on straw mats. The women covered their private parts with grass and straw, but they also wore shawls that hung to the waist or in some cases to the knees.[40]

During the time the four travelers were waiting for the rain to subside and the floodwaters to recede, Castillo saw an Indian wearing a horseshoe nail and the buckle from a sword belt as ornaments around his neck. Castillo asked him about the metal objects, and the Indian—who didn't know their origin—replied that they came from the sky. He said he had obtained the objects from men with beards, like Castillo himself, who also came from the sky. Using signs and gestures, the Indian endeavored to explain that the bearded men had come to the nearby river riding on the backs of monstrous animals and brandishing metal weapons, and they had speared two local Indians. Hiding his interest, Castillo asked what had become of the bearded men. The Indian replied that they had gone to the sea and submerged themselves in the water, and then they had gone away overland. He had watched the bearded men until nightfall and was frightened by what he saw. Although Castillo didn't fully comprehend the Indian's story, he recognized that it concerned other Christians, and he and his three Christian companions thanked God for the information. At the same time, the four men acknowledged that they had little hope of meeting these other Christians. They understood the Indian's story to pertain to Spanish maritime explorers who had come by ship up the Pacific coast and sailed on to some other location.[41]

Most route interpreters agree that the place where Castillo saw the items of European manufacture was on the Río Yaqui. When he wrote his *Relación*, Cabeza de Vaca drew upon information he received after reconnecting with other Spaniards, and he said Castillo saw the buckle and nail near "the river to which Diego de Guzmán arrived." At the time Castillo saw the metal objects, neither he nor Cabeza de Vaca had ever heard of Diego de Guzmán, but that Spanish captain had taken possession of the Río Yaqui in 1533. For several years thereafter, the river marked the northern boundary of Spanish penetration in what is now northwestern Mexico.[42]

As soon as Cabeza de Vaca and his companions were able to cross the swollen river that probably was the Yaqui, they pressed on southward, spurred by the news of other Christians. Their course was parallel to the coast, but as had been the case when they moved down the Texas coast toward the Río Pánuco, they maintained a prudent ten- to twelve-league distance from the shore. The countryside they passed through was almost completely deserted, and they saw burned settlements and other signs of devastation. The few Indians they encountered were thin and covered with sores, and Cabeza de Vaca describes them as "timid and sad." These Indians talked of little other than the bearded men who had "destroyed and burned the villages and carried off half the men and all the women and boys." The bearded men had invaded the area three times, each time carrying people away. Most of the native survivors had fled eastward into the mountains. Those Indians who remained in their coastal homeland had gone into hiding and lived furtively like wild animals. They did not dare to sow crops or work the land.[43]

Cabeza de Vaca and his companions heard the stories about the bearded raiders with mixed emotions. Although they were elated by the evidence of their proximity to other Christians, Cabeza de Vaca writes, "It was a thing that gave us great sorrow, seeing the land very fertile and very beautiful and very full of waterways and rivers, and seeing the places deserted and burned and the people so emaciated and sick, all of them having fled and in hiding." The four travelers moved forward cautiously because they didn't know how their Indian escorts would react if they encountered Spanish cavalrymen. Cabeza de Vaca says he feared that the Indians on the frontiers of Christian territory "would treat us cruelly and make us pay for what the Christians were doing to them." He must have worried also about the way in which armed cavalrymen might deal with four naked medicine men and their Indian escorts. He and his companions informed their escorts that they wished to move southward into the country of the bearded men in order to tell them to stop killing and enslaving Indians. The plan seemed to please the Indians. Perhaps they thought the Children of the Sun had the power to make other bearded men obey their commands.[44]

Despite their fear of the mounted raiders, the people of the Sonoran coastal plain came out of hiding one by one and gathered together to receive the Children of the Sun. They seemed to revere the bearded healers even more highly than had those Indians who had never previously seen a bearded man. The fugitive people had little food to offer their guests other than tree bark and roots, but they gave the travelers what they had, including even their straw sleeping mats. They also gave them beads and robes they had hidden from the bearded raiders. The fugitives undertook to lead the Children of the Sun forward on their journey, but instead of taking them directly southward along the coastal plain, they took them eastward into the foothills of the Sierra Madre Occidental.[45]

The new escorts led the travelers through rugged terrain to a camp in a cleft of the mountains. Many refugees from the burned coastal settlements had gathered in this hideaway where, because it was nearly inaccessible to horses, they felt relatively safe. The refugees received the Children of the Sun with pleasure and presented them with more than two thousand loads of maize, each of the size that one man might carry, and the four travelers turned this food over to their escorts. The following day, according to their customary procedure, the healers sent messengers to a settlement that was three days ahead, instructing them to prepare the people there for the arrival of the Children of the Sun. The healers followed slowly after the messengers, escorted by refugees from the mountain hideaway, and along their way they saw campsites where they inferred that other Christians had slept. At some point, the healers caught up with their messengers, who were so upset they could scarcely speak. They had visited the settlement to which the Children of the Sun had sent them, but they had found it deserted and had failed to locate new hosts for the healers. All the people of the region had fled. The previous night, the messengers had hidden behind some trees and watched as several bearded men kept guard over a group of Indians in chains. When the Indians escorting Cabeza de Vaca and his companions heard this report, many turned back to warn their kinsmen and friends of the proximity of bearded slave-hunters. Others, however, refused to leave the Children of the Sun. Some had walked with them for a hundred leagues and were far from their homes. To calm their followers, the healers decided to go no farther that day.[46]

The following morning, the group set off for the campsite where the messengers had seen bearded men guarding Indians in chains. They spent one night on the road and arrived at their objective the next evening. Cabeza de Vaca and his companions saw signs of horses, including picket stakes and, no doubt, horse dung. The camp was near a river that, as Cabeza de Vaca later learned, was known to his Spanish contemporaries as the Río Petatlán. This river, known today as the Río Sinaloa, flows southwestward from the Sierra Madre Occidental into the Gulf of California. Before reaching the river, the travelers had passed from the present-day Mexican state of Sonora into the state of Sinaloa. Cabeza de Vaca gauges the distance between the campsite where he and his companions found evidence of horses and the place where Castillo had seen the buckle and the horseshoe nail as eighty leagues. However, if the one place was on the Río Sinaloa and the other on the Río Yaqui, the actual distance can only have been around

165 miles. Cabeza de Vaca may have overestimated the distance because he and his companions had traveled from the one river to the other by way of the mountain hideaway.[47]

Cabeza de Vaca says that when he and his Christian companions were sure that other Christians were nearby, "we gave many thanks to God our Lord for wanting to take us out of so sad and wretched a captivity. And may the pleasure we felt on this account be judged by every man when he considers the time we spent in that land and the dangers and hardships we endured." Cabeza de Vaca urged Castillo and Dorantes to hurry with him in pursuit of the other Christians, but they both excused themselves on account of fatigue. No doubt they feared what might happen when they finally encountered their compatriots. Cabeza de Vaca was irritated with the captains and observed that "each one of them would be able to do it better than I, on account of being hardier and younger." He was determined to pursue the horsemen, however, and he recruited Estevanico and eleven Indians to accompany him. Meanwhile, Castillo and Dorantes would endeavor to reassemble those Indians who had fled in fear of the bearded slavers.[48]

Cabeza de Vaca, Estevanico, and their eleven escorts went a distance of ten leagues and along the way found three places where the horsemen had camped. The pursuers moved quickly and soon caught up with the men they were tracking. There were four of them, and they were armed with lances and harquebuses. When the leader of the horsemen spotted what seemed to be a dozen Indians coming toward him, he called upon his men to prepare their harquebuses for firing.[49]

TEN

New Spain

The bearded horsemen who confronted Cabeza de Vaca and his party had been searching beyond the frontiers of what they knew as the province of Nueva Galicia for Indians to press into slavery. Although the area had once been dotted with villages, however, they had not captured or even seen an Indian for fifteen days. Cabeza de Vaca must have called to the slavers, for he later reported: "[They] experienced great shock upon seeing me so strangely dressed and in the company of Indians. They remained looking at me a long time, so astonished that they neither spoke to me nor managed to ask me anything. I told them to take me to their captain."[1]

Their captain, Diego de Alcaraz, was camped half a league away beside the Río Petatlán. Cabeza de Vaca must have informed Alcaraz that he was one of four survivors of a group of three hundred men Pánfilo de Narváez had led into the interior of La Florida. Two of the others, Captain Alonso del Castillo and Captain Andrés Dorantes, were encamped with a large group of Indians some ten leagues to the north. Alcaraz must have been pleased with this information. He and his men were beginning to run short of food, and he saw Indians not only as potential slaves but also as producers and suppliers of food. The captain delegated three of his horsemen and fifty Indian slaves to go with Estevanico to fetch Castillo, Dorantes, and the Indians they had with them.[2]

Meanwhile, Cabeza de Vaca must have had questions for Alcaraz. Where exactly were they? What was the date? Alcaraz said his camp was thirty leagues north of San Miguel de Culiacán, which was both the nearest Spanish settlement and the northernmost outpost in Nueva Galicia, a newly established province in the viceroyalty of New Spain. Founded only five years earlier, Culiacán was some two hundred leagues northwest of México, the city formerly known as Tenochtitlán that was now the capital of the viceroyalty. When Cabeza de Vaca left Cuba in 1528, neither Culiacán nor the province of Nueva Galicia existed, and although the territory conquered by Cortés had been known as New Spain, it had not been organized as a viceroyalty. During the years Cabeza de Vaca had been out of touch with the Spanish-speaking world, the extent of the territory incorporated within New Spain had grown considerably. Spaniards now controlled not only the coast of the Gulf of Mexico as far north as the Río Pánuco but also the Pacific coast as far north as Culiacán.[3]

Although Cabeza de Vaca had once aimed for the outpost on New Spain's northeastern frontier, he had arrived at an outpost on its northwestern frontier. He and his companions had walked from the shores of the North Sea almost to the shores of the South Sea. In our terms, they had walked from the Gulf of Mexico almost to the Gulf of California. Cabeza de Vaca estimated that since he and his companions had parted from the Avavares the previous summer, they had been traveling continuously for ten months and had walked two hundred leagues, or six hundred miles. His estimate, however, was too low. The distance from their starting point in southeastern Texas to Alcaraz's camp on the Río Petatlán (today's Río Sinaloa) is at least nine hundred miles as the crow flies, but the four men had gone far north of the straight line that can be drawn between their starting and ending points. After they first sighted mountains, they had walked northwestward up the drainage valley of the Rio Grande to somewhere near the confluence of that river with the Río Conchos. From there they had walked westward to Corazones and then turned southward. Their route had probably taken them from Texas through the present Mexican states of Tamaulipas, Nuevo León, Coahuila, Chihuahua, and Sonora into Sinaloa.[4]

Cabeza de Vaca asked to make a written record before an *escribano* certifying that he, the royal treasurer of the Narváez expedition, had emerged from the wilderness. He was honoring the custom, common among Spaniards at that period, of recording and notarizing all significant events and actions. He was also fulfilling his obligation as the senior surviving officer of the ill-fated expedition. Unfortunately, the notarized document has not survived, nor has any record of the date, but it was definitely in 1536 and probably in April.[5]

The date may have come as something of a shock to Cabeza de Vaca. He had long ago lost track of calendar time, but he had been wandering in the unmapped North American interior for the eight years since Easter 1528. He had left Spain in 1527, so nine years had passed since he last saw his wife, who had probably given him up for dead. During his years of wandering, Cabeza de Vaca had become middle-aged. In 1536 he was between forty-four and fifty-one years old. He gave thanks to Jesus Christ his Redeemer for having brought him so far and for preserving his life through countless hardships and dangers.[6]

Cabeza de Vaca would later reflect, however, that just when he thought his hardships had come to an end, new ones arose. He and Alcaraz probably began to annoy each other almost immediately. Alcaraz must have looked contemptuously on Cabeza de Vaca's nakedness, and the explorer must have looked at the slave-hunter in horror and disgust. It must have galled him that the first of his countrymen he had encountered in eight years should be trafficking in slaves. During the past several weeks as he was drawing ever closer to the territory controlled by Spaniards, Cabeza de Vaca had fretted over the devastation his compatriots were wreaking upon the land and its indigenous people. Although he had interacted as a boy with his grandfather's slaves from the Canary Islands and had seen Indian slaves in Hispaniola and Cuba during the winter of 1527–28, the explorer had subsequently learned how it felt to be enslaved. He knew that he, Dorantes, Castillo, and Estevanico could neither have made their long journey nor even have survived without the help of Indians.[7]

Five days after Alcaraz dispatched Estevanico, the African returned with Captains Castillo and Dorantes and six hundred Indian men, women, and children. Estevanico may not yet have perceived it, but now that he had reentered a world in which white men were masters, he would suffer a significant loss of status. The Indians among whom he and his Spanish companions had been living regarded the four men as roughly equal. Alcaraz, however, regarded Estevanico as an African slave. Even the dynamics of Estevanico's relationship to Dorantes, who legally owned him, and to Castillo and Cabeza de Vaca were subtly changed. The four men had been partners during the time when their lives depended on mutual cooperation, and because of his ability to communicate with Indians, Estevanico had been a valuable part of the team. But now his Spanish companions needed to make their way in a Spanish-speaking world.[8]

Alcaraz must have smiled when he saw the six hundred Indians. Four hundred of them were people that Castillo and Dorantes had persuaded to come out of hiding. Their homes were along the Río Petatlán, but they had retreated into the mountains out of fear of Alcaraz and his men. The other two hundred came from various places the Children of the Sun had passed through, including even Corazones, a hundred leagues to the north. All six hundred Indians trusted the healers to protect them from the slave-hunters.[9]

Unlike the four healers, Alcaraz and his men seem not to have understood any Indian languages whatsoever. They communicated with their slaves via an Indian interpreter. Alcaraz entreated Cabeza de Vaca and his companions to call upon the newly arrived Indians to supply him and his men with food. Accordingly, the four sent messengers back northeastward into the mountains to retrieve provisions the Indians had buried there. The messengers soon returned bearing sealed clay jars filled with maize, plus bows and arrows, bison robes, and the five emerald arrowheads given previously to Dorantes. The Children of the Sun received everything and distributed the maize equitably among all the hungry people, Indians and Spaniards alike.[10]

Cabeza de Vaca began to suspect Alcaraz, however, of intending to enslave the six hundred Indians his companions had brought to the camp. Some of the Indians told him that Alcaraz had sent his interpreter among them with stories designed to discredit the Children of the Sun. The interpreter had said that three of the four men were Spaniards like Alcaraz himself, but whereas Alcaraz and his slavers were "the lords of the land," the four naked travelers were "people of ill fortune and no worth." According to Cabeza de Vaca, the Indians answered the interpreter by saying "[that Alcaraz and the slavers] were lying, because we [the Children of the Sun] came from where the sun rose, and they from where it set; and that we cured the sick, and that they killed those who were well; and that we came naked and barefoot, and they went about dressed and on horses and with lances; and that we did not covet anything but, rather, everything they gave us we later returned and remained with nothing, and that the others had no other objective but to steal everything they found and did not give anything to anyone." It is noteworthy that in reporting the conversation, Cabeza de Vaca refers to himself and his companions as "we" and to Alcaraz and his men as "they."[11]

Cabeza de Vaca and his companions endeavored to strike a bargain with Alcaraz in order to prevent him from enslaving their Indian supporters. They gave the slave-hunter everything the Indians had brought down from the hills, including the bows, arrows, and bison robes. The bows, which Cabeza de Vaca describes as "Turkish bows," were probably made of buffalo or elk horn and strung with buffalo sinew. In exchange for these gifts, Alcaraz promised that he and his men would not harm the Indians or trouble them in any way and that he would allow the local Indians to return in peace to their deserted villages and farms. He stipulated, however, that the Indians should feed his men and their horses whenever the Spaniards passed through the Río Petatlán area. Alcaraz then delegated Lázaro de Cebreros, three other horsemen, and a small group of Indian slaves to escort the four naked travelers southward to the Spanish settlement of San Miguel de Culiacán.[12]

The Indians, however, were unwilling to trust Alcaraz. The four hundred from the Río Petatlán area feared to resume farming. The two hundred from more distant settlements did not wish to part with the Children of the Sun or to leave them with either Alcaraz or Cebreros. They wanted to deliver the four men to native people like themselves who would revere them appropriately. They also wanted to recoup their losses. Some weeks earlier they had lost goods to the people who brought the Children of the Sun to them, and now they had lost maize, bison robes, and bows to Alcaraz. Although the four healers could not compensate the Indians, they tried to assure them that all was well. They would go with Cebreros to the chief of the Spaniards, and they would urge him to halt the persecution of native people. The Indians reluctantly began to withdraw, but they were harassed by Alcaraz's men. Cabeza de Vaca says that he and his companions "suffered many annoyances and great disputes" with the slave-hunters and that they parted from Alcaraz in anger. In the confusion and ugliness of the situation, Dorantes inadvertently lost his five emerald arrowheads.[13]

The four naked travelers set off southward with Cebreros and the men of his party, but they soon discovered that Alcaraz had played a dirty trick on them. Cebreros and his associates led the travelers into arid, trackless terrain where they became lost in dense and thorny chaparral. After two days without water, seven of the Indian slaves in the party died of thirst. Cabeza de Vaca rued his own naïveté. He later learned that soon after he and his companions left Alcaraz's camp, the slaver resumed his regular practice of hunting for Indians. As a result, most of the indigenous people of the Río

Petatlán area again fled into the mountains. Cabeza de Vaca says the experience taught him "how much men's thoughts deceive them, for we went to them seeking liberty and when we thought we had it, it turned out to be so much to the contrary." He adds: "And in order to remove us from conversation with the Indians, they led us through areas depopulated and overgrown so that we would not see what they were doing nor their conduct, because they had conspired to go and attack the Indians whom we had sent away reassured and in peace." Again, and this time more directly, Cabeza de Vaca refers to himself and his companions as "we" and to the slavers as "they." Although he had not come to identify with the Indians, he was now finding it difficult to identify with his fellow Spaniards.[14]

Cebreros led the four travelers for twenty-five leagues through miserable and deserted country and then brought them to a village of Indians who had made peace with the Spaniards. Cebreros took leave of the travelers there and went on ahead to the Spanish settlement of San Miguel de Culiacán. He must have informed officials there of the reappearance of four survivors of the Narváez expedition, for Melchior Díaz, the *alcalde mayor* (chief magistrate) of Culiacán, soon marched out to meet them at the Indian village where they were resting. In his capacity as *alcalde mayor* and on behalf of Nuño Beltrán de Guzmán, the governor of Nueva Galicia, Díaz welcomed the travelers to the Culiacán area and offered them his hospitality. He listened attentively to their stories, and with them, he gave thanks to God for their deliverance from the wilderness. He admired a buffalo robe the men had brought with them, and he expressed displeasure when they told him of the treatment they and their Indian supporters had received from Alcaraz and his slave-hunters.[15]

Díaz must have valued, as Alcaraz had not, the skills that Cabeza de Vaca and his companions had acquired for communicating with Indians. The *alcalde mayor* wished to undo the damage that the slave-hunters had done to the local area. Most of the local Indians had retreated from their coastal villages into the Sierra Madre Occidental and, from there, were making war upon the Spaniards who were occupying their home territory. Díaz wanted to resettle the displaced Indians in their proper villages and to work out a cooperative arrangement whereby all might live together peacefully, since the Spanish settlers of Culiacán needed the foodstuffs that Indian farmers might supply. The *alcalde mayor* solicited the aid of the travelers and entreated them to invite the displaced Indians to a conference at the peaceful Indian village where the four men were staying. He had the wisdom not to suggest meeting the Indians at the Spanish settlement of San Miguel de Culiacán. Díaz promised the travelers that he would guarantee the safety of all Indians who took part in the conference.[16]

The four men were reluctant at first to undertake Díaz's task. Cabeza de Vaca seems to have wished to return as quickly as possible to Spain to report to Emperor Charles V on the fate of the Narváez expedition. He noted also that he and his companions had dismissed their Indian escorts at Alcaraz's camp, and they no longer had Indians with them who knew them in their capacity as healers. The only Indians who had accompanied them to Culiacán were Alcaraz's slaves. But two of these slaves, as it happened, were natives of the Culiacán area and were related to the displaced Indians with whom Díaz hoped to negotiate. The two slaves had been at Alcaraz's camp when Estevanico led Castillo, Dorantes, and six hundred Indians there from out of the hills. The two slaves had spoken with some of the six hundred and learned from them of the miraculous cures the Children of the Sun had performed. The slaves had also seen that the ceremonial gourd rattles the four men carried were the insignia of their authority. Cabeza de Vaca entrusted one of these rattles to the two slaves and sent them as messengers to muster their brethren in the hills. He also directed the slaves to return to the Río Petatlán area and to call out whatever Indians were attempting to resettle their villages there. Those Indians would recognize the rattles as a sign the slave messengers were acting on behalf of the Children of the Sun.[17]

After seven days the slave messengers returned to the village Díaz had chosen as the conference site. With them, the messengers brought eighteen Indians who, although indigenous to the Culiacán area, had been driven away from their homes by the slave-hunters. Three of the eighteen were chiefs among their people. The slave messengers reported, however, that they had been unable to find any Indians near the Río Petatlán, because Alcaraz had chased them all back into the hills.

Cabeza de Vaca and his companions communicated with the Indian conferees by means of signs and the trading language, Primahaitu, which they had learned in the course of their overland journey. They also made use of interpreters whom Díaz supplied. Díaz gave robes and other presents to the eighteen Indian conferees. The Children of the Sun probably flourished their gourd rattles, and the Indians, recognizing the four men as healers, gave them turquoises and plume feathers. The conference must have been conducted with great ceremony and with many pauses for translation back and forth. A Spanish *escribano* made an official record of the proceedings. The four healer-mediators told the Indians that they had come "on behalf of God who is in heaven" and had carried His message to the many people they had met in the course of a great journey that had lasted many years. Díaz called for a reading of the Requerimiento, thereby informing the Indian conferees that they were now subject to the pope and the Spanish crown. The healer-mediators called upon the Indian conferees to serve God and Emperor Charles V, who ruled over the three Spanish kingdoms of Castile, Aragón, and Navarra, and many other lands besides. They told the Indians that if they agreed to accept Christianity and to serve God and the emperor, the Spaniards of San Miguel de Culiacán would accept them as brothers and cease enslaving them. If they resisted, however, the Spaniards not only would enslave them but would send them to labor in faraway places.[18]

The Indian conferees listened attentively and responded that they were willing to serve the Spanish God and the Spanish emperor. They said they already gave reverence to a man in the sky called Aguar, who had created the world and made the rain to fall. The healer-mediators said that Aguar and the Christian God were one and the same and that henceforth, whenever the Indians wished to call upon Aguar, they should address him by his Spanish name, "Dios." The Indians agreed to do this. Then the Children of the Sun directed the Indians to bring their people down from the mountains, to repopulate their abandoned villages, and to live in peace with their Spanish brothers in San Miguel de Culiacán. The healers said that, in each of their villages, the Indians should set aside one building for use as a church and should mark this building with a cross. Whenever Spaniards came to their villages, the Indians should put aside their weapons and come out to greet them with crosses in their hands and food for both the Spaniards and their horses. In this way, the Spaniards would recognize the Indians as fellow Christians and as brothers. The Indians said they would do everything the healers directed, and Melchior Díaz, in his capacity as *alcalde mayor* of San Miguel de Culiacán, swore a solemn oath to prevent all those under his command from enslaving any Indians who accepted Christianity. The conference probably concluded with a banquet and the exchange of more presents. In a final gesture of beneficence, Díaz freed the two Indian slaves who had summoned the three chiefs and fifteen other Indians to the conference. These two former slaves then returned with the eighteen conferees to where their people were hiding in the mountains.[19]

Soon afterward a multitude of Indians came down from the highlands and reinhabited their villages. They quickly fulfilled their agreement to erect crosses, and many Indians brought their children to San Miguel de Culiacán to be baptized. Captain Alcaraz came into town and told Melchior Díaz that Indians were also repopulating the Río Petatlán area and building churches there. Díaz ordered Alcaraz to discontinue his slaving operations.[20]

Cabeza de Vaca had come to believe that if Spaniards were to succeed in pacifying the Indians of the New World, in securing their cooperation, and in converting them to Christianity, they must win the Indians with kindness rather than force. He had long dreamed of returning to Spain, and he hoped one day to advise the emperor that Spaniards must not enslave Indians, nor abuse them, nor drive them from their lands. The explorer dreamed also of succeeding Pánfilo de Narváez as governor of La Florida—the vast territory north of New Spain that he had reconnoitered. Cabeza de Vaca must have felt that he knew La Florida and its people better than any possible rival for Narváez's position and that he was the best-qualified person to establish a Spanish colonial government in the territory. He had proved that he had excellent negotiating skills, and the conference at Culiacán would henceforth be his model for how best to deal with Indians. The explorer knew it would be difficult, however, for a man like himself, who had come naked and empty-handed out of the wilderness, to impress the emperor with his worth and his ability to undertake new ventures on the crown's behalf. Convincing the emperor that La Florida deserved further Spanish investment would also be difficult.[21]

While he was in Culiacán, Cabeza de Vaca probably discussed Indian slavery with Melchior Díaz, and the *alcalde mayor* probably informed him about recent changes in Spanish law. Indian slavery had been outlawed by royal order in 1530, but in 1534 Charles V had again made it possible for Spaniards in two situations to own Indian slaves. The first situation was that the Spaniard had captured the Indian in the course of a war certified to be just. The second was that the Indian was already a slave to an Indian master, and the Spaniard had acquired him or her either through purchase or in lieu of tribute. Acquiring slaves in either of these ways was not difficult. On the one hand, Indians were frequently required to pay tribute to their Spanish overlords, and on the other, any Indians who resisted Spanish authority were inviting the Spaniards to make war upon them. In Nueva Galicia, for example, those Indians who had abandoned their homes, fled to the mountains, and taken up arms against the Spaniards were liable to be enslaved by any Spaniard who could capture them. Díaz's predecessor as *alcalde mayor* of Culiacán had been tried, convicted, and later pardoned for branding and selling Indian slaves.[22]

In any discussion between Díaz and Cabeza de Vaca about Indian slavery, the name of Nuño Beltrán de Guzmán must have come up. Guzmán, both in his present position as governor of Nueva Galicia and in his previous position as governor of Pánuco, had become notorious for his mistreatment of Indians. Cabeza de Vaca was probably already familiar with Guzmán's name. In 1525, two years before the Narváez expedition left Spain, the emperor had appointed Guzmán to be governor of Pánuco. Guzmán had left Spain in 1526 and assumed his duties in Pánuco in 1527.[23]

In 1528 Guzmán was appointed to preside over the first Audiencia of New Spain, and in 1531 he was appointed to govern Nueva Galicia. By the present year of 1536, he had become one of the most powerful men in New Spain and enjoyed nearly as much power as the newly appointed viceroy, Antonio de Mendoza, and as Hernán Cortés, now known as the Marqués del Valle de Oaxaca. But Guzmán had incurred the enmity of both Cortés and Juan de Zumárraga, the archbishop of New Spain. That the extent of Spanish-controlled territory on New Spain's northern frontier had grown so considerably during Cabeza de Vaca's eight years in the wilderness was partly due to Guzmán's boldness—or ruthlessness. Guzmán was responsible for the burned settlements Cabeza de Vaca and his companions had seen on their journey southward from the Río Yaqui to Alcaraz's camp on the Río Petatlán. Guzmán had founded the settlement of San Miguel de Culiacán in 1531 and had authorized its Spanish residents to take slaves, justifying his action on the ground that this was "a new land and the residents very much in debt."[24]

In the course of his earlier governorship in Pánuco, Guzmán had sent out slaving expeditions and exported captive Indians from his province to the islands of Cuba, Jamaica, and Hispaniola. Because the native Taínos on those islands had almost all died, slaves were in demand to work in Spanish gold mines and on Spanish plantations. Archbishop Zumárraga said of Guzmán in Pánuco: "When he began to govern this province, it contained 25,000 Indians, subjugated and peaceful. Of these he has sold 10,000 as slaves, and the others, fearing the same fate, have abandoned their villages." Zumárraga's estimate of 10,000 slaves may be high. Other records indicate that, from 20 August 1527 to 6 September 1529, some 5,800 Indian slaves were shipped under abominable conditions from Pánuco to the Caribbean Islands. Before shipment, most of these slaves, including children possibly as young as six, were branded on the face.[25]

In addition to Zumárraga, others who criticized Guzmán's policies were Bartolomé de las Casas and Gonzalo Fernández de Oviedo y Valdés. Oviedo would describe Guzmán as a governor "who came to be despised as quickly as any other." Las Casas would characterize him as a "butcher" who perpetrated "outrage upon outrage" during his term as governor of Pánuco. According to the historian, "[Guzmán] saw to the depopulation of the entire province, for he took to branding any number of free men as slaves, in the same way as we have seen others do before him, and bundling them on to vessel after vessel for transport to the island slave markets of Cuba and Hispaniola where they would fetch a better price. He also bartered one mare against eighty locals: against, that is, eighty members of the human race." Las Casas, like Zumárraga, may have inflated his numbers, for Guzmán is on record as having decreed that no one in Pánuco could exchange more than fifteen slaves for a horse.[26]

In 1528 Charles V had created the Audiencia of New Spain in order to shift power away from Hernán Cortés. The emperor appointed Guzmán to serve as the first president of the new administrative court. During his term as president, Guzmán made himself notorious by undertaking a brutal war of conquest and by executing a wealthy native lord, the Cazonci of Michoacán. The Cazonci had once been nearly as prominent as Aztec emperor Montezuma, and Michoacán had been one of the most powerful Indian polities in pre-Columbian Mexico.[27]

In May of 1529 Guzmán and the subordinate judges of the Audiencia declared war on the previously pacified people of Jalisco, who were resisting paying tribute to the Spaniards. Archbishop Zumárraga objected that the war Guzmán was about to launch would be unjust. Guzmán's chief concern, however, seems to have been that Michoacán lay between Jalisco and the Spanish-controlled city of México. In August, Guzmán summoned the Cazonci to México and held him hostage there while the native lord attempted to ransom himself with silver and gold. Guzmán was imitating Cortés, who had gained an advantage over the Aztecs by holding Montezuma as his hostage. In December, Guzmán departed from México en route to Jalisco, taking the Cazonci and some four hundred armed Spaniards with him. To force the native lord to give up more of his treasure, Guzmán had him tortured. According to Bartolomé de las Casas, the men who carried out Guzmán's orders placed the Cazonci in fetters, and "they then lit a brazier under the soles of his feet and had a lad with a hyssop filled with oil sprinkle them from time to time to ensure a nice even roasting." Las Casas continues: "On one side of the hapless victim stood one tormentor holding an armed crossbow pointed at his heart, while on the other stood a second holding a wild dog which constantly snapped at him and which would have torn him to pieces in the twinkling of an eye." Under torture, the Cazonci confessed to a variety of crimes against the Spaniards. Ultimately, Guzmán had him dragged behind a horse to a place of execution and then burned.[28]

After executing the Cazonci, Guzmán went on to Jalisco, which, according to Las Casas, was "one of the most fertile and wonderful parts of the New World" and "home to a huge number of people." There, Las Casas says: "[Guzmán] burned towns and cities to the ground, seized the local lords, torturing them and enslaving all those he could lay his hands upon. He led away thousands in chains, burdening women who had recently given birth with his baggage and that of his wicked companions so that, what with the huge loads they had to carry and the hunger they were forced to endure, they could no longer carry their children as well and were forced to leave them by the side of the road where they perished in huge numbers."[29]

After subduing Jalisco, Guzmán continued marching northward through Nayarit and into Sinaloa. He laid waste to much of the region, burning native settlements and pressing the inhabitants into slavery. He treated the Indians cruelly, placing some in chains and others in stocks. He took a thousand Indians with him to carry his baggage, and when he had no more use for them, he left many of them permanently stranded in places far from their homes. By 1531 he had gained control of the Pacific coastal plain all the way from Jalisco to the Culiacán valley. The area Guzmán had conquered became known as the province of Nueva Galicia, and he was named its governor. He immediately founded four Spanish settlements in the province, including San Miguel de Culiacán on its northern frontier and Compostela, its capital, in Jalisco.[30]

Hernán Cortés claimed that Guzmán had devastated parts of Nueva Galicia that he, Cortés, previously had pacified. In 1533 Guzmán sent an expedition northward from Culiacán that penetrated as far into Sonora as the Río Yaqui. At that time the country between Culiacán and the Río Yaqui was dotted with twenty to twenty-five Indian villages, each with one to three hundred houses made from straw mats. One Spaniard who participated in the 1533 expedition observed that the Indians living between Culiacán and the Río Yaqui were great archers and cultivated maize, beans, melons, and a kind of seed they made into bread. But when Cabeza de Vaca traveled southward through the same area in 1536, he observed that many of the villages had been burned and the country was deserted. Captain Diego de Alcaraz, whom Cabeza de Vaca met at the Río Petatlán, had participated in Guzmán's conquest of Nueva Galicia.[31]

Compostela, Guzmán's capital, was one hundred leagues south of Culiacán on the main route to México, the capital of the viceroyalty. If Cabeza de Vaca was ever to get home to Spain, he would have to go by way of Compostela and meet Guzmán face-to-face. Melchior Díaz, the *alcalde mayor* of Culiacán, warned Cabeza de Vaca that the journey to Compostela would be dangerous. All the country between Culiacán and Compostela was depopulated because its native people had abandoned their settlements and were at war with Guzmán and the Spaniards. Díaz advised Cabeza de Vaca and his companions to delay their departure for Compostela until they could travel with a large party of armed men.[32]

The four men did as Díaz advised and remained in Culiacán until 15 May. They traveled under the protection of twenty Spanish horsemen for the first forty leagues of their journey and with six Spaniards and five hundred Indian slaves for the remaining sixty leagues to Compostela. It must have saddened Cabeza de Vaca to see so many slaves. In the course of their long journey from the Gulf of Mexico, he and his companions had encountered no hostile Indians until they arrived in Nueva Galicia.[33]

When the survivors of the Narváez expedition arrived in Compostela, probably in June, they were welcomed to the provincial capital by Governor Nuño Beltrán de Guzmán. He was anxious to learn whatever the four men could tell him about the territories on the northern frontier of his province. In one of his first gestures of hospitality, he presented each of the naked travelers with a new suit of European-style clothing. He then accommodated the four men in quarters furnished with European-style beds. Several days passed before Cabeza de Vaca could tolerate wearing his new clothes. He and his companions, who long had been used to sleeping on the ground, also found it difficult to readjust to beds.[34]

Cabeza de Vaca was too prudent to criticize a powerful man like Guzmán openly. And yet the governor must have annoyed him in much the same way as the slave-hunter Alcaraz had done. In the reports he would give to

Viceroy Antonio de Mendoza and to Emperor Charles V, Cabeza de Vaca would confine himself to describing the devastation he had witnessed in Nueva Galicia, without ascribing responsibility to Guzmán. The explorer would manage, nevertheless, to contrast his own actions with those of the governor. He had seen the effects of Guzmán's 1530–33 expedition of conquest. Between the Río Yaqui and the Río Petatlán, he had seen burned and deserted villages and spoken with terrorized Indians, and from San Miguel de Culiacán to Compostela, he had seen deserted land whose indigenous inhabitants were engaging in guerrilla war with the Spaniards. But at Culiacán, Cabeza de Vaca had negotiated a peace treaty for Melchior Díaz with a group of displaced Indians. Thus, whereas Guzmán's ruthlessness had led to the depopulation of large areas of Nueva Galicia, Cabeza de Vaca had succeeded in pacifying and resettling some of the Indians Guzmán had driven away.[35]

After spending ten to twelve days in Compostela as Guzmán's guests, Cabeza de Vaca and his companions set off for the city of México. As it happened, Guzmán was enjoying his last days of power. On 20 January 1537 he would be arrested and subjected to a *residencia* regarding his governorship of Nueva Galicia. Following that inquiry into his official conduct, he would spend more than eighteen months as a prisoner in México and then be recalled to Spain, where he would remain under house arrest for the rest of his life.[36]

The distance from Compostela to México was some 120 leagues. To Cabeza de Vaca and his companions, this last stage of their great journey must have seemed like a victory lap. The four men quickly perceived that they had gained celebrity status, and they may have shed their European clothing to dramatize their identity as survivors of the Narváez expedition. Cabeza de Vaca noted that many Spaniards "came out to see us along the roads and gave thanks to God our Lord for having delivered us from so many dangers." The travelers arrived in México on Sunday, 23 July 1536. To get to the city from where their overland journey began on the central Texas coast, they must have walked at least 2,500 miles and perhaps as many as 2,800. Cabeza de Vaca estimated that in the long course of their travels "by land and through the sea on the rafts and another ten months that we went through the land without stopping once we were no longer captives," they had covered two thousand leagues.[37]

México, the capital of New Spain and the seat of its viceroy, was located in a shallow basin ringed by mountains, including the twin volcanoes of

Popocatepetl and Iztaccihuatl. The Spaniards were raising a new Spanish city on the ruins of the Aztec one they had destroyed. Cortés had built a fortress, a defensive wall, and a series of watchtowers. Other new buildings included churches, monasteries, and many adobe houses.[38]

The Narváez expedition survivors were welcomed to the city by Viceroy Antonio de Mendoza and Hernán Cortés. The two great men extended their hospitality to the travelers and presented them with new clothing. Again Cabeza de Vaca must have marveled at the changes that had taken place during the years he had been out of contact with the Spanish world. The office of viceroy was a new one, and Mendoza, a high-ranking Castilian nobleman, was the first man to serve in the position. He had assumed his viceregal duties late in 1535, only months before Cabeza de Vaca arrived in the capital city. Cortés had been in Spain at the time the Narváez expedition left Cuba, and his career at that point was in decline. After defeating the Aztecs in 1522, Cortés had received a royal appointment as governor, captain general, and chief judge of New Spain. But in 1526 he was subjected to a *residencia*, his governorship was suspended, and he was recalled to Spain. Emperor Charles V subsequently elevated Cortés to the nobility, granting him the title of Marqués del Valle de Oaxaca, but he never restored the conquistador to his office as governor. Instead, the emperor vested authority first in the Audiencia of New Spain and then in its new viceroy.[39]

Perhaps the most earthshaking of all the changes that had occurred during Cabeza de Vaca's absence was that Francisco Pizarro had conquered Peru in 1532 and seized the wealth of the Incas. If Cabeza de Vaca hadn't learned of this already in Culiacán or Compostela, he must have learned it soon after arriving in the capital.[40]

On 25 July, two days after arriving in México, the Narváez expedition survivors joined in celebrating the annual festival of Santiago, the patron saint of Spain. When the four men appeared in the city's principal church, they wore only the deerskins in which they had traveled; the skins covered their private parts but little else. After the religious services, the four probably joined in games, feasting, drinking, and dancing. Bernal Díaz del Castillo, who attended similar festivities in México in 1538, said the fiestas were grander than anything he had seen in Spain. Viceroy Mendoza and the Marqués del Valle de Oaxaca cosponsored bullfights, jousting games, and other lavish spectacles. The jousting games, which involved two opposing teams, had originated among the Muslims of Spain and North Africa.

As the game was played in New Spain, one team dressed as Christians and the other as Moors. Each player was mounted and armed with a shield and a flexible wooden lance, which was not designed to do serious harm. The teams would process into the plaza where the contest was to be staged, then face each other from opposite sides of the square, charge forward at full tilt, and hurl their lances at one another. Spectators judged the players on their skills with the lance and shield and on their horsemanship.[41]

Among those who saw Cabeza de Vaca and his companions standing nearly naked in church on the feast day of Santiago was Alonso de la Barrera, who had sailed to La Florida with Narváez but remained with the ships when the ill-fated governor and the three hundred men of his overland party set off into the Florida interior. At least two other men who had stayed with the ships were now also in the city of México. From these other veterans of the Narváez expedition, Cabeza de Vaca learned that the men and women of the maritime party had searched for nearly a year up and down the Florida coast for the men of the overland party, and during that time they had found a great bay near Narváez's initial landing site. This body of water was one hundred leagues from Havana, Cuba, and many scholars believe it was Tampa Bay.[42]

Soon after their arrival in the capital, Cabeza de Vaca and his companions spoke lengthily with Viceroy Mendoza, Hernán Cortés, and Archbishop Zumárraga. Mendoza and Cortés wanted information about the lands the four travelers had explored. Cortés had already sent three maritime expeditions up the Pacific coast beyond the Spanish frontier. In the course of the third of these expeditions, he had laid claim to what now is known as Baja California. In 1539, after his talks with the survivors of the Narváez expedition, Cortés would send out a fourth expedition that would map both coasts of the Gulf of California and determine that Baja California was a peninsula.[43]

Cabeza de Vaca spoke with Archbishop Zumárraga about his dealings with Indians. Following these conversations, Zumárraga would write a treatise opposing the enslavement of Indians and using "the experience of those who came with Narváez" as a positive example of how to win Indians to cooperate with Spaniards. As it happened, Zumárraga would not be the only clergyman to point approvingly to the men "who came with Narváez." The great champion of Indian rights, Fray Bartolomé de las Casas would, in his *Apologética historia sumaria*, cite Cabeza de Vaca as an authority on negotiating productively and peacefully with Indians. Cabeza de Vaca would note, in his reports to Viceroy Mendoza and Emperor Charles V, that during the eight years he had spent in North America, he had seen no idolatry and no instances of human sacrifice. He would make a special point of this, for he knew that idolatry and sacrifice could provide grounds for Spaniards to enslave Indians.[44]

Viceroy Mendoza asked the three hidalgos among the Narváez expedition survivors to prepare both a report of their experiences and a map of the lands they had seen. They complied with both requests, but neither the report nor the map has survived. In providing the information, they encountered a problem. If they said too little, they risked losing Mendoza's attention and assistance. If they said too much, they risked triggering a mad rush of conquistadors into the lands they had reconnoitered. And yet, in choosing to work within the Spanish official system, the hidalgos had already determined their priorities. News of their return would spread quickly across New Spain and inspire many Spaniards to try to capitalize on the information they had gathered.[45]

As it happened, the hidalgos probably said too much. Or perhaps, as he listened to their testimony, Mendoza heard what he wanted to hear. Undoubtedly, many Spaniards who heard about their testimony at second hand allowed their imaginations to run wild. Pedro de Castañeda de Nájera, a chronicler of the Coronado expedition, reported that Cabeza de Vaca, Dorantes, and Castillo created false expectations by telling "the good Don Antonio de Mendoza how, through the lands they had traversed, they obtained interpreters and important information regarding powerful pueblos with houses four or five stories high, and other things quite different from what turned out to be the truth."[46]

The hidalgos told Mendoza about the Indians of the maize villages who lived in permanent houses and cultivated squash, beans, and cotton as well as maize. They told him what they had heard about the people who lived in large, permanent villages in the mountains in the north, had copper and turquoises, and engaged in long-distance trade. They told him about mineral resources in the lands they had explored. Dorantes, they said, had been given both a copper bell and five "emerald" arrowheads. Cabeza de Vaca said he had heard from Indian informants that pearls could be found on the coast of the "South Sea." He reported that in the mountains between Corazones and the Río Petatlán he and his companions had found evidence of "gold and antimony, iron, copper, and other metals." In the same region, he said, they had seen "signs of mines of gold and silver."[47]

To Viceroy Mendoza, the information about the advanced Indian societies in the maize villages and in the mountains to their north was probably the most remarkable news the survivors of the Narváez expedition provided. The viceroy may have imagined that these societies were as wealthy as those of the Aztecs and the Incas. At any rate, he resolved to explore the country the travelers described. Cabeza de Vaca said the Indian settlement of Corazones, where Dorantes had received the emerald arrowheads, was the gateway to the prosperous region in the north. Beyond Corazones, he said, were "more than a thousand leagues of populated land."[48]

Even though no copies now exist, the report that Cabeza de Vaca, Castillo, and Dorantes prepared for Viceroy Mendoza in 1536 is known by scholars today as the *Joint Report*. The three hidalgos probably gave verbal testimony before an *escribano* who transcribed their first-person narratives into the third person of an official written report. The information the three provided came solely from their memories, for they had had no means to make records along their way. Cabeza de Vaca, as royal treasurer of the Narváez expedition and the highest-ranking of its survivors, seems to have provided most of the information. Dorantes seems to have added information about events that occurred in Texas during the time he lived apart from Cabeza de Vaca. Castillo may have provided additional information, or he may simply have confirmed with his signature that what his colleagues said was true.[49]

Several copies of the *Joint Report* seem to have been made, and although none has come down to us, the report served as the source for the surviving accounts of the Narváez expedition. Viceroy Mendoza is known to have had one copy of the *Joint Report* and to have sent it to Emperor Charles V. Cabeza de Vaca must have retained a second copy and used it as a basis for his 1542 *Relación*. He sent a third copy to the Audiencia of Santo Domingo, which turned it over to Oviedo. The royal historian used this copy as the source for the account of the Narváez expedition that he included in his *Historia general y natural de las Indias*.[50]

Oviedo seems to have copied the material of the *Joint Report* in much the form that he found it, and then to have interpolated commentary of his own. He remarked, for example, on the fate of Pánfilo de Narváez and his unfortunate armada, saying: "Things of great grief and sadness occurred, and even miracles were worked by the few who escaped or survived after having suffered innumerable shipwrecks and dangers, as can be gathered from the story that was sent to this Royal Audiencia resident in this city of

Santo Domingo by the three *hidalgos* named Álvar Núñez Cabeza de Vaca, Andrés Dorantes and Alonzo del Castillo." Oviedo's account is in the third person, as the *Joint Report* must also have been. The royal historian's text provides some details not present in Cabeza de Vaca's *Relación*, especially concerning the experiences of Dorantes. Oviedo's text also provides a kind of check upon the *Relación*, for although Dorantes and Castillo as well as Cabeza de Vaca attested to the *Joint Report*'s accuracy, the two captains had no part in substantiating the *Relación*. Any detail that appears in the *Relación* and not in Oviedo's account is therefore open to question. Oviedo preferred the *Joint Report* to the *Relación*, noting: "I take as being valid the account given by the three. It is clearer than the other, which only one of them made and had printed."[51]

In the fall of 1536, after he spoke with the Narváez expedition survivors and read the report the three hidalgos had composed, Viceroy Mendoza tried to persuade at least one of them to lead a new expedition to the prosperous region north of Corazones. In a letter to Emperor Charles V, Mendoza wrote that one of the men might "render great service to your Majesty if he were sent with forty or fifty horsemen to lay bare the mysteries of that region." Mendoza probably offered Cabeza de Vaca the opportunity to serve the emperor in that way, but if so, the erstwhile royal treasurer declined. Leading a reconnaissance force of fifty horsemen was not, for him, a sufficiently attractive proposition. Cabeza de Vaca must have known, moreover, that Mendoza's power to sponsor an exploratory expedition was limited. The explorer seems to have wanted his next commission to come directly from Charles V. A royal commission, Cabeza de Vaca must have calculated, would give him more authority than one from the emperor's viceroy.[52]

ELEVEN

Further Explorations

In October of 1536, after he had rested in the city of México for two months, Cabeza de Vaca attempted to return to Spain. Before leaving Spain nine years earlier, he had received instructions to inform the emperor "extensively and particularly of every matter." So he was now duty bound to report to Charles V on what he knew concerning the Narváez expedition. According to a Portuguese gentleman who met Cabeza de Vaca in 1537 in Spain, the explorer was hoping to persuade the emperor to appoint him to succeed Narváez as governor of La Florida. Among the items Cabeza de Vaca gathered to take with him on his homeward journey were at least one and probably two copies of the *Joint Report* that he, Castillo, and Dorantes had recently completed. The former royal treasurer traveled sixty-six leagues from the capital of New Spain to Veracruz, the principal port on its gulf coast, and booked passage on a ship. But before he could embark, a storm capsized the vessel. Having then no choice but to overwinter in New Spain, he returned to its capital city.[1]

On 11 February 1537, Viceroy Antonio de Mendoza wrote to the emperor expressing the hope that the Narváez expedition survivors would be rewarded suitably for the services they had performed. The viceroy noted that he had already sent the emperor a copy of the *Joint Report* the men had prepared, and that Cabeza de Vaca and Dorantes would shortly be sailing to Spain in order to report to the emperor directly. Apparently, Castillo had no desire either to return to Spain or to engage in further explorations of

North America. Viceroy Mendoza had already arranged a marriage for him to a wealthy widow.[2]

Cabeza de Vaca returned to Veracruz with Dorantes during the Lenten season. At the seaport, they found three ships bound for Spain, and they booked passage on one of them. The ships would sail in convoy for greater security. French privateers preyed on Spanish shipping, with the approval of the French government, and many Spanish vessels had been lost to the corsairs. The two explorers waited through Easter for a favorable wind, but when the ship upon which they were to sail began to take on water, Cabeza de Vaca transferred to the more seaworthy of its sister ships. On 10 April 1537 the three ships left Veracruz, with Cabeza de Vaca a passenger on one and Dorantes on another. The three ships kept together for 150 leagues, but two of them leaked so badly that they were forced to return to Veracruz. Cabeza de Vaca's ship alone went forward.[3]

On 4 May, Cabeza de Vaca's ship anchored at Havana, Cuba. Because of the access it afforded to the Florida Straits and the Gulf Stream, Havana had become an important port, and most Spanish ships bound for Spain from the Caribbean stopped there to take on food and supplies. Cabeza de Vaca and his shipmates waited at Havana almost a month, hoping their two sister ships would catch up, but they never did. Their own ship was carrying gold and silver worth 300,000 *castellanos* (the equivalent of at least 135 million *maravedíes*), and its captain hesitated to cross the Atlantic alone. A few weeks earlier, a French privateer had boldly entered Havana's harbor and looted three Spanish ships.[4]

While in Havana, Cabeza de Vaca sent a copy of the *Joint Report* to the Audiencia of Santo Domingo, the Spanish administrative court on the nearby island of Hispaniola. Because the Audiencia had jurisdiction over the northern rim of the Gulf of Mexico and La Florida, Cabeza de Vaca, as the senior-surviving officer of the Narváez expedition, was accountable to the court and owed it a report. The Audiencia subsequently turned its copy of the *Joint Report* over to Gonzalo Fernández Oviedo y Valdés, the royal historian of the Indies, who resided in Santo Domingo.[5]

On 2 June the ship on which Cabeza de Vaca had booked passage left Havana and set its course for Spain. The explorer must have regretted sailing without Dorantes, but he may have persuaded himself that his friend would meet him in Spain later that year. Cabeza de Vaca's ship was caught in a storm off Bermuda but weathered it and sailed on. Then, twenty nine days after leaving Havana, as the ship was nearing the Portuguese-controlled

Azores, it was confronted by a French privateer. The French captain had already captured a Portuguese slave ship and used it as well as his own vessel to menace the captain and crew of the Spanish ship. Toward evening, the Spaniards caught sight of nine additional sails but were unable to determine whether the distant ships were friends or foes. When night fell, the French privateer was within cannon range of the Spanish ship and could easily have captured it, but its captain put off doing so until daylight. At sunrise, Cabeza de Vaca and his shipmates found themselves very close to the nine ships they had spotted the previous evening, and these proved to be a Portuguese armada. In view of the overwhelming opposition, the French privateer released its captive Portuguese slave ship, put out oars, and hastened away. The Portuguese armada, however, mistook Cabeza de Vaca's Spanish vessel for another French privateer and prepared to do battle. The captain of the Spanish ship quickly saluted the armada and identified himself as a friend. The Portuguese fleet commander then offered the Spanish ship his protection and escorted it onward to Terceira, in the Azores. Cabeza de Vaca and his shipmates rested at the island for fifteen days.[6]

While they sojourned at Terceira, a ship arrived there from the Spanish province of Río de la Plata in South America. Pedro de Mendoza, the provincial governor, had been returning to Spain to seek assistance for his colony but had died at sea before reaching the Azores. Cabeza de Vaca spoke with some of the men who had been traveling with Mendoza, but he cannot have guessed that Río de la Plata would soon become important to him personally.[7]

The explorer and his shipmates sailed from Terceira to Portugal under the protection of the Portuguese armada and arrived in Lisbon on 9 August 1537. From there, Cabeza de Vaca made his way to Spain. He must have rejoined his wife, but we can only speculate about the character of the relationship the two were able to reestablish after their ten-year separation.[8]

That autumn, Cabeza de Vaca must have attended to his domestic and financial affairs and worked on the report he planned to present to the emperor. He had probably retained a copy of the *Joint Report* to use as an outline for the longer and more detailed account of the Narváez expedition that he was now endeavoring to prepare. Judging from the finished *Relación* he published in 1542, he seems to have had several goals in mind. Because he was actively seeking a new royal appointment, he strove to document the services he had already performed for the crown. He strove also to portray himself as a man of sound judgment, worthy of the emperor's trust, and therefore tried to absolve himself of any possible blame for the expedition's failure. Finally, he tried to persuade the emperor that the best way to induce the Indians to accept Christ and the dominion of the Spanish crown was to treat them justly and with kindness.[9]

In October of 1537, Cabeza de Vaca and his cousin Pedro Estopiñán Cabeza de Vaca prepared a *probanza* (notarized testimonial) concerning the services performed by their grandfather, Pedro de Vera. It was not uncommon for a vassal to petition his overlord for rewards or preferment that ought to have gone to a deserving ancestor. To Álvar Núñez Cabeza de Vaca, the services Pedro de Vera had performed for the Catholic Kings in conquering the island of Gran Canaria may have seemed more obviously worthy of reward than any service he personally had performed for Charles V in North America.[10]

At some point after his return to Spain, however, Cabeza de Vaca must have learned he had no hope of using either the record of his services on the Narváez expedition or the record of his grandfather's services in Gran Canaria in any campaign to win the governorship of La Florida. That governorship had already been granted to Hernando de Soto. On 20 April 1537, De Soto had received a royal contract authorizing him to "conquer and settle" La Florida, including all the lands between the Río de las Palmas and the tip of the Florida Peninsula. Ironically, De Soto received his *capitulaciones* just ten days after Cabeza de Vaca departed from Veracruz on his homeward voyage to Spain. The news of the emperor's contract with De Soto must have dismayed Cabeza de Vaca, and he must bitterly have regretted the circumstances that had prevented him from reaching Spain sooner. But he likely would not have competed effectively with De Soto in any case. De Soto was enormously rich, and to the cash-strapped Emperor Charles V, money was very persuasive.[11]

De Soto had participated in the conquest of Peru and had collected 180,000 *cruzados* (or the equivalent of 67.5 million *maravedíes*) as his share of the Inca treasures. He had served the crown in the Indies since 1513, when, at about the age of fourteen, he had gone with the expedition of Pedrárias de Ávila to Castilla del Oro, or modern-day Panama. Later, in Nicaragua, De Soto became wealthy through trafficking in Indian slaves. As a lieutenant to Francisco Pizarro in 1532, De Soto played a key role in the capture of the Inca emperor Atahualpa. De Soto returned to Spain in 1536 to marry a daughter of Pedrárias de Ávila and to seek a royal appointment to govern Quito or Guatemala or some other Spanish province in the New World. When he arrived at the Spanish royal court, De Soto spent his money lavishly. Charles V rewarded him by appointing him governor of Cuba and granting him the contract he had given more than a decade earlier to Pánfilo de Narváez. De Soto agreed to conquer and settle La Florida at his own expense. According to two of the chroniclers of his expedition, he spent most of the loot he had taken from Peru on his Florida enterprise.[12]

On 8 November 1537, seven months after De Soto received his *capitulaciones*, Cabeza de Vaca was summoned to appear at the royal court to report on "all the things he had seen and learned about the province of *Florida*." Emperor Charles V was residing in Valladolid in late 1537, so Cabeza de Vaca presented himself in that city.[13]

At the time of his arrival in Valladolid, the anonymous Portuguese *caballero* referred to as the Gentleman of Elvas was also at the Spanish royal court. The Gentleman would journey to La Florida with De Soto and become one of the principal chroniclers of his expedition. In his account of that venture, the Gentleman reports that Cabeza de Vaca came to the Spanish court with "a written relation of what he had seen in Florida." Perhaps this written relation was the *Joint Report* he had coauthored with Dorantes and Castillo. More likely, it was the revised report he had been working on since his return to Spain. When De Soto and his associates asked Cabeza de Vaca about La Florida, the explorer said: "Most of what I saw there I leave for discussion between myself and his Majesty." He had, according to the Gentleman of Elvas, made a pact with Andrés Dorantes "not to divulge certain things which they had seen," because the two men were hoping to return to La Florida and Cabeza de Vaca had come "to Spain to beg the government from the emperor." The explorer described "the wretchedness of the land and the hardships he had suffered," but according to the Gentleman of Elvas, he indicated to two of his kinsmen who were considering going to La Florida that "it was the richest land in the world" and that they should sell their patrimonies and go with De Soto, "for in so doing they would act wisely." When Cabeza de Vaca met at last with Charles V and delivered his report, its substance leaked out. According to the Gentleman of Elvas, the explorer told the emperor that "he had found cotton cloth, [and] he had seen gold and silver and precious gems of much value." Cabeza de Vaca's report and his general behavior, the Portuguese gentleman asserts, stimulated so much interest in La Florida that more men clamored to sail with De Soto than the commander could accommodate.[14]

According to the Gentleman of Elvas, De Soto offered a position on his staff to Cabeza de Vaca, who considered accepting it but ultimately declined. He told his kinsmen that "if he had given up going with De Soto, it was because he expected to ask for another government and did not wish to go under the banner of another." He had already gone to La Florida under the banner of Pánfilo de Narváez and had suffered the consequences of the commander's foolish decisions. He had declined to explore the North American wilderness under the banner of Viceroy Mendoza. He wished to return to the New World under his own banner.[15]

Cabeza de Vaca gave De Soto some information, however, about the parts of La Florida he had explored. In particular, he told De Soto about the large bay on the Gulf coast of the Florida peninsula one hundred leagues north of Havana and about the availability of maize in Apalachee territory. De Soto seems to have decided on the basis of this information to land his fleet on Florida's Gulf coast and to visit the Apalachee chiefdom. Cabeza de Vaca told De Soto about the hunger Narváez and his men experienced in La Florida, and this information seems to have prompted De Soto to take pigs with him to North America. Cabeza de Vaca must have told De Soto that Indians had perceived him and his companions as *hijos del sol*, or Children of the Sun, for De Soto subsequently represented himself to Indians as the son of the sun.[16]

On 7 April 1538, De Soto set sail for the New World from Sanlúcar de Barrameda, the same port from which Pánfilo de Narváez had departed eleven years earlier. Cabeza de Vaca, meanwhile, must have returned to Jerez de la Frontera to resume writing his account of his North American adventures.[17]

De Soto, like Narváez before him, left Sanlúcar with approximately six hundred men. But whereas Narváez sailed in five caravels, De Soto had nine or ten ships. He took along more than two hundred horses and thirteen pregnant sows. The pigs multiplied so that they numbered three hundred within a few months of his arrival in Florida, and they provided his men amply with bacon. Like Narváez before him, De Soto sailed from Spain to the Canary Islands and then Cuba, arriving there on 7 June 1538. Since Charles V had appointed him governor of Cuba, De Soto planned to use the island as a base from which to explore the North American mainland, and he would sojourn in Cuba for nearly a year before proceeding to

La Florida. He learned while in Cuba that Viceroy Antonio de Mendoza was preparing to mount an overland expedition from New Spain to the territory that the Narváez expedition survivors had reconnoitered.[18]

Much had happened in New Spain since Cabeza de Vaca's departure from the viceroyalty. After failing to reach Havana, Andrés Dorantes returned to Veracruz. While there, he received a letter from Viceroy Mendoza, offering him the opportunity to lead an expedition to the country north of Nueva Galicia, but Dorantes declined the commission. Perhaps he was honoring his pact with Cabeza de Vaca to wait for the emperor to authorize them to return to La Florida together. In 1539 Viceroy Mendoza wrote to the emperor, reporting that he had consulted with Dorantes many times about the prospective expedition, without persuading him, adding, "[I have] spent considerable money in providing what was necessary for his journey, and I do not know how it was that the plan fell through and the undertaking was abandoned." Despite his disappointment, Mendoza arranged for Dorantes to marry a wealthy widow.[19]

In the end, both Dorantes and Alonso del Castillo settled permanently in New Spain. What is known about their later lives derives from *probanzas* attesting to various services they performed for the viceroy and the Spanish crown. In the case of Dorantes, another source of information is a report written in 1604 by his son, Baltasar. Andrés Dorantes became master of a prosperous *encomienda* in Atzalán-Mexcalcingo, near Veracruz and Mexico's Gulf coast. The *encomienda* was worked by 1,608 Indians and consisted of a central hacienda and six satellite farms that produced cotton, honey, beans, chickens, fish, and maize. Dorantes and his wife became parents to one son and three daughters. The veteran of the Narváez expedition fought under the banner of Viceroy Mendoza in the Mixton War of 1541–42. He died, probably in New Spain, sometime in or before 1560.[20]

Castillo became master of an *encomienda* in Tehuacán, an area about a hundred miles southeast of the city of México. He lived in the capital city with his wife and their daughters and held various administrative and judicial positions there. On 3 December 1547, Castillo filed a *probanza* in support of his application to serve on the city's municipal council, but the application was denied. There are no further records concerning Castillo.[21]

Since all three of the Spaniards who survived the Narváez expedition refused to undertake additional reconnaissance for Mendoza, the viceroy turned to the expedition's fourth survivor. In a 1539 letter to Charles V, Mendoza reported: "I retained a negro who had come with Dorantes."

According to Francisco Vázquez de Coronado in a letter of 15 July 1539, Mendoza purchased Estevanico. According to another source, Mendoza offered Dorantes five hundred pesos for his slave, but Dorantes refused the money and presented Estevanico to the viceroy as a gift. We can only guess at what Estevanico thought of the transaction, but he was to play a more prominent role in history than either Dorantes or Castillo. Mendoza described Estevanico as a "persona de razón" (person of reason), but although he employed the African as a guide, he did not appoint him to lead the reconnaissance party he was preparing to send northward. Instead, Mendoza gave the lead position to a Franciscan friar, Marcos de Niza.[22]

Fray Marcos had previously served the Spanish crown in Guatemala and Peru. He had witnessed the conquest of the Inca Empire and acquired some knowledge of "cosmography and navigation." On 20 November 1538, Viceroy Mendoza issued written instructions to Fray Marcos, directing him to "penetrate the land in the interior." The friar was to leave from the settlement of San Miguel de Culiacán, which was still the northernmost Spanish settlement in Nueva Galicia, and head northward, reversing the route of the survivors of the Narváez expedition. Mendoza referred to Estevanico by the surname of his former master, instructing Fray Marcos to "take along Esteban de Dorantes as guide" and commanding the African to obey the friar. Mendoza also directed Francisco Vázquez de Coronado, the acting governor of Nueva Galicia, to provide Fray Marcos with Indian porters and guides. The friar left Culiacán on 7 March 1539.[23]

Fray Marcos says that Indians called him Sayota, or "man from heaven," and came to him to be healed. He celebrated Easter at a place he called Vacapa, which he says was forty leagues from the sea. From Vacapa, he sent Estevanico northward, instructing him to explore the country fifty to sixty leagues ahead. Since the African could not read or write, Fray Marcos told him that if he found anything of moderate interest, he was to send the friar a small cross, the size of the span between a man's outstretched thumb and forefinger. If he found something of greater interest, he was to send a cross the size of two spans. And if he found something truly stupendous, he was to send a large cross and to come in person to tell the friar what he had seen. According to Fray Marcos, Estevanico took some Indians with him, plus two greyhounds from Castile and a quantity of trade goods. The African carried a gourd rattle, as he had done on his journey from Texas with Cabeza de Vaca, Castillo, and Dorantes. Fray Marcos says that "the gourd had some strings of jingle bells, and two feathers, one white and the other red."

Hernando de Alarcón, who participated in the 1540 Coronado expedition, says Estevanico "wore bells, and feathers on his ankles and arms, and carried plates of various colors."[24]

Four days after Estevanico left Vacapa, Fray Marcos received messengers from him bearing a cross the size of a man. The messengers said Estevanico had heard reports of seven large and wealthy cities in a land called Cíbola, where the houses were built of limestone, three and four stories high, and terraced like a wedding cake, and the doorways of the richest houses were decorated with turquoise. The messengers urged the friar to set out at once to follow his African guide.[25]

Fray Marcos left Vacapa two days after Easter, spent three days on the road, and then met the Indians who had informed Estevanico about the seven cities. They estimated the friar could reach the first of the seven in thirty days. Estevanico had not waited for him as directed, but had pressed forward, no doubt enjoying his freedom from a European master. The African and the Indians of his advance party seem to have been traveling rapidly, whereas the friar paused often to rest, to talk to Indians, and to perform various religious duties. After four or five more days of travel, Fray Marcos came to a pueblo where the people were dressed in cotton robes and bedecked in turquoises. They presented him with deer, rabbits, quail, maize, piñon nuts, buffalo hides, and some finely crafted pottery bowls. The friar claims that, like Cabeza de Vaca before him, he refused to keep anything.[26]

The Indians told Fray Marcos that Cíbola had houses ten stories high. They said he was marching on a course parallel to the coast of the nearby sea. But after pursuing this course through an unpopulated region for four or five more days, the friar met people who told him that the coast had turned sharply westward. He says he went to verify this, found it was so, and measured the latitude, calculating it to be thirty-five degrees. Thirty five degrees, however, is approximately the latitude of present-day Flagstaff, Arizona, and Albuquerque, New Mexico. The Gulf of California reaches its northern limit at approximately thirty-two degrees.[27]

Fray Marcos continued following after Estevanico, who from time to time sent him additional large crosses. On 9 May the friar entered another unpopulated region. Twelve days later he encountered an Indian whom he knew to have been with Estevanico. The Indian was drenched in sweat and appeared very agitated. He told Fray Marcos that when Estevanico and the Indians of his advance party were one day short of the first city of Cíbola, the African sent messengers ahead with his gourd, as he had learned to do while traveling with Cabeza de Vaca, Castillo, and Dorantes. When the messengers arrived in the first city, they showed the gourd to its chief. He seized it angrily, threw it to the ground, and ordered the messengers to leave his city, threatening that if they or anyone in their party returned, he would kill them all.[28]

When the messengers rejoined Estevanico and told him of the chief's threats, the African appeared unperturbed. He continued onward to Cíbola, but when he arrived there, its people took away all his trade goods and shut him in a large house. They held him and his supporters there all night, without giving them anything to eat or drink. The Indian who gave Fray Marcos this information had managed to slip away and conceal himself. In the morning, from his place of concealment, he saw Estevanico fleeing, pursued by men from Cíbola who were shooting arrows at him. The Indian did not see what happened to Estevanico, but he knew that many of the Indians in the African's advance party were killed.

When he heard this news, Fray Marcos claimed, "I feared not so much to lose my life as not to be able to return and report on the greatness of the country, where God, our Lord, can be so well served, His holy faith exalted, and the royal patrimony of his Majesty increased." The friar distributed trade goods to his Indian supporters, no doubt to ensure their loyalty, and continued on his journey. In a short time, he met two other Indians who had been with Estevanico. They were wounded and bloodstained, and although they could not say for certain whether Estevanico was dead, they believed he was. They said Cíbola was one day away.[29]

Fray Marcos withdrew for an hour and a half to pray. He told his Indian companions that he was determined to see Cíbola, and he would later assert that he got close enough to the city to see that it was on a plain at the foot of a hill and that its houses were terraced, had flat roofs, and were built of stone. He would later tell Viceroy Mendoza that "the city is larger than the city of Mexico" and that the land "is the greatest and best of all that have been discovered." The friar heaped up a pile of stones, erected a small cross at the top, and took possession of Cíbola in the name of Emperor Charles V. Then using all the haste he could muster, he retraced his steps to Compostela. Along the way, he spotted a verdant valley stretching eastward toward the Sierra Madre Occidental. Indians told him that the valley held much gold and that its inhabitants worked the gold to "make it into vessels, and jewels for the ears, and into little blades with which they wipe away their sweat." Fray Marcos did not pause to verify this information. He simply set up two crosses and took possession of the valley.[30]

He arrived in Compostela at the end of June and was back in the city of México by August. He prepared a written *relación*, and on 2 September 1539 he swore before Viceroy Mendoza and an *escribano* that every word of it was true. His report, however, seems both exculpatory and self-aggrandizing. Coronado expedition chronicler Pedro de Castañeda de Nájera says that Fray Marcos was sixty leagues from Cíbola when he learned of the death of Estevanico and that, at that point, the friar turned back south. Carl Sauer, who attempted in the 1930s to reconstruct Fray Marcos's route, notes that the friar's report on his itinerary is vague. Sauer contends that the Franciscan cannot have covered as much territory in the time he had available as he claims to have done and that he probably went no further than the Cananea plateau in the region of the present international border between Mexico and Arizona. On the other hand, Sauer argues that Estevanico did reach Cíbola. Other scholars are of the opinion that Estevanico cannot have gone so far, but if Sauer is correct, the African was the first man of the Old World to visit the present states of Arizona and New Mexico.[31]

In addition to Fray Marcos's account of Estevanico's death, several others exist. Sancho Dorantes de Carranza, the grandson of Andrés Dorantes, reports that Estevanico was "shot through with arrows like a Saint Sebastian."[32]

In another account, Francisco Vázquez de Coronado, who retraced Estevanico's footsteps to Cíbola, claimed he found evidence that the African had reached at least one of the seven cities. The seven, which proved to be six Zuni pueblos in present-day New Mexico, were not nearly so grand as Fray Marcos had led Coronado to expect. In August of 1540, Coronado wrote from one of these pueblos to report that "the death of the negro is perfectly certain, because many of the things which he wore have been found." Referring to the inhabitants of the Zuni pueblo and to those of a fortress called Chichilticale, which both Coronado and Estevanico had visited, Coronado said of the African: "The Indians say that they killed him here because the Indians of Chichilticale said that he was a bad man, and not like the Christians who never kill women, and he killed them, and because he assaulted their women, whom the Indians love better than themselves."[33]

If we can accept it as true, Coronado's account of the death of Estevanico may shed light on the character of the relationships the African and his three Spanish companions formed with women during the course of their overland journey in 1535–36. Perhaps the four men routinely asked for and received the favors of women. At the time of his death, Estevanico may have been repeating behavior patterns he had acquired while traveling with Cabeza de Vaca, Castillo, and Dorantes. On the other hand, since Estevanico is the only one of the four who seems to have had trouble with women, it could be that the four men together exercised more circumspection than the African did on his own. Both of the Coronado expedition chroniclers, Pedro de Castañeda de Nájera and Juan de Jaramillo, say that Estevanico reached Cíbola. Castañeda says that the African asked the leading men of Cíbola "for turquoises and women" and that "they considered this an affront and determined to kill him."[34]

That Estevanico was killed on account of a woman or that he abused women is not certain, however. Hernando de Alarcón, who participated in the Coronado expedition, heard a different story from an Indian in 1540 about the way in which Estevanico met his death. Alarcón's informant said that for a time the chief of Cíbola had kept a greyhound that the African gave him. The chief had asked Estevanico whether he had any brothers, and the African replied that "he had an infinite number, that they had numerous arms, and that they were not very far from there." The informant added: "Upon hearing this, many chieftains assembled and decided to kill him so that he would not reveal their location to his brothers."[35]

Still another account of Estevanico's death was preserved by the Zunis through their oral tradition. The story, which supports the theory that Estevanico reached Zuni territory, was collected by Frank Hamilton Cushing, an anthropologist from the Smithsonian Institution who lived among the Zunis from 1879 to 1884. Cushing's informants told him that Estevanico was killed at Kiä-ki-me, a Zuni pueblo whose ruins are in western New Mexico. Their story includes references to "Black Mexicans" in the plural, as if other black men had been with Estevanico. Cushing translated into English what his Zuni informants told him:

A long time ago, when roofs lay over the walls of Kiä-ki-me, when smoke hung over the housetops, and the ladder-rounds were still unbroken—It was then that the Black Mexicans came from their abodes in Everlasting Summerland. One day, unexpected, out of "Hemlock Cañon," they came, and descended to Kiä-ki-me. But when they said they would enter the covered way, it seems that our ancients looked not gently on them, but with these Black Mexicans came many Indians of Sóno-li, as they call it now, who carried war feathers and long bows and cane arrows like the Apaches, who were enemies of our ancients; therefore these our ancients, being always bad tempered and quick to anger, made fools of themselves after their fashion, rushed into their town and out of their town, shouting, skipping and shooting with sling-stones and arrows and war clubs. Then the Indians of Sóno-li set up a great howl, and then they and our ancients did much ill to one another. Then and thus, was killed by our ancients, right where the stone stands down by the arroyo of Kiä-ki-me, one of the Black Mexicans. . . . Then the rest ran away, chased by our grandfathers, and went back toward their country in the Land of Everlasting Summer. But after they had steadied themselves and stopped talking, our ancients felt sorry; for they thought, "Now we have made bad business, for after a while, these people, being angered, will come again." So they felt always in danger and went about watching the bushes. By and by they did come back, those Black Mexicans, and with them many men of Sóno-li. They wore coats of iron and even bonnets of metal and carried for weapons short canes that spit fire and made thunder.

The Zunis had good reason to watch the bushes. When Fray Marcos returned to the city of México in August 1539, his report on his reconnaissance mission to Cíbola generated great excitement. Viceroy Mendoza appointed Francisco Vázquez de Coronado, who was then the governor of Nueva Galicia, to lead a follow-up expedition to Cíbola.[36]

Meanwhile, in May of 1539, two months after Fray Marcos left Culiacán on his northbound journey, Hernando de Soto set sail from Havana for La Florida and—like Narváez before him—made landfall somewhere in the vicinity of Tampa Bay. De Soto disembarked his men and animals near the Indian settlement of Ucita and soon discovered a survivor of the Narváez expedition, Juan Ortiz, living nearby among Indians. Ortiz joined De Soto and served for the next two and a half years as his principal interpreter. Because of what had happened to Narváez after he lost contact with his ships, De Soto stationed several ships at Tampa Bay, but he sent his largest ships back to Cuba.[37]

De Soto's route through Florida roughly paralleled that of Narváez, but the precise coordinates of the one *entrada* are no clearer than those of the other. Like Narváez, De Soto marched from Tampa Bay up Florida's Gulf coast to Apalachee Bay, but historians disagree about where he camped and which Indian communities he encountered. In October, De Soto entered the territory of the Apalachee chiefdom and located what seems to have been its principal town. Shortly thereafter his men found the remains of Narváez's camp at the Bay of Horses. De Soto spent the winter of 1539–40 in Apalachee territory.[38]

De Soto's itinerary included, in addition to Florida, the present states of Georgia, North and South Carolina, Tennessee, Alabama, Mississippi, Arkansas, Texas, and Louisiana. At the Indian settlement of Piachi, near the Alabama River, Indians showed De Soto's men a dagger that had belonged to Doroteo Teodoro, the Greek on the Narváez expedition who went with Indians to seek water and never returned. At four locations, De Soto and his men fought major battles with Indians and inflicted heavy casualties upon them. In the battle of Mabila, in the present state of Alabama, between 2,500 and 3,000 Indians lost their lives. In May of 1541, De Soto came for the first time upon the Mississippi River, which his men judged to be half a league wide. Juan Ortiz died the following winter, leaving De Soto without an interpreter. De Soto fell ill in the spring and died on 21 May 1542 after naming Luis de Moscoso to succeed him as captain general. To conceal De Soto's death from the Indians, Moscoso weighted his body and sunk it in the Mississippi River.[39]

The new captain general and his officers decided to return to Spanish civilization and to do so by traveling westward overland, as Cabeza de Vaca had done. By October they were somewhere in east Texas at a place called Naçacahoz, and their maize was all but gone. They heard reports that other Christians were nearby, and they interrogated an Indian woman who claimed "that she had seen Christians and that she had been in their hands but had escaped." Moscoso sent fifteen horsemen with the woman to seek out the other Christians, but after they had gone three to four leagues, "the Indian woman who was guiding them said that all she had said was a lie."[40]

Moscoso and his captains concluded that the area farther to the west was the land Cabeza de Vaca had said was inhabited by "Indians who wandered about like Arabs without having a settled abode anywhere, subsisting on prickly pears, the roots of plants, and the game they killed." Moscoso doubted his ability to sustain his army in such a land, so he decided to return to the Mississippi River. The army spent the winter at an Indian settlement and labored all the while to build seven brigantines. On 2 July they launched their boats and set off downriver, abandoning five hundred

Indian porters and concubines in strange and hostile territory. On 10 September 1543, Moscoso and 311 ragged survivors of the De Soto expedition succeeded, as Narváez had not, in reaching the Río Pánuco and the Spanish settlement of Santisteban del Puerto. Their countrymen at Santisteban received them joyfully and sent word to Viceroy Mendoza of their miraculous delivery from the wilderness.[41]

Between 1540 and 1542, two Spanish expeditions had explored North America at the same time, both operating within the present borders of the United States. Both had been authorized by the emperor, but whereas the De Soto expedition of 1539–43 had been organized in Spain, the Coronado expedition of 1540–42 was organized in New Spain under the supervision of Viceroy Mendoza. De Soto had sought to conquer and settle La Florida, while Coronado sought to discover and pacify the seven cities of Cíbola. Both commanders used information provided by the survivors of the Narváez expedition, and Moscoso and Coronado seem at some point to have got wind of the other's proximity.[42]

The woman Moscoso interrogated in east Texas in 1542 probably was the "painted Indian woman" who, according to a chronicler of the Coronado expedition, ran away from one of Coronado's captains and then came "into the possession of some Spaniards from Florida." If Moscoso had not concluded that the woman was lying, he might have picked up Coronado's trail and established an overland route from Florida to New Spain. Coronado missed an equally tantalizing opportunity when, somewhere in the Great Plains, he and his men met an old, blind Indian. According to a chronicler, "[The Indian] gave us to understand by signs that, many days before, he had seen four others of our people near there and closer to New Spain. Thus we understood and assumed them to be Dorantes, Cabeza de Vaca, and the ones I have mentioned." But since Cabeza de Vaca, even during his years as a wandering merchant, never penetrated as deeply into the central heartland of the present United States as both Coronado and De Soto did, the four Spaniards whom the old Indian told Coronado he had encountered had probably come into the area with De Soto.[43]

Besides the two main accounts of the Coronado expedition—by Castañeda and Jaramillo, both of whom served as horsemen in Coronado's army, additional information concerning the expedition comes from letters, including some written by Coronado himself, and from the testimony of witnesses at the *residencias* of Coronado and of his lieutentant, García López de Cárdenas.[44]

Coronado recruited some three hundred Spaniards and eight hundred Indians for the expedition to Cíbola, and on 22 February 1540 he mustered his men in Compostela. Fray Marcos de Niza was to accompany him as a guide. Among others who took part in the expedition were two men Cabeza de Vaca had met in 1536: the slave-hunter Diego de Alcaraz and the *alcalde mayor* of Culiacán, Melchior Díaz. Both these men lost their lives in the course of the expedition.[45]

The first destination on Coronado's itinerary was the settlement of San Miguel de Culiacán on Nueva Galicia's northern frontier. From there the captain general set off for Cíbola on 22 April, with an advance guard of seventy-five horsemen and thirty foot soldiers, leading them northeastward across present Arizona and into present New Mexico along what he later described as "a very bad trail." On 6 July he and his advance guard reached the first of the seven cities, which modern scholars believe was the Zuni pueblo of Hawikuh. They captured it the following day, but in the course of the action, Coronado was battered by rocks and received an arrow wound in the foot.[46]

Coronado sent a letter to Viceroy Mendoza on 3 August 1540, expressing his anger at Fray Marcos de Niza. The captain general complained that the friar had "not told the truth in a single thing that he said" and that "everything is the opposite of what he related." The seven cities, Coronado lamented, had turned out to be "seven little villages." Pedro de Castañeda accused Fray Marcos of telling "glowing tales of what the negro Esteban had discovered and what they had heard from the Indians." According to the chronicler, the curses that some of Coronado's disillusioned men "hurled at Fray Marcos were such that God forbid they may befall him." The friar was escorted back to Nueva Galicia because he "did not consider it safe to remain in Cíbola."[47]

Coronado established his winter camp at a place called Tiguex in New Mexico's Rio Grande valley, and the main body of his army joined him there. He acquired the services of a Plains Indian interpreter who told tales of gold and silver in his distant homeland: a fabulous place called Quivira. The interpreter, whom the Spaniards called El Turco, or "the Turk," promised to lead Coronado to Quivira in the spring. But during the winter of 1540 in what became known as the Tiguex War, the Spaniards fought several battles in the valley. Captain García López de Cárdenas captured the pueblo of Arenal, imprisoned most of its population, and, in the most infamous atrocity of Coronado's *entrada*, had twenty-five to thirty prisoners burned at the stake. Other prisoners from Arenal lost their lives when they attempted to escape.[48]

On 23 April 1541, Coronado set off from Tiguex for Quivira. Nine days later he came to plains he described as "so vast that in my travels I did not reach their end, although I marched over them for more than three hundred leagues." On the plains, he encountered New World cattle (buffalo) in such a quantity that he said "it would be impossible to estimate their number." Coronado and his men followed El Turco through the present states of Texas, Oklahoma, and Kansas—all the way, perhaps, to the Great Bend of the Arkansas River—but when they didn't find anything that matched the interpreter's stories of Quivira, they garroted him. Late in the year, the expeditionary army returned to its camp at Tiguex and spent a second winter there.[49]

The following spring, Coronado was trampled by a horse, and he ordered a retreat to New Spain. The army set off in April 1542 on its return journey, carrying the injured captain general in a litter. As soon as they reached Culiacán, they disbanded. Coronado went on to the city of México, but Viceroy Mendoza received him coldly. The viceroy had invested a great deal of money in the expedition and had recouped nothing.[50]

Coronado was subjected to a *residencia* regarding his conduct of the expedition. Lorenzo de Tejada, a judge of the Audiencia of New Spain, was appointed to investigate various cruelties that Coronado and his men were alleged to have perpetrated "against the natives of the lands through which they passed." In 1544 Coronado testified before Tejada and answered questions about the Tiguex War and the execution of El Turco. On 19 February 1546, Coronado was exonerated of all charges relating to the Cíbola expedition.[51]

Captain García López de Cárdenas was not so lucky. After the conclusion of the Cíbola expedition, he returned to Spain to take control of his family estate. He was imprisoned in Madrid on 7 January 1546 on criminal charges brought against him for his actions in the Tiguex War. The captain denied ordering the burning of any Indians and said that whatever happened at Tiguex "was done in the heat of battle." On 20 December 1549, Cárdenas was found guilty, fined, sentenced to additional prison time, and banished from the Indies. He appealed his conviction, and although his sentence was reduced, he ended up spending a total of seven years in jail.[52]

Coronado lost far fewer expeditionary personnel than did Narváez and De Soto, but his *entrada*, like theirs, ended in failure. None of the three expeditions made any profit for its investors or for the conquistadors who participated. None of the three succeeded in establishing a permanent Spanish presence in what is now the United States. Europeans would not establish a foothold in this territory until 1565, when the Spanish founded an enduring settlement at St. Augustine in Florida. Jamestown, the first permanent English settlement, would be founded in 1607; and Santa Fe, New Mexico, the second permanent Spanish settlement, in 1608.[53]

The De Soto expedition seems to have had an especially injurious impact upon the Native American populations it encountered. During the years between 1559 and 1561, when some veterans of the expedition returned under the leadership of Tristán de Luna to western Florida, Alabama, and Georgia, they were shocked by the changes they saw. Villages along the Alabama and Coosa Rivers that had appeared rich and populous when De Soto visited them had either been abandoned or suffered serious population decline. In 1682, when René-Robert Cavelier, Sieur de la Salle, and his men traveled up the Mississippi River in canoes, they saw only some ten Indian settlements in an area where De Soto had seen fifty. By the first decades of the seventeenth century, European diseases had also decimated the area north of San Miguel de Culiacán (in present-day Sinaloa and Sonora) that Guzmán, Cabeza de Vaca, and Coronado had all visited.[54]

During the time when De Soto and Coronado were commencing their *entradas*, Cabeza de Vaca was in Spain, writing his *Relación*. He must have finished the report sometime before the end of 1540. A colophon at its conclusion states that it was "printed in the magnificent, noble, and very ancient city of Zamora" and that the printing was completed on 6 October 1542.[55]

Cabeza de Vaca seems to have conceived of Charles V as the primary reader of his *Relación*, and in the course of its pages, he addresses the emperor seven times. In a prefatory epistle, after saluting the emperor as "Your Sacred Caesarian Catholic Majesty," the explorer reflects upon the role that fortune plays in men's lives. He says that although he had anticipated that his deeds in service to his sovereign "would be as illustrious and self-evident as those of my ancestors," adverse fortune had prevented him from doing as he had aspired. He explains that "since no expedition of as many as have gone to those lands ever saw itself in such grave dangers or had such a wretched and disastrous end as that which God permitted us to suffer on account of our sins, I had no opportunity to perform greater service than this, which is to bring to Your Majesty an account of all that I was able to

Frontispiece from *La Relación que dio Álvar Núñez Cabeza de Vaca de lo acaescido en las Indias en la armada donde iva por governador Pánphilo de Narbáez, desde el año de veinte y siete hasta el año de treinta y seis que bolvió a Sevilla con tres de su compañía*, 1542. Rare Books Division, The New York Public Library, Astor, Lenox and Tilden Foundations.

observe and learn in the nine years that I walked lost and naked through many and very strange lands." Cabeza de Vaca asks the emperor to receive his *Relación* "in the name of service, because this alone is what a man who came away naked could carry out with him." He notes that he made a point of observing "the locations of the lands and provinces and the distances among them" and of noting "the foodstuffs and animals that are produced in them, and the diverse customs of many and very barbarous peoples with whom I conversed and lived." In the explorer's opinion, the information he had collected was "not trivial" and should prove useful to those who might go in the emperor's name "to conquer those lands" and bring their inhabitants "to knowledge of the true faith and the true Lord and service to Your Majesty."[56]

Again addressing the emperor directly, Cabeza de Vaca expresses his hopes for the Indians, praying: "May God our Lord in his infinite mercy grant, in all the days of Your Majesty and under your authority and dominion, that these people come and be truly and with complete devotion subject to the true Lord who created and redeemed them." The explorer adds that he is certain "that it will be so, and that Your Majesty will be the one who is to put this into effect." Cabeza de Vaca makes bold, however, to advise the emperor that "it is clearly seen that all these peoples, to be drawn to become Christians and to obedience to the Imperial Majesty, must be given good treatment, and that this is the path most certain and no other."[57]

Before publishing his *Relación*, Cabeza de Vaca attested to its truth and signed it with his name. Writing the report was an important part of his quest for a new royal appointment, and within its pages, he portrays himself as a man who understands the native people of the New World and who, because of his demonstrated ability to deal with them in a Christian manner, might be of continued service to the emperor. During the years the explorer was working on the *Relación* in Spain, he made frequent appearances at court. For a time he assisted Martín de Orduña, the attorney for the late Pedro de Mendoza, in looking after the attorney's interests in Río de la Plata. His work with Orduña may have given Cabeza de Vaca the idea of succeeding Mendoza as governor of the South American province. The explorer must have solicited for the position, because on 18 March 1540, two and a half years after his return from North America, he signed a contract with the Spanish royal crown, authorizing him to take over as governor and captain general of the province of Río de la Plata.[58]

TWELVE

Río de la Plata

C abeza de Vaca probably enjoyed a proud moment when he signed his royal contract, but his title to govern the province of Río de la Plata was not as clear as he would have liked. It depended on the fate of Juan de Ayolas, the acting governor of the province. If Ayolas was dead, Cabeza de Vaca was to take over as governor and captain general of Río de la Plata, and he was to be the *adelantado* (military commander or governor) of any new lands he might bring under Spanish control. He was to have a twelfth part of the revenue of Río de la Plata and to receive an annual salary of 2,000 ducats (the equivalent of 750,000 *maravedíes*). However, he was to advance 8,000 ducats of his own money to finance his expedition to South America and purchase supplies for his province. If Ayolas was not dead, however, Cabeza de Vaca would not become governor. He would simply be reimbursed for his expenses and granted a six-year monopoly on trade with Río de la Plata. In either case, Cabeza de Vaca was to have jurisdiction for twelve years over the island of Santa Catalina, which was off the coast of Brazil but belonged to the Spanish crown and had already served as a base for several European ventures of exploration.[1]

Cabeza de Vaca's *capitulaciones* specified that the indigenous people of Río de la Plata were to be treated in a Christian fashion, and the newly appointed governor probably accepted this injunction with all the idealistic enthusiasm of a man who has not yet got his feet wet. He aspired to give the Indians of his province good treatment, but he also hoped to Christianize them and subject them to the jurisdiction of the Spanish royal crown. Like most Spaniards of his generation, Cabeza de Vaca believed that Indians would be better off living as Christians under Spanish rule. He saw Christianity as the one true religion and saw the civilization of Spain as superior to the indigenous civilizations he had encountered in the New World.[2]

The new governor was to sail to South America within six months of the signing of his *capitulaciones*. Unlike Pánfilo de Narváez, who in 1527 had been appointed to govern an area no European had previously explored, Cabeza de Vaca was to govern an established colony. Spaniards were already living in Río de la Plata and had already developed interests there. Cabeza de Vaca was a seasoned veteran when it came to dealing with New World Indians, but his skills at dealing with his own compatriots were not as well proved.[3]

The province he was to govern was not well mapped, but its rivers had made it accessible to Europeans who had begun exploring its territory when Cabeza de Vaca was a young man in Spain. The province had been given the name "Río de la Plata" (River of Silver) because the first Europeans to make their way up its rivers were searching for silver they believed was somewhere in the South American interior. According to the Spanish crown, the province stretched northward along South America's Atlantic seaboard from the Straits of Magellan to Portuguese-controlled Brazil and extended westward to Peru. It consisted—at least in theory—of the modern nations of Argentina, Uruguay, and Paraguay and contested portions of Brazil. The northern and western limits of the province were not clearly defined, but the Spanish crown was interested in containing Portuguese expansion and in extending Spanish sovereignty as far as possible.[4]

The gateway to Cabeza de Vaca's province was the estuary still known today as the Río de la Plata, which forms the wedge between the present nations of Argentina and Uruguay and receives the waters of the Río Paraná and the Río Uruguay. Together these rivers and their tributaries channel as much water as all the rivers of Europe combined and constitute a drainage system second in South America only to the Amazon. The Paraná, the fourteenth-longest river in the world, rises in Brazil and flows for more than 3,000 miles before it enters the Río de la Plata estuary. In the Guaraní language spoken by many inhabitants of the area drained by the river, "Paraná" means "Father of the Waters." The Río Uruguay, which flows for slightly less than 1,000 miles, meets the Río Paraná near its outlet. Ocean tides ebb and flow for 120 miles up both rivers.[5]

A third river, the Río Paraguay, is important in the history of the colonization of the Río de la Plata region. The Paraguay is the principal tributary of the Paraná and the fifth-largest river in South America. It rises in Brazil and meanders for some 1,500 miles before meeting the Paraná. In Guaraní, the word "Paraguay" can refer both to a colorful plumed bird and to a plumed headdress.[6]

At the time of Cabeza de Vaca's appointment to govern Río de la Plata, the principal Spanish settlements in the province were Buenos Aires (now the capital of Argentina) and Asunción (now the capital of Paraguay). Buenos Aires is situated near the Río Paraná's outlet. Asunción, some 300 to 350 leagues (1,000 miles) upriver from Buenos Aires, is situated on the eastern bank of the Río Paraguay about 150 miles above its confluence with the Paraná.[7]

The Río Paraguay acts as a natural dividing line that separates the fertile eastern part of the present nation of Paraguay from a sparsely populated western region known as the Chaco. The land east of the river supports both farms and forests. In contrast, the Chaco is a poorly drained desert that is both arid and subject to seasonal flooding. It stretches from the Río Paraguay clear to the foothills of the Andes and extends over the western two-thirds of the nation of Paraguay and into parts of Argentina and Bolivia. To the immediate west of the river, the Chaco is a grassy savanna tufted with palms and other trees. Farther to the west, the vegetation becomes spinier. On both sides of the present border between Bolivia and Paraguay, the Chaco supports a dense and almost impenetrable thorn forest. At the time of first European contact, the Chaco was inhabited by nomadic hunter-gatherers.[8]

The headwaters of the Río Paraguay lie within the world's largest inland swamp, a region known as the Pantanal. This region floods annually when its rainy season begins in November, and it remains flooded through March. Even during the dry season, from May through October, the Pantanal is very marshy. Today the Pantanal is an adventure travel destination and attracts the kind of tourist who desires to see jaguars and anacondas in their natural habitat. At the time of first European contact, the vast swamp was—like the Chaco—inhabited by nomadic hunter-gatherers.[9]

In the sixteenth century, the land extending from the Río Paraguay eastward to the Brazilian coast and southward into Uruguay was inhabited by Guaraníes. These people were farmers who lived in semipermanent villages and practiced slash-and-burn agriculture, cultivating maize, cassavas, three kinds of potatoes, and cotton. Archeological evidence collected in Brazil indicates that they sometimes practiced cannibalism. At the time of European contact, their population may have numbered 1.5 million. There are Guaraníes living today in Paraguay and southern Brazil, but all the subtribal groups mentioned by the sixteenth-century chroniclers have disappeared. The Guaraní language belongs to one of the major language families of South America.[10]

Indians of other cultural and linguistic groupings were interspersed throughout the Guaraní region, but from the point of view of the sixteenth-century Spaniards who colonized Río de la Plata, the Guaraníes were the most congenial group of indigenous people living there. Near Buenos Aires, the indigenous people were hunters and gatherers who, because the incoming Spaniards threatened their lifestyle, attempted to repulse the invaders. The hunting-and-gathering peoples of the Chaco and the Pantanal also resisted the Spaniards. The agricultural Guaraníes, however, allied themselves with the Spaniards and supplied them with both food and labor. The Guaraníes valued the alliance because of the military support that the Spaniards, with their horses and guns, could give them in their wars with their traditional Indian enemies.[11]

The history of the colonization of Río de la Plata begins in 1511–12, when the Portuguese Estéban Froes became the first European captain to visit the Río de la Plata estuary. In 1516 Captain Juan Díaz de Solís, sailing for the Spanish crown, anchored in the same estuary with three ships and seventy men. Solís and several men incautiously went ashore and were killed by Indians. The surviving crew members sailed northward but lost a ship and several more men on the island known to later explorers as Santa Catalina. Most of the remaining men succeeded in returning to Spain and reporting their discoveries.[12]

However, a few of Solís's men—significantly including the Portuguese Alejo García—were inadvertently stranded at Santa Catalina. They found Guaraní Indians on the island and the nearby mainland, and García learned to speak their language. Groups of Guaraníes had been conducting raids into the foothills of the Andes since the end of the fifteenth century, and García joined his Guaraní friends in such a raid. The group marched westward to the Río Paraguay, ascended the river, then skirted the Chaco desert and turned westward again. Ultimately, the raiders must have reached the silver-mining area in the eastern highlands of the present nation of Bolivia. García never returned to the Atlantic coast, and his death is shrouded in mystery, but before he disappeared from history, he sent Guaraní couriers with a message and samples of gold and silver for his European shipmates at Santa Catalina Island. In his message, García told of a white king (El Rey Blanco) and a mountain of silver (Sierra de la Plata). The white king may have been the Grand Inca, and the Sierra de la Plata probably was the rich hill in Bolivia that Spaniards would later know as the *cerro rico de Potosí*. García's shipmates in Santa Catalina would pass the information about the silver mountain along to Sebastian Cabot, the next European captain to visit the island. Because of these stories, Cabot would bestow the name "Río de la Plata" on the region and on the great estuary that separates the present nations of Uruguay and Argentina. Cabot would also give the name "Santa Catalina" to the island where he met the survivors of the Solís voyage.[13]

Cabot was Genoese, but his voyage was licensed by the Spanish crown. With two hundred men in three large ships and a caravel, he left Spain on 3 April 1526, a year ahead of the Narváez expedition to La Florida. In October he anchored off Santa Catalina Island but ran his flagship aground. His intended destinations were the Moluccas and China, but when he heard from Solís's men about Alejo García and his mountain of silver, Cabot altered his itinerary. Eight or nine of his officers objected to the alteration, so the captain marooned them on an island near Santa Catalina.[14]

Early in 1527, Cabot sailed into the Río de la Plata estuary. Mooring his two larger ships there, he headed up the Río Paraná with the caravel and a smaller vessel. At the confluence of the Carcarañá and Paraná Rivers, Cabot built a fort, which he named Sancti Spiritus. He left a garrison at the fort and continued his explorations of the Río Paraná and the Río Paraguay, observing that both rivers were broad and deep but full of islands and treacherous currents. He and his men encountered Indians of many ethnicities, including Guaraníes wearing headdresses of colorful macaw feathers. Through trade with Indians, Cabot obtained some objects of silver and gold, which probably originated in the Andes but fueled his hopes of finding more treasure.[15]

Cabot's river explorations were tedious and laborious. In the absence of favorable winds, his men often had to kedge their vessels. A couple of men would row ahead in a skiff, secure a long rope to a tree, and signal their shipmates to haul on the line and pull the larger craft forward. They would then find another tree and repeat the process. Food was difficult to obtain, and Cabot and his men were frequently harassed by Indians.[16]

When Cabot received word late in 1529 that Indians had killed most of the garrison he had left at Sancti Spiritus, he decided to return to Spain. He lost one of his larger ships along the Uruguayan coast, and although he saw smoke signals made by the crew, he refused to go to their rescue. He reached Seville on 22 July 1530, together with only twenty-five of his original two hundred men and some sixty South American Indians. Cabot had opened a route into the South American interior, but he never managed to produce an accurate map of the territory he had reconnoitered. He brought stories back to Spain about the mountain of silver he had tried to find.[17]

Two years later, Francisco Pizarro seized the Inca emperor Atahualpa and began sending Inca treasure home to Spain. In 1534, as a result of both Pizarro's successes and Cabot's stories of the silver mountain, Pedro de Mendoza contracted with Emperor Charles V to conquer, settle, and govern Río de la Plata. Mendoza must have hoped to find a treasure equivalent to Pizarro's. The new governor was a wealthy member of a noble Spanish family and cousin to the Antonio de Mendoza who would later serve as viceroy of New Spain.[18]

Unfortunately for Pedro de Mendoza, he had contracted syphilis in the course of a military action in Italy, and in the words of one of his soldiers, "he was always melancholy, weak, and ill." In August 1535, at around the time Cabeza de Vaca was beginning his overland journey from Texas to New Spain, Mendoza set sail from Spain with twelve ships and two thousand prospective colonists. Historian Gonzalo Fernández de Oviedo y Valdés saw him depart and said that his "was a company that would appear to good advantage in Caesar's army and in all parts of the world." Among the men who sailed with Mendoza were Juan de Ayolas, Domingo Martínez de Irala, Juan de Salazar de Espinosa, Gonzalo de Mendoza, Alonso Cabrera, Felipe de Cáceres, García Venegas, Pero Hernández, and Martín de Orúe, all of whom would later become significant to Cabeza de Vaca. Since Mendoza was aiming to establish a colony, he took women to Río de la Plata, including both Spanish ladies and African slaves. Wealthy banking houses in Flanders and Germany helped finance the expedition, and as a consequence, eighty Flemish and German mercenaries accompanied Mendoza.[19]

One of these mercenaries—a Bavarian harquebusier named Ulrich Schmidt—would remain in South America until 1552 and later write an account of his experiences. It was Schmidt who described Governor Mendoza as "always melancholy, weak, and ill." The harquebusier gives valuable information about the early colonial development of Río de la Plata, but his allegiance was to his military commander—Domingo Martínez de Irala—and he would have little sympathy for Cabeza de Vaca.[20]

After stopping in the Canaries, Mendoza and his fleet crossed the Atlantic and sailed into the Río de la Plata estuary. The colonists founded Buenos Aires near the head of the estuary, but life in the new settlement was difficult. Disease, starvation, and warfare with the local Indians all took a toll on the European settlers. The hunting-and-gathering lifestyle of the local people put them at odds with the Europeans. The Indians used bolas—weapons consisting of a length of rope with a stone ball at each end—that when thrown around the legs of a horse, were very effective at bringing the animal down.[21]

After a battle in which Indians burned four Spanish ships, only 560 of Mendoza's men remained alive. Knowing that the future success of his colony depended upon his securing a steady food supply, Mendoza was anxious to find and establish cooperative relations with Indians who cultivated crops. He also hoped to find Cabot's Sierra de la Plata. Leaving only 160 men at Buenos Aires, Mendoza sailed with the other 400 men up the Río Paraná and reoccupied the fort that Cabot had built at Sancti Spiritus. Two of the men who accompanied him would assume positions of leadership in the fledgling colony: Juan de Ayolas and Domingo Martínez de Irala. Ayolas was a gentleman and Mendoza's lieutenant governor. Irala was a captain from the province of Vizcaya in the Basque region of Spain. He did not enjoy high social status, but he was able and audacious and quickly acquired power.[22]

Mendoza directed Ayolas to go upriver to scout out the country and search for silver and gold. Ayolas took 170 men, including Captain Irala, in two brigantines and a caravel up the Río Paraná to its confluence with the Río Paraguay. He then proceeded up the Paraguay and observed that much of its eastern side was inhabited by Guaraní farmers.[23]

Ayolas continued upriver into the Pantanal, and on Candlemas Day, 2 February 1537, he established a port at a place he called Candelaria in honor of the day. Although the exact location of Candelaria is not now known, Irala says that it was in the territory of the Payaguá Indians, at latitude 19°40′ south. At Candelaria, Ayolas encountered an Indian who claimed that some thirteen years earlier he had accompanied Alejo García—the Portuguese survivor of the Solís expedition—to the fabled Sierra de la Plata. The Indian offered to guide Ayolas there and said the silver mountain lay westward, beyond the formidable Chaco desert. Leaving Captain Irala at Candelaria in command of 33 men and the ships, Ayolas set off westward into the Chaco on 12 February with 130 Spaniards and his Indian guide.[24]

Two months later, on 20 April, Governor Mendoza—on account of his infirmities—departed with two ships for Spain. He left a garrison of 250 men at Buenos Aires, which, because of its strategic location at the gateway to the Río Paraná, he saw as vital to the defense of his colony. He placed the colony under the command of Juan de Ayolas, but since the lieutenant governor had not yet returned from the Chaco, Mendoza sent Captain Juan de Salazar de Espinosa upriver in two brigantines to search for him. On 23 June, Salazar met Irala at Candelaria, and the two captains searched briefly for Ayolas. They soon abandoned their efforts because, as Irala later reported, he and his men were short of food and his brigantines needed repair.[25]

Alonso Cabrera accompanied Mendoza on his homeward voyage, but the melancholy governor never reached Spain. As Cabeza de Vaca learned during his layover in the Azores, Mendoza died aboard his flagship on 26 July 1537 and was buried at sea. Cabrera arrived in Spain in August and reported Mendoza's death. He then secured a royal appointment for himself as inspector of mines for Río de la Plata. He also obtained a *cédula real* (royal order) designating Juan de Ayolas as governor—if he had returned from the Chaco. If Ayolas had not returned, the *cédula* authorized Cabrera to convene the Christians of the province to elect an interim governor. The *cédula* was dated 12 September 1537 and signed by the queen.[26]

While Cabrera was busy with diplomatic affairs in Spain, a group of conquistadors defeated a number of Guaraníes on a hill called Cerro Lambaré, on the east bank of the Río Paraguay. Ulrich Schmidt, who participated in the battle, noted that the Guaraníes were "wonderful warriors." Lambaré, the Guaraní chief, was killed in the conflict. Today a colossal bronze statue representing the chief stands atop Cerro Lambaré to commemorate Paraguay's Guaraní heritage. Present-day Paraguay is officially bilingual, with Spanish and Guaraní as its two national languages. Paraguay and Peru are currently the only nations in South America to have given official status to indigenous languages.[27]

After Lambaré's death, the Guaraníes sued for peace and secured it by presenting six women to the commander of the Spanish forces and two women to each of his men. Sealing a peace treaty with a gift of women was a Guaraní custom, and the native people were hoping thereby to forge kinship ties with the Spaniards, many of whom soon acquired sizeable harems

Bronze statue memorializing sixteenth-century
Guaraní chief Lambaré, at Cerro Lambaré
in Asunción, Paraguay. Photograph by Juris
Zagarins.

of Guaraní wives. Captain Irala married all seven daughters of a Guaraní
chief in a single ceremony. Schmidt admired the Guaraní women and said
it was possible to buy a woman from her father, brother, or husband for
the price of "a shirt or a bread knife, or a small hoe, or some other thing of
that kind."[28]

The Guaraníes lived in patrilineally related extended-family groups.
Their villages, which consisted of four to eight thatched rectangular long-
houses arranged around a central plaza, were encircled by two or three
wooden palisades and a series of moats. The Guaraníes made pottery and
baskets, and they wove hammocks from cotton or palm fiber. Both the men
and the women went naked, but chiefs and shamans wore cloaks made of
feathers. Guaraní men wore plugs in their lower lips, and they shaved the
crowns of their heads to create a tonsure like that of a Franciscan friar. The
women had intricate tattoos on their faces and breasts. The men hunted
and fished, burn-cleared the fields, and saw to community defense while
the women planted and harvested the crops, transported water, cooked,
and cared for the children. Many Guaraníes smoked tobacco, and they
celebrated big events—such as a victory in war, or a successful hunt or
harvest—with drinking fests. Schmidt noted that the Guaraníes made wine
from honey. He also observed that they "eat man's flesh if they can get it"
and would ritually devour the prisoners they captured in war.[29]

Schmidt and the majority of his fellow Europeans were inclined to remain in Guaraní territory and live off the labor and produce of the Indians.

The harquebusier reported that "the country and the people pleased us very well, as did also their food, for we had not seen nor eaten better bread during the last four years, fish and meat having been our only sustenance." According to Schmidt, the Guaraníes were "more able to endure work and labour than the other natives." For their part, the Guaraníes desired the Europeans' support in their wars with the Guaycurúes to the west and the Payaguás to the north.[30]

Shortly after the battle of Cerro Lambaré, Captain Juan de Salazar de Espinosa established a colonial settlement at a place he named Nuestra Señora de la Asunción in honor of the day of its founding—the feast day of the Assumption of the Virgin, 15 August 1537. Thus, Asunción was established twenty-eight years before Saint Augustine, Florida (the oldest permanent European settlement in what is now the United States), and ninety-three years before Boston. In Asunción today a statue in the Plaza de la Independencia honors Salazar as the city's founder.[31]

Salazar chose a site for the new settlement near Cerro Lambaré on a bluff overlooking a bay formed by a natural breakwater on the eastern side of the Río Paraguay. Assisting him in establishing the settlement were most of the surviving Europeans of Mendoza's colony, as well as the Guaraníes of Cerro Lambaré. The Europeans and their Guaraní in-laws built a fort of wood, stone, and red Paraguayan soil, and then the Europeans settled down with their Guaraní wives on small ranches near the fort. Their houses were made from wood or adobe, with roofs of thatch, and the entire community was enclosed within a palisade. Situated at latitude 25°17′ south—nearly two degrees below the Tropic of Capricorn—Asunción is in South America's subtropical zone. The Europeans of the new settlement estimated Asunción to be 350 leagues upriver from Buenos Aires and 120 leagues downriver from the frontier outpost at Candelaria, where Ayolas had last been seen. Captain Irala occasionally took his brigantines from Asunción to Candelaria, but because the Payaguás in that area were hostile, he never lingered there for long.[32]

In 1539 Alonso Cabrera arrived back in Buenos Aires from his diplomatic mission to Spain, bringing with him the *cédula* he had obtained from the queen and some two hundred additional Spanish colonists. When Cabrera reached Buenos Aires, he learned that Lieutenant Governor Ayolas was still lost somewhere in the Chaco, that Buenos Aires was still beleaguered by Indians, and that most of the Spanish settlers of Río de la Plata were now living in Asunción. Cabrera therefore sent royal comptroller Felipe de Cáceres and a small delegation of provincial representatives, including the *escribano* Martín de Orúe, back to Spain with this latest news. Cáceres was to ask the Royal Council of the Indies for additional reinforcements and supplies. The information that Cáceres brought to Spain would be the most recent news Cabeza de Vaca would have from Río de la Plata before he sailed for South America. One of the great problems of colonial administration in the sixteenth century was the length of time required for officials, news, and authorizing documents to cross the Atlantic. Even for news to travel between Buenos Aires and Asunción could take months.[33]

On 19 June 1539, Cabrera brought the *cédula* to Asunción. Since the whereabouts of Juan de Ayolas were still unknown and the *cédula* empowered the Christians of Río de la Plata to elect an interim governor to act in his stead, Cabrera called them together and they elected Captain Domingo Martínez de Irala. According to Schmidt, who never learned to spell Irala's name correctly, "it seemed good to us Christians to elect Martin Domingo Eijolla for our chief commander." On 31 July, Irala assumed his new position. He would remain in command of the province until Cabeza de Vaca arrived in Asunción. Meanwhile, the captain continued to patrol the Paraguay and Paraná rivers in his brigantine gunboats. Shortly after he took over as interim governor, he led the Spaniards and their Guaraní allies in a successful war against the Agaz Indians. After their victory, the Guaraníes butchered and ate their Agaz prisoners. Irala, according to a Spanish eyewitness, did not flinch.[34]

On 16 January 1540, Irala returned to Candelaria to search yet again for the missing Ayolas. It was then the rainy season in the Pantanal, and water levels in the huge swamp were high. Irala interrogated six of the local Payaguás, and he interviewed a Chané Indian youth whose people lived in a country far to the west. The youth, whom the Spaniards called Gonzalo, said he was the sole survivor of a group of Chanés whom Ayolas had conscripted as porters. Both Gonzalo and the Payaguás told Irala that Ayolas and all 130 of his men were dead. After leaving Candelaria in 1537, Ayolas had marched westward through swampy country and had penetrated far into the unmapped interior of South America. He and his men reached a large settlement where, the Indians said, they found "much silver and gold and sheep of the kind that are in Peru [llamas]." Ayolas acquired some of the silver and gold and compelled Gonzalo and the other Chané porters to carry it to Candelaria. The lieutenant governor succeeded in returning to the outpost, but he and his men were ill and exhausted, and they had expended all their gunpowder. The Payaguás ambushed and slaughtered them all. They also killed the Indian who had accompanied Alejo García to the Sierra de la Plata and had served Ayolas as his guide. The massacre seems to have occurred in June or July of 1538, and by his own account, Irala learned of it early in 1540. Shortly thereafter, Irala directed the relevant officials to open Ayolas's will and settle his estate. Martín de Orúe reported that Irala "understood very well what had happened and the sad end that Captain Juan de Ayolas and the Christians with him had suffered."[35]

Early in 1540, around the time Irala learned conclusively of Ayolas's death, Felipe de Cáceres and the members of his delegation were in Spain bringing news to the emperor and the Royal Council of the Indies of the probable death of Ayolas and reporting on conditions in Río de la Plata. Since Cáceres had left South America in 1539, he could not have known with certainty that Ayolas was dead. The comptroller painted a grim picture of economic hardship in Río de la Plata and the sufferings of its European settlers. He warned that unless they received reinforcements and supplies, the settlers might all perish. He pleaded that a new governor be appointed in Ayolas's stead and sent to Río de la Plata with the needed reinforcements and supplies. After careful deliberation, the Council of the Indies selected Álvar Núñez Cabeza de Vaca, a seasoned veteran of the Indies, to undertake the task.[36]

On 18 March 1540, Cabeza de Vaca signed his contract to lead a relief expedition to Río de la Plata and to take over, if Ayolas was dead, as governor of the colony. If the fate of Ayolas remained unknown when Cabeza de Vaca arrived in Río de la Plata, the *capitulaciones* stipulated that he was to "assume the governance of the said province as his [Ayolas's] lieutenant governor, named by us, to use and exercise the title in his name, notwithstanding any other deputy that he might have left, even though this person might have been approved by us and elected by the Spanish settlements or the captains or their men." Thus, the question of whether or not Ayolas was dead would have serious consequences for Cabeza de Vaca. If Ayolas were only presumed dead, Cabeza de Vaca would not have a clear title to the governorship. It was therefore in the interest of Irala, as interim governor, to keep what he knew about the fate of Ayolas hidden from his royally appointed rival. From Irala's point of view, the most problematic clause in Cabeza de Vaca's *capitulaciones* was the one stipulating that Cabeza de Vaca was to assume the governorship "notwithstanding any other deputy" who might be serving in the office.[37]

Untangling the history of Cabeza de Vaca's governorship is complicated because his rivals and his supporters produced contradictory accounts of what happened. Among the major primary sources are the *Relación general* that Cabeza de Vaca submitted to the Council of the Indies on 7 December 1545 and the *Comentarios de Álvar Núñez Cabeza de Vaca* that his secretary—Pero Hernández—published in 1555. Other sources are Ulrich Schmidt's narrative and Book XXIII of Oviedo's *Historia general y natural de las Indias.* Domingo Martínez de Irala and various other men also reported in writing upon events that occurred in Río de la Plata while Cabeza de Vaca was governor.[38]

In May, shortly after receiving his royal contract, Cabeza de Vaca journeyed to Seville to prepare for his expedition to South America. Although he was contractually obligated to spend only 8,000 ducats of his own money, he actually spent 14,000, borrowing some of that total on credit. He acquired two large ships and a caravel, forty-eight horses, and provisions for both his voyage and his colony. The largest of his ships, *La Capitana*, had a burden of 350 tons and was to serve as his flagship. Cabeza de Vaca stocked his ships with armaments, ammunition, medicines, cloth and clothing, ship biscuit, wine, olive oil, flour, and other foodstuffs. He also purchased wine necessary for the celebration of the mass. For the Indians he expected to encounter, he bought gifts and trade goods, including shirts, hats, blankets, axes, knives, scissors, fishhooks, and mirrors. Cabeza de Vaca engaged pilots and sailors and paid their salaries himself. One of these pilots, Gonzalo de Acosta, had sailed to and from Río de la Plata with Governor Mendoza. Cabeza de Vaca also recruited four hundred men-at-arms and provided each with a double set of armaments.[39]

Before leaving Spain, Cabeza de Vaca completed the *Relación* of his experiences in North America and placed the manuscript in the hands of a book merchant and two printers. In October of 1542, these three men would publish the *Relación.*[40]

Cabeza de Vaca remained in Seville from May through September and then proceeded to Cádiz. The Atlantic seaport is only some twenty miles from Jerez de la Frontera, so the newly appointed governor probably traveled frequently between Cádiz and his hometown. On 2 December 1540, when he was between forty-eight and fifty-five years of age, he set sail from Cádiz for South America. Among the things Cabeza de Vaca took with him were a manuscript copy of his *Relación* and a copy of his family genealogy.[41]

Among the four hundred men in his company were his cousin Pedro Estopiñán Cabeza de Vaca, his nephew Alonso Riquelme de Guzmán, and several other Jerezanos from his hometown. Returning to Río de la Plata with Cabeza de Vaca were Felipe de Cáceres and Martín de Orúe. Pedro Dorantes, nine priests, a Flemish drummer, four Africans, two Indians, and half a dozen women also sailed with the expedition. Dorantes, newly appointed as royal quartermaster for Río de la Plata, should not be confused with the Narváez expedition survivor Andrés Dorantes.[42]

Nine days after leaving Cádiz, Cabeza de Vaca arrived at the island of La Palma in the Canaries and purchased a second caravel. He also stopped at the Cape Verde Islands because his flagship, *La Capitana*, was leaking so badly that it had to be unloaded and repaired. Martín de Orúe later asserted that Cabeza de Vaca did not purchase the caravel in La Palma but commandeered it, and that he commandeered supplies in the Cape Verde Islands. According to Orúe, Cabeza de Vaca sent seventy men to board a merchant ship in Cape Verde and seize flour, vinegar, canvas, and oars.[43]

When the repairs to *La Capitana* were completed, Cabeza de Vaca set off to cross the Atlantic. Somewhere between Cape Verde and the equator, he and his shipmates began to see an unfamiliar set of constellations, including the Southern Cross. When their supplies of fresh water were so low that only three of the one hundred barrels they had brought from Cape Verde remained, the new governor and his fleet reached the Brazilian coast. In the predawn hours before they sighted land, a cock—which had been brought from Cádiz and had crossed the ocean in a mute and disconsolate fashion—began to crow. The sailors credited the cock with alerting them to the proximity of dangerous rocks upon which they might have foundered. Cabeza de Vaca paused briefly to take on fresh water, and on 29 March 1541, some four months after he left Cádiz, he arrived at Santa Catalina, the island over which he was to have jurisdiction for twelve years. The new governor ordered all his people to disembark, and he offloaded the twenty-six horses that had survived the ocean voyage. He then took formal possession of Santa Catalina in the name of His Majesty Charles V. Using their navigational instruments, the company's pilots estimated the island to be at latitude 28° south. In actuality, it lies between 27°22′ and 27°50′ south and thus is approximately two degrees farther south than Asunción.[44]

The natives of Santa Catalina were Guaraníes, and their population on the island at the time of first European contact is estimated at four thousand. Guaraníes also occupied the nearby mainland and much of the area extending westward from the Brazilian coast to the Río Paraguay and Asunción. Cabeza de Vaca's chief pilot, Gonzalo de Acosta, spoke the Guaraní language and served as the new governor's interpreter. And since Cabeza de Vaca knew from dealing with Indians in North America that gifts were important in establishing diplomatic relations, he presented gifts to the Guaraní leaders. In return, the Guaraníes built houses for the new governor and his people.[45]

Two Franciscan friars, Bernardo de Armenta and Alonso Lebrón, were living nearby on the Brazilian mainland, having arrived in South America in 1538 with Alonso Cabrera. They now came to Santa Catalina seeking the protection of the new governor, saying that their Indian neighbors were trying to kill them. But the friars would soon become Cabeza de Vaca's adversaries.[46]

In May of 1541, late in the South American autumn, Cabeza de Vaca sent Felipe de Cáceres in a caravel to Buenos Aires to investigate the feasibility of taking the whole company there. Cáceres was familiar with Buenos Aires and in the previous year had traveled from there to Spain. In 1541, however, bad weather and unfavorable winds prevented him from entering the Río de la Plata estuary, and he returned to Santa Catalina with little to report to Cabeza de Vaca.[47]

At around the same time, eight or nine other Spaniards arrived at Santa Catalina in a small stolen boat. They were fleeing from Buenos Aires, and when Cabeza de Vaca offered them his hospitality, they warned him there was much warfare in Buenos Aires between Christians and Indians. Only some 70 Christians remained in Buenos Aires since most of the 350 to 400 Christian settlers of Río de la Plata were now residing in Asunción. The fugitives claimed that the royal officials in Asunción were dealing unjustly with both Christians and Indians and were creating much dissatisfaction in the province.[48]

The fugitives also told Cabeza de Vaca that Lieutenant Governor Ayolas and all 130 of his men had been killed by Payaguás on the upper Río Paraguay. When Ayolas returned from his exploratory expedition to the river port of Candelaria, he was counting on finding Irala there with the brigantines left in his charge. But unfortunately for Ayolas, the captain had abandoned his post. According to the current gossip, Irala was eighty leagues downriver dallying with the daughter of a Guaraní chief. Cabeza de Vaca must have heard what the fugitives told him with mixed feelings. On the one hand, the news of the massacre of the Ayolas party was deeply disturbing; on the other hand, the death of Ayolas cleared Cabeza de Vaca's title to the governorship of Río de la Plata.[49]

The new governor was impatient to reach Asunción and to succor its European settlers with the supplies and reinforcements he was bringing. The fugitives warned him, however, that in the South American winter, it would be difficult to reach Asunción from Buenos Aires. The alternative— to march to Asunción from the Brazilian coast—seemed to offer Cabeza de Vaca a quicker means of achieving his objectives. Moreover, if he made an overland *entrada*, he could secure Spanish control of the territory he crossed and protect it from possible incursions by the Portuguese from the portions of Brazil they controlled. Fray Bernardo de Armenta, who knew something from the local Guaraníes about the country to the west, encouraged Cabeza de Vaca to make the *entrada*. Pedro Dorantes, the royal quartermaster, pointed out that some twenty years earlier, Alejo García had marched from Santa Catalina with Guaraní guides to a fabulous Sierra de la Plata. Dorantes encouraged Cabeza de Vaca to seek out García's route.[50]

Felipe de Cáceres, however, objected to the proposed *entrada*. At this early stage in their relations, the royal comptroller was already emerging as an antagonist to the new governor. Cáceres would later swear that from the time Cabeza de Vaca left Cádiz, he had styled himself as governor—even though his appointment was provisional—and had insisted upon being called "your lordship." In view of Cáceres's objections to the *entrada*, Cabeza de Vaca sent Pedro Dorantes to the mainland to seek a road into the interior. The quartermaster was gone three and a half months and then returned to Santa Catalina with a favorable report of the land he had explored. He had crossed a range of mountains and subsequently followed the course of the Río Ytabucú. People living near the river had assured him that it afforded the best means of reaching their country from the Atlantic coast. Cabeza de Vaca decided to take most of his men overland to Asunción via the route Dorantes had reconnoitered. The two friars, Armenta and Lebrón, insisted on going along. Cabeza de Vaca had wished them to remain at the coast to instruct and sustain their native converts, but they refused to do so. This was the first of many disagreements the governor would have with the friars.[51]

Cabeza de Vaca divided his company into overland and seagoing parties and prepared to leave Santa Catalina. He would command the overland party of 250 harquebusiers and crossbowmen, the two friars, and the twenty-six surviving horses. The seagoing party, under the command of his cousin Pedro Estopiñán Cabeza de Vaca, would ferry the overland group from Santa Catalina to the mainland and then sail to Buenos Aires. Estopiñán's party of 140 people included all the Jerezanos and all the women. No doubt Governor Cabeza de Vaca thought of Estopiñán and the Jerezanos as the most trustworthy persons to put in charge of a sensitive mission. But in hindsight, given the antagonism he encountered when he reached Asunción, the new governor may have wished that he had kept some loyal Jerezanos at his side.[52]

Felipe de Cáceres seems to have joined the seagoing party. In light of the comptroller's earlier objection to the *entrada*, this is not surprising. Cabeza de Vaca entrusted him with a number of artillery pieces that were too heavy for overland transport. Cáceres would later be accused of having done "everything possible" to keep the new governor from assuming his office. It would be said that Cáceres had traveled apart from Cabeza de Vaca in order to reach Asunción ahead of him and persuade the Spaniards there not to receive him as their governor.[53]

On 18 October 1541, early in the South American spring, Cabeza de Vaca presented the Guaraníes of Santa Catalina with many shirts and hats and crossed from the island to the mainland. He had arranged for a group of Guaraníes to accompany his overland party as porters and guides. It took the new governor and his men nineteen days to cross the range of mountains Pedro Dorantes had reconnoitered, because they had to cut roads as they went. Cabeza de Vaca walked as he had done in North America and later said: "I always went on foot and without shoes in order to encourage the men so they would not be dismayed, because in addition to the travails of the journey in clearing trees and making roads and bridges to cross the rivers, which were many, we suffered great and excessive difficulty." After crossing the coastal mountains, the expeditionary army came to an area inhabited by Guaraníes. These people raised poultry, kept parrots as pets, fished, and hunted for such game as deer, boars, tapirs, and pheasants. They greeted the army with food, and in return Cabeza de Vaca gave them shirts and other presents. Since the region had not previously been visited by Europeans, he took possession of it on 29 November 1541 in the name of Emperor Charles V. An *escribano* drew up a deed of possession, and Cabeza de Vaca honored his paternal grandfather, Pedro de Vera, by calling the newly acquired land the province of Vera. According to sources unfriendly to the new governor, he then had his coat of arms engraved on a large stone.[54]

On 1 December, Cabeza de Vaca and his army came to the Río Iguazú, which they would cross at least twice. The Iguazú rises in the coastal mountains of Brazil and flows westward for some 380 miles before emptying into the Río Paraná. After a short pause while the pilots sounded the depths of the river, Cabeza de Vaca continued marching through his province of Vera, stopping along the way at several Guaraní settlements. The sometimes considerable distances between these settlements presented a problem for the governor because he was relying on Guaraní farmers to supply his army with food. He and his men found it simpler to buy provisions from the Indians than to hunt or forage on their own. The terrain they were crossing was a vast forested plain, watered by many rivers. The Spaniards saw wild boars and monkeys and probably saw blossoming jacaranda and lapacho trees as well. The province of Vera, Cabeza de Vaca observed, "is the best country in the world and has the best waters, rivers, arroyos, springs, fields, and groves that I have seen, and provides much opportunity for hunting, and seems well suited for colonization and the raising of livestock of all sorts." Describing its Guaraní inhabitants as farmers who "raise geese and fowls like those in Spain," he added: "They are a domestic people, friendly to the Christians, and with a little trouble could be brought to accept our holy Catholic faith."[55]

Through interpreters, Cabeza de Vaca spoke with the leading men of each community on his route. The Indians supplied his army with honey, poultry, flour, and maize, and in return Cabeza de Vaca gave them scissors and knives. Sometimes the Guaraníes provided so abundantly that he returned some of the commodities, as he had learned to do in North America, for redistribution to the native people. According to Pero Hernández, who chronicled but did not participate in the expedition, Cabeza de Vaca was generous with the Guaraníes, "especially with their chief[s], to whom, besides paying the price of the commodities which they brought, he gave many presents, and did them many favours and treated them so well that the fame went through the land and the province, and all the natives laid aside their fear and came to see and to bring all they had, and they were paid for it as aforesaid."[56]

Cabeza de Vaca not only insisted upon paying for everything but also was strict with his men regarding their behavior. He ensured that they camped well away from Indian settlements, and he kept his men from trafficking privately with the Guaraníes, from entering their houses, and from bothering their women. His strictness, however, caused grumbling among some of the men, who later complained that, in the course of the *entrada*, the governor had monopolized all trade with the Indians. Cabeza de Vaca would later report to the Royal Council of the Indies: "All the men I carried in my company in the said discovery were new people, inexperienced in the dealings and customs of the Indians, for which reason, on account of keeping them from occasions of disorder wherein we would have conflict with them [the Indians], they [my men] gave me great difficulties, which I suffered more than the burdens of traveling and dismounting and building bridges."[57]

As Cabeza de Vaca had seen during his journey across North America, the Indians used the arrival of the Europeans as an occasion for dancing and feasting. The Guaraníes, who had never seen horses before, were fearful of the Spaniards' mounts and attempted to tame them by offering them honey, poultry, and other inappropriate delicacies, telling the horses that if they behaved well they would receive more treats.[58]

Whenever Cabeza de Vaca conferred with Guaraníes, he sought information from them about the terrain ahead. At one settlement, he learned that, some time earlier, a group of Guaraní warriors had killed a group of Portuguese explorers near the confluence of the Iguazú and Paraná rivers. At another settlement, he conversed with a Christian Indian who had lived among the Spaniards in Asunción. This Indian now agreed to serve Cabeza de Vaca as his guide. The governor therefore discharged the Indians who had been escorting him, rewarded them for their service, and sent them home again. As was his practice in North America, he took care not to displace any Indian too far from his home territory.[59]

Cabeza de Vaca made some effort to map and keep a record of his army's route. At one Guaraní settlement the men visited in December, his pilots measured the latitude as 24°30′ south, or approximately one degree below the Tropic of Capricorn. The Spaniards were east and somewhat north of Asunción, and they were west and north of Santa Catalina Island. Sixteenth-century pilots had no way of determining longitude, but the army was moving in the direction of the sunset.[60]

In mid-December the army passed through a region where its progress was impeded by rivers, marshes, and huge thickets of bamboo-like reeds. The men of the vanguard had to cut a road through the reeds, and on one day they had to construct eighteen bridges. When the army finally reached a friendly Guaraní settlement, Cabeza de Vaca decided to pause there to rest his men and celebrate the Feast of the Nativity. When they resumed marching, the men entered a region of alternating mountain ridges and river valleys choked with reeds. For several days they came to no Indian settlement, and although they occasionally killed game such as deer and boars, the men complained of hunger. Cabeza de Vaca discovered, no doubt with the help of his Indian guides, that if he opened the stalks of the reeds, edible grubs could be found inside. Pero Hernández reports: "In the hollows of these reeds there were some white worms, about the length and thickness of a finger; the people fried these for food, obtaining sufficient fat from them to fry them in very well; all ate of them, and thought it excellent food." Cabeza de Vaca had learned long before not to be squeamish about unfamiliar foods, and he likely set an example for his men by eating his share of worms with a show of gusto.[61]

The expeditionary army again came upon Guaraní settlements in early January of 1542. However, the two friars—Bernardo de Armenta and Alonso Lebrón—had gone ahead of the main body of Spaniards and traded privately with the Indians, so when Cabeza de Vaca reached the settlements, the native people had little left to offer him. The governor warned the friars not to repeat this behavior, but they defied him. Because of their position as clerics, Cabeza de Vaca declined to punish them, but the friction between him and the friars was exacerbated.[62]

In mid-January, Cabeza de Vaca wrote to the royal officials in Asunción to inform them that he was coming by order of His Majesty Charles V to assume leadership of the province of Río de la Plata and to bring reinforcements and supplies to its Spanish settlers. Cabeza de Vaca directed the officials to send two brigantines up the Río Paraná to meet him and his army. He wanted the brigantines for security because of what he had heard about the killing of Portuguese explorers near the confluence of the Paraná and the Iguazú. Cabeza de Vaca sent his letter to Asunción via Indian couriers.[63]

On 31 January the expeditionary army arrived again on the banks of the Río Iguazú. They had crossed the river once before, and Cabeza de Vaca knew that crossing it this time was going to be dangerous. His first concern was to avoid the fate of the Portuguese explorers, but he also knew from native informants that shortly before meeting the Paraná, the Río Iguazú would fan out broadly and plummet into a deep gorge. Cabeza de Vaca summoned his officers to a council meeting to talk about the challenges ahead. He also directed his pilots to measure the latitude, and they found it to be 25°30′ south, which is roughly the correct latitude for the Iguazú Falls. The falls, which straddle the present border between Argentina and Brazil, are eight miles upriver from the point where the Río Iguazú flows into the Paraná. Today, at the confluence of these rivers, the three nations of Argentina, Brazil, and Paraguay come together.[64]

Together with Niagara in North America and Victoria in Africa, the Iguazú is one of the world's three greatest waterfalls. Niagara channels the largest volume of water and has a steadier flow than the seasonally variable Victoria and Iguazú, and Victoria, at 354 feet, is the highest of the three. But Iguazú is the widest—with a 10,000-foot rim supporting more than 250 visually distinct cataracts. It is two-tiered, with an intermediate shelf of basalt that breaks the cascade of water. The heart of the Iguazú Falls is a tight horseshoe of rock over which water plunges more than 230 feet into the Garganta del Diablo, a "devil's throat" of foam, spray, and rainbows. Swallows nest behind the curtains of water, and surrounding the falls is a subtropical rain forest frequented by ring-tailed coatimundis, toucans, capuchin monkeys, and large blue butterflies. Those who come upon the falls from upstream are nearly on top of them before hearing them, because the gorge into which the river leaps acts as a sound baffle. The plume of spray from the Garganta del Diablo, however, is visible from a good distance away. Pero Hernández says that "the spray rises two spears high and more above the fall." By "spears," he must have meant the distance to which a spear can be thrown.[65]

In consultation with his officers, Cabeza de Vaca decided to try to secure both sides of the Río Iguazú. He bought canoes from the local Indians and divided his men into overland and canoeing parties. The governor chose to lead the eighty men who would use the canoes to cross the river above the falls and portage around them. The remaining men and the horses would remain on the near side of the river and find an overland route around the falls. Below the falls, each party would defend the other from possible attack by Indians. After they had negotiated the Río Iguazú, both parties would use the canoes to cross the Paraná.[66]

The current of the Río Iguazú above the falls is very swift. When Cabeza de Vaca's party reached the far shore, they had to carry their canoes for more than a quarter of a league before they could reenter the river. As planned, they rendezvoused below the falls with their comrades of the overland party. A great number of Guaraní warriors wearing war paint and parrot feathers and armed with bows and arrows had assembled near the confluence of the Iguazú and Paraná rivers, but the arrival of the horses and of Spaniards from two directions disconcerted the Indians and kept them from attacking. Cabeza de Vaca spoke through interpreters with the Guaraní warriors and appeased them by distributing gifts to the chiefs. In the end, the Guaraníes agreed to help him and his men cross the Río Paraná. The river was

Cabeza de Vaca points to the Iguazú Falls in the fifth of eight panels from *Paseo Murales: Costa con historia Álvar Núñez Cabeza de Vaca* in Puerto Iguazú, Argentina. The murals, dated 2005, were created in polychrome plaster relief by Daniela Almeida and Hector Kura. Photograph by Juris Zagarins.

deep, rapid, and full of whirlpools, and Cabeza de Vaca estimated its width as equivalent to the maximum shot of a crossbow. But such a crossbow shot would be extraordinary, because just below its confluence with the Río Iguazú, the Río Paraná is six-tenths of a mile wide. Cabeza de Vaca ordered that the canoes be lashed together in pairs and used as rafts for transporting the horses. It took six hours for the entire army to cross the Paraná. During the crossing, one raft was upset and one Spaniard drowned.[67]

On the western side of the river, Cabeza de Vaca formally took possession of the Paraná in the name of His Majesty Charles V. His pilots again measured the latitude. They were roughly due east of Asunción, which is 190 miles from the confluence of the Iguazú and the Paraná. Today one of the constituent cataracts making up the total marvel of the Iguazú Falls is known as Salto Álvar Núñez, in Cabeza de Vaca's honor. A bronze plaque there credits the explorer with being the *descubridor* (discoverer) of the falls.[68]

Cabeza de Vaca was disappointed to find that the brigantines he had requested from the royal officials in Asunción were nowhere in evidence. About thirty of his men were too ill to continue the overland journey, and he had hoped to transport them to Asunción in the brigantines. Of necessity, he decided to send the sick men and an escorting group of fifty crossbowmen and harquebusiers downriver on the rafts constructed for crossing the Paraná. Pedro Dorantes, however, protested against sending any men on the rafts.[69]

After the departure of the rafting party, Cabeza de Vaca and his remaining men set off for Asunción. They crossed several rivers and large marshes and paused often to build bridges. Along the way, they met Guaraníes who supplied them with provisions. Cabeza de Vaca compensated them all, and he later testified that throughout his *entrada* he paid the Indians for everything they gave him and his men.[70]

As they neared Asunción, Cabeza de Vaca and his men met a Guaraní messenger who spoke Castilian Spanish. He said he was a Christian and that Interim Governor Irala had sent him to meet them. A short time later the army met a Spanish messenger who also brought greetings from Asunción. This second messenger told Cabeza de Vaca that the letter he had sent to the royal officials had reached them and they were expecting his arrival. The messenger informed the new governor, once again, of the death of Juan de Ayolas but also conveyed the surprising news that Buenos Aires had been abandoned. In June of 1541, Irala and Alonso Cabrera, the royal inspector of mines, had ordered the evacuation of the city and had moved its Christian population to Asunción. Cabeza de Vaca had received his last news of Buenos Aires in May of 1541 from the fugitives he had entertained at Santa Catalina Island. What he was now hearing caused him grave concern because in October of 1541 he had sent Pedro Estopiñán Cabeza de Vaca and his seagoing party of 140 men and women from Santa Catalina to Buenos Aires. Since the settlement was deserted and possibly in the hands of Indians, Estopiñán's party might be in danger. The new governor sent the Spanish messenger back to Asunción to inform the royal officials there of his imminent arrival.[71]

At nine o'clock in the morning of 11 March 1542, Álvar Núñez Cabeza de Vaca and his expeditionary army arrived in Asunción. In the five months since they had left Santa Catalina Island, the men had marched four hundred leagues. Their only casualty was the man who drowned while crossing the Río Paraná. Cabeza de Vaca would later boast that his men had caused no disturbance among the Indians and that he had left the entire region from Santa Catalina to Asunción "in peace." He had accomplished a major feat in opening an overland route to Asunción from the Brazilian coast.[72]

THIRTEEN

Asunción

The European residents of Asunción, most of them heavily bearded and dressed in leather and locally woven cotton, came out to greet their new governor in the road and to welcome him to their settlement. They thanked him for bringing reinforcements and supplies. After abandoning the seaport of Buenos Aires, they had despaired of receiving aid from Spain. Three years had passed since they had seen any new Spanish faces. At the time of Cabeza de Vaca's arrival, some 300 Europeans were living in Asunción. But with the approximately 250 Spaniards the governor brought with him, the European population of the settlement nearly doubled. The date of Cabeza de Vaca's arrival, 11 March, was late in the South American summer and near the end of the rainy season, which, in the area of Asunción, generally runs from December to April. The daily high temperature in March may have reached the low nineties on the Fahrenheit scale.[1]

On his first day in Asunción, Cabeza de Vaca met ceremonially with Interim Governor Irala and the two royal officials who were in Asunción. Like most Spanish provinces, Río de la Plata had four royal officials: in order of seniority, the *tesorero* (treasurer), the *contador* (comptroller), the *factor* (quartermaster), and the *veedor* (inspector of mines). Only *factor* Pedro Dorantes and *veedor* Alonso Cabrera can have been present at the first meeting between Cabeza de Vaca and the leaders of the Spanish community he had come to govern. Dorantes, a newcomer to Río de la Plata, had crossed the Atlantic with Cabeza de Vaca and marched with him to

Asunción. The other three officials had all come to Río de la Plata with the late governor Pedro de Mendoza. Cabrera had collaborated with Irala in evacuating Buenos Aires in 1541. Felipe de Cáceres, the comptroller, had carried news to Spain and then returned to South America with Cabeza de Vaca, but he had declined to march with him from Santa Catalina and had sailed with Pedro Estopiñán Cabeza de Vaca to Buenos Aires. García Venegas, the acting *tesorero*, had taken three brigantines and gone to rescue the men whom Governor Cabeza de Vaca had sent down the Río Paraná on rafts.[2]

The *escribano* Pero Hernández was present at the initial meeting between Cabeza de Vaca and the leaders of Asunción. Hernández had come to Río de la Plata with Governor Mendoza and would soon become Cabeza de Vaca's secretary and one of his most loyal defenders. He would write two accounts of the new governor's term in office. Hernández was born in 1513, so when Cabeza de Vaca arrived in Asunción, he was twenty-eight or twenty-nine years old.[3]

Others who were present at the initial meeting included the mayor of Asunción and various clergymen, magistrates, and military officers. Cabeza de Vaca presented his authorizing documents to Irala and the royal officials. The documents, which bore the imperial seal of Charles V, were read out loud. According to Hernández, all the Spaniards present at the gathering, including Irala, recognized Cabeza de Vaca as their royally appointed governor and captain general. Irala turned the official insignia of justice over to Cabeza de Vaca, who, following standard protocol, redelivered them, in the name of Charles V, to the magistrates in charge of administering justice in the province.[4]

Apparently there was disagreement, however, concerning whether Cabeza de Vaca was the governor or merely the acting governor of Río de la Plata. Irala later reported to the emperor:

> [Cabeza de Vaca] showed us a *provision* of Your Majesty in which it was ordered that in case of the death of the Governor Juan de Ayolas, we should obey him as governor of this country; and because we had no more certainty about the death of Juan de Ayolas than what the Chane boy had said, because he had said that some Christians had remained in his land, and he might still have been alive there among them, we would not receive him by virtue of this *provision*. Then he showed us another one in which your Majesty ordered that in case of doubt of the life or

death of Juan de Ayolas, we should receive him [Cabeza de Vaca] as his deputy and in Your Majesty's name. After seeing this, he was obeyed and received in accord with his *provisiones*.

Irala seized upon the clause in Cabeza de Vaca's *capitulaciones* specifying that the royal appointee was to succeed Ayolas as governor if, and only if, Ayolas was known to be dead. If any doubt existed concerning the fate of Ayolas, Cabeza de Vaca was merely to be the acting governor. Although Irala had learned conclusively in 1540 that Ayolas was dead, he now insisted that Mendoza's lieutenant might still be alive somewhere in the country of the Chané Indians. Pedro Dorantes sided with Irala and wrote to the emperor, explaining that he and the other royal officials refused to accept Cabeza de Vaca as more than their acting governor. Insisting that he was indeed the governor, Cabeza de Vaca maintained that at the time of his arrival in Asunción, the death of Ayolas was common knowledge, and he even had Pero Hernández certify that Ayolas was dead. As long as the fate of Ayolas was officially unknown, however, Cabeza de Vaca's title to the governorship was unclear, and he could not claim the full powers to which he was entitled.[5]

Irala and Cabeza de Vaca were obvious rivals, and Irala had the advantage of being well established in Asunción and surrounded by friends who wished to restore him to power. To him and to many of his supporters, Cabeza de Vaca and the newcomers he brought with him were greenhorns and agents of unwelcome change.[6]

The royal officials were also at odds with the new governor, but the problems between them and him were primarily economic. Río de la Plata had a subsistence economy based on Indian labor. In default of the gold and silver they all hoped to find, the European settlers of the province were trading in IOUs or using a barter system whereby, for example, twenty-five pieces of iron weighing eight ounces each were equal in value to one Indian girl. Some of the European settlers were very nearly destitute, and they complained to Cabeza de Vaca that the resident royal officials Alonso Cabrera and García Venegas were levying unjust and unreasonable taxes. Cabrera and Venegas had seized the armaments and even the clothing of those Spaniards who were too poor to pay their taxes, leaving the men naked and unarmed, and the officials had jailed other tax defaulters. According to Pero Hernández, when Cabeza de Vaca arrived in Asunción, "the governor found everything disorganised, the Christians in poor circumstances and without arms, and the inhabitants complaining of the extortionate behaviour of the officers, who, to advance their personal interests, had most unjustly levied tribute and a new tax, contrary to the custom of Spain and the Indies, to which they gave the name of *quinto*." Cabrera and Venegas claimed to be collecting the *quinto real* (king's fifth) on behalf of Emperor Charles V, but because their salaries were in arrears, they were keeping the money for themselves. The officials had imposed their *quinto* tax on the local fishing industry, on pelts and other items bought from the Indians, and on commodities like maize, butter, and honey. Cabeza de Vaca acknowledged that no gold or silver was available with which to pay the officials' salaries, but he sided with the destitute settlers. Soon after coming to Asunción, he distributed clothing, weapons, and other necessities to the neediest Europeans, supplying the items at his own expense. He then set limits on the taxes the royal officials could collect. He also directed the mayor of Asunción, the constables, and the provincial *escribano* not to collect their customary fees until the province was on a sounder economic footing.[7]

Naturally, the royal officials resented the new governor's actions. Pero Hernández reports that the officials were "prompted by a bad spirit" toward Cabeza de Vaca and "strove to do him all the harm they could." Pedro Dorantes, the newly arrived quartermaster, quickly joined his more seasoned colleagues in opposing the governor. In a letter to the emperor, Dorantes argued that the *quinto* was rooted in local law and custom. He also complained that Cabeza de Vaca had not consulted sufficiently with him and the other royal officials.[8]

And yet when serious matters were afoot, the new governor's procedure was to call the royal officials, the military captains, and the local clergymen into council, give them information, and ask for their advice. The governor charged an *escribano* with recording the deliberations and required the officers and clergymen to certify their opinions with their signatures. But if his advisers gave him hopelessly conflicting opinions, Cabeza de Vaca did as he best saw fit.[9]

The military captains under Cabeza de Vaca's command included Juan de Salazar de Espinosa, Domingo Martínez de Irala, Gonzalo de Mendoza, Francisco de Ribera, Hernando de Ribera, and Juan Romero. Most of the local clergymen supported Cabeza de Vaca, but others, like Bernardo de Armenta and Alonso Lebrón, did not. Among those who opposed the governor were three priests and a friar who became angered by his insistence that they live virtuously.[10]

During his first days in Asunción, Cabeza de Vaca did what he could to assist those members of his expeditionary army who had not entered the Spanish settlement with him. His first concern was for the eighty men he had sent down the Río Paraná on rafts. Irala reported that upon receiving Cabeza de Vaca's letter from the field, he had dispatched García Venegas with three brigantines to the new governor's aid. As it happened, the eighty Spaniards of the rafting party, both the sick and the able-bodied, arrived in Asunción about a month after Cabeza de Vaca did. They had suffered many hardships and much harassment from Indians, but they had eventually met with Venegas and his brigantines. They lost only one man who was killed by a large cat that the Spaniards identified as a tiger.[11]

Meanwhile, Cabeza de Vaca was also concerned about the 140 men he had sent from Santa Catalina Island to Buenos Aires under the command of Pedro Estopiñán Cabeza de Vaca. In late April the governor sent Captain Juan Romero with two brigantines downriver to Buenos Aires, directing Romero to join with Estopiñán and his men in rebuilding and repopulating the seaport since its security was vital to the Europeans residing in Asunción. After Romero's departure, Cabeza de Vaca ordered the building of two more brigantines to be sent to Buenos Aires as well.[12]

Cabeza de Vaca then turned his attention to matters that were nearer at hand. Several Guaraníes complained to him about bad treatment they were receiving from Europeans. The governor wanted good relations with the Guaraníes, for, according to Pero Hernández, the European settlers depended on them "for their means of subsistence" and could not have continued in Asunción without it. Cabeza de Vaca remembered the devastation caused by Spanish slavers on the northwestern frontier of New Spain, and he meant to prevent anything like it from occurring in Río de la Plata. He was later to testify that the Christians of his South American province, "especially some of the captains, the royal officials and their friends, committed grievances and cruelties against Indians and their women and children," killing some and forcing others to work without pay.[13]

In an early effort to rectify the situation, the governor summoned all the Christian clergymen to a meeting in Asunción and had those parts of his royal charter concerning the treatment of Indians read aloud. He charged the clergymen with spreading the gospel to the Indians and protecting them from ill use by Europeans. He also directed the clergymen to set a good moral example for both Europeans and Indians and, in particular, to guard their own behavior with Indian women. Cabeza de Vaca asked the clergymen to inform him of any abuses perpetrated by Europeans against Indians. Then he distributed the items to the clergymen that he had brought for their special use, including vestments, a barrel of sacramental wine, and flour for the sacramental bread. Finally, he gave them a building site and directed them to begin constructing a church.[14]

Cabeza de Vaca wished to prevent his compatriots from treating the Indians as slaves and from taking their property, children, or women by force, and he wanted the Europeans to pay the Indians for their labor. But his wishes concerning paying the Indians would prove difficult to implement for two reasons. First, the Europeans did not possess enough items of value to sustain a wage economy. Second, the local Guaraníes were already committed to the Europeans in ways that had nothing to do with wages. They valued the advantage that their alliance with the Europeans gave them over their traditional Indian enemies, and they were related to the Europeans by marriage. Before Cabeza de Vaca's arrival, the Guaraníes had given the Europeans some seven hundred women. These women provided their European husbands not only with sexual services but also with domestic and agricultural work. And since Guaraní culture obliged relatives to provide one another with kinship labor, the women's brothers and fathers worked for their European in-laws as well. In Guaraní culture, moreover, the number of wives a man had was a sign of his status. Some Europeans made a point, therefore, of amassing large harems, and a few possessed thirty, forty, or even fifty women. Irala, as Cabeza de Vaca later charged, had an especially large harem. Pero Hernández reported that Irala had "carnal access" to many Indian women, including some who were sisters or cousins or otherwise related, and he guarded them jealously "as though they were his legitimate wives." By 1545 mestizo children in Asunción numbered between four hundred and six hundred, and in 1550, by Irala's count, there were three thousand. Cabeza de Vaca's nephew Alonso Riquelme de Guzmán would one day father children by one of Irala's mixed-race daughters. In the new social order, as the Guaraní women quickly perceived, a woman's status was improved if she bore mixed-race rather than purely Indian children.[15]

To Cabeza de Vaca, polygamy was a "grave sin and offence against God." He was especially dismayed that some of his Spanish compatriots were violating Christian taboos against incest by having sexual relations with groups of sisters, with a mother and her daughter, or with an aunt and her niece. He also charged that "some Indian women, although they were Christian,

Cabeza de Vaca "defends the Indians and issues laws against the abuse of natives" in the seventh of eight panels from *Paseo Murales: Costa con historia Álvar Núñez Cabeza de Vaca* in Puerto Iguazú, Argentina. The murals were created in polychrome plaster relief by Daniela Almeida and Hector Kura in 2005. Photograph by Juris Zagarins.

were bartered and exchanged as if they were slaves." The women themselves accepted polygamy, however, and may have preferred a domestic arrangement in which they had blood ties to their co-wives. On 5 April 1542, Cabeza de Vaca issued the first of a series of edicts concerning treatment of the Indians. He decreed that no Indian, male or female, could be sold or traded without a license. No women who were related by blood could live together in the household of any Christian. No weapon was to be sold or traded to an Indian. No Indian could be forced to sell property against his will, and any sale of land by an Indian to a European was subject to the governor's review. In addition, Cabeza de Vaca imposed a curfew on the Europeans and barred them from entering the dwellings of the Indians. Offenders were subject to fines, imprisonment, or service as oarsmen in the brigantines. As Cabeza de Vaca later testified, these measures made him odious to many of his compatriots.[16]

The governor also moved to restrict the behavior of the Guaraníes, particularly with respect to cannibalism. Pero Hernández describes how the Guaraníes brought war captives to their villages, fattened them, and even allowed them to enjoy the sexual favors of Guaraní women. When a captive was sufficiently fat, the women adorned him with feathers and necklaces and began singing and dancing around him. Then the Guaraní men appeared on the scene. Hernández describes what would follow:

> The Indian considered the bravest among them now takes a wooden sword in his hand, called in their language *macana*, and leads the captive to a place where he is made to dance for one hour; the Indian then advances, and with both hands deals him a blow in the loins, and another on the spine to knock him down. It happens sometimes that after striking him six blows on the head they cannot kill him, so hard are their heads, though this two-handed sword is made of very tough, heavy, black wood, and the executioner is strong enough to kill an ox with a single blow.

If the executioner failed, little boys dispatched the victim with hatchets. Amidst general merrymaking, the women would divide the body and cook it in earthenware pots. The ensuing feasting lasted for several days. The chief executioner would take the name of the dead man in commemoration of the event.[17]

On 29 April, Cabeza de Vaca summoned the Guaraníes to meet with him and the Christian clergymen, and in this meeting he outlawed the practice of cannibalism. He told the Guaraníes he had been sent by Emperor Charles V to protect them and to lead them to the Christian faith. If they submitted to the authority of the emperor, accepted Christianity, and gave up the practice of cannibalism, he assured them they would receive good treatment from the local Christians. They would be paid for their labor, and no Christian would take their property by force. If the Guaraníes continued to eat human flesh, however, Cabeza de Vaca threatened to make war on them because cannibalism was "a sin and a grave offence against God." The governor concluded the meeting by presenting the Guaraníes with shirts, caps, and lengths of fabric.[18]

On 10 July a delegation of Guaraníes appeared before Cabeza de Vaca to complain about their enemies, the Guaycurúes, who lived in the Chaco desert on the western side of the Río Paraguay. "Guaycurú" was a collective term for several bands of nomadic fishermen, hunters, and gatherers who shared a language and culture. The Guaraníes said that when they went to the river to fish, the Guaycurúes would attack them.[19]

The Agaces, a Guaycurú band living near Asunción, possessed dugout canoes that they used for both fishing and piracy. A favorite practice among them was to capture a lone Guaraní and extort a huge ransom from his relatives. Even if the ransom was paid, they would sometimes behead their prisoner and mount his head on a pole on the riverbank for all to see. Before Cabeza de Vaca arrived in Asunción, Irala had made war on the Agaces and concluded a peace with them, but they had violated the agreement. When the Agaces heard that a new governor had arrived, several of their chiefs came to Asunción to swear allegiance to him and restore peaceful relations with their Spanish neighbors. Cabeza de Vaca welcomed their overtures and told them that so long as they kept the peace, he would regard them as friends, but if they broke the peace again or bothered the Guaraníes, he would punish them without mercy. He stipulated that the Agaces were not to travel on the Río Paraguay at night, to trespass on Guaraní or Spanish territory, or to harass any Spanish or Guaraní fishermen. The Agaces also were to free any Guaraní captives they held. The Agaces agreed to all these terms, and as Cabeza de Vaca had learned to do when negotiating with Indians in North America, he gave them gifts.[20]

A more pressing threat was posed by another group of Guaycurúes who had attacked a Guaraní settlement at Caguazú. Cabeza de Vaca sent Martin de Almenza, a priest who understood their language, and fifty armed Spaniards to negotiate with the Guaycurúes. Almenza returned to Asunción eight days later, reporting that he had tried to resolve the problem but the Guaycurúes had driven him away. Almenza and his brother clergymen gave Cabeza de Vaca their opinion, in writing, that war against the recalcitrant Indians was justified.[21]

Leaving Gonzalo de Mendoza and a garrison of 250 men to defend Asunción, the governor set out on 12 July 1542 with 200 foot soldiers and 12 horsemen to deal with the Guaycurúes. He allowed his soldiers to bring their women as burden-bearers, and he used two brigantines to ferry his army to the western side of the Río Paraguay. They rendezvoused there with their Guaraní allies, whose force numbered ten thousand men. Pero Hernández says of the Guaraní warriors: "It was wonderful to see the order they kept, and their preparations for war, all of them armed with bows and arrows, adorned with parrots' feathers, and painted with divers colours. They had musical instruments, which they use in battle, such as timbals and trumpets, cornets, etc."[22]

Cabeza de Vaca sat down with the Guaraní leaders to feast on venison and the meat of rheas, large ostrichlike birds. Each of the Guaraní leaders recognized him as commander in chief and presented him with a brightly painted bow and an arrow fletched with parrot feathers. The army was at the edge of the Chaco desert, with the river behind them and a flat, seemingly endless savanna ahead. Cabeza de Vaca sent out Guaraní scouts who returned the next day to say that the Guaycurúes were five to six leagues away and, using their traditional method of driving out game, had set fire to the grasslands. The Guaycurúes seemed unaware of the proximity of their Spanish and Guaraní foes.[23]

Upon receipt of this intelligence, the army set off in pursuit of the Guaycurúes. Pero Hernández gives an account of their march:

> The Indians went together in a troop extending over a league in length, all arrayed in parrots' feathers, and with bows and arrows. In front of them was the advanced guard, and behind came the main body, the governor and the cavalry, followed by the Spanish infantry, arquebusiers and crossbowmen. After these came the women, bearing the munitions and provisions of the Spaniards. The Indians carried their own supplies. In this order they marched till mid-day, when they rested under some large trees, where they all halted and partook of some refreshment. After this, they resumed the march, led by the Indian guides, along footpaths, where the quantity of deer and ostriches was amazing. . . . [A]ll kept their ranks, the Guaranís in advance numbering some ten thousand men, all painted and bedizened with necklaces of beads and plumes, and plates of copper, which glistened marvellously well in the sun.[24]

At dusk, Cabeza de Vaca set a strict watch, ordering his crossbowmen to keep their bows strung and his harquebusiers to keep their guns loaded and fuses lit. As the darkness thickened, a large cat—either a puma or a jaguar—caused a panic among the men. Several harquebusiers fired their weapons, wounding a few Guaraníes and scattering the rest. In the confusion, Cabeza de Vaca himself was fired upon twice, and the bullets "grazed the skin of his face." Pero Hernández later charged that "these shots were certainly fired maliciously with intent to kill him [the governor], and to please Domingo de Irala, whom he had deprived of the command of the province." Despite the danger to himself, Cabeza de Vaca succeeded in rallying the Guaraníes and restoring calm.[25]

Later that night, a scout returned to the Spanish and Guaraní camp and reported that four thousand Guaycurúes were camping three leagues away. Cabeza de Vaca ordered his troops to advance quietly. He directed the Guaraníes to paint white crosses on their chests so that the Spaniards would recognize them on the battlefield as friends. The Spanish cavalrymen fastened breastplates on the horses and filled their mouths with grass so that the animals could not arouse the enemy by neighing.[26]

At dawn the allied forces surrounded the Guaycurú camp. The Guaycurúes beat their drums in alarm, shot volleys of arrows, and hurled burning logs at their foes. Crying "Santiago!"—the traditional Spanish battle cry—Cabeza de Vaca led a cavalry charge into the camp. The Guaycurúes torched the camp and fled, under cover of the smoke, into the underbrush. But as they retreated, they killed two Spaniards and a dozen Guaraníes. According to Pero Hernández, the Guaycurúes decapitated their victims: "This operation is performed by the aid of two or three teeth of a fish called the *palometa* [piranha], which bites fish-hooks in two. These teeth are attached to a small stick. The Guaycurús, holding their prisoners by the hair of the head, pass this instrument round their neck, and with a twist or two of the head, completely sever it from the body, and carry it off by the hair." In the heat of the battle, a Guaycurú warrior flung himself against Cabeza de Vaca's horse and plunged three arrows into the animal's neck, but a nearby horseman came to the governor's aid. Cabeza de Vaca and his cavalrymen then rounded up some four hundred Guaycurú prisoners, but as the allied forces marched back to Asunción, other Guaycurúes picked off a thousand Guaraní stragglers.[27]

Cabeza de Vaca refused to allow his Spaniards to enslave, or his Guaraní allies to eat, any of the Guaycurú prisoners. Instead, he selected one of the prisoners as a messenger, gave him presents, and sent him to summon his kinsmen to a conference. The man returned four days later with twenty Guaycurú chiefs. Speaking through an interpreter, a Guaycurú spokesman said: "No people has ever conquered us, and we never thought we should be conquered by anyone. Now we have found others more valiant than ourselves, and we have come to place ourselves in their power and be their slaves. You are the chief of the Spaniards, command us and we will obey your orders." Cabeza de Vaca answered that what he desired was for the Guaycurúes to submit to Spanish authority, accept the Christian religion, and cease harassing their Guaraní neighbors. He offered to release all four hundred of his war prisoners if the Guaycurúes agreed to his terms.[28]

Pero Hernández reports that the Guaycurúes not only accepted the governor's terms but also helped supply Asunción with fish and game from that time forward. They brought these commodities, along with barbecued meats and animal skins, to an outdoor market on the banks of the Río Paraguay and traded with the Guaraníes for maize, manioc, peanuts, bows, and arrows. Hernández describes a typical gathering:

> Two hundred canoes crossed the river together for this market, laden with all these things; and it was the finest thing in the world to see them cross. The celerity of their movements is such that they sometimes collide with one another, and all the merchandise falls into the water. Then the Indians to whom this happens, and those awaiting them on the bank, burst into fits of laughter, and the jokes and merriment continue all the time the market is being held. They come to this market in full paint and in their feathers.

Cabeza de Vaca's enemies would later accuse him, however, of having killed four thousand Guaycurúes during the course of the 1542 war and of having destroyed nine Guaycurú encampments.[29]

Soon after he returned from the battlefield, Cabeza de Vaca received a report from Gonzalo de Mendoza, the captain he had left in command of the garrison at Asunción. During the governor's absence, Mendoza said, a delegation of six Apirús had sought to initiate an alliance between their people and the Spaniards. The Apirús were yet another group of Guaycurúes, and Mendoza had mistrusted them and made hostages of their delegates. A more troubling matter was that the Agaces had violated the terms of the peace treaty they had concluded with Cabeza de Vaca. While the governor was away, they had attempted to burn Asunción and had carried off a number of Guaraní women. Mendoza was holding thirteen or fourteen Agaz prisoners.[30]

To address the first problem, Cabeza de Vaca interrogated Mendoza's Apirú hostages. But when they promised to submit to Spanish authority, he released them, gave them presents, and promised to protect them. Several days later, a larger delegation of Apirús called on him. They had brought Apirú women and begged the governor to seal their alliance by accepting the women as his wives. Because of his efforts to contain the polygamous arrangements of his compatriots, however, Cabeza de Vaca could not afford to take the women into his household. He accepted them only as hostages and entrusted them to the care of clergymen who were to instruct them in Christian doctrine. A friar who knew Cabeza de Vaca's character later reported that the governor never touched an Indian woman.[31]

To address the problem with the Agaces, Cabeza de Vaca consulted with his officers and clergymen, and they agreed that a war against the Agaces was justified. They also declared that Mendoza's Agaz prisoners should be hanged, so—perhaps to demonstrate that he was not soft on Indians—Cabeza de Vaca condemned the prisoners to death. He selected Domingo Martínez de Irala to lead the war against the Agaces, for despite his rivalry with the captain, he recognized Irala's expertise as a field commander. In the ensuing war, Irala and his Spanish and Guaraní forces killed many Agaces, and the Guaraníes ate their Agaz captives.[32]

At some point during Cabeza de Vaca's first year in Asunción, he stripped Martín de Orúe of his office as provincial *escribano* and replaced him with Pero Hernández, who had been serving as the governor's secretary. Cabeza de Vaca cited Orúe's "insufficiency and inability" as the cause of his dismissal. Orúe became the governor's implacable enemy and went on to write a negative account of Cabeza de Vaca's administration of Río de la Plata that Gonzalo Fernández de Oviedo y Valdés incorporated into the twenty-third volume of his *Historia general y natural de las Indias*. Among other things, Orúe would report that "within a short time [of his arrival in Asunción], Cabeza de Vaca earned the dislike both of the people he brought with him and of those he found in the land." Orúe, like Irala, was a Basque from Vizcaya, in northern Spain.[33]

Throughout his first months in office, Cabeza de Vaca continued to worry about the safety of the men he had sent to Buenos Aires under Estopiñán's command, even though Juan Romero and two brigantines had already gone to their aid. The two additional brigantines the governor had commissioned were now ready, and Cabeza de Vaca sent them to Buenos Aires on 25 July 1542, under the command of Gonzalo de Mendoza.[34]

The governor then ordered the construction of a caravel and ten more brigantines. He intended to send the caravel to Spain to inform the emperor of what was happening in Río de la Plata. He planned to take the brigantines up the Río Paraguay and into the uncharted region in the northwest where first Alejo García and then Juan de Ayolas were said to have found gold and silver.[35]

As his long treks from Texas to Mexico and from Santa Catalina to Asunción indicate, Cabeza de Vaca enjoyed exploring. He dreamed of serving his emperor by extending the territory Charles V had appointed him to govern. But Cabeza de Vaca's more pressing need was to find the wherewithal to meet his administrative and diplomatic expenses. He had contracted with Charles V to bear the costs of his government himself. And yet, soon after arriving in Asunción, Cabeza de Vaca had put limits on the collection of taxes. Now he was running short of the goods he had brought from Spain as presents for Indians—he had already given many items away, at his own expense, both to Indians and to needy Spaniards. Furthermore, he wanted to continue paying the Indians for their labor. But in order to do all that he wanted, he needed a source of revenue. The economic potential of his province seemed limited unless he could discover and develop the mineral resources reputed to originate somewhere in the northwest.[36]

The governor called his officers and clergymen into council, and they agreed he should make an *entrada* into the country to the northwest. He also consulted his Guaraní allies and asked them to furnish him with guides. Aracaré, a Guaraní chief from the upper Río Paraguay, offered his personal services. Cabeza de Vaca deputized three Spaniards who knew the native languages to go with Aracaré into the Chaco on an overland reconnaissance mission. The governor also ordered Captain Irala to go with three brigantines and ninety men up the Río Paraguay to the frontier outpost at Candelaria to collect information about the upper reaches of the river, the native people living there, the availability of foodstuffs, and the whereabouts of gold and silver. The governor directed Irala to return to Asunción in three and a half months.[37]

On 20 October, near the onset of summer and the rainy season, Irala and his three brigantines set off for Candelaria. Aracaré and the three Spaniards of the overland reconnaissance party went with him. Eight days later the party arrived at Las Piedras, a river-port seventy leagues upriver from Asunción. Aracaré and the three Spanish explorers disembarked and set off westward into the Chaco.[38]

Twenty days after leaving Asunción, however, the three Spanish explorers returned to the Spanish settlement. From Las Piedras, they reported, they had marched westward for four days. But as they marched, Aracaré had ordered his Indians to burn the fields on either side of their route. This, according to the Spaniards, had signaled other Indians to harass them. Aracaré told his Indians to desert the Spaniards, who were "evil," and to avoid showing them the country. Thus, the three men could give Cabeza de Vaca little information that would assist him in planning his *entrada*.[39]

The governor therefore sent four other Spaniards to reconnoiter the Chaco with a different group of Guaraní guides. The men set off on 15 December for Las Piedras and, from there, marched westward for thirty days, experiencing great hunger along the way. They had nothing to eat except wild thistles and herbs. Aracaré and his people harassed them until they too returned to Asunción.[40]

Since Aracaré had previously declared his allegiance to the Spanish crown, Cabeza de Vaca saw his actions as treasonous. He knew that if he permitted one Guaraní chief to defy Spanish authority, others would follow. He indicted Aracaré on charges that he had "impeded the discovery of the land" and, following standard legal procedure, had the indictment served on the rebellious chief. According to Pero Hernández, notifying the chief of the charges against him was a "dangerous commission, because Aracaré came out with arms in his hands, followed by a number of friends and relations, with the intent to kill the Spaniards sent to him." Cabeza de Vaca obtained the written consent of the royal officials and condemned Aracaré to death. Carrying out the sentence was going to be another "dangerous commission," so the governor sent a letter to Captain Irala—the strongman upon whom he had to rely yet again—and assigned the task to him.[41]

On 20 December 1542, in the midst of these difficulties with Aracaré, Pedro Estopiñán Cabeza de Vaca and his party arrived in Asunción from Buenos Aires in a convoy that included their ship's boat and the four brigantines the governor had sent to their rescue. With Estopiñán were the royal comptroller, Felipe de Cáceres, and the captains of the brigantines: Juan Romero and Gonzalo de Mendoza. While the group was traveling upriver to Asunción, Cáceres had made an unhappy wager in a game of cards or dice and lost the artillery pieces the governor had entrusted to his care. Cabeza de Vaca demanded the guns from the winning gamblers and placed them in the joint charge of the four royal officials. A few days later, Cáceres—with the approval of his three brother officers—wagered the artillery pieces again, and again lost them.[42]

Estopiñán reported that he had set off from Santa Catalina for Buenos Aires the year before, as his cousin, the governor, had directed. The voyage was difficult because of contrary winds and the death of his pilot en route. When Estopiñán and his people finally arrived in Buenos Aires, they found a ship's mast planted upright near the waterfront and carved with the words "aquí está una carta," or "here is a letter." The letter, which had been placed there in June of 1541, was in a hole bored in the mast. Signed by Interim Governor Irala and inspector of mines Alonso Cabrera it stated that Buenos Aires had been abandoned and its people evacuated to Asunción.

It also stated that Irala and Cabrera were leaving a large cache of maize and beans in a house on a nearby island for anyone who could read their message. Thus, Estopiñán found himself in a precarious position. He and his people had little to eat except the maize left by Irala and Cabrera, and they were harassed continuously by the local Indians. The Spaniards began making their way up the Río Paraná toward Asunción, but they soon met Captain Romero and returned with him to Buenos Aires. They were later joined there by Captain Mendoza and his two additional brigantines. But although Estopiñán, Romero, and Mendoza had all received orders from the governor to secure Buenos Aires, a series of disasters, including Indian attacks, floods, and an earthquake, forced them to abandon the seaport. Buenos Aires would remain a ghost town until 1580.[43]

On 4 February 1543, two months after Estopiñán's arrival in Asunción, a fire broke out there, apparently from an accidental cause. Cabeza de Vaca ordered the sounding of the alarm. No Spaniards lost their lives, but 200 of Asunción's 250 houses, the church, five thousand measures of maize, and other property and livestock were destroyed. So far as he was able, the governor resupplied the destitute settlers with food and goods from his own reserves. He directed the Spaniards to rebuild their houses with brick and adobe rather than wood and straw, and he ordered the rebuilding of the church, assisting in the reconstruction with his own hands. According to one clergyman, the governor had never in many months missed a day of mass.[44]

Two to three weeks after the fire, Captain Irala returned to Asunción with his three brigantines. He had traveled 250 leagues up the Río Paraguay, pushing deep into the Pantanal and well beyond the outpost at Candelaria. On 6 January 1543, the Feast of the Three Kings, he had established a new outpost at latitude 16°50′ south, calling it Puerto de los Reyes in honor of the Magi. The people living in the vicinity of the outpost were farmers. They possessed samples of gold and silver, and they told Irala that the best route to the region from which these metals originated lay westward through their territory. Irala made a three-day reconnaissance march and found the country sufficiently fruitful to supply a large army of explorers. He also encountered a band of Guaraníes who had traveled with Alejo García to the Sierra de la Plata. They said that to march from where they lived to the land of gold and silver would require fifteen days. On his return downriver, Irala had received the letter from Cabeza de Vaca directing him to hang Aracaré. Irala had carried out the order but had met resistance from

Aracaré's friends and relations. As it happened, Cabeza de Vaca—and not Irala—would later be charged with tyranny for his role in the execution of the Guaraní chief.[45]

On 24 May, three months after Irala's return, Cabeza de Vaca called his officers and clergymen together to finalize plans for his *entrada*. Irala's talk of gold and silver must have mesmerized them all, but some of the officers warned that the recent fire and the annual flooding of the Río Paraguay posed obstacles. Because of the fire, many settlers had lost equipment and provisions that were necessary for an expedition of exploration. On the other hand, these very losses were a reason why they desperately needed to find gold and silver. Cabeza de Vaca, being a relative newcomer to South America, may not have understood how serious a problem seasonal flooding could pose. During the rainy season from November through March, the water level on the upper Paraguay and in the Pantanal could rise by ten feet. Irala's recent journey to Puerto de los Reyes had occurred during the hot and rainy months of October through February. Irala advised Cabeza de Vaca to undertake his *entrada* in the winter months of June, July, and August.[46]

The governor readied his ten new brigantines and sent Captain Gonzalo de Mendoza to purchase provisions from the Guaraníes. Mendoza soon ran into trouble, however. Two Guaraní chiefs, Guaçani and Aracaré's brother Tabaré, rose in rebellion against the Spaniards. Guaçani and Tabaré burned settlements and blocked roads to impede Mendoza's efforts to collect and transport provisions.[47]

On 8 June, Cabeza de Vaca again called his officers and clergymen into council, and they urged him to take military action against the rebellious chiefs. The governor hoped to avoid war, but he sent Captain Irala with four brigantines and 150 men to Mendoza's relief. Cabeza de Vaca supplied Irala with presents to distribute to the chiefs and directed him to try to resolve the situation by peaceful means. If he had to use force, Irala was to do as little damage as possible.[48]

When Irala arrived in their territory, he summoned Guaçani and Tabaré to a conference. But the chiefs had anointed their arrowheads with poisonous herbs, and they laughed at the captain's overtures. Irala made war on them, killed many Guaraníes, and seized Tabaré's wives and children as hostages. Later he reported to the emperor that he had suppressed the rebellion "with great difficulty and danger to myself, because it was first necessary to destroy the *pueblos*, which were surrounded with thick palisades and had more than seven or eight thousand Indians inside." He added: "They killed four of my Christians there and wounded more than forty; but I left them all in peace and all the *principales* of the country reduced to obedience to Your Majesty." Guaçani and Tabaré agreed to appear before Cabeza de Vaca. He forgave them but warned that if they rebelled again, he would punish them mercilessly. Before dismissing them, he gave them presents. The newly pacified Guaraníes soon supplied Captain Mendoza with the maize and manioc flour the governor needed for his *entrada*.[49]

But before Cabeza de Vaca could complete his preparations, the two Franciscans, Bernardo de Armenta and Alonso Lebrón set off for the Brazilian coast on the road the governor had opened. Having long sparred with Cabeza de Vaca, the friars were intending to go to Spain to lodge charges against him. According to Pero Hernández, they acted "out of jealousy and hatred towards the governor, and in order to hinder his exploration and discovery of the country, so that his service to the king might be of no effect." Matters came to a head when Cabeza de Vaca learned that the friars had taken thirty-five young Guaraní women to serve as porters on their journey. The friars may have had licentious relations with these women, although ostensibly they had been instructing them in Christian doctrine. The fathers of the girls came to Cabeza de Vaca to inform him that the girls had gone with the friars against their will and to ask him to restore the young women to their families. The governor sent men to apprehend the friars and oblige them to return to Asunción. The friars were found to be carrying letters for the emperor from the royal officials in which they defended the *quinto* tax that Cabeza de Vaca had abolished, and accused the governor of overstepping his authority. The friars and royal officials had hoped to persuade Charles V to replace Cabeza de Vaca with Irala and to appoint Armenta as bishop of Río de la Plata. Upon discovering the letters, Cabeza de Vaca placed the friars under house arrest. He imprisoned the royal officials, suspended them from office, and initiated legal proceedings against them. A clergyman, Francisco González Paniagua, thought that Cabeza de Vaca should have hanged the royal officials and the friars. But the governor, who was reluctant to hang any Spaniard, exercised his customary forbearance.[50]

Two of the royal officials, Alonso Cabrera and García Venegas, were held in jail for a considerable time. The other two, Pedro Dorantes and Felipe de Cáceres, were released on bail. Cabeza de Vaca required them to participate in his *entrada* so that he could keep them under his personal surveillance. Cáceres, however, was the only one who actually participated. Dorantes set off on the *entrada*, but when his horse died soon afterward, he returned to Asunción. In his subsequent statements regarding the flight of the rebellious friars, Cabeza de Vaca asserted that Irala as well as the royal officials had played a part, but Irala was never charged. The captain professed his desire to serve the governor, and because he had scouted out the territory around Puerto de los Reyes, Cabeza de Vaca accepted him as a participant in the *entrada*.[51]

Before he left Asunción, the governor appointed Captain Juan de Salazar de Espinosa as his lieutenant governor, placed him in command of a garrison of two hundred foot soldiers and six horsemen, and directed him to defend Asunción and maintain good relations with the local Indians. Cabeza de Vaca also directed Salazar to supervise the completion of the caravel the governor intended to send to Spain.[52]

FOURTEEN

The Search for Gold and Silver

O n 8 September 1543, after attending mass in the newly rebuilt church, Cabeza de Vaca embarked upon his *entrada*, heading up the Río Paraguay toward the region that Irala had recently reconnoitered, and where first Alejo García and then Juan de Ayolas had disappeared. Only a year and a half had elapsed since Cabeza de Vaca's arrival in Asunción. The weather on the morning of 8 September was good. The governor launched an armada that included his ten new brigantines and 120 Guaraní canoes, but according to his detractors, he arrogantly displayed his coat of arms on his flagship. He commanded a force that included four hundred harquebusiers and crossbowmen, twelve horsemen, several clergymen, 1,200 Guaraní archers, and many women who would serve as burden-bearers. Pero Hernández describes the scene: "[The Indians] produced a wonderful effect, in their war paint adorned with plumes and feathers, and wearing on their brows plates of metal, so that when the sun shone they glittered marvellously. The Indians said they wore these plates in order that they might so glitter and dazzle the eyes of the enemy; and they went forth with loud cries and shouts, all as merry as possible."[1]

The Río Paraguay meanders lazily across an almost level plain, but the men had to row or tow their brigantines upstream. They stopped frequently at Indian settlements to confer with the residents and purchase provisions. At one settlement, Cabeza de Vaca recruited a Guaraní interpreter who knew the language of the Payaguá Indians. Shortly thereafter, the governor and his army entered the country of the Payaguás. These people were fishermen and pirates, and the Spaniards mistrusted them because they had killed Juan de Ayolas. Cabeza de Vaca directed his men to keep their vessels close together and to moor the canoes to the brigantines at night. He slept ashore with most of his men, and their camp each evening stretched for a league along the riverbank. The men lit campfires, and everyone had plenty of fish, game, and fruit to eat. The Guaraníes killed capybaras, which are large aquatic rodents. The Spaniards used their horses to hunt deer, tapirs, and boars.[2]

On 12 October the army arrived in Candelaria, the port that Juan de Ayolas had established in 1537 and used as the base for his ill-fated expedition into the Chaco. Cabeza de Vaca's pilots measured the latitude as 21°40′ south. Although, according to Irala, Candelaria was at 19°40′ south, the governor and his army must have been in the Pantanal and near the place where the present nations of Paraguay, Bolivia, and Brazil come together.[3]

The following morning, seven Payaguá warriors presented themselves on the riverbank, and Cabeza de Vaca sent seven Spaniards and his Guaraní interpreter to confer with them. The Payaguás asked if the newly arrived Spaniards were the same men who had come into their country several years before. The Spaniards had anticipated this question and taken the precaution of concealing Captain Irala, whom the Payaguás might have recognized. Upon hearing that the Spaniards were under the command of a new governor, the Payaguás asked to be brought before him. They told Cabeza de Vaca that their chief wished to be his friend. They confirmed that their people had killed Juan de Ayolas, and they asked to be pardoned for the crime. They said their chief had preserved everything that had belonged to Ayolas, including the gold and silver objects his porters had carried, and he would turn everything over to the new Spanish governor. The Payaguás said their chief was highly respected, and when he wished to spit, someone near him would cup his hands so that he might spit into them. Cabeza de Vaca said he wished to speak to the chief and to live in peace with the Payaguás. He gave presents to the seven emissaries, and they promised to return with their chief the next day.[4]

Cabeza de Vaca waited four days, but the Payaguá chief never appeared. The governor's Guaraní interpreter said the Payaguás were a sly and deceitful people and were probably moving their old people, women, and children farther up the Río Paraguay. He advised Cabeza de Vaca to pursue them, because they would be heavily burdened and the likelihood of over-taking them was good.

Cabeza de Vaca chased the Payaguás a long way, but ultimately they moved away from the river into country he chose not to enter. Then, in order not to alarm the Indians living upriver, the governor divided his armada in two, placing five brigantines and sixty canoes in each group. He took command of the vanguard and placed Captain Gonzalo de Mendoza in charge of the rearguard. He instructed the captain to treat the Indians well and to pay them for whatever supplies they provided.[5]

The vanguard entered the country of the Guajarapos, who lived north of the Payaguás, on the west bank of the Río Paraguay. The Guajarapos dressed in animal skins, tattooed their faces, and pierced their ears and lips. They lived by farming, hunting, and fishing. At one settlement, thirty Guajarapos came out in canoes to speak with the governor and give him fish and game. Cabeza de Vaca gave them presents, told them a second group of Spaniards and Guaraníes was following, and asked them to receive the second group as friends. They promised to do so, but they warned the governor that the rainy season would soon begin. The rivers would flood and the waters would engulf all but a few high places, which would become islands in a vast lagoon. After three or four months, the floodwaters would recede, but the land would be covered in mud.[6]

Cabeza de Vaca and his vanguard came to a place where a sizeable tributary flows into the Río Paraguay. Beyond that, they came to a place where they encountered whitewater and then to a place where the river divided into three streams. One of these flowed from a large lake, and the other two reunited beyond a long island. But farther upstream the river separated into so many channels that it was impossible to say which was the main water-way. Cabeza de Vaca pursued a channel that the natives knew as Yguatú, and he ordered that three large crosses be erected at its entrance so that Captain Mendoza and the rearguard would know how to proceed.

The country became increasingly marshy. Cabeza de Vaca and his party came to a group of large bell-shaped rocks rising from the river. Irala recognized them as landmarks on the way to the outpost he had established at Puerto de los Reyes. Soon after passing the rocks, the vanguard anchored in a lagoon near villages inhabited by the Sacocis, Xaqueses, and Chanés. Cabeza de Vaca sent soldiers and an interpreter to invite the Indians to a conference. The Indians assured the governor that he was near Puerto de los Reyes, but they warned him it would be difficult to reach the outpost because the Río Yguatú was presently too shallow for the brigantines.[7]

The following morning, Cabeza de Vaca directed his men to take up their oars and return to the river. When the water became only knee-deep, he ordered everyone to disembark and carry or push their vessels upstream. The canoes presented no problem, and the Guaraníes helped the Spaniards haul their brigantines through the shallows. According to Irala, Puerto de los Reyes was located at 16°50′ south, and according to Cabeza de Vaca, at 17°50′ south, so its exact location cannot now be determined. It must have been deep in the Pantanal swamp, somewhere north of the present nation of Paraguay and near the present border between Brazil and Bolivia.[8]

A large Indian settlement consisting of eight hundred houses was near the Spanish outpost, and many people had assembled on the riverbank to greet the Spaniards and their Guaraní allies. Cabeza de Vaca told them via an interpreter that he had been sent by His Majesty Charles V to win them to the Christian religion. He promised that if they accepted Christ and Spanish authority, he would protect them and treat them as friends, and he demonstrated his goodwill by distributing gifts. Then, in the name of Charles V and in the presence of his officers and an official *escribano*, Cabeza de Vaca formally took possession of the area. He charged his clergymen both with instructing the Indians and with building a church in that place, and he ordered his men to erect a large wooden cross on the riverbank.[9]

On 10 November, Cabeza de Vaca commended Domingo Martínez de Irala for his "capacity, ability and fidelity" and appointed him to serve as his *maestre de campo*. The governor, who could neither trust Irala nor do without him, charged the captain with administering justice, pacifying the land, and overseeing all dealings with Indians. Cabeza de Vaca directed his men to pay the local Indians for any commodities they provided and to refrain from molesting them or entering their houses. Using his personal resources, he purchased food from the Indians and distributed it among his men. The Indians, meanwhile, offered a hundred young women to the Spanish captains. Apparently, the governor allowed his officers to accept the women's services.[10]

The Spaniards, using a form of their word for "ear," described the local Indians as Orejones because they pierced and stretched their earlobes until they hung to their shoulders and could accommodate large vegetable-ivory disks. The Orejones were short-statured, and although the women were adept at spinning cotton, both they and the men went naked. The German harquebusier Ulrich Schmidt noted that the women were "nice-looking" and wore "a grey stone of crystal, thick and long as a finger, in their lips." The Orejones were farmers, as well as hunters and fishermen, and they grew maize and manioc. They raised poultry, both to eat and as a protection against crickets. These insect pests bred in the thatch of the people's houses and ate their blankets and furs, but the geese and other fowls devoured the crickets. In another defense against crickets, the Orejones stored their furs in large earthenware jars during the day. Ants, both red and black, were also a problem, and the Orejones knew of no remedy for their painful sting. At night the Indians penned their poultry to protect them from the many vampire bats that roosted along the river. The Spaniards soon found they had to protect their own livestock from the bats, which bit their horses on the ears and bit off the teats of the brood sows so that the piglets could not suck. The bats also bit human beings, generally on a toe or the tip of the nose. While Cabeza de Vaca slept aboard a brigantine one night, he left a foot uncovered, and a bat bit him. He was not wakened by pain but by a sensation of coldness in his leg, and he found his bedclothes soaked in blood.[11]

The Orejones venerated wooden idols. Cabeza de Vaca said that their idols were of the devil, and he urged the Orejones to burn them and to worship the Christian God instead. The Indians reluctantly began to burn their idols, but they quickly became frightened and said their traditional gods would punish them. When the Christian church at Puerto de los Reyes was finished, however, the Orejones willingly attended mass.

Cabeza de Vaca attempted to learn from the Orejones and other local people—including the Sacocis, Xaqueses, and Chanés—where gold and silver might be found and whether there were roads leading to it. The Sacocis and Xaqueses lived north of the Guajarapos and south of a people called the Arrianicosies, and two Chané settlements were four leagues (twelve miles) from Puerto de los Reyes. A generation earlier the Chanés had come into the Pantanal with Alejo García, and they showed Cabeza de Vaca some European glass beads the Portuguese explorer had given them. Juan de Ayolas had used Chané porters in his attempt to carry gold and silver out of their distant homeland, but a Chané youth was the sole survivor of that party. Cabeza de Vaca met with the local Chanés, distributed presents among them, and asked their chief for information. The chief told him what he knew, but he could say little concerning distances or the location of settlements. He was aware of Guaraníes living somewhere in the neighborhood who had raided settlements in the foothills of the western mountains. He thought they were living near the Xarayes, whose land was upstream on the Río Yguatú. The Xarayes possessed gold and silver but were enemies of the Chanés. The Chané chief told Cabeza de Vaca that the country of the Xarayes was not presently accessible by brigantine, but that men in canoes could arrive there in eight to ten days.[12]

Cabeza de Vaca decided to send two Spaniards, Héctor de Acuña and Antonio Correa, and several Indians to the country of the Xarayes. He directed them to seek out any Guaraníes who might be living nearby, and he entrusted the envoys with caps for the chiefs of both the Xaray and Guaraní communities.[13]

On 15 November, a week after Cabeza de Vaca reached Puerto de los Reyes, Captain Mendoza arrived there with the five brigantines and sixty canoes of the rearguard. Mendoza had had trouble with the Guajarapos along the way. Cabeza de Vaca was angered by this news because he had made a compact of friendship with the Guajarapos, and they had promised to treat the men of his rearguard as friends. He soon learned, however, that Mendoza and his men were partly to blame for the trouble they had had. Mendoza had taken a piece of cloth from a Guajarapo without paying for it. And the *escribano*, Martín de Orúe, had manacled a Guajarapo for stealing an ax. In retaliation, the Guajarapos killed five or six Spaniards who were onshore towing a brigantine upstream. Afterward the Guajarapos said that the Spaniards were cowards and their skulls were soft, and they urged their neighbors to join them in driving the Spaniards away. Cabeza de Vaca worried about the damage the incident would do to his army's reputation for invincibility.[14]

Héctor de Acuña and Antonio Correa returned to Puerto de los Reyes eight days after they left and reported that they had reached the country of the Xarayes. But they had often had to wade through knee-deep or waist-deep mud, and they had run short of both fresh water and provisions. When they arrived at their destination, five hundred Xarayes came out to greet them. The men adorned themselves with parrot feathers and blue paint and wore aprons made of beads. They also wore heavy lip plugs, which distended their lips in a manner the Spaniards found hideous. The women wore cotton garments. The chief, whose name was Camire, sat on a cotton hammock, surrounded by three hundred of his people. A Guaraní who was living among the Xarayes served as interpreter. The chief explained through the interpreter that he had heard good reports of the Spanish governor, who was known far and wide for his generosity, and that whatever the governor might desire, he and his people would provide. Acuña and Correa presented Camire with the cap Cabeza de Vaca had sent to him, and they told the chief their governor desired information about the region where gold and silver might be found, the best road to that region, the distance the Spaniards would have to travel, and the names of the peoples whose settlements they would pass through. Camire replied that he knew nothing of any roads. For two months of each year, the surrounding countryside was flooded and travel in any direction was impossible. He offered, however, to let his Guaraní interpreter go with the Spaniards as their guide. Acuña and Correa then asked Camire for directions to the settlement of the Guaraníes they had been told were living nearby. Camire said those Guaraníes were his enemies, but that, in the morning, he would provide guides to conduct the Spaniards to them. That night Camire had hammocks slung in his own house for Acuña and Correa, and he offered them each a girl to sleep with, but they were tired and declined the girls.[15]

The next morning, the two Spaniards were wakened by the sound of drums. Camire led them out to where six hundred of his warriors in war paint and feathers had assembled. He warned the Spaniards that if they went without an escort to the settlement of the Guaraníes, the Guaraníes would kill them. The Spaniards saw that if they accepted the escort, however, they would have no chance of speaking with the Guaraníes and might provoke a skirmish. They decided, therefore, to return directly to Cabeza de Vaca. Camire seemed pleased by this outcome, and he gave them a headdress made of parrot feathers to take back to their governor. Acuña and Correa returned to Puerto de los Reyes with the Guaraní who had served as their interpreter.

Cabeza de Vaca received the interpreter with great kindness. The man said he was a native of Itatí, a Guaraní settlement on the Río Paraguay. When he was a boy, he had traveled upriver with his father and many other Guaraní warriors and then marched westward in search of plunder. Somewhere in the remote west the group had found gold and silver, but the local people repulsed them, slew many of them, and drove the others away. The Guaraníes retreated to the country of the Xarayes, but the interpreter was now the sole survivor of his group. He had taken a Xaray wife and settled in with her people. He did not remember from his boyhood adventure that he and his kinsmen had followed any road. The country they had explored was heavily forested, and his kinsmen had opened a road by felling trees. The interpreter said he was willing to guide the Spaniards to the country he had explored as a boy.[16]

Cabeza de Vaca convened his officers and clergymen, and they agreed he should march into the uncharted country to the west. Captain Irala, Felipe de Cáceres, three hundred harquebusiers and crossbowmen, ten horsemen, and roughly a thousand Guaraníes would accompany him. Captain Juan Romero and the remainder of the men would stay in Puerto de los Reyes to guard the brigantines. Cabeza de Vaca gave each man, Spaniard and Guaraní alike, forty pounds of flour and enough other provisions to last for twenty days.[17]

On 26 November 1543, Cabeza de Vaca and his expeditionary army set off westward toward the Andes. On the first day of their journey, their interpreter-guide led them along a little-used path through a wooded area. But by the second day, the forest had become so nearly impenetrable that Cabeza de Vaca had to send twenty men in advance to clear the way. Other men foraged for food, but a kind of fruit they found caused everyone who ate it to vomit or suffer from diarrhea. After five laborious days, the interpreter-guide began to express embarrassment. He said it was a long time since he had seen the country the Spaniards were seeking, and he did not remember how to proceed. On the ninth day of the expedition the explorers came upon a dwelling inhabited by fourteen Guaraníes who had come into the area with Alejo García. These Guaraníes could give Cabeza de Vaca no information about a route to the land of gold and silver, but they said they had kinsmen living nearby who knew the way. The governor sent two Spanish scouts and an interpreter to find these more knowledgeable Guaraníes.[18]

The scouts had to traverse thickly forested country, and in some places the vegetation was so dense that they had to crawl on their hands and knees. Cabeza de Vaca and his men followed slowly after them, but although they hacked at the underbrush all day, the path they cleared was only as long as the distance to which a stone can be hurled from a sling. During that miserable day, the typically heavy rains of the season commenced. The governor worried that the gunpowder his men were carrying would be spoiled. He ordered the men to camp that night in the same rude shelters in which they had slept the night before.[19]

The men must have sat in their shelters and grumbled. Ulrich Schmidt complained that Cabeza de Vaca "was not the right sort of man" to lead the expedition and that "all the officers and soldiers hated him for his perverse and rigorous carriage towards the men." Some of the officers, including Irala and Cáceres, seem to have begun hatching plots. Cabeza de Vaca later claimed that Irala and Cáceres were planning to kill him if a scuffle should arise with the Indians and afford them the opportunity.[20]

After several wet days, the scouts returned with a new Guaraní guide from the settlement they had visited. The new guide said the nearest settlement beyond his own was atop a high hill called Ytapoa Guazú. The guide said he had visited the hilltop settlement several times in order to obtain arrows that could be found there, but he had not gone there in a long time. The last time he had been there, he had seen the smoke of many campfires rising from the surrounding countryside and had feared that unfriendly people were moving into the area. He said that reaching the hilltop settlement would require sixteen days or more of difficult travel through densely forested and unpopulated terrain and that the army might encounter hostile Indians at the end.[21]

Cabeza de Vaca convened his officers and clergymen, but the meeting was tense. The officers pointed out that provisions were running low, for although they had brought food that should have lasted twenty days, the men had profligately consumed most of it already. The officers said it could easily take more than sixteen days to reach Ytapoa Guazú since Indians were poor at estimating distance. If Cabeza de Vaca forced the men to go forward, they might all die of starvation. The officers insisted upon returning to Puerto de los Reyes for additional supplies. One of the clergymen later wrote that some of the officers acted "maliciously" in requiring the governor to abort his *entrada*. Pero Hernández accused the governor's enemies of wishing to prevent him from discovering gold and silver. According to Hernández, they were jealous "because in three days he had discovered a country and a route, while those who had lived in the country for twelve years had not been able to accomplish it." Irala, Cáceres, and their supporters knew that if Cabeza de Vaca succeeded in finding precious metal, he would win the emperor's favor and secure his title to govern Río de la Plata.[22]

Cabeza de Vaca told his officers the food reserves at Puerto de los Reyes were not sufficient to enable them to try a second time to reach Ytapoa Guazú. And the Indians living near the port would not be able to supply additional provisions until after the next harvest. The governor reminded his officers that, as the Guajarapos had cautioned several weeks earlier, the rainy season, which had now begun, was likely to produce flooding and make further exploration impossible. The officers warned the governor that if he refused to turn back to Puerto de los Reyes, they would require him—in the name of Emperor Charles V—to do so. Cabeza de Vaca finally had to give in to his officers and order a return to their base. But even though the officers forced him to return, the hypocritical Martín de Orúe later claimed that he did so "against the will of all."[23]

The most Cabeza de Vaca was able to do to extend his explorations was to send Captain Francisco de Ribera, six other Spaniards, and eleven Indians on a reconnaissance mission to Ytapoa Guazú with the new Guaraní guide. The governor and most of his men arrived back in Puerto de los Reyes eight days after they reversed their course. They had been away from their base for less than three weeks. Cabeza de Vaca, according to Pero Hernández, was "much dissatisfied at having gone no farther."[24]

Captain Juan Romero, the commander of the garrison at Puerto de los Reyes, reported that while the governor and the majority of his men were away, a coalition of Indians led by the Guajarapos had attempted to massacre the Christians at the outpost and gain possession of the brigantines. Cabeza de Vaca swiftly summoned all the local chiefs and, in the presence of his officers and clergymen, threatened to make war on them if they again broke their agreement. He reminded the chiefs of the presents he had already distributed, and he gave them colorful caps as additional presents. The chiefs renewed their pledges of friendship, but they also took note of the Spaniards' weakness.[25]

As Cabeza de Vaca had anticipated, provisions at Puerto de los Reyes were running low. He had some two thousand persons under his command—including his Spanish and Guaraní fighting men and their women—and only enough food to sustain them for another ten to twelve days. He sent his interpreters to the nearby Indian settlements to buy supplies, but the interpreters returned empty-handed. They reported that the only people in the area with surplus provisions were the Arrianicosies, who lived near some large lagoons north of the Sacocis and Xaqueses.[26]

Cabeza de Vaca convened his officers and clergymen, and they told him that the men were so hungry they were threatening to disband. The officers advised the governor to send armed men to the village of the Arrianicosies to seize the needed provisions. Cabeza de Vaca disliked the proposal, but the hunger of his men made him desperate. He supplied Captain Gonzalo de Mendoza with beads, knives, iron wedges, and fishhooks to use as barter and sent him at the head of 120 Spaniards and 600 Guaraníes to deal with the Arrianicosies. The governor gave the captain these instructions:

> You shall use the utmost diligence and care that, in all places you may pass through inhabited by friendly Indians, none of your men should use violence, or maltreat the natives. All that you take, and all that they give you, must be paid for to their satisfaction, and leave no cause of complaint. When you arrive at the villages you shall ask for the commodities you require for the sustenance of your men, offering payment, and entreating the Indians with kind words. Should they decline to provide you with what you want, you shall repeat your request twice, thrice, or as often as you think right, offering payment beforehand. Should they then refuse to give it, you shall take it by force, and, if resistance be offered you, shall make war upon them, for the hunger we suffer from justifies us in resorting to these extreme measures. In all that may happen afterwards you shall use such moderation as becomes the service of God and His Majesty.[27]

Mendoza departed on 15 December, and within a few days he reported via courier that he had established a base. He had sent an interpreter to the Arrianicosies to ask them to sell food, but they had driven him away, saying they would neither sell food to the Spaniards nor allow them to trespass on their land. The Arrianicosies were allied with the Guajarapos, who had told them that the Spaniards were cowards and could be easily killed. Mendoza followed his instructions and sent his interpreter to the Arrianicosies a second time, but again they drove him away.

Mendoza then went with all his men to seize the food they needed. A large number of Indians came out against them and shot arrows at them. The Spanish harquebusiers returned fire and killed two Indians, causing the others to flee into the forest. Mendoza's men looted the Arrianicosi village, taking maize, peanuts, and enough other commodities to feed the Spaniards and their Guaraní allies for three months. The captain sent after the Arrianicosies, offering to pay them for the things his men had taken. The Arrianicosies refused to be reconciled, however. They torched their village and, with their Guajarapo allies, continued to harass Mendoza's men.[28]

Felipe de Cáceres later asserted that it was Mendoza who burned the village and that the captain killed many more than two Arrianicosis. Another eyewitness, however, confirmed Mendoza's account of the confrontation.

Cabeza de Vaca testified that no more than one or two Indians were killed, no more than eighty small straw houses were burned, and nothing was taken from the Arrianicosis except the food the Spaniards needed.[29]

Meanwhile, ever since Cabeza de Vaca's return from his aborted exploratory expedition, the rain had continued to fall. The rivers rose, lakes swelled, and dry land receded. The Pantanal became the mother of all swamps. The local people said the rains would continue for four months. Most of the Indians withdrew to whatever high ground they could find. Some of them moved their families and household goods into large canoes in which they would live for the remainder of the rainy season. In one section of each such canoe, the householders heaped earth for a hearth and a cooking fire. When conditions permitted, the Indians living in such canoes would land on high ground to hunt deer and tapirs.[30]

Late in December the Indians living near Puerto de los Reyes advised Cabeza de Vaca that the Río Yguatú had risen sufficiently to allow a brigantine to ascend at least as far as the country of the Xarayes. These same informants said that the Xarayes possessed surplus food. Héctor de Acuña and Antonio Correa had already made contact with the Xarayes and their chief, Camire, in November. Cabeza de Vaca now sent Captain Hernando de Ribera (not to be confused with the Francisco de Ribera, who was reconnoitering Ytapoa Guazú) with a brigantine and fifty-two men to renew contact with the Xarayes. The governor supplied the captain with an interpreter and presents for the Indians and ordered him and his men to stay aboard the brigantine. Ribera was to allow only the interpreter to disembark and confer with the Xarayes. One of the men who went with Hernando de Ribera was the harquebusier, Ulrich Schmidt.[31]

In mid-January 1544, Captain Francisco de Ribera returned to Puerto de los Reyes and reported that although he and his men had failed to reach Ytapoa Guazú, they had discovered a rich country whose people were well supplied with both foodstuffs and precious metals. Ribera and all six of the Spaniards in his party were wounded, and only three of the eleven Guaraníes who had set out with them had remained with them. After parting from Cabeza de Vaca, the captain and his men had followed their Guaraní guide westward for twenty-one days, cutting their path each day through dense vegetation. On good days they cleared a league, but on bad days only a quarter of that distance. They sustained themselves by hunting and by gathering fruit and honey. On the twenty-first day, they came to the banks of a westward-flowing river from which they took many fish. According to their guide, Ytapoa Guazú was on a hill near this river. Ribera and his men crossed the river, found fresh footprints on the other side, and followed them to a place where Indians were harvesting maize. One of these Indians, who wore gold earrings and a silver lip plug, addressed them in a language they could not understand. The Indian took Ribera by the hand and led him toward a large house made of wood and straw. As the captain and his men approached the front door, they saw women carrying objects out of the house through an opening they had cut in the thatch. The objects included cotton cloth, baskets of maize, and silver plates, bracelets, and hatchets. The man with the gold earrings invited Ribera and his men to enter the house, and he offered them maize wine. The servants or slaves who poured the wine were Orejones and spoke a language that was familiar to some of the men of Ribera's party. The Orejones said that the man with the gold earrings and his family were Tarapecosies. They also said that other Spaniards were living nearby at a place that might be reached in three days. Ribera and his men had likely penetrated almost to the Andes and narrowly missed making contact with Spaniards based in western Bolivia or Peru.[32]

Ribera grew uneasy because he could see more and more warriors gathering outside. He estimated that there were three hundred of them, armed with bows and arrows and wearing war paint and feathers. He directed his men to leave the house at once, and he indicated to his host that he was going to fetch other Spaniards who were waiting nearby. But when the captain and his men were only a stone's throw from the house, the Tarapecosies began to shoot at them. Ribera showed Cabeza de Vaca some of the arrows, which he had brought back to Puerto de los Reyes. The captain and his men had taken cover in the forest, but they all sustained wounds. They retraced their steps to the place where they had parted from Cabeza de Vaca, arriving there in twelve days, nine days less than the time they spent covering the same distance on their outward journey. The chief obstacle on their return trip was a lagoon whose water had been only knee-deep when first they crossed it but was now over a man's head. To cross the lagoon the second time, they had to construct rafts. Ribera estimated that the total distance from the territory of the Tarapecosies to Puerto de los Reyes was some seventy leagues.[33]

A small group of Tarapecosies happened to be living near the Spanish outpost. Cabeza de Vaca sent for them, and they said the arrows brought by Francisco de Ribera were made in their distant homeland. They speculated that the Tarapecosies the captain had encountered had acted not out of hostility toward the Spaniards but out of hostility toward their Guaraní guides. If the Spaniards were to return with an interpreter who understood their language, matters would be different. Cabeza de Vaca's informants speculated that their kinsmen had acquired their gold and silver through trade with other Indians. Some Spaniards showed them a brass candlestick and a gold ring and asked them which was more like the yellow metal their kinsmen possessed. The Tarapecosies pointed to the gold ring. The Spaniards then showed them a tin plate and a silver cup. The Tarapecosies pointed to the silver cup and said their kinsmen possessed vases, plates, bracelets, crowns, and hatchets made from this kind of white metal.

Cabeza de Vaca began planning a large *entrada* to the land of the Tarapecosies. Ribera warned, however, that the intervening country was likely to remain flooded for several more weeks. Another problem was that many of the Spaniards and their Guaraní allies were ill with fever and chills. The disease was probably malaria, but the Spaniards thought its source was the water, which was becoming more and more brackish as the rainy season advanced.[34]

Hoping to mount a new exploratory expedition, Cabeza de Vaca recalled Gonzalo de Mendoza from the country of the Arrianicosies. The captain reported via courier that the Arrianicosies continued to rebuff his friendly overtures and that many of his men were ill with the same fever that was afflicting the men at Puerto de los Reyes. Mendoza returned to the Spanish outpost in late January, bringing four hundred Arrianicosi captives with him. Cabeza de Vaca saw the captives as a burden, and as he didn't want to have to feed them, he said they should be released. The governor, however, was now suffering from fever and shivering fits, and his secretary, Pero Hernández, was also ill. There were no longer enough healthy men at Puerto de los Reyes to stand guard.[35]

On 30 January 1544, Captain Hernando de Ribera returned to Puerto de los Reyes from his mission to the Xarayes, but Cabeza de Vaca was too ill to receive his report. Ribera would not report on his discoveries until much later, but after setting off on 20 December, he and his men had ascended the Río Yguatú in their brigantine. In the country of the Xarayes, the captain had spoken with the Xaray chief and obtained information about the terrain. Then, although Cabeza de Vaca had ordered him to stay aboard his brigantine, Ribera had left the vessel in a place of safety with ten men to guard it and had taken his other forty men overland with a Xaray guide. The explorers followed the course of a river that, according to their guide, had its source in the western mountains. The land they traversed was flat but flooded, and they waded through water sometimes up to their knees and sometimes up to their waists. Ultimately, they reached a populous country whose inhabitants cultivated the soil. The Spaniards measured the latitude as 14°20′ south. The Indians of the area presented Ribera with feathers and told him that to the northwest, a ten-day march away, were warrior women living in large towns under the command of a female chief. These women lived near a large lake called the House of the Sun, and they possessed great quantities of yellow and white metal. Other towns lay beyond, some inhabited by black men with beards and some by people who wore clothing embroidered with silver and gold. These people bred "great sheep" (llamas), both for their wool and for use as beasts of burden. In the far west were tall mountains and then salt water. All the land to the west was ruled by one great chief, and there were white men with beards—much like Captain Ribera himself—living in that country.[36]

When Ribera heard about the warrior women living in the west, he understood them to be the Amazons of Greek mythology. In reality, the women were probably the Incas' "virgins of the sun." Much of the information Ribera received seems to have pertained to the Inca Empire. The single great chief was almost certainly the Grand Inca, although by the 1544 date of Ribera's reconnaissance, the last Inca emperor was dead and Spaniards were in control of his domain. The large lake that Ribera's informants described was probably Lake Titicaca, which lies on the border between the present nations of Bolivia and Peru and, in Ribera's day, was the site of a great Temple of the Sun. Hernando de Ribera seems, like Francisco de Ribera a few weeks earlier, to have penetrated nearly to the Andes and narrowly to have missed connecting with other Spaniards.[37]

Ulrich Schmidt, who marched with Hernando de Ribera, gives another account of the reconnaissance mission. Schmidt's focus is largely on the native women he encountered. The harquebusier found one group of women to be "very fair and vener[e]ous, very amiable, and very hot too." He says of the women in another group: "They are absolutely naked, and are beautiful after their manner, and also commit transgressions in the dark." He claims that upon Ribera's return to Puerto de los Reyes, Cabeza de Vaca very nearly had the captain hanged. Schmidt admits: "On this journey each of us plundered nearly two hundred ducats' worth of Indian cotton mantles and silver, having secretly bartered these for knives, paternosters [rosaries],

Reception of Hernando de Ribera by the king of the Xarayes. Engraving by Theodore de Bry, from *Collectiones peregrinationum*, Frankfurt, 1599. Courtesy of The Hispanic Society of America, New York.

scissors, and looking glasses." According to Schmidt, Cabeza de Vaca seized the illegally traded items and imprisoned Ribera. Perhaps the governor was angry with the captain for disobeying his orders not to disembark from his brigantine. Yet no eyewitness other than Schmidt reports on a conflict between Cabeza de Vaca and Ribera. In view of the captain's loyalty to the governor during the ensuing weeks and months, Schmidt's story seems less than credible.[38]

Since Cabeza de Vaca was too ill to receive Ribera's report, he was probably too ill to have the captain hanged. He was also too ill to deal effectively with the local Indians. Some of them were complaining that, despite the governor's orders, Spaniards and Guaraníes were entering their houses and taking their possessions by force. The Sacocis and Xaqueses, who had previously pledged their friendship to Cabeza de Vaca, now perceived his weakness and allied themselves with the Guajarapos in a terror campaign against the Spaniards. The Sacocis lived on a large island, known to the Spaniards as Paradise Island, which was about a league from Puerto de los Reyes. One morning when a group of Spaniards and Guaraníes were fishing, a party of hostile Indians carried them forcefully to Paradise Island, where they butchered and ate them. Soon afterward a group of hostiles set fire to Cabeza de Vaca's camp. When the governor's men ran out to save the camp, the hostiles abducted several of them and ate them. The next day, the hostiles launched a major attack and killed or captured fifty-eight Spaniards. Cabeza de Vaca immediately demanded the release of the captives, but the hostiles replied that the land was theirs and the Spaniards and Guaraníes had no right to fish there. The hostiles threatened to kill all of the Spaniards and their allies if they did not leave immediately.[39]

To Cabeza de Vaca, both the treachery of the formerly friendly Sacocis and Xaqueses and their cannibalism were serious offenses. According to laws that were current when he left Spain, enslavement was a just and appropriate punishment for those Indians who either ate human flesh or reneged on their compacts of friendship with Christians. In February, Cabeza de Vaca called his officers and clergymen into council, and with their concurrence, he declared war upon the Guajarapos, Sacocis, and Xaqueses. With the express approval of the clergymen, the governor authorized his men to make slaves of any of the rebellious Indians they might capture.[40]

In his report on the incident, Cabeza de Vaca says he pacified the Sacocis, Xaqueses, and Guajarapos and made sure they could do him and his men no further damage. Neither he nor Pero Hernández gives many details, however. The governor's detractors, on the other hand, accuse him of using excessive cruelty to quell the rebellion. Comptroller Felipe de Cáceres claims that three thousand Sacocis, Xaqueses, and Guajarapos were killed. Other detractors assert that a village of nine hundred houses on Paradise Island was destroyed and that sixteen villages were looted. On 4 March 1544, Cabeza de Vaca is alleged to have ordered the manufacture of a branding iron for use on those hostile Indians taken as slaves. Schmidt says Cabeza de Vaca sent 150 Spaniards and 2,000 Guaraníes in four brigantines to Paradise Island and ordered his forces to kill "all [enemy] persons from forty to fifty years of age." Schmidt had previously stated, however, that because the whole region surrounding Puerto de los Reyes was so unhealthy, he "did not find a single Indian who was forty or fifty years of age." Schmidt says that Cabeza de Vaca's forces looted and burned Paradise Island and took two thousand prisoners. He concludes, "God knows that we did them wrong," but given that the governor and most of his men were ill, the har-quebusier's story seems exaggerated.[41]

Cabeza de Vaca would later testify that "all the wars made in that land were made because of information about the crimes the Indians had committed and because they had rebelled and because they had killed Christians and because of the war they continually waged, and these wars were made with the advice and consent of His Majesty's officials, the clergymen, the captains, and others, and in all these wars, the Christians behaved temperately and did not depopulate the villages." He insisted that "if there were any depopulation, it was because these same Indians burned three or four villages of their own will." He added that the Indians often resorted to burning their houses, "because they were made of straw and could be rebuilt in a day, being small and set up on four poles."[42]

The governor's detractors claimed that his difficulties with the Sacocis, Xaqueses, and Guajarapos stemmed from his arrogance and unfitness to govern. Cabeza de Vaca and his supporters maintained that his difficulties were caused by the greed of many of his men. In particular, Cabeza de Vaca later asserted, Captain Irala and his cronies were robbing the natives.[43]

By March the floodwaters that had engulfed the Pantanal began at last to recede, but many fish were left gasping in shrinking pools, and the stench of rotting fish became unbearable. The expeditionary army had spent the better part of four months at Puerto de los Reyes, and the governor and most of his men continued to suffer from the illness that had been plaguing them for weeks. They were also tortured by swarms of mosquitoes. In mid-March, Felipe de Cáceres, as the royal comptroller, issued a *requerimiento* to Cabeza de Vaca, demanding that he return with all his men to Asunción. Cáceres listed seven arguments in support of this demand. First, the Spaniards and their allies were ill, and the Guaraníes were likely to desert if they were kept too long from their proper homes. Second, the army did not have sufficient food, and the South American winter was coming on. Third, the local people were hostile and would constitute a danger to any garrison left at Puerto de los Reyes. Additionally, the rain and high water were serious impediments to further exploration. The surrounding country was heavily forested, and the men of the various reconnaissance parties had discovered that, for a long distance, it was uninhabited. The people of the region to the west were hostile—as could be seen from the way the Tarapecosies in particular had repulsed Captain Francisco de Ribera. And, finally, the brigantines needed repair. Cáceres concluded by threatening that if Cabeza de

Vaca did not immediately return to Asunción, he would write to Emperor Charles V.[44]

Cabeza de Vaca later learned that Cáceres and Irala were plotting to kill him if he refused to return to the Spanish settlement. They knew that if he succeeded in finding gold and silver, he would secure his hold on power. Cáceres and Irala walked around the Spanish camp, buttonholing soldiers, telling each one that Cabeza de Vaca had called him a thief or a traitor, and enjoining the man not to go forward under the governor's leadership. Cabeza de Vaca asserted that Irala took men aside and told them: "The governor has taken an oath before God that he will have you hanged because you are a villainous traitor." When Cabeza de Vaca got wind of the plot against his life, he instituted a legal process against Irala, whom he identified as the "chief mutineer." However, the illness of the governor and his *escribano*, Pero Hernández, delayed the proceeding. Meanwhile, Irala's friends warned him that if Cabeza de Vaca were to die in the field, Captain Juan de Salazar de Espinosa would succeed him as governor. Before leaving Asunción, Cabeza de Vaca had named Salazar as his lieutenant governor, stipulating that the captain was to hold the position until the governor returned. If Irala wished to succeed Cabeza de Vaca, he would have to allow him to return to Asunción.[45]

Cabeza de Vaca responded carefully to Cáceres's *requerimiento*. He wanted to continue searching for the gold and silver that would put the colony and his administration on a sounder economic footing. Although he and many of his men were ill, he expressed the hope that "God should be pleased to restore them to health, and the waters should subside to enable them to undertake the exploration of the country." If they waited a little longer, he argued, they might "enter the land and take out the gold and silver which there is in the land, and in great quantity." The governor agreed, however, to consult with his officers and clergymen. Two of the captains said they were willing to wait another month at Puerto de los Reyes. But even Captain Francisco de Ribera, who had seen great riches in the country of the Tarapecosies, advised the governor to return to Asunción for the sake of everyone's health. Other captains repeated the arguments Felipe de Cáceres had enumerated in writing. The governor bowed at last to the will of his officers and agreed to return to the Spanish settlement.[46]

Cabeza de Vaca would not allow his officers or men to take their local concubines out of the area, however. The governor said that carrying the women into exile would offend both God and the women's fathers and that the women must be returned to their families. Pero Hernández reported: "The natives were well satisfied with this measure, but the Spaniards were greatly discontented, some of them felt ill-disposed towards him [the governor], and from that time he was detested by the majority." Irala and Cáceres began to talk again of killing the governor. They saw his actions as arrogant and as a threat to their prerogatives.[47]

Meanwhile, Cabeza de Vaca convened the local chiefs one last time. He gave them presents and informed them that although he was leaving Puerto de los Reyes, he would soon return. He later reported that he left the native people of the area "in total peace and concord."[48]

On 24 March 1544, Cabeza de Vaca and his army embarked on their return journey. Many of the men were too sick either to man the oars or to defend themselves. The Guajarapos attacked the armada as it passed through their country and killed one Spaniard and several Guaraníes before the Spaniards could fire their cannons. On 8 April, the Tuesday of Holy Week, the armada arrived in Asunción. It took Cabeza de Vaca and his men only twelve days to reach the Spanish settlement, although the same journey upstream had taken them two months. The governor was weak from his illness, and he soon took to his bed, giving his attention only to the most pressing matters of business.[49]

Lieutenant Governor Juan de Salazar de Espinosa reported that he and his garrison had been harassed continuously by the Agaces. The rebellious Indians had burned Guaraní settlements, seized foodstuffs and other valuables, and kidnapped women and children. On a brighter note, Salazar had nearly completed the caravel the governor had ordered him to build. Cabeza de Vaca directed him to finish it quickly because he wanted to send it to Spain with a report for His Majesty Charles V.[50]

FIFTEEN

Mutiny

Irala and the royal officials quickly refined their plans to oust Cabeza de Vaca. According to Pero Hernández, the royal officials "hated" the governor "because he refused to consent to things done against the service of God and the king." They recruited a hundred of their friends, telling them, "The governor wants to rob you and take your goods and Indian women—and have you for slaves." Like Irala, many of the conspirators were Basques from Vizcaya in northern Spain. The disgruntled *escribano* Martín de Orúe was a Vizcayan, and so was Pedro de Oñate, a servant in the governor's household. Cabeza de Vaca had come heartily to dislike the Vizcayans, and in the *Relación general* he would write the following year, he would rarely mention Irala without adding the epithet *vizcaíno* after his name. In Spanish literature of that period, the figure of the *vizcaíno* was frequently employed as an object of ridicule.[1]

The conspirators set their plans in motion on the night of 25 April 1544, only a little more than two weeks after Cabeza de Vaca's return to Asunción, and only slightly more than two years after his initial arrival in the Spanish settlement. On the night of the coup, some thirty armed mutineers surrounded the governor's house. His servant Pedro de Oñate admitted ten to twelve of them, and they burst in shouting, "Libertad, libertad, viva el rey!" They carried harquebuses with lighted fuses, armed crossbows, and naked swords. Cabeza de Vaca, still ill and weak, was in bed. Mutineers aimed a harquebus and a poisoned dart at his breast. All four of the royal officials—García Venegas, Alonso Cabrera, Felipe de Cáceres, and Pedro Dorantes—took part in the governor's arrest. Irala kept a low profile, but it was clear to Pero Hernández, Juan de Salazar de Espinosa, and others that he had conspired against the governor. Mutineers dragged Cabeza de Vaca, dressed only in his shirt, out of his house and into the street.[2]

Some of his friends were attracted by the commotion, and when they understood what was happening, they drew their swords and attempted to defend the governor. But the mutineers forced him into García Venegas's house, shut him in a small dark room, fettered his ankles, and held him under guard. Venegas, Orúe, and other mutineers then returned to the streets and ordered the governor's friends to disperse.[3]

When he later reported on his arrest, Cabeza de Vaca referred to the men who mutinied against him as Comuneros, using the term that had been applied during his youth in Spain to those who rebelled against the king. During the revolt of the original Comuneros in 1520–21, Cabeza de Vaca had supported the king, as—in his code of honor—a faithful vassal should do. For Cabeza de Vaca, the term "Comunero" had the ugly connotations of disloyalty and treason, and a man who mutinied against his governor was giving offense and doing grave disservice to the king who had placed that governor in office. Cabeza de Vaca saw his own supporters as loyal "servants of His Majesty." The mutineers endeavored to avoid the appearance of treason by chanting, "Liberty, liberty! Long live the king!"[4]

Soon after arresting Cabeza de Vaca, the Comuneros arrested Juan Pavón—the *alcalde mayor* of Asunción—and the *alguaciles* (constables), all of whom had close ties to the governor. Martín de Orúe seized the staff of office from Pavón, pulled his beard, and called him a villain and a traitor. The Comuneros dragged Pavón and the constables to the public jail and clamped them by their necks in the stocks. Shouting "Libertad, libertad!" the Comuneros then freed a condemned murderer and other criminals whom Cabeza de Vaca had imprisoned. One of the freed prisoners, Hernando de Sosa, became the deposed governor's chief jailer. Sosa hated Cabeza de Vaca because the governor had imprisoned him for striking an Indian. Pero Díaz del Valle, who supported Irala and had served under him as *alcalde mayor*, was reappointed to his former position. Two other Comuneros were appointed to replace the jailed constables.[5]

The Comuneros also arrested Pero Hernández, who was both Cabeza de Vaca's secretary and the provincial *escribano* for Río de la Plata. They seized documents that were in his keeping, including the criminal processes

Cabeza de Vaca had initiated against the royal officials the previous spring and the *probanzas* of witnesses. The Comuneros took Hernández to Irala's house, insulted him, chained him, and set watch over him. Martín de Orúe reclaimed the office of provincial *escribano*, which he had held before Cabeza de Vaca took it from him and gave it to Hernández. The Comuneros then paraded through the streets, beating a drum and shouting, "Liberty, liberty! Long live the king!" They imposed a curfew on Asunción, declaring that "anyone going out of doors will be considered a traitor and condemned to death."[6]

The Comuneros returned to the residence of the governor late on the night of the mutiny, rifled his papers, and confiscated his valuables. They also seized the Indian women who were serving in his household and redistributed them among themselves. According to Pero Hernández, the property confiscated from Cabeza de Vaca was worth more than 100,000 *castellanos*. The Comuneros used the property as bribes to persuade undecided persons to support the mutiny.[7]

The following day, the royal officials called for the residents of Asunción to assemble in front of Irala's house. There an *escribano* read a statement declaring that Cabeza de Vaca was a tyrant and a traitor and had intended to seize everyone's possessions. He had been arrested in order to prevent him from abusing his power. After the statement was read, the royal officials directed those present to join them in their chant of "Liberty, liberty! Long live the king!" The royal officials then presided over an election in which Irala was chosen as lieutenant governor and captain general of Río de la Plata. According to Pero Hernández, Irala had the support of the royal officials because he "would always do what they bade him." Ulrich Schmidt says that Irala was elected "not only because he had formerly governed the country, but especially because most of the soldiers were satisfied with him."[8]

Irala and the royal officials dismantled the caravel that Juan de Salazar de Espinosa had nearly completed and used planks from the ship to construct doors and windows for their houses. They also scuttled the ten brigantines that had carried Cabeza de Vaca and his expeditionary army to and from Puerto de los Reyes. Irala and the royal officials were hoping to keep the news of their mutiny from reaching Spain, but they soon regretted having destroyed the ships. Irala needed the brigantines to patrol the rivers and conduct further exploration. He and his coconspirators must have managed to salvage some of the vessels, for Cabeza de Vaca later reported that by March of 1545, they had a caravel and four brigantines at their disposal. Irala announced soon after the mutiny that he intended to mount a new expedition to Puerto de los Reyes to continue the search for gold and silver. Pero Hernández accused him and his coconspirators of planning to use whatever gold or silver they might find to purchase the emperor's consent to the regime change in Río de la Plata. Hernández said of the mutineers: "Should they not succeed in finding gold, they would not return [to Spain], as they feared punishment; yet it might happen that they found so much of the precious metal that the king, in return for it, would make them a present of the country."[9]

Those residents of Asunción who openly objected to the incarceration of Cabeza de Vaca, including three clergymen, were thrown into prison. A young hidalgo was publicly bastinadoed for plotting to free the governor. If two or three of Cabeza de Vaca's friends were seen speaking together, Comuneros would disarm them and order them to disperse. The deposed governor was kept under four padlocks in Venegas's house, and although the house was made of straw, a strong palisade, with the end of each wooden stake anchored in the ground, was set up around it to prevent Cabeza de Vaca's friends from tunneling under the walls. No one—neither friend nor foe—was allowed to see the imprisoned governor. Nor were his servants allowed to attend to him. Hernando de Sosa, whom the mutineers had liberated from jail, guarded Cabeza de Vaca day and night. Four other guards, whose salaries were paid with the imprisoned governor's money, stood watch outside the door and on the roof of the Venegas house. Fifty men were quartered nearby to prevent Cabeza de Vaca's friends from attempting to rescue him. Because they knew that their actions might be construed as treasonous, the Comuneros barred their doors, built stockades around their houses, barricaded the streets, went armed at all times, and set spies to report on what people were saying. At night, sentries patrolled the streets of Asunción to prevent people from congregating.[10]

Some of the Comuneros wished to send Cabeza de Vaca to Spain, but they could not do so without a ship. Other Comuneros wished to kill him, but because he had powerful friends, they feared to take his life. The governor's friends were clamoring so loudly for proof he still lived that the royal officials were forced to procure his signature and show it to his supporters. One of these supporters, Captain Juan de Salazar de Espinosa, procured a promise from the royal officials that they shortly would free Cabeza de Vaca, and although—according to the deposed governor—they never intended to fulfill the promise, they managed to appease Salazar and gain time. Both Cabeza de Vaca and the mutineers had to maneuver carefully, for each side was afraid of the other. The deposed governor said his captors had "their weapons always in their hands." At one point, he got wind of a plot to poison his food, and for many days he did not dare to eat anything that was brought to him. And yet he saw that "neither did the said Comuneros have a moment of security or rest." He later reported that "the said officials knew clearly that if I were killed in prison, my friends would kill them."[11]

The royal officials did all they could to prevent the deposed governor from communicating with his supporters. Anyone wishing to enter the Venegas residence had to undergo a security check, and every day one of the new constables inspected the property to ensure that no one was tunneling under the walls. García Venegas warned that if any attempt were made to rescue Cabeza de Vaca, he would kill the deposed governor and throw his head to the would-be rescuers. Meanwhile, Cabeza de Vaca continued to suffer from the illness he had contracted at Puerto de los Reyes. The room in which he was confined was dark and so damp that grass grew under his bed. He asked to be freed from his chains, claiming that their chief purpose was to annoy him.[12]

Despite all the measures taken to prevent communication, Cabeza de Vaca's friends managed to keep in touch with him. Juan, an Indian formerly in the governor's service, carried letters rolled inside a piece of hollow cane that he threw through Cabeza de Vaca's window. In July of 1544, however, someone other than the deposed governor caught the piece of cane. Captain Hernando de Ribera and a clergyman, Francisco González Paniagua, were suspected of having written the letters it contained. Another go-between was the Indian woman who brought Cabeza de Vaca his meals. This woman was stripped naked by the deposed governor's guards each evening before they admitted her to his presence. The guards examined her mouth, ears, and private parts and cut off her hair to prevent her from concealing messages. Even so, she managed to carry letters under her toes. The letters were written on thin paper, rolled tightly in a tube, and covered with wax. She managed to carry letters from Cabeza de Vaca out to his friends in the same way. The royal officials suspected the woman of carrying messages, and so they watched her and noted with whom she spoke. According to Pero Hernández, the officials employed an even more unsavory stratagem for uncovering her methods: "They chose four of the more youthful of their party to seduce the Indian woman—not a difficult task, for these women are not sparing of their charms, and consider it an affront to deny their favors to anyone; they say, moreover, that they have received them for that purpose. These four youths accordingly intrigued with her and gave her many presents; but they could never make her divulge her secret during the whole of their intercourse, which lasted eleven months." The letters the Indian woman brought to Cabeza de Vaca informed him of what was happening outside and what his friends were doing on his behalf. According to his friends, most of the people in Asunción supported him but feared to try to rescue him, because of the threats Venegas had made against his life. Cabeza de Vaca urged his friends not to attempt a rescue, arguing that many people would be killed.[13]

One item the Indian woman succeeded in smuggling out of his prison was a document Cabeza de Vaca signed on 23 January 1545, naming Juan de Salazar de Espinosa as his lieutenant governor and empowering the captain to govern Río de la Plata in his stead. Cabeza de Vaca's supporters had urged him to transfer his authority to Salazar and thus to enable the captain to free him from incarceration. Apparently, however, Salazar hesitated to accept the power Cabeza de Vaca was attempting to transfer, knowing that to do so would provoke violence, and he hid the document he possessed.[14]

Meanwhile, García Venegas and Alonso Cabrera were attempting to force Cabeza de Vaca to name Irala as his lieutenant governor. But the deposed governor refused to cede power to a Comunero, and he told the royal officials that if they wanted a new governor, he would appoint Captain Salazar to the position. Venegas responded that since they already had made Irala their governor, they could not unmake him. The royal officials would have liked Cabeza de Vaca to ratify their action, but if he would not, they considered the power they had conferred upon Irala to be sufficient. Venegas insisted that at the moment the royal officials had arrested Cabeza de Vaca, the royal provisions naming him as governor of Río de la Plata had lost their force, so the officials were no longer obliged to comply with anything he said.[15]

Irala and the royal officials feared Charles V might construe their actions as treasonable, but the emperor was on the far side of the Atlantic, and it would be difficult for him to sort out what exactly had happened in Río de la Plata. Authority resided in Spain, but because of the huge distances involved, power belonged to those in the kingdom's American colonies who could seize it. The coup leaders hoped to persuade Charles V that Cabeza de Vaca had behaved tyrannically and mistreated the Indians.[16]

During the summer of 1544, the royal officials—Cabrera, Cáceres, Dorantes, and Venegas—held two legal inquiries concerning Cabeza de Vaca's conduct in office. The first involved the deposed governor's alleged display of his personal coat of arms on his flagship during his voyage to Puerto de los Reyes. The royal officials said that Cabeza de Vaca should have flown the royal arms instead. The second inquiry had to do with alleged attempts by Cabeza de Vaca to set himself above the emperor. The royal officials accused him of having said, "I am the king and ruler of this land," and of having said that royal commands lost their force south of the equator. They said he had directed his associates to address him as "king, prince and natural lord." To support their accusations, the officials collected *probanzas* from four dozen witnesses. Cabeza de Vaca asserted that the witnesses were bribed. Both he and Pero Hernández complained that the words of witnesses who testified in the deposed governor's favor were not recorded. Witnesses seem to have been chosen because they supported Irala and the royal officials. Or perhaps the witnesses feared reprisal if they testified for the governor and against the officials. It is also possible that the witnesses told the truth when they said Cabeza de Vaca carved his coat of arms on a stone on a beach in Brazil and flew his coat of arms from the mast of a brigantine. Such actions show pride, but they do not show treason. Captain Hernando de Ribera, who supported the deposed governor, claimed that the legal proceedings against him were conducted "with great cunning, falsehoods and bribes, presents and promises."[17]

Cabeza de Vaca, meanwhile, cherished the hope of someday mounting a legal case against Irala and the royal officials. Much as he had noted everything in North America that he might one day report to his king, he now noted everything he might someday use against the mutineers. Although the royal officials had imposed martial law on Asunción, the period of Cabeza de Vaca's imprisonment was marked by general lawlessness. From the letters that were smuggled to him, Cabeza de Vaca learned of crimes and brawls that were occurring outside his prison cell, and he later reported on several of these incidents:

Francisco de Mansylla killed Cristobal Simón. Juan Riquel killed García de Villalobos. Juan Richarte cut off the hand of a caulker named Nicolás Simón. Mendez threw a lance at Diego Vezino. Luis Vasco maimed two fingers on the hand of García de Villamayor. Captain Diego de Abrigo stabbed Miguel de Urrutia, a Vizcayan, in the head. Captain Camargo maimed the right hand of Roque Caravallo. Captain Agustín de Campos wounded the hand of Blas Núñez. . . . And each day there were many other scandals and disturbances. And Francisco de Sepúlveda killed his daughter. And Juan Venialbo wounded master Miguel, a carpenter. Fernando de Sosa gave a sword blow to the thigh of Juan Fernández. And Martín de Orúe drew a sword against Sancho de Salinas, constable of the community, at which the said Sancho de Salinas threw down his staff of office, saying that since his office was held in such low esteem, he would not carry it any more.

Pero Hernández reported that during a celebration of the mass, one of the Vizcayans groped the breasts of an Indian woman. He accused another man of having raped a seven-year-old Indian girl. The *escribano* also noted that, in a fit of jealousy, Irala had Diego Portugués hung by his genitals. Fray Juan de Salazar of the Order of Mercy reported that Asunción had become "a town of more than five hundred men and more than five hundred thousand disorders, all in disservice to God and His Majesty."[18]

Relations between the Spaniards and the Indians deteriorated as well. Irala and the royal officials wanted free trade with the Indians and more freedom to exploit them, and they overturned many of the measures Cabeza de Vaca had put in place to protect the indigenous people. Pero Hernández says of Irala and the royal officials: "[They] gave public permission to all their friends and partisans to go into the villages and huts of the Indians and take by force their wives, daughters, hammocks, and other of their possessions, a thing contrary to the service of His Majesty and the peace of the country. While this was going on they would scour the country, strike the Indians blows with sticks, carry them off to their houses, and oblige them to labour in their fields without any remuneration." Another eyewitness reports that Irala and the royal officials robbed the Indians, "taking their pregnant wives and those recently delivered of children, separating infants from their breasts and taking their children for their service." Some Indian women were so badly treated that they hanged themselves.[19]

In an effort to beguile the Indians, Irala and the royal officials authorized them to resume eating human flesh. They told the Indians they had imprisoned Cabeza de Vaca because he had attempted to outlaw cannibalism. According to other witnesses, however, the Indians rejected this explanation and clamored for Cabeza de Vaca's release. The witnesses reported that "all the Indians of the said province had good relations with the governor, and when they learned of his imprisonment, they all wept and even wanted to liberate him from prison."[20]

Some Indians abandoned their settlements and moved far from Asunción. Still others, including the Agaces and some Guaraníes, took up arms against the Spaniards. Ulrich Schmidt says, "When the Carios [Guaraníes], who had formerly been our friends, perceived that we Christians were disunited, and had such false and treacherous hearts one towards another, they were not at all pleased, for they thought that every realm that is divided in itself and cannot agree must be destroyed. They therefore held a council, and agreed that they would kill us and drive us out of their country." The Guaraní chief Tabaré revolted against Spanish authority and skirmished with the Spaniards for a year and a half until Irala suppressed the revolt. Schmidt, who fought with Irala, says that the Christians slaughtered a great number of Tabaré's people.[21]

In the years to follow, the mistreatment of Indians in Río de la Plata would continue, and maltreatment would continue to spark uprisings among the native people. According to a 1561 report, fifty thousand Indians died in the course of these uprisings. Epidemic diseases, including a smallpox outbreak in 1559, also took a toll. Within three decades of the arrival of Europeans in Río de la Plata, most of the full-blood Guaraníes had disappeared. They were replaced in the social demographic by their mestizo children.[22]

During the period of Cabeza de Vaca's incarceration, Indians were not the only ones to flee from the tyrannical new regime in Asunción. Some fifty Spaniards withdrew to the Brazilian coast via the road the deposed governor had opened. Most of these Spaniards were Cabeza de Vaca's supporters, but two who were not were the Franciscans Bernardo de Armenta and Alonso Lebrón. The friars had attempted to leave Asunción in 1543 to carry charges against Cabeza de Vaca to Spain, but because they were also attempting to take Indian women away from their homeland, Cabeza de Vaca had stopped them. The friars subsequently had backed Irala and the royal officials in the coup against the governor. Now, with Irala's approval, the friars set off for the Brazilian coast, accompanied by five or six armed Spaniards and forty Indian women who served them as burden-bearers. As had been the case in 1543, the women went under duress. The friars forced them to wear chains, and the women cried as they marched away. Armenta, who hoped to become bishop of Río de la Plata, carried a letter he had written to Charles V in October of 1544, charging that while Cabeza de Vaca was governor, "there were made many wars, deaths and arrests unjustly against many Indian nations, without having cause or reason for it." The friars also carried letters for the emperor from the royal officials. However, Armenta and Lebrón never reached Spain. Armenta died in 1546 at Santa Catalina Island. Lebrón embarked for Spain but was lost at sea.[23]

Meanwhile, some of Cabeza de Vaca's supporters—including Pero Hernández—took refuge in the church in Asunción. There, on 28 January 1545, Hernández completed his *Relación de las cosas sucedidas en el Río de la Plata*. He would later manage to smuggle the report out of the province.[24]

Because of the dissension that the imprisonment of Cabeza de Vaca was causing, Irala and the royal officials decided to deport him to Spain. They hastened to repair some of the vessels they previously had scuttled. But when the deposed governor's supporters got wind of the plan, they protested so loudly that the leaders of the new ruling junta had to ask Cabeza de Vaca to quiet them. He agreed to cooperate, but not until his adversaries swore not to imprison any more of his friends and to release those currently in detention. His supporters were not easily silenced, however, and they insisted that if the deposed governor were sent to Spain, at least two of the royal officials should accompany him and appear with him before Charles V. Irala and the royal officials, who knew they needed someone to represent their case to the emperor, selected Alonso Cabrera and García Venegas for the task. Gonzalo de Acosta, who had piloted Cabeza de Vaca on his outward voyage to South America, would pilot him home. The *escribano* Martín de Orúe would go to Spain as well. According to Cabeza de Vaca, Orúe was chosen because he was especially gifted with "the crafty power of those who deceive."[25]

The deposed governor's supporters spoke secretly with the carpenters who were preparing the vessel that would carry Cabeza de Vaca to Spain. They arranged that the carpenters would hollow a space in the vessel's hull in which to conceal documents. The governor's supporters gathered those of his papers they had managed to preserve, including a report Cabeza de Vaca had written in prison and smuggled out with the help of the Indian woman who brought him his meals. No doubt Pero Hernández added his recently completed *Relación* to the cache of documents. Several of the governor's other supporters wrote letters to the emperor, expressing their good opinions of Cabeza de Vaca and of his conduct in office. Captain Hernando de Ribera defended the governor in a letter of 25 February 1545 and charged those who overthrew him with disservice to God and the king.

Another of Cabeza de Vaca's friends complained that under the new regime "we are tyrannized away from obedience to His Majesty." The governor's supporters encased all the clandestine documents in a cloth bag and dipped it in wax. The carpenters placed the packet in the cavity they had prepared and covered it with a timber they nailed in place. One of the sailors was made privy to the secret so that when the vessel arrived in Spain, he could uncover the documents.[26]

On 3 March 1545, Captain Hernando de Ribera appeared secretly before the *escribano* Pero Hernández and reported—under oath and before witnesses—about the exploratory journey he had made from Puerto de los Reyes between 20 December 1543 and 30 January 1544. Because Cabeza de Vaca had been ill when Ribera returned from his reconnaissance mission and because of the governor's subsequent arrest, the captain had never had an opportunity to give him an official report. Now, in view of Cabeza de Vaca's imminent deportation, Ribera wished to make his report and send it with the other secret documents to the emperor in Spain. The captain reported on the many wonders he had seen or heard about, including the Amazons, the "great sheep" (llamas) of the western mountains, and the people who wore clothing embroidered with silver and gold.[27]

At the same time, Irala and the royal officials were also writing reports to send to Charles V along with the *probanzas* they had collected the previous summer. They hoped to justify their actions, win the emperor's support, and secure their grasp on power. According to Pero Hernández, "they wrote things that never happened and were entirely untrue." Someone complained, for example, that on his journey to Puerto de los Reyes, Cabeza de Vaca had taken along a camp bed and other unnecessary luggage. But given the governor's proven ability to endure hardship, this charge seems spurious. Felipe de Cáceres claimed in a letter of 7 March 1545 that Cabeza de Vaca had arrogantly and inappropriately styled himself as governor from the moment in 1540 when he left Cádiz. Cáceres also accused Cabeza de Vaca of having monopolized trade with the Indians and of having burned eleven Indian settlements near Puerto de los Reyes "wherein died more than three thousand souls without cause or just reason." Irala wrote to the emperor on 1 March 1545, claiming that the royal officials in Río de la Plata had never accepted Cabeza de Vaca as more than provisionally their governor. Irala reported that "since it seemed to Your Majesty's officials and to all the men that [the governor] was going beyond his instructions in many of the things pertaining to your service and the pacification of the land, and that he had not carried out what he had contracted with Your Majesty to do, they arrested him and threw him in jail and are going to give an account of all; and in the meantime, since it seemed to them that it was suitable for Your Majesty's service and the pacification of the country, they demanded that I accept the position of governor's deputy." Irala also informed the emperor that he was preparing to launch another *entrada* in quest of the Sierra de la Plata that Alejo García, Juan de Ayolas, and Cabeza de Vaca had all attempted to find.[28]

On 4 March 1545, an inventory was made in Asunción of Cabeza de Vaca's personal goods. Among the things the governor was credited with possessing were a black velvet suit, a pair of gloves, fourteen handkerchiefs, his family genealogy, and a manuscript copy of his *Relación* concerning the Narváez expedition. The royal officials sent many of the papers they had seized from Cabeza de Vaca to Spain for inspection by officers of the Royal Council of the Indies.[29]

During the night of 7 March 1545, three of the royal officials—Cabrera, Venegas, and Dorantes—appeared in the deposed governor's cell, together with several harquebusiers. By this time, Cabeza de Vaca had been incarcerated for eleven months. It had been nearly three years since he first came to Asunción, and nearly five years since he received his royal contract to govern Río de la Plata. He was weak from his long confinement and burdened by the chains around his feet, but two strong men dragged him from his bed and carried him into the street. When Cabeza de Vaca saw the sky, which he had not seen for eleven months, he begged his captors to let him give thanks to God. They allowed him to pray and then carried him to the harbor, where several vessels lay at their moorings. Armed Comuneros, with the fuses of their harquebuses lit, were posted at the head of every intersecting street along the way. Other armed Comuneros were posted at the doors of the homes of the deposed governor's supporters. Despite these measures, a crowd quickly gathered. Cabeza de Vaca was forced to board a vessel that he says was a caravel.[30]

The royal officials demanded again that Cabeza de Vaca appoint Domingo Martínez de Irala as his lieutenant governor, but he refused. Instead he shouted in a voice loud enough for any of his sympathizers in the growing crowd to hear: "Señores, be my witnesses that I name as my lieutenant governor and captain general of this province, in the name of His Majesty, Captain Juan de Salazar." Venegas brandished his dagger, clapped his free hand over the deposed governor's mouth, and wounded him slightly in the temple. Even so, Cabeza de Vaca managed to protest: "I did not come to this province for anything more than to die in the service of God and His Majesty." The royal officials forced him into the cabin prepared for him in the poop of the vessel, and they confined him there with chains that prevented him from moving. Cabrera, Venegas, Orúe, and the other Comuneros who were to journey with him took their places on the deck of the caravel, all carrying harquebuses with lighted fuses.[31]

Cabeza de Vaca asked that two of his servants be allowed to accompany him and attend to him on his journey. But although two servants—one a Spaniard and the other an Indian—were allowed to embark, Venegas called them traitors, threw them off the caravel, and made them board one of three brigantines that were to escort the larger vessel downriver. Three other supporters of Cabeza de Vaca were forcibly embarked as prisoners: Pero Hernández, Juan Pavón (the former *alcalde mayor*), and Luis de Miranda (a clergyman). Hernández, who had taken refuge in the church, seems to have been arrested there. Pavón and Miranda were brought to the harbor from prison. Francisco de Paredes and Fray Juan de Salazar of the Order of Mercy, both of whom supported the deposed governor, were permitted to board the caravel. The two men had sold their property in Río de la Plata and wished to return to Spain. No other friends of Cabeza de Vaca were allowed to embark. Many of the Comuneros who traveled in the small convoy were Basques from Vizcaya.[32]

Early on the morning of 8 March, the crews of the caravel and its escort-ing brigantines unmoored their vessels and headed down the Río Paraguay toward the Río Paraná and the Río de la Plata estuary. Cabeza de Vaca's two servants were required to man the oars of the brigantine that carried them downriver.[33]

On 13 March, Juan de Salazar de Espinosa attempted to claim power with the document Cabeza de Vaca had signed on 23 January, naming him as lieutenant governor. Salazar waited until Cabeza de Vaca had left Asun-ción before revealing that he possessed the document. Pero Hernández, who thought Salazar might have done more to aid the deposed governor, claimed that "if Captain Salazar had wished it the governor would not have been arrested, and still less would they have been able to take him out of the country." On 14 March, Salazar—who seems to have hoped to placate the mutineers—issued a pardon to "whatever persons might have been, and are, guilty in [Cabeza de Vaca's] imprisonment, and might have been, and are, rebels and disobedient." Salazar named Irala as the "chief aggressor and guilty one in the said crime." He also named Cáceres and Dorantes, the two royal officials remaining in Asunción, as guilty parties. Irala and the two officials had Salazar arrested. They also arrested the deposed governor's cousin Pedro Estopiñán Cabeza de Vaca, and they sent both prisoners downriver in a brigantine that pursued the earlier convoy.[34]

After the expulsion of Governor Cabeza de Vaca, even Ulrich Schmidt, who disliked him, says that the civil order in Río de la Plata deteriorated. Schmidt reports: "And when Albernunzo Cabessa de Bacha was sent to Spain there was discord among us Christians, and soon we fought day and night, so that any one would have thought that the devil governed among us; no man was safe from the other."[35]

The deposed governor was held under armed guard during the whole of his journey downriver. The two men who prepared and served his meals were Comuneros from Vizcaya, and Cabeza de Vaca detected arsenic three times in his food. One of his guards confirmed that Irala and the royal officials wanted him killed when he was far from his friends in Asunción but before he reached Spain. As antidotes for poison, Cabeza de Vaca carried a bottle of oil and a piece of what Pero Hernández describes as "the horn of a unicorn." For several days, the deposed governor refused to eat, and he begged that his own servants prepare his meals. Cabrera and Venegas refused to allow this, and at last hunger compelled Cabeza de Vaca to accept the food his captors offered.[36]

On 2 April the brigantine bearing Captain Salazar and the deposed governor's cousin caught up with the convoy it was pursuing. Salazar, with fetters on his feet, was transferred to the caravel on which Cabeza de Vaca was confined. With the addition of Salazar, there were twenty-seven persons aboard the small vessel.[37]

On 24 April, after a voyage of more than a month, the convoy arrived at San Gabriel Island at the head of the Río de la Plata estuary. The brigantines, under the command of a Comunero, prepared to part from the caravel and return upriver to Asunción. Although Francisco de Paredes and Fray Juan de Salazar had been told that they could travel onward to Spain, Cabrera and Venegas forced them to return to Asunción in the brigantines. The two royal officials refused to take Paredes and the friar across the Atlantic, where they might testify in defense of the deposed governor. The officials forced Cabeza de Vaca's two servants to return upriver as well. However, Pero Hernández, Pedro Estopiñán Cabeza de Vaca, and Captain Juan de Salazar de Espinosa were remanded for deportation to Spain. Before the caravel left San Gabriel, someone whose identity Álvar Núñez Cabeza de Vaca never learned threw a scrap of paper through the tiny window of the cabin in which he was confined, thereby informing him of the existence of the hollow cavity in the ship's hull and of the documents hidden inside.[38]

Although the caravel was small for an ocean voyage, it proceeded into the open Atlantic. Rather than follow the coast northward to Brazil, Cabrera and Venegas decided to head directly for the Azores. They might have taken on additional supplies in Brazil, but Pero Hernández says they "dreaded being arrested and brought to justice as rebels against their king."[39]

Three days after they had put out to sea, a storm hit the caravel and—except for some fish, flour, lard, and fresh water—most of the provisions it was carrying were spoiled. According to Pero Hernández, this turn of events unnerved Cabrera and Venegas:

> [They] said that God had sent them this terrible tempest as a punishment for the wrongs and injustice they had made their prisoner suffer. They resolved, therefore, to take off his chains and let him out of prison. Alonso de Cabrera filed them asunder, García Venegas kissed his feet, though Cabeza de Vaca would not allow it. They said openly that God had sent them those four days' sufferings as a retribution for the wrongs they had done him. They acknowledged they had grievously wronged him, and that all their depositions were false; that the malice and jealously they bore him prompted them to administer two thousand false oaths.

Hernández reports that as soon as Cabrera and Venegas took "the chains off the governor the sea and wind subsided, and the tempest, which had lasted four days, calmed down." The two officials begged Cabeza de Vaca to pardon them, acknowledged him as their governor, and promised that they and everyone aboard the caravel would do whatever he might command. Cabrera and Venegas must have been terrified by the prospect of facing Charles V, for they begged their captive not to say anything to the emperor about the mutiny or their role in it, but only to request aid and supplies for Río de la Plata. Cabeza de Vaca replied that he would give a faithful account to His Majesty of all that had occurred. Cabrera and Venegas then proposed returning to Río de la Plata, and they assured Cabeza de Vaca he would be received there as governor and obeyed. Cabeza de Vaca said he preferred to go to Spain and to report there about what had happened. The two officials proposed going to the king of Portugal and begging him to intercede for them with Charles V. Cabeza de Vaca insisted he would appear before his proper king, rather than present himself to a foreign monarch.[40]

The caravel maintained its northeasterly course. But because so many of the ship's provisions had been damaged, the entire company was on short rations for the remainder of the voyage. On 16 July 1545, after nearly three months at sea, the tiny ship arrived at the Portuguese-controlled island of Terceira in the Azores.[41]

Cabeza de Vaca had visited Terceira in 1537 on his return from North America to Spain, so he knew the island and may have had friends there. Cabrera and Venegas brought him forcibly ashore to face the local legal authorities, but before he left the caravel, Cabeza de Vaca broke into the hidden compartment in its hull and removed the documents his supporters had placed inside. When Cabrera and Venegas discovered the hole in the hull, they became very upset. They had not imagined that any letter or document had been smuggled out of Río de la Plata to give information against them.[42]

Before a Portuguese judge, Cabrera and Venegas accused Cabeza de Vaca of having looted ships in the Portuguese-controlled Cape Verde Islands during the winter of 1540–41 on his outward voyage to South America. According to Pero Hernández, the royal officials wanted the judge "to arrest the governor, so as to prevent him from giving information to His Majesty of the crimes and disorders they had committed," but the judge dismissed the case. Someone warned Cabeza de Vaca that Cabrera and Venegas were plotting to kill him, and he managed to elude them and to avoid returning to their caravel. On 24 July 1545, Cabeza de Vaca wrote to Charles V from Terceira, informing the emperor that he would shortly arrive in court to make a full report on the situation in Río de la Plata and the mutiny against him. He saluted the emperor's "Sacred Caesarian Catholic Majesty" and styled himself as one who "kisses the royal hands and feet."[43]

As it happened, Charles V was not in Spain. In his absence, Crown Prince Philip was serving as regent, and he and the Spanish royal court were residing in Madrid. A memorandum sent from the Casa de Contratación in Seville on 2 September 1545 provided the prince and his ministers with the following information:

A small ship has arrived from Río de la Plata, carrying Alonso Cabrera, inspector of mines, García Venegas, deputy treasurer, Gonzalo de Acosta, royal pilot, and twenty-four or twenty-five others. They were bringing as prisoner the governor Álvar Núñez Cabeza de Vaca to present before the Council [of the Indies] with certain reports and charges against him; the royal officials of that province sent him as a prisoner. The first land after leaving there at which they stopped to take refreshment was the island Terceira. Others aboard the ship took off the governor, who did not want to travel with them [i.e., the royal officials], and he came in another caravel to Cádiz.[44]

To reach Cádiz, Cabeza de Vaca had traveled to Lisbon on a Portuguese ship. Cabrera and Venegas embarked from Terceira directly for Spain and arrived there in late August, eight days ahead of the deposed governor. Cabeza de Vaca wrote from Cádiz to the Casa de Contratación to urge its officers to arrest Cabrera and Venegas, but the officers declined to do so. At the same time, they refused fully to credit the reports of Cabrera, Venegas, or Orúe, "because they all come lined up against the governor." Both Cabeza de Vaca and his adversaries made their ways posthaste from southern Spain to Madrid, but Cabrera and Venegas arrived there first. They immediately presented themselves at court and accused Cabeza de Vaca of having "gone to the King of Portugal to inform him about those countries beyond the sea." Because Cabeza de Vaca had traveled to Spain by way of Lisbon, his enemies were able to claim that he had revealed Spanish secrets to a foreign monarch.[45]

SIXTEEN

The Royal Court

Before Madrid became the capital of Spain in 1561, the royal court and the various royal councils simply followed the emperor (or his regent if the emperor was out of the country) as he moved from one city to another. In the fall of 1545 the Royal Council of the Indies—the arm of the Spanish government that had jurisdiction over Río de la Plata—was assembled in Madrid, since the regent, Prince Philip, was in residence in that city. Cabeza de Vaca arrived in Madrid soon after Alonso Cabrera and García Venegas did. All three men were ordered to remain within the jurisdiction of the royal court, and all three were required to post bail. Cabrera and Venegas deposited with the appropriate officials of the Royal Council of the Indies the documents they had brought from Río de la Plata. Among these documents were the *probanzas* obtained in Asunción the previous year, attesting to Cabeza de Vaca's misconduct as governor.[1]

Ultimately, the matter of Cabeza de Vaca's removal from office would spawn four separate legal inquiries. The first was a criminal proceeding brought by Alonso Cabrera and García Venegas against Álvar Núñez Cabeza de Vaca concerning his conduct in office. The second was a reciprocal action brought by Cabeza de Vaca against Cabrera and Venegas. The third was a suit brought against Cabeza de Vaca by Martín de Orduña, who claimed to be the heir of Juan de Ayolas. The fourth was a suit brought by Cabeza de Vaca against Martín de Orúe, the provincial *escribano* for Río de la Plata.[2]

Cabeza de Vaca was not the first Spanish colonial official to be sent home from the Americas in chains. Nor was he the first to face charges stemming from his official actions. Christopher Columbus was sent to Spain in chains after his third voyage to the New World. Hernán Cortés was suspended in 1526 from his office as governor of New Spain and subjected to a *residencia*, and although Charles V subsequently bestowed an aristocratic title upon him, the emperor never reappointed Cortés to his governorship. Nuño Beltrán de Guzmán, whom Cabeza de Vaca had met in Nueva Galicia, was arrested in 1537 and deported to Spain, where he remained under house arrest for the rest of his life. Francisco Vázquez de Coronado and his lieutenant García López de Cárdenas were both subjected to *residencias* after their unsuccessful search for the seven cities of Cíbola. Coronado was absolved of most charges, but Cárdenas underwent a legal ordeal in Spain that dragged on for years.[3]

The prosecutor who handled the case against Cárdenas, Juan de Villalobos, also handled the case against Cabeza de Vaca. Villalobos indicted Cárdenas on 7 January 1546 for atrocities against friendly Indians in the course of the 1540 Tiguex War. Coronado's lieutenant was held prisoner for the six years (from 1546 to 1551) that his case was in litigation. On 20 December 1549, the Royal Council of the Indies convicted him of gross misconduct and ordered him to pay a fine of 800 gold ducats (or the equivalent of 300,000 *maravedíes*) and "to serve his Majesty with his person, arms, and horse at Orán [in North Africa] at his own cost for the time and period of thirty months." Cárdenas appealed, but although his sentence was reduced, his conviction was upheld.[4]

Juan de Villalobos was the *fiscal* (chief prosecuting attorney) of the Council of the Indies. He had studied at the University of Salamanca and served as a judge in both Hispaniola and New Spain. In Spain he had served as an inquisitor before accepting his position with the Council of the Indies. Like Cabeza de Vaca, Villalobos had been born in Jerez de la Frontera, and the two men were approximately the same age. But although Villalobos may have had some sympathy for Cabeza de Vaca, matters that were beyond the prosecutor's control complicated the ousted governor's case. In 1542, while Cabeza de Vaca was in South America, the emperor and his Council of the Indies had promulgated a set of Leyes Nuevas, or New Laws, which prohibited the enslaving of Indians for any reason. During the time Cabeza de Vaca's case was in litigation, the New Laws made the Council of the Indies especially sensitive to any question of alleged mistreatment of Indians in Spain's American colonies.[5]

Much of what we know about Cabeza de Vaca's legal struggles and about the last years of his life is based on documents filed in his case. Apparently his wife was still living when he returned to Spain in 1545, because in subsequent documents Cabeza de Vaca twice claims that she exhausted her monetary resources to preserve his good name. We do not know, however, which of the spouses ultimately outlived the other. We know that on 7 September 1545, Pero Hernández gave written testimony in Madrid concerning events in Río de la Plata. Hernández had traveled with Cabeza de Vaca from Terceira, via Lisbon and Cádiz, to Madrid. And we know that on 22 September, Juan de Salazar de Espinosa wrote to the emperor from Lisbon.[6]

Throughout that fall, Cabeza de Vaca worked on composing a *Relación general* concerning his governorship and the mutiny against him. He defended his actions in Río de la Plata and vilified Irala and the Comuneros. He stressed that when he arrived at Santa Catalina Island in 1541, Juan de Ayolas—Mendoza's lieutenant governor—was known to be dead. Cabeza de Vaca insisted that he had always paid the Indians for any commodities they supplied, and had ordered his men to pay them for their labor. He had never made war against Indians without first securing the advice and consent of his officers and clergymen. On 7 December 1545 he submitted his *Relación general* to the *señores* of the Royal Council of the Indies. On its title page, he styled himself as *adelantado*, governor, and captain general of the province of Río de la Plata. On its final page, he swore that "in everything I have told the truth as before my king and lord I am obliged to do."[7]

On 3 February 1546, Martín de Orduña, the purported heir of Juan de Ayolas, sued Cabeza de Vaca for control of the resources of Río de la Plata. Orduña had helped finance the 1535 Mendoza expedition and had invested heavily in the province. By suing Cabeza de Vaca, he must have hoped to recoup some of the money he had invested. Cabeza de Vaca had worked with Orduña during the period between his return from North America in 1537 and his departure for South America in 1540. During that time, Governor Pedro de Mendoza was known to be dead, but the fate of his lieutenant, Juan de Ayolas, was unknown.[8]

At around the time Orduña filed his suit, the Council of the Indies indicted Cabeza de Vaca on thirty-four criminal charges. The prosecutor, Villalobos, had drawn up the charges after reading the *probanzas* and other documents Cabrera and Venegas had brought from Río de la Plata. Villalobos arranged the charges more or less chronologically, beginning with crimes Cabeza de Vaca was alleged to have committed on his outward voyage to South America.[9]

On his outward voyage, Cabeza de Vaca was alleged to have robbed certain Canary Islanders and to have looted two merchant ships in the Cape Verde Islands. In the course of his overland *entrada* from Santa Catalina Island to Asunción, he was alleged to have monopolized trade with the Indians, to have robbed the Indians, and to have abandoned thirteen Spaniards who were too ill to continue the overland march. Other charges were that he had failed to bring enough supplies to Asunción to meet the needs of its settlers, he had turned twenty-five friendly Indians over to the Guaraníes to be eaten, he had mistreated the Indians of his province, and he had allowed Indian girls to be bought and sold. He had hanged the Guaraní chief Aracaré tyrannically, without first holding a trial. He had used "a medal engraved with his own device, a cow's head," for the purpose of summoning Indians. He had monopolized trade with the Guaraníes and established "such a low price-scale that the Guaraníes would rather eat their slaves than sell them." He had failed to enforce the laws he had enacted. He had killed four thousand Indians in the course of his war with the Guaycurúes and destroyed nine villages. He had killed three thousand Indians in his war with the Sacocis, Xaqueses, and Guajarapos, had branded others as slaves, and had looted sixteen villages. He had flown his own coat of arms rather than the king's from the mast of his brigantine during his journey to Puerto de los Reyes. He had burdened his men (both Spaniards and Indians) so heavily that his search for gold and silver had to be aborted. He had said, "I am the prince and master in this land." He had engraved his coat of arms together with the king's. He had seized property without remunerating the owners, taken property from the dead, interfered in private business, and manipulated the local tax laws to his advantage. He had obstructed the work of the royal officials and prevented them from writing to the emperor. He was also alleged to have committed unspecified acts of cruelty, arrogance, and greed.[10]

Cabeza de Vaca hired an attorney to defend him against these charges. In February, on order of the Royal Council of the Indies, Cabeza de Vaca was arrested and incarcerated in Madrid's public jail. He petitioned to be placed under house arrest instead, and on 19 April, after depositing a bond of 1,000 ducats (or 375,000 *maravedíes*), he was transferred from the jail to a private house in Madrid. That spring or summer, Cabeza de Vaca lodged a criminal complaint against Cabrera and Venegas, charging them with violent aggression against his person and unlawful seizure of his property. He contended that the evidence against him that they had brought to Spain, and particularly the *probanzas* collected in Asunción in 1544, had been obtained through fraudulence, bribery, and coercion.[11]

On 10 May 1546, Crown Prince Philip granted Cabeza de Vaca 120 days to prepare his defense. The prince issued a *cédula real* addressed to "all the cities and places of these our realms," informing them of the particulars of the case and directing them to assist any of Cabeza de Vaca's legal representatives who might appear before them within the next 120 days. If called upon to do so, the judges were to subpoena witnesses and to examine them in the presence of two *escribanos*, one appointed by the defense and the other by the prosecution. If the prosecutor for the Council of the Indies failed to supply an *escribano* within three days, the judge was to examine the witnesses before Cabeza de Vaca's *escribano* alone. The judge was to ask each witness his name, his place of residence, and whether he was related to anyone involved in the case. If a witness spoke in answer to any question, the judge was to ask him how he knew the information he gave and whether he knew it by direct experience or by hearsay. The *probanzas* were to be taken down in writing, signed by the judge and both *escribanos*, sealed in an official manner, and turned over to Cabeza de Vaca's representative for delivery to the Council of the Indies. Cabeza de Vaca's representative was to pay the judge and the *escribanos* the customary fees for their services.[12]

Cabeza de Vaca and his supporters immediately began gathering *probanzas* in eighteen cities in His Majesty's realms and preparing an *interrogatorio*, or series of questions to be used in examining witnesses. Altogether they compiled seventy-six such questions. Three of them had to do with the time frame in which the death of Ayolas became known to the various parties in the dispute. Other questions concerned the way Indians had been treated in Asunción and other areas under Cabeza de Vaca's control. Questions 68 and 69, for example, were as follows:

68. Is it not the case that in all the time he was governor, he prevented any Spaniard from doing damage [to the Indians], and is it not the case that he punished any Spaniard who mistreated them?

69. Is it not the case that during the time he governed the said province, he paid the Indians and ordered his men to pay them for all the

provisions they supplied, even if the Indians provided the items, through trade or other means, of their own free will, which pleased the Indians greatly?

Cabeza de Vaca sought through his questions to demonstrate that when he had made war against Indians, he had followed the accepted Spanish principles for the just conduct of war. He also attempted to justify his having enslaved some Indians.[13]

Cabeza de Vaca collected *probanzas* throughout the summer of 1546. Hearings were held for this purpose in Madrid, Andújar, Santiponce, Jerez de la Frontera, and Seville. However, most of those who might have testified on the ousted governor's behalf were in South America, and Cabeza de Vaca found it difficult to gather witnesses in Spain who had firsthand knowledge of events in Río de la Plata. Among the witnesses who spoke in his defense were the three men who had been expelled from Asunción with him: Pero Hernández, Pedro Estopiñán Cabeza de Vaca, and Captain Juan de Salazar de Espinosa. Other veterans of the Indies also came forward to speak for the ousted governor. Among these were Alonso de Montalbán, Pedro de Heredia, Andrés de Cobasrubias, and Andrés de Tapia. Although none of these men had been in Río de la Plata, Montalbán and Heredia had served in other parts of South America, and Cobasrubias and Tapia had served in New Spain. The evidence provided by these friendly witnesses, however, seemed paltry in comparison with the evidence presented by Cabeza de Vaca's enemies.[14]

Among the eyewitnesses testifying against the ousted governor were Cabrera, Venegas, Orúe, and the pilot Gonzalo de Acosta—all of whom had escorted him to Spain in chains. Acosta testified that "Domingo de Irala is so much loved that every one would die for him." Acosta's words and those of the other hostile witnesses were backed up by the four dozen signatures on the *probanzas* the royal officials had collected in Asunción in 1544 and sent with Cabrera and Venegas to Spain.[15]

The Council of the Indies, which had an executive function as well as a judicial one, made administrative decisions for Río de la Plata while Cabeza de Vaca's case was in litigation. On 22 July 1547 the council named Juan de Sanabria to replace Cabeza de Vaca as governor and captain general of the province and ruled that "because of the differences and matters that were exhibited between Álvar Núñez Cabeza de Vaca and the people who were in the province, he was brought a prisoner to these kingdoms, and he is not to return again to the province because it is not suitable that he go back to it." As it happened, Sanabria died in 1549 before he could take office. For this reason, and because Cabeza de Vaca was embroiled in legal proceedings, Domingo Martínez de Irala would manage to hang on to power in Río de la Plata.[16]

In 1547–48 Irala would succeed in crossing the uncharted area from the wetlands of the Pantanal to the Bolivian highlands, but he would find that Bolivia's silver mines had already been claimed by rival Spaniards from Peru. In 1545 these Peruvian Spaniards had discovered a mountain containing rich silver ore at a place they called the *cerro rico de Potosí*. When Irala arrived in the area and found other Spaniards in control, he sent messengers to Lima to meet with the governor of Peru. The governor received the messengers but ordered them and Irala to return posthaste to Río de la Plata. Oviedo, the royal historian of the Indies, would later conclude that Río de la Plata had been "improperly named, since never in it has silver been found or seen, nor is it known to the present time that any is there."[17]

In 1555, Emperor Charles V would confirm Irala as governor of Río de la Plata, but the Vizcayan would serve only briefly in the office. He died in 1557 at around the age of seventy. Today the front facade of Asunción's cathedral bears a sculptural relief depicting Irala embracing a Guaraní warrior and several Guaraní women. Perhaps the carving commemorates the sixteenth-century mingling of Spanish and Guaraní blood. Perhaps it celebrates Irala as the father of his country. One has only to peruse a Paraguayan phone book or to stroll through the Recoleta Cemetery in present-day Asunción to see that many Paraguayans bear or have borne Irala's surname. John H. Parry and Robert G. Keith, the editors of *New Iberian World*, describe Irala as "the very archetype of South American dictator."[18]

As for Cabeza de Vaca, he petitioned successfully in September 1546 to be freed from house arrest and treated instead as a "prisoner of the court." His new legal status required him simply to remain within proximity to the Council of the Indies. A year later, on 7 September 1547, Juan de Salazar de Espinosa testified in Madrid on Cabeza de Vaca's behalf. On that same date, Cabeza de Vaca was freed from the loose detention under which he had been held during the year he had "the court for his prison." He was required to pay a 1,000-ducat bond and to promise that he would appear before the Council of the Indies within thirty days whenever summoned. He was released to his bondsman and told that he now had "the kingdom for his jail."[19]

Sculptural relief depicting Domingo Martínez de Irala embracing a Guaraní warrior. The panel, mounted on the front facade of Asunción's Catedral de Nuestra Señora de la Asunción, was donated by the government of Spain in 1965. Photograph by Juris Zagarins.

In 1546 and 1547, Gonzalo Fernández de Oviedo y Valdés was in Spain on official business. Half a dozen years earlier the historian had transcribed and commented on the *Joint Report* that Cabeza de Vaca, Dorantes, and Castillo had prepared in 1536. He had produced a six-chapter account of the Narváez expedition and incorporated it in his *Historia general y natural de las Indias*, where it appears in Book 35. During his time in Spain, Oviedo met with Cabeza de Vaca twice. At their first meeting, which took place in Madrid, the two men discussed Cabeza de Vaca's experiences in North

America. At their second meeting, in Aranda del Duero, they discussed his experiences in South America. The royal historian also examined a copy of the *Relación* that Cabeza de Vaca had published in 1542. Oviedo described it as the *segunda relación* in contrast to the *Joint Report*, which he saw as the *primera relación* of the Narváez expedition. He preferred the *Joint Report* because Dorantes and Castillo, as well as Cabeza de Vaca, had testified to its accuracy. After meeting with Cabeza de Vaca, Oviedo added a seventh chapter to his account of the Narváez expedition. He begins this seventh chapter by stating that Cabeza de Vaca "is a trustworthy person," and then he itemizes those details that appear in the explorer's published *Relación* but not in the earlier *Joint Report*. He points out, for example, that the name "Malhado" (Evil Fate) appears only in the *Relación*, and he asks why Cabeza de Vaca gave the island such a name "since on that island the Christians were well treated." The royal historian notes that, in the published *Relación*, "Cabeza de Vaca says that through all that land that includes the mountains they saw great signs of gold and galena, iron, copper, and other metals," and Oviedo notes that "I would like to have this more clearly stated and a longer explanation of it."[20]

Oviedo took a stern view of Cabeza de Vaca's actions as governor of Río de la Plata. He met with Martín de Orúe and García Venegas as well as with Cabeza de Vaca to talk about what had happened in South America. Orúe gave Oviedo a copy of a report he had written on the history of the European exploration and settlement of Río de la Plata, and Venegas vouched for its accuracy. The report is invaluable with respect to the Solís, Cabot, Mendoza, and Ayolas expeditions, but it is unsympathetic to Cabeza de Vaca. Orúe claims, among other things, that "within a short time [of his arrival in Asunción], Cabeza de Vaca earned the dislike both of the people he brought with him and of those he found in the land." The *escribano* also reports that Cabeza de Vaca mistreated the Indians of his province and destroyed a settlement of nine hundred houses near Puerto de los Reyes. Oviedo used Orúe's report as his principal source for his account of Cabeza de Vaca's governorship and of the mutiny against him. He acknowledged that Orúe and Venegas were "notorious rivals and enemies of the governor, Cabeza de Vaca," but he stood by Orúe's words and declared that "in the end, what has occurred is what is said." Even so, Oviedo expressed some sympathy for the ousted governor. He describes him as "fatigado e pobre" (tired and poor) and reports that "[he] seeks justice against his rivals, and it is pitiable to hear him and know what he has suffered in the Indies." Oviedo completed his history of Río de la Plata in January 1549, and it appears in Book 23 of his *Historia general y natural de las Indias*. The first nineteen books of the *Historia* had been printed in 1535. The two sections that relate to Cabeza de Vaca were not published until the nineteenth century.[21]

On 17 December 1549, Cabeza de Vaca brought suit against Martín de Orúe for offenses the *escribano* had committed against him in South America. Orúe was imprisoned after the suit was filed, but he petitioned to return to Río de la Plata. His petition was granted on 25 January 1553, and he returned to South America in 1555. Captain Juan de Salazar de Espinosa had returned to Río de la Plata in 1550. Alonso Cabrera and García Venegas both came to bad ends, according to Pero Hernández: "Garcia de Venegas, who was one of those who had arrested the governor, died a sudden, terrible death, his eyes having fallen out of his head, and he never declared the truth of what had passed. Alonso Cabrera, the supervisor, his accomplice, lost his reason, and in a fit of frenzy he killed his wife at Loxa."[22]

Another death that had an impact on Cabeza de Vaca's case was that, on 8 September 1550, of Juan de Villalobos, the chief prosecutor for the Council of the Indies. His successor, Martín Ruiz de Ágreda, was not appointed until 13 June 1551. In the meantime, three interim prosecutors filled Villalobos's position.

On 18 March 1551, while one of these interim prosecutors was in office, the Council of the Indies—meeting in Valladolid—pronounced its judgment on Cabeza de Vaca. Six ministers of the council affirmed the following with their signatures:

> We find that for the guilt which appears in the said suit against the said Álvar Núñez Cabeza de Vaca we must condemn him, and we condemn him to the perpetual deprivation of the said office of governor and adelantado of the provinces of the said Río de la Plata, and of all the right and property which the said Álvar Núñez alleged he held in the said governorship; and likewise we suspend him perpetually from the office of governor, adelantado, or any other judicial office in all the Indies of His Majesty. . . . And further we condemn him to perpetual banishment from all the said Indies under penalty of death, and further we condemn him for the five years next following to serve His Majesty in Oran [in Barbary, now Algeria] with his arms and horse at his own expense, and he must remain in the said service for the said time under penalty of the doubling of the said time of the said five years. And we maintain

the rights of the persons injured according to the charges of the said suit, that they may seek compensation for injuries received from the said Álvar Núñez and take action for their payment as and before whom they may see fit.

After this harsh sentence was delivered, Cabeza de Vaca was again made a prisoner of the court.[23]

On 6 April 1551, Cabeza de Vaca appealed the decision. He pointed to the length of time he had already been detained at court and to the financial difficulties he was suffering as a result both of the seizure of his goods in Río de la Plata and of his legal expenses. Cabeza de Vaca claimed, "I have no means to buy food nor to prosecute my case, and I am much in debt for all I spent for my fleet and to bring help to those lands whose officials seized me and sent me back naked." The ousted governor added, "And I swear by God and by this cross that I know of no one who will lend me anything because my poverty is notorious." On 11 April the council affirmed its decision but released Cabeza de Vaca, upon his payment of a large bond, from confinement. On 22 November, Cabeza de Vaca petitioned to reopen his case, and in December the council's newly appointed prosecutor, Martín Ruiz de Ágreda, granted him 120 days to gather new evidence. During the allotted time, the ousted governor gathered additional *probanzas* from some nineteen witnesses. Although these *probanzas* documented little that was substantive, they attested that Cabeza de Vaca was held in great esteem in his native Jerez de la Frontera, that he and his wife were nearly destitute, and that he had performed military service in Europe as a young man.[24]

By now Cabeza de Vaca had spent more than six years in court. He was at least fifty-nine years old and may have been in his mid-sixties. The Council of the Indies seems to have appreciated that he was an aging man from a respectable social background who enjoyed the support and esteem of friends in his hometown. Perhaps for these reasons, on 23 August 1552 the council lightened its sentence against him, amending the terms of his banishment, both from the Indies and to Oran. The council decreed that "the condemnation of perpetual banishment from the Indies made by our said sentence be and be understood to refer to the governance and provinces of Río de la Plata and nowhere else and, with regard to our said sentence condemning the said Álvar Núñez to service in Oran with his arms and horse at his own cost for five years, that, taking into account the new *probanzas* taken before us and presented by the defendant in his appeal, we should and we do revoke the said sentence with regard to the said condemnation to such service." Although Cabeza de Vaca's deprivation of his titles as governor and *adelantado* of Río de la Plata and his liability for court costs remained in force, the council had effectively exonerated him of the criminal charges brought against him.[25]

Pero Hernández viewed the reduction of Cabeza de Vaca's sentence as tantamount to an acquittal. However, the *escribano* lamented the loss of the money the ousted governor had expended in and for Río de la Plata: "After keeping him eight years under arrest at court, he was set at liberty and acquitted. He was relieved of his governorship for divers reasons; for his enemies said that if he returned to punish the guilty, he would have occasioned more troubles and dissensions in that country. He therefore lost his appointment, besides other losses, without receiving any compensation for all the money he had spent in relieving the Spaniards, and in his voyage of discovery."[26]

After the reduction of his sentence, Cabeza de Vaca remained at court in an effort to gain restitution for his lost property. He petitioned for reimbursement for the six brigantines, four other small vessels, two houses, various fields, horses, and domestic goods that Irala and the royal officials had confiscated. Pedro Estopiñán Cabeza de Vaca testified in 1554 that his cousin had held property in Río de la Plata worth "a hundred thousand ducats." The former governor never entirely gave up on the legal battles stemming from his years in South America, and as late as 8 November 1555 he was still filing documents pertaining to his case. During his frequent appearances at court, he also represented the interests of Jerez de la Frontera. He received some compensation for his services to his hometown, and it is clear that he commanded respect there. He also seems to have become an accepted and respected figure at court. In particular, he became friendly with two of the court's most learned men, Antonio de Rojas y Velasco and Honorato Juan, both of whom served as tutors to the young Infante Don Carlos, the son of Prince Philip and grandson of Charles V.[27]

In the early 1550s, Cabeza de Vaca was much involved with a book that he and his former secretary, Pero Hernández, were working on together. The book was to be Cabeza de Vaca's legacy, a monument to his service in the Indies, and the means of restoring his good name. It would also provide him with a context in which to argue that the Indians of the New World should be treated in a just and Christian fashion. The book's title was to be *La relación y comentarios del governador Álvar Núñez Cabeza de Vaca, de lo acaescido en las dos jornadas que hizo a las Indias* (*The Report and Commentaries of the Governor Álvar Núñez Cabeza de Vaca, of What Happened on the Two Journeys He Made to the Indies*). Its first part would be a new edition of the *Relación* that Cabeza de Vaca had published in 1542 concerning the Narváez expedition. The much longer second part would be the narrative Hernández was writing about Cabeza de Vaca's years in Río de la Plata. In a nod to Julius Caesar's classic *Commentarii de bello Gallico*, Hernández would call his book the *Comentarios*. Just as in his account of the Gallic War, Caesar had memorialized and defended his generalship, Hernández would memorialize and defend Cabeza de Vaca's governorship.[28]

In composing the *Comentarios*, Hernández worked closely with Cabeza de Vaca. The latter probably understood that because of the controversy surrounding his governorship, he could not defend himself in print as effectively as an eyewitness like Hernández, narrating in the third person, could do. In a "Prohemio" (Proem) that he wrote for the combined *Relación y comentarios*, Cabeza de Vaca says he entrusted the writing of the *Comentarios* to Hernández and that the *escribano* "wrote them with great diligence and truth." Possibly Hernández was little more than an amanuensis. He had two written sources for his book, but his own *Relación de las cosas sucedidas en el Río de la Plata*, completed in Asunción on 28 January 1545, was a less important source than the *Relación general* that Cabeza de Vaca had presented to the Council of the Indies on 7 December 1545.[29]

In the *Comentarios*, Hernández characterizes Cabeza de Vaca as both firm and fair, arguing that the governor dealt justly and humanely with the Guaraníes and other Indians of his province and that his wars against the Guaycurúes and against the Sacocis, Xaqueses, and Guajarapos were just. The *escribano* claims that Cabeza de Vaca's protection of the rights of the Indians aroused the resentment of many of his Spanish subordinates, and he places most of the blame for what went wrong in Río de la Plata on Irala and the royal officials. As an epilogue, Hernández appends Hernando de Ribera's report on his reconnaissance mission of 1543–44, which treats of Amazon women and people with clothing embroidered in silver and gold. By appending the report, Hernández implies that Cabeza de Vaca was on the right track and might have found gold and silver if Irala and Cáceres had not forced him to abort his *entrada*.[30]

Perhaps at Cabeza de Vaca's request, Hernández suppressed some of the more lurid accusations he had made against Irala and the royal officials in his 1545 *Relación de las cosas*. The *escribano* does not say in the published

Comentarios, as he had in his 1545 report, that at the time of Lieutenant Governor Ayolas's return to Candelaria, Irala was eighty leagues downriver, dallying with a Guaraní beauty. He does not say that Irala looked the other way when a man related to both Alonso Cabrera and García Venegas raped a seven-year-old Indian girl. He does not mention that, during a celebration of the mass, Irala allowed one of his supporters to grope the breasts of an Indian woman, or that Irala hung Diego Portugués by his genitals.[31]

Hernández not only suppressed ugly details but also added new material to the *Comentarios* that was not present in his sources. In particular, he added a great deal of local color. Some of the new material—such as that concerning Guaraní cannibalism, the method by which the Guaycurúes decapitated their enemies, and the houseboats in which the people of the Pantanal lived during flood season—has ethnographic value. Other new passages—including the descriptions of the Spanish and Guaraní army advancing against the Guaycurúes, of the Spanish and Guaraní armada departing for Puerto de los Reyes, and of the floating market on the Río Paraguay—present vivid pictures of life and military pageantry in Río de la Plata. Hernández may have drawn on his own memory for some of the new material, but he must also have received information from Cabeza de Vaca. The *escribano* never saw the Iguazú Falls, for example, so the observation that "the spray rises two spears high and more above the fall" must have come from the former governor. Hernández did not march with Cabeza de Vaca from the Brazilian coast to Asunción, so he must have learned from the former governor that he and his men ate worms along the way. Cabeza de Vaca seems to have wanted the combined *Relación y comentarios* to be both educational and entertaining. He had argued in his 1542 account of the Narváez expedition "that all men desire to know the customs and practices of others."[32]

While Hernández was working on the *Comentarios*, Cabeza de Vaca was revising his 1542 *Relación* for republication. The aging explorer made relatively few changes, but among those he authorized were one that made his book more accessible to readers and two that aggrandized his own role in his story. To make his book more accessible, Cabeza de Vaca divided it into thirty-eight chapters and gave each one a descriptive heading. In the first case in which he aggrandized himself, he asserted that after he removed an arrowhead from the chest of an Indian, the scar from the incision "looked like nothing more than a crease in the palm of one's hand." In the second case, he made himself, rather than Andrés Dorantes, the recipient of five emerald arrowheads at the Indian settlement of Corazones. Cabeza de Vaca also added the detail that the members of his Mariames host family were all blind in one eye and the observation that divorce was simple among the Indians of the Texas coast. He added the word *naufragios*, meaning "shipwrecks" or "disasters," to his title. The word helps emphasize the role that adverse fortune played in his life, and although it does not appear on the title page of the combined *Relación y comentarios*, it is included in the heading for the table of contents of the *Relación* and in the running head at the top of each of its pages. The new heading for the table of contents was "Tabla de los capítulos contenidos en la presente relación y naufragios del governador Álvar Núñez Cabeza de Vaca."[33]

On 21 March 1555, Cabeza de Vaca was granted a royal license to print the *Relación y comentarios*. Within the text of the license, the aging explorer is identified as a "resident of the city of Seville." He had not needed a license in 1542 to print the first edition of his *Relación*, but a royal edict issued in 1554 had made it mandatory for an author or his agent to obtain a license from the Council of Castile before publishing a book in that kingdom. Cabeza de Vaca's license was endorsed by the Infanta Juana, acting for her father, the emperor. The princess authorized the publication of the *Relación* and the *Comentarios* together, declaring that "the one book and the other were on the same subject, and it was advisable that the two should be put into one volume."[34]

From Cabeza de Vaca's point of view, publishing the second edition of the *Relación* together with the first edition of the *Comentarios* enabled him to use the narrative of his successes in North America to bolster the record of his governorship in Río de la Plata, and to use the account of his good dealings with the Indians of North America to defend the record of his dealings with the Indians of South America. In the *Relación*, Cabeza de Vaca comes across, in contrast to Pánfilo de Narváez, as a man of sound judgment. In the *Comentarios*, he comes across, in contrast to Domingo Martínez de Irala, as a man of integrity. Ultimately, because Cabeza de Vaca published an account of the events surrounding his governorship, and Irala did not, his version of the story prevailed over his rival's.[35]

The *Relación y comentarios* was published in 1555 in the city of Valladolid. On its title page, Cabeza de Vaca styled himself as the governor and *adelantado* of Río de la Plata, although these titles had been rescinded three years earlier. He addressed the *Relación y comentarios* to a broad audience of educated readers and armchair travelers and not simply, as was the case with the 1542 edition of the *Relación*, to the emperor and a handful of Indies specialists. The division of both the *Comentarios* and the new edition of the *Relación* into chapters makes this clear. So do the many passages in both books on the customs and lifeways of the Indians. But nowhere is it clearer that Cabeza de Vaca hoped to entertain and edify a broad audience than in the "Prohemio" he wrote to the 1555 volume.[36]

Cabeza de Vaca opens the "Prohemio" with a dedication to "the most serene, very high and very powerful lord, the Infante Don Carlos." The dedicatee was then just ten years old. Explaining to Prince Carlos that he published the *Comentarios* together with the *Relación* "so that the variety of matters treated in the one part and the other, as well as the variety of my deeds, might detain your highness pleasurably in this reading," Cabeza de Vaca asserts, "It is certain that nothing more delights readers than the variety of things and times and turns of fortune, which, although distasteful at the time one experiences them, are agreeable when one recalls them to memory or reads about them." Cabeza de Vaca is addressing not only the prince but, through him, also the boy's father and grandfather, Prince Philip and Charles V, and the broad audience of readers the explorer hopes to "detain pleasurably." He boasts of the variety of his deeds, but he assigns a large role in his story to fortune. In the dedicatory epistle with which Cabeza de Vaca had introduced his 1542 *Relación*, he had assigned an equally large role to fortune and had apologized for not having succeeded in performing any greater service for his emperor than to write an account of all he had seen and learned. He argued that the smallness of his success was caused, not by personal shortcomings, "but only by fortune, or more certainly through no fault of one's own, but only by the will and judgment of God, where it happens that one may come away with more notable services than he expected, while to another everything occurs so to the contrary that he cannot demonstrate any greater witness to his intention than his diligence." Fortune had not smiled upon Cabeza de Vaca on either of his voyages to the New World, but as he says in his "Prohemio," his adventures were agreeable to him in recollection and would, he hoped, entertain his readers.[37]

In the "Prohemio," Cabeza de Vaca both praises the Infante Don Carlos and instructs him in those precepts that should make him "a wise, just, strong, truthful, prudent, liberal, magnanimous, merciful, humane, gentle, beneficent, amiable, Christian king." The aging explorer expresses the hope that his book might nurture a desire in the young prince to draw the

Indians of the New World "to the light of the evangelical truth of Jesus Christ, not permitting them to spend more time in darkness and blindness or subject to the tyranny of demons." He argues that the Spaniards "who have discovered so many new provinces, abounding in all the good things in nature," were "chosen by God to be the executors and instruments of evangelization in all the Occident, where enlarging the kingdom of the gospel enlarges their kingdoms and fiefdoms, titles and fame." In Cabeza de Vaca's view, spreading Christ's word was the justification for extending Spain's empire, and the extension of the empire was the reward for spreading the gospel. He describes evangelism as "necessary work" and notes that although in his case the envy of his detractors had prevented him from engaging fully in this necessary work, the emperor and the crown prince had defended him and preserved his good name. The explorer declares that "even when envy operates to impede and hinder such necessary work, the clear virtue and merits of such princes will defend us, if God gives us the peace and tranquility that abounds in the times of good kings." Clearly, Cabeza de Vaca was grateful to Charles V and his son and to the ministers who served them on the Royal Council of the Indies for having retracted the most humiliating portions of their original judgment against him. The explorer seems never to have wavered in his loyalty to his emperor.[38]

In the remarks he addresses to the Infante Don Carlos, Cabeza de Vaca praises not only the prince's father and grandfather but also the prince's tutors, Antonio de Rojas y Velasco and Honorato Juan. Rojas y Velasco is commended for his "very ancient and very illustrious lineage" and for his "great Christianity, prudence, modesty, and experience in the service of the royal persons and their concerns"; and Honorato Juan, for his "great and deep learning of the Greek and Latin authors, and natural and moral philosophy, and the discipline of mathematics." Although not so well educated as Rojas y Velasco or Honorato Juan, Cabeza de Vaca valued learning. The three men had become friends, and there can be little doubt but that the two courtiers were "detained pleasurably" by Cabeza de Vaca's stories of his deeds and the turns in his fortune. In many ways, the young prince's tutors represented the ideal audience for the *Relación y comentarios*.[39]

Fray Bartolomé de las Casas, the champion of Indian rights and of peaceful evangelization, was another reader who was favorably impressed with Cabeza de Vaca's story. In his *Apologética historia sumaria*, which Las Casas completed in 1561, the friar used ethnographic information from the explorer's book to support his own argument that all the people of the world, including the native people of America, "enjoy the benefit of very good, subtle and natural intellects and most capable understanding." Las Casas pointed approvingly to Cabeza de Vaca's statement in the *Relación* that he found no instances of either human sacrifice or idolatry during the whole of his journey across North America. He also commented approvingly on Cabeza de Vaca's assertion that the Indians he encountered were spiritually ready to receive Christianity.[40]

One reader who was not pleased by Pero Hernández's *Comentarios* was the Bavarian harquebusier Ulrich Schmidt, who had returned to Europe from Asunción in 1554. In 1567, twelve years after the publication of the *Relación y comentarios*, Schmidt published *A true and agreeable description of some principal Indian lands and islands, which have not been recorded in former chronicles, but have now been first explored amid great danger during the voyage of Ulrich Schmidt of Straubing, and most carefully described by him.* The book seems to have been ghostwritten, but the harquebusier furnished it with a map and eighteen illustrations by the Flemish engraver Theodore de Bry. Schmidt endeavored to disparage Hernández's account of events in Río de la Plata and to defend the actions of Domingo Martínez de Irala. Perhaps because of the book's lurid descriptions of cannibalism and of Indian women who "commit transgressions in the dark," it became one of the most widely read travel books of the sixteenth century.[41]

On 16 January 1556, not long after the publication of the *Relación y comentarios*, Charles V handed the crowns of Castile and León over to his son, the crown prince, who was known thereafter as Philip II. Philip was the king who, in 1588, would send a Spanish armada against England. More immediately, on 15 September 1556, he bestowed the meager amount of twelve thousand *maravedíes* on Cabeza de Vaca "for help to be cured of his illness."[42]

The document of 15 September 1556 is one of the last concerning Cabeza de Vaca to be filed in his lifetime. Another document, written by historian Alonso Gómez de Santoya around 1560, states that Cabeza de Vaca "died in Valladolid, a completely poor caballero." The precise date of Cabeza de Vaca's death is not now known, but that is not surprising, considering that we do not know the date of his birth either.[43]

There are conflicting views of the veteran explorer's final years. Morris Bishop, the author of *The Odyssey of Cabeza de Vaca*, says both that the explorer died in "obscurity, shame, and the conviction of failure" and that he died "penniless, old, and broken-hearted." Rolena Adorno and Patrick

Charles Pautz, the authors of *Álvar Núñez Cabeza de Vaca: His Account, His Life, and the Expedition of Pánfilo de Narváez*, disagree. They point to Cabeza de Vaca's amicable relations with Prince Carlos's tutors and argue that such influential courtiers are not likely to have befriended the explorer if he had become a truly pathetic figure.[44]

Adorno and Pautz have discovered that, on 13 March 1559, Álvar Núñez Cabeza de Vaca and Pedro Sierra Granado cosigned a ransom agreement drawn up in Jerez de la Frontera to secure the freedom of the veteran explorer's cousin Hernán Ruiz Cabeza de Vaca. In the agreement, both Sierra Granado and Álvar Núñez Cabeza de Vaca are identified as residents of Jerez de la Frontera, so although the explorer was living in Seville in 1555 when he received his license to print the *Relación y comentarios*, he must subsequently have reestablished residence in his hometown. His cousin Hernán Ruiz had been captured in an action against the Ottomans in North Africa and was being held captive in Algiers. The agreement specified that the ransom amount could not exceed 130 ducats of gold. A notation, added to the document on 19 May 1559, indicates that Álvar Núñez Cabeza de Vaca put up a bond for the stipulated ransom money. The document indicates that the explorer was not entirely impoverished during his final years and that, when he needed to, he could still raise a sizeable amount of money. Although he had claimed in the course of his legal battles that he was destitute, he may have exaggerated the extent of his poverty (as was customary in Spain at that time) in order to win the sympathy of the court.[45]

After 19 May 1559, Álvar Núñez Cabeza de Vaca disappears from the historical record. No documents concerning his death or burial have survived. Since he was resident in Jerez de la Frontera in 1559, he probably died there. If he died in Valladolid, as Alonso Gómez de Santoya reported, his body would likely have been transported to Jerez for burial. Burial records exist for the explorer's grandfather Pedro de Vera, but none have been found for either of the explorer's parents. Pedro de Vera was laid to rest in 1506 in the royal chapel in the Convento de Santo Domingo in Jerez. He had purchased his tomb in 1474, adorned it with his coat of arms, and pledged an annual sum of 10,000 *maravedíes* for its upkeep. On 16 March 1506, shortly after his death, his heirs pledged an additional 50,000 *maravedíes* to the Convento and acknowledged that don Pedro had "wanted and intended his children and heirs and grandchildren and descendants and great-grandchildren to be buried there." Teresa Cabeza de Vaca, the mother of the Indies explorer, stated in her will (filed on 1 August 1509) that she wished to be buried beside her late husband, Francisco de Vera, in the Vera family vault in the Convento. Her wishes were probably honored, and in all likelihood her son—Álvar Núñez Cabeza de Vaca—was interred near his parents in the same vault. Unfortunately, during modifications made to the Convento de Santo Domingo in 1750, Pedro de Vera's coat of arms was removed from the royal chapel it had graced for more than 200 years.[46]

The great monument to Álvar Núñez Cabeza de Vaca, of course, is the *Relación y comentarios*. The publication of the book in 1555 must have brought tremendous pleasure to the veteran explorer, and a measure of solace to his final years. I think he must have died a reasonably happy man. He had survived to tell his tale and was blessed with at least sixty-seven years of life. He had come home again to Jerez de la Frontera, and he enjoyed the respect of people there and of some men in high places in the royal court. Additionally, the stiff sentence imposed on him had been overturned. I like to think that sometimes of an evening during the final period of his life, Cabeza de Vaca sat by a fountain in his native Jerez, enjoying a glass of the local sherry, talking with friends about the Indies, and watching the swifts soar and tumble in the darkening skies.

Glossary

adelantado The military commander or governor of a frontier district.

alcalde A municipal judge.

alcalde mayor The chief magistrate of a town.

Audiencia A royal appellate court.

braza The distance measured by a man's outstretched arms, equivalent to 5.5 feet or roughly a fathom.

caballero A knight.

capitulaciones Contractual agreements.

Casa de Contratación The House of Trade, founded in Seville in 1503.

castellano A gold coin weighing 1.6 ounces and equivalent to 450–490 *maravedíes*. Also called *peso de oro*.

cédula real A royal order.

cerro A hill.

Comunero (1) A participant in the 1520–21 effort to win more autonomy for Spanish cities and towns; (2) a participant in the 1544 mutiny against Cabeza de Vaca.

contador A comptroller.

converso A Christian convert of Jewish descent.

cruzado A gold coin worth 375 *maravedíes*; equivalent to a ducat.

ducat A gold coin worth 375 *maravedíes*; equivalent to a *cruzado*.

encomendero A Spanish colonist to whom an *encomienda* was granted.

encomienda A grant to a Spanish colonist of rights to receive tribute or labor from a group of Indians.

entrada An armed entry into a territory; an armed expedition of exploration.

escribano A scribe or notary.

factor A quartermaster.

harquebus   A matchlock gun.

hidalgo   A person belonging to the lowest level of the Spanish nobility.

legua (**league**)   The walking distance covered in an hour, roughly equivalent to three miles.

maestre de campo   A chief of staff.

maravedí   A Castilian coin of small value. Thirty-four *maravedíes* were equal to a silver *real*. Eleven *reales* and one *maravedí* (or 375 *maravedíes*) were equal to a gold ducat. According to J. H. Elliott, a Spanish laborer's wages in the early sixteenth century were 15 to 20 *maravedíes* per day (*Imperial* 117). According to Samuel Eliot Morison, pilots and master mariners were paid 2,000 *maravedíes* per month (*Admiral* I: 139).

Mesoamerica   A region extending from central Mexico into Guatemala, Belize, Honduras, and Nicaragua.

mestizo   A person of mixed parentage, usually of European and Indian descent.

peso de oro   A gold coin weighing 1.6 ounces and equivalent to 450–90 *maravedíes*. Also called *castellano*.

plus ultra   The motto of Charles V, meaning "more beyond."

probanza   An oral testimony sworn before a notary public.

quinto real   (1) A royal tax equivalent to a fifth of the income accruing from a venture; (2) a tax imposed by the royal officials in Río de la Plata.

Reconquista   The effort from A.D. 711 to 1492 to liberate the Iberian Peninsula from the Moors.

relación   An official report.

Requerimiento   (1) The legal proclamation requiring Indians to accept the dominion of the pope and the Spanish crown; (2) a legal mandate served by one official on another.

residencia   An investigation at the end of an official's term of service into his conduct in office.

Río de las Palmas   A river in northeastern Mexico known today as the Río Soto la Marina.

Río Petatlán   A river in northwestern Mexico known today as the Río Sinaloa.

Royal Council of the Indies   The supreme judicial council governing colonial Spanish America, founded in 1524.

tesorero   A treasurer.

veedor   An inspector of mines.

Notes

PREFACE

1. The attribution to Verrazano is from Mann 44.

2. The quotation is from page f57v of the Adorno & Pautz translation of Cabeza de Vaca's *Relación* (known hereinafter as R), which appears in volume I of their *Álvar Núñez Cabeza de Vaca: His Account, His Life, and the Expedition of Pánfilo de Narváez*.

3. I have used the 1999 Adorno & Pautz translation of Cabeza de Vaca's *Relación*, which is printed face-to-face with the Spanish original. I have retained Adorno & Pautz's page numbering system in my notes. This system preserves the foliation of the original 1542 Zamora edition of the *Relación*. Thus, Adorno & Pautz head each transcribed Spanish page with a notation, such as Z:f3r, identifying the Zamora edition, folio number, and side of the leaf (recto or verso). The facing English translation is simply headed f3r. I have also used the 1974 Hedrick & Riley translation of Oviedo's account of Cabeza de Vaca's experiences in North America and the 1891 Domínguez translation of Hernández's *Comentarios*.

4. In his preface to *Knights of Spain* (xvi, 484n2), Hudson acknowledges that he borrowed the concept of the braided narrative from David Hackett Fischer, "The Braided Narrative: Substance and Form in Social History," in *The Literature of Fact*, ed. Angus J. S. Fletcher (New York: Columbia University Press, 1976), 109–33.

5. Among the most useful are Chipman; Krieger; Campbell & Campbell; Hoffman "Narváez"; Reséndez; and Adorno & Pautz.

CHAPTER 1. JEREZ DE LA FRONTERA

1. Throughout this chapter, I have relied heavily on J. H. Elliott, *Imperial Spain, 1469–1716* (1963, 2002). Information here is from Elliott *Imperial* 24, 31, 63, 125; Milanich & Milbrath "Another World" 6; Morison *European* 43.

2. Quotation from Adorno & Pautz I: 295. Information from Adorno & Pautz I: 340.

3. Quotations from R (f67r). Information from Adorno & Pautz I: 298–99, 330, 343–50.

4. Adorno & Pautz I: 298–99; Bishop 8; Hedrick & Riley vi.

5. The story of Alhaja comes from Adorno & Pautz I: 302–303; Bishop 4. Although it may be only a story, Adorno & Pautz have noted that a long line of Cabeza de Vaca's ancestors took part in the Reconquista (I: 298–99, 330). See the genealogical charts in Adorno & Pautz I: 306, 314–15, 324.

6. Adorno & Pautz I: 341; Bishop 3.

7. The generalization about the rights of victors to enslave the vanquished is from Elliott *Imperial* 69. Other information from Adorno & Pautz I: 325–26, 330–31, 340–41, III: 75; Bishop 3.

8. Elliott *Imperial* 58–59.

9. Adorno & Pautz I: 327, 329–31.

10. Elliott *Imperial* 58; Benjamin 24; Hudson 9, 31.

11. Quotation from Adorno & Pautz I: 332. Information from Adorno & Pautz I: 326–29; Bishop 5–7; Elliott *Imperial* 69.

12. Quotations from Adorno & Pautz I: 329, 341. Information from Adorno & Pautz I: 296, 332.

13. Elliott *Imperial* 31–34, 63, 113–17.

14. Quotations from "Bartolomé de las Casas" (35). Information from Morison *Admiral* I: 341, 345; Hanke 20.

15. Quotation from Benjamin 94. Information from Cohen 127n; Pagden "Introduction" xvi–xvii; Elliott *Imperial* 69.

16. Quotations from Machiavelli 67–68. Information from Elliott *Imperial* 77, 107.

17. The figure of two thousand casualties is from Bakewell & Holler 86. Other information from Elliott *Imperial* 106–107, 218–19.

18. Cohen 129n; Crosby 67, 75; Elliott *Imperial* 70; Bakewell & Holler 118.

19. Quotation from Pagden "Introduction" xx. Information on the *encomienda* system from Yeager 842–43; Elliott *Imperial* 70; Hanke 19; Bakewell & Holler 114. Information on the demise of the Taínos from Debo 20; Benjamin 129.

20. Quotation from Hanke 20. Hanke's *The Spanish Struggle for Justice*, incidentally, is the classic work on the effort of sixteenth-century Spaniards to justify Spain's empire to themselves and to the world. Other information from Hanke 19, 25; Elliott *Imperial* 70; Adorno & Pautz III: 335; Pagden "Introduction" xvi–xvii.

21. Elliott *Imperial* 130, 135–39.

22. Adorno & Pautz I: 330–31, 339–40, 342, 346.

23. Adorno & Pautz I: 336, 345–46, 351, 365.

24. Hudson 7; Crosby 79; Elliott *Imperial* 64; Paniagua 3, 6; Adorno & Pautz II: 391; Morison *Admiral* I: 342.

25. Griffith 36; Casas 50n67.

26. Plague casualties from Benjamin 129. Other information from Hudson 11; Hanke 90.

27. Morison *Admiral* I: 193; Bishop 3; Adorno & Pautz I: 341–42, 351; Elliott *Imperial* 33.

28. Quotation from Adorno & Pautz I: 360. Information from Adorno & Pautz I: 350–51, 356; Bishop 9.

29. Quotation from Adorno & Pautz I: 366. The casualty figure for the battle of Ravenna is from Bishop 9. Other information from Adorno & Pautz I: 360–66; Elliott *Imperial* 133; Diamond 358; Weddle 186.

30. Adorno & Pautz I: 353–58.

31. Adorno & Pautz I: 331, 357; Elliott *Imperial* 57, 63, 79, 122, 182–83, 186–87; Pagden "Introduction" xlii; Clayton, Knight & Moore I: 176n8; Calvert 706, 710, 714, 718, 722, 726.

32. Espinosa 42, 46, 48, 61–62; Elliott *Imperial* 134, 139–42, 144–45; Benjamin 161.

33. Elliott *Imperial* 146; Elliott "Cortés" xxiv; Espinosa 60–61; Benjamin 161.

34. A *peso de oro* was a gold coin weighing 1.6 ounces and equivalent to 450–90 *maravedíes* (Adorno & Pautz I: 271n1). Other information from Cortés 40–46; Elliott "Cortés" xx, xxv–xxvi; Weddle 115.

35. Bainton 38, 59–61; Elliott *Imperial* 163; Espinosa 7, 24.

36. Elliott *Imperial* 151–55; Espinosa 66–67, 71–72; Adorno & Pautz I: 361.

37. Elliott *Imperial* 156–59; Elliott "Cortés" xxix; Espinosa 88–91.

38. Quotation from Pupo-Walker 132. Information from Adorno & Pautz I: 359, 361–62, 367–68; Bishop 9–10.

39. Adorno & Pautz I: 359; Elliott *Imperial* 106, 116; Bishop 10.

40. Elliott *Imperial* 159, 164–65; Espinosa 32, 84, 73, 139, 142, 177, 205, 276.

41. Rosenthal 204.

42. Quotation from Cortés 48. Information from Cortés 158; Diamond 373; Hudson 32; Adorno & Pautz III: 211–13, 228, 239, 245, 257; Weddle 55; Benjamin 130; Elliott "Cortés" xi–xiii.

43. Adorno & Pautz III: 298; Pagden "Translator's Introduction" lviii.

44. Adorno & Pautz I: 323, 360, 372, 376, II: 6; Bishop 25; Covey 9; Pupo-Walker 130.

45. Adorno & Pautz I: 373, 375; Bishop 26. Thirty-four *maravedíes* were equal to a silver *real*, and 375 *maravedíes* were equal to a gold ducat (Elliott *Imperial* 125).

46. Quotations from Adorno & Pautz III: 3–4. Information from Adorno & Pautz I: 374.

Chapter 2. Pánfilo de Narváez

1. Quotation from O (37). Information from Adorno & Pautz I: 372, II: 16; Goodwyn 152.

2. Casas quotation from Adorno & Pautz III: 205. Díaz quotation from Adorno & Pautz III: 206. Oviedo quotations from O (2–3). Information from Bishop 17.

3. Weddle (25) says Narváez accompanied Columbus on his second voyage, but Adorno & Pautz (III: 208) question this. Other information from Weddle 27; Rosenblat 64; Adorno & Pautz III: 209, 213, 280; Johnson I: 62; Cortés 449n1.

4. Quotations from Casas 9–10. Information on the Taíno population from Olsen 3; Benjamin 23; Wilson ix; Bakewell & Holler 110–11. Other information from Weddle 14; Benjamin 18; Deagan 49; Pagden "Introduction" xix.

5. Quotations from Casas 29. Casualty figures from Casas 29; Weddle 37. Other information from Casas 28–29; Pagden "Introduction" xix, xxi; Weddle 26, 29–30.

6. Cortés 117; Weddle 80.

7. O (1); Cortés 52; Adorno & Pautz III: 213, 218, 223–24, 253–54; Casas 42n54; Elliott "Cortés" xii–xiii, xv, xxiii–xxiv.

8. Cortés 113, 118–19; Díaz 257, 261–64, 281.

9. Quotation from Díaz 288. Information from Cortés 126; Díaz 287–94; Elliott "Cortés" xxvi; Adorno & Pautz III: 255.

10. Quotations from Díaz 190–91. Population figure for Tenochtitlán from Clendinnen 18. Other information from Cortés 83, 110–11; Clendinnen 20; Elliott *Imperial* 186.

11. First quotation from Díaz 293. Second pair of quotations from Léon-Portilla 93. Information from Crosby 46–47, 49; Elliott "Cortés" xxiii.

12. Adorno & Pautz III: 208, 257.

13. O (3); Adorno & Pautz II: 62.

14. Quotation from Adorno & Pautz II: 6. Information from O (3).

15. Quotations from Adorno & Pautz II: 31–32.

16. To distinguish it from present-day Florida, I shall refer to the vast territory Narváez was authorized to explore, conquer, and settle as La Florida. Information from Adorno & Pautz II: 32; Weddle 14.

17. Weddle 40–42, 45–48; Adorno & Pautz III: 216; Hudson 32.

18. On the attribution of the map to Pineda, see Adorno and Pautz III: 238, 241–42. Other information from Adorno & Pautz II: 31–32, III: 267–69; Weddle 99–101, 148.

19. Milanich & Milbrath "Another World" 15; Weddle 100; Adorno & Pautz II: 66, III: 267.

20. Cortés 94; Adorno & Pautz II: 31, III: 267–68.

21. Adorno & Pautz II: 31; Weddle 105, 132; Chipman *Spanish Texas* 27; Hudson 403.

22. Adorno & Pautz argue that Narváez's goal was "to settle on the Río de las Palmas" (II: 72). They deduce this (II: 62) from Cabeza de Vaca's statement that Narváez hired his chief pilot because he "had been in the Río de las Palmas" (R:f5r). Other information from Adorno & Pautz II: 31–32, 74, III: 278; Weddle 156; Chipman *Spanish Texas* 27.

23. Quotation from Adorno & Pautz II: 14. Information from Casas 33; Adorno & Pautz II: 12–14; Hanke 33–36, 111–12; Pagden "Introduction" xxv.

24. R (f3r); Adorno & Pautz II: 15, 23–25.

25. Adorno & Pautz I: 374–75, II: 22, 58.

26. R (f3r, f15v); Adorno & Pautz II: 51, 56–59, 409, 425; Hudson 7, 50, 67; Bishop 26–27.

27. R (f12v, f65v); Adorno & Pautz II: 18, 25, 57, 131; Bishop 28.

28. Lyon "Niña" 59, 62; Morison *Admiral* I: 106, 109–11; Adorno & Pautz II: 16, 26, 67; Bishop 29; Guillermo 23.

29. Morison *Admiral* I: 160, 162, 176–83, 186; Benjamin 70.

30. R (f10r, f15r); Lyon "Niña" 64; Morison *Admiral* I: 123; Deagan 51; Adorno & Pautz II: 56, 113; Weddle 163.

31. Adorno & Pautz I: 375, II: 26, 425.

32. R (f65v–f66r).

33. Adorno & Pautz I: 350, II: 41–42; Bishop 28.

34. R (f3r); Adorno & Pautz I: 378; Bishop 29; Morison *Admiral* I: 123–24; Weddle 164–65; Hudson 50.

CHAPTER 3. THE CARIBBEAN

1. In my notes, I refer to Cabeza de Vaca's *Relación* as R and to Oviedo's account as O. The information here is from R (f67r); O (7); Hedrick & Riley v; Clayton, Knight & Moore I: 249.

2. The length and itinerary of a typical voyage are from Adorno & Pautz II: 47.

3. To reconstruct the probable details of the voyage, I have relied particularly on Samuel Eliot Morison's *Admiral of the Ocean Sea*; see vol. I: 120, 123, 168–69. Other information from Lyon "Niña" 62.

4. Morison *Admiral* I: 137, 153, 160, 165, 172, 182–83.

5. R (f3r); Adorno & Pautz II: 394, III: 13–15; Weddle 165; Burkholder & Johnson 45–46.

6. Morison & Obregón 99–102.

7. R (f3r–f3v); Debo 20; Ewen & Williams 70; Adorno & Pautz II: 47; Weddle 165.

8. First quotation from Casas 21. Second quotation from León-Portilla xxvii. Information from R (f3r); Adorno & Pautz II: 20–21; Weddle 165; Crosby 76–77, 80; Hudson et al. "Tristán de Luna" 125.

9. African slaves were first introduced into the Caribbean region in 1501 (Adorno & Pautz II: 415). Information on the Taíno population from Benjamin 131. Other information from R (f3r); Adorno & Pautz II: 19, 47–48; Ewen & Williams 70.

10. Hoffman "Ayllón's Discovery" 36; Hudson 33–35; Adorno & Pautz III: 273–74.

11. Hoffman "Ayllón's Discovery" 41–43; Hudson & Chaves Tesser 4; Chaney & Deagan 166.

12. R (f3r); Adorno & Pautz II: 45, III: 211; Wilson 53.

13. Quotation from Elvas in Clayton, Knight & Moore I: 52–53. Information from Johnson I: 61, 81, 103, 123; Adorno & Pautz III: 211; Guillermo 35–36.

14. Quotations from Elvas in Clayton, Knight & Moore I: 52. Information from Hudson 50, 53.

15. Quotations from Elvas in Clayton, Knight & Moore I: 54. Information from Clayton, Knight & Moore I: 52–53, 182–83n28; Johnson I: 43; Adorno & Pautz II: 222; Morison *Admiral* II: 447–49, 456, 459, 463; Morison & Obregón 62, 66, 70; Crosby 4, 6, 9.

16. Johnson I: 8–9, 32; Morison *Admiral* I: 227, II: 449; Morison & Obregón 51, 59, 70, 72.

17. Adorno & Pautz II: 58–59, 61; Morison *Admiral* I: 139; Hanke 6.

18. Information about Porcallo's abuse of the Taínos is from Adorno & Pautz II: 50 and from Elvas in Clayton, Knight & Moore I: 53–54. Other information from R (f3v); Adorno & Pautz II: 49, 54; Clayton, Knight & Moore I: 184–85n40.

19. R (f3v); Adorno & Pautz III: 213; Johnson I: 111; Morison *Admiral* II: 454–55.

20. R (f3v); Guillermo 35; Johnson I: 124; Morison & Obregón 68.

21. R (f3v–f4r).

22. R (f4v–f5r); Adorno & Pautz II: 53–54; Johnson I: 124; Casas 10n; Covey 10.

23. R (f4v–f5r); Adorno & Pautz II: 53.

24. R (f5r); Morison *Admiral* II: 459.

25. My favorite definition of a league—the distance a person can walk in an hour—is from Espinosa 308. Information about the *legua legal* and the *legua común* is from Hudson xvi. However, Adorno & Pautz (I: 25n2) say that in the early sixteenth century a Spanish league measured 4.8 kilometers, or a little over 3 miles. Krieger (42) says that the Spanish judicial league was the equivalent of 2.634 miles. The calculations concerning Cabeza de Vaca's league are from Adorno & Pautz II: 82.

26. O (7); Adorno & Pautz II: 54.

27. For the Arawakan words that appear in the *Relación*, see R (Z:f3v, Z:f6r, Z:f6v, Z:f17v, Z:f25v, Z:f29v). Other information from Casas 10n; Guillermo 15n, 41n, 51; Crosby 170; Johnson I: 8; Wilson 19, 28, 57, 59, 120; Deagan 49, 52–53; Morison & Obregón 50–51.

28. O (7); Adorno & Pautz II: 55, III: 3–4. Information about the Julian calendar is from Adorno & Pautz I: 93n5; Hudson xvi.

29. R (f5r–f5v). Information about brigantines is from Morison *European* 549–50. Morison notes, however, that although English translations generally use the word "brigantine" for the sixteenth-century vessel known to Cabeza de Vaca as a *vergantín*, this vessel was different from the two-masted one known to English speakers in the seventeenth and eighteenth centuries as a brigantine (*European* 560n).

30. Quotation from R (f5r–f5v). On the basis of this quotation, Adorno & Pautz argue that the Río de las Palmas was Narváez's primary destination (II: 67–68, 74–75). Other information from Adorno & Pautz II: 31, 56; Weddle 132, 204; Hoffman "Narváez" 53. On the identity of Miruelo, see Adorno & Pautz II: 62–69.

31. R (f5v); O (7); Adorno & Pautz II: 55–56, 70, 113.

32. Adorno & Pautz II: 56, 114.

33. R (f5v); Adorno & Pautz II: 70; Morison & Obregón 72; Morison *Admiral* II: 463.

34. R (f5v); Adorno & Pautz I: xxvii, II: 45, 70, 72–73; Reséndez 80–82.

CHAPTER 4. FLORIDA

1. Quotation from R (f6v). The estimate that Narváez was more than nine hundred miles from Río de las Palmas is from Krieger 25. Information about Easter Sunday is from Bishop 33n6. Other information from R (f5v, f66v); O (7); Adorno & Pautz II: 71–75, 83.

2. Adorno & Pautz II: 38, 65–66, 74, 152, III: 245, 268–69; Weddle 132.

3. R (f7v); Adorno & Pautz II: 71, 139–40, III: 219, 235, 270–75; Hudson *Knights* 32; Milanich *Florida's Indians* 138.

4. Quotations from R (Z:f5v, Z:f7v). Information from Adorno & Pautz II: 74; Hoffman "Narváez" 71n21.

5. R (f5v–f6r); O (7–8).

6. Quotations from R (f66v). Information from R (f6r); O (8).

7. Hoffman "Narváez" 66–67; Adorno & Pautz II: 83; Mitchem "Initial" 52; Mitchem "Artifacts" 103–108; Clayton, Knight & Moore I: 6–7; Milanich *Florida* 72; Ewen "Anhaica" 110.

8. Hoffman ("Narváez" 67) says the most likely anchorage was in Boca Ciega Bay. Bishop (34) says the landing was in Pinellas County "just north of St. Petersburg." Weddle (205) and Reséndez (268n26) both locate the landing at Sarasota Bay. Adorno & Pautz (II: 78) say that a landfall on Pinellas Peninsula is "the most convincing response to a question to which a verifiable answer does not exist."

9. The estimate of Florida's Native American population in 1513 is from Milanich *Florida* 1. Other information from Milanich *Florida* 28; Milanich *Florida's Indians* 99; Scarry "Late Prehistoric" 17–18; Hudson 420, 424.

10. Simpson; Perry 185–89.

11. Perry 188; Milanich *Florida* 28, 71–77; Mitchem "Initial" 49; Hudson 69.

12. R (f6r); O (8).

13. Reséndez (267–68n23) argues that Narváez would not have taken possession of the land if he were not certain that it lay within the territory his *capitulaciones* entitled him to conquer and settle and that therefore he must have known he was on the Florida side of the Río de las Palmas. Other information from R (f6r); O (8); Adorno & Pautz I: 325, II: 13–14.

14. R (f6r); Hudson 65.

15. Adorno & Pautz (II: 84) propose that the Bay of the Cross was Old Tampa Bay. Reséndez (85), who argues that Narváez made landfall at Sarasota Bay, proposes that it was greater Tampa Bay. Quotation from R (f6r–f6v). Information from R (f15v); O (8).

16. Quotations from R (f6v). Information from O (8–9); Adorno & Pautz II: 64–67, 75–77, 80–81. Adorno & Pautz argue that the port Miruelo "had said he knew" was the Río de las Palmas (II: 67).

17. R (f6v–f7r, f65v); Adorno & Pautz I: 37n1.

18. Milanich *Florida* 28, 73–75.

19. R (f7r); O (9).

20. Quotation from Adorno & Pautz III: 291. Information from R (f7r); Clayton, Knight & Moore I: 74, 229, 230, 273; Richter 21, 23–24.

21. R (f7r, f66v); O (9–10).

22. Quotations from Elvas in Clayton, Knight & Moore I: 57.

23. R (f7r–f7v, f65v); Adorno & Pautz II: 72, 94.

24. R (f7r–f7v); O (10); Adorno & Pautz II: 76.

25. Quotations from R (f8r).

26. Quotation from R (f7v). Information from R (f8v); O (10).

27. R (f7v–f8r); O (11).

28. R (f8r); Adorno & Pautz II: 155.

29. Quotation from O (10). Information from Adorno & Pautz II: 234.

30. Quotation from R (f8v). Information from R (f8r, f66r).

31. Quotation from R (f65v). Information from R (f8v, f66r).

32. R (f8v–f9r, f66r).

33. R (f10r, f15r); Diamond 76; Hudson *Knights* 68–69.

34. Díaz 8, 57, 392; Hudson 67–69; Tarassuk & Blair 104–105; Clayton, Knight & Moore I: 234, 293; K. Howard 62.

35. R (f9r); Adorno & Pautz II: 107; Hoffman "Narváez" 59.

36. Quotations from R (f11v). Information from R (f9r). Both Hoffman ("Narváez" 67) and Adorno and Pautz (II: 81) argue that because Cabeza de Vaca does not mention Tampa Bay and the Manatee River as obstacles, Narváez and his men must have started from Pinellas Peninsula.

37. O (12); R (f9r); Hudson 92; Call & Stephenson 14, 18.

38. Adorno & Pautz (II: 112) credit Buckingham Smith (1871) with identifying the Withlacoochee. Other information from R (f9r); Adorno & Pautz II: 141.

39. Milanich *Florida* 135; Mitchem "Initial" 56.

40. R (f9r–f9v); Adorno & Pautz II: 112.

41. R (f9v); Hudson 97–98.

42. R (f9v); Adorno & Pautz II: 112.

43. R (f9v–f11r); O (12).

44. R (f10r).

45. Adorno & Pautz II: 137–38; Milanich *Florida* 80, 122.

46. Quotation from Bishop 40. Information from Lyon "Menéndez's Plan" 152; Milbrath 198–99.

47. R (f10r).

48. R (f10r, f22r). Adorno & Pautz (II: 115) credit Buckingham Smith (1871) with identifying the Suwannee.

49. R (f10r–f10v); Milanich *Florida* 120–21.

50. Quotations from R (f10v). Information from R (f11r).

CHAPTER 5. APALACHEE

1. R (f10v–f11r); O (12); Adorno & Pautz II: 119, 132, 138.

2. Quotation from R (f11r). Information from R (f10v); O (12).

3. R (f7r, f10r); Milanich *Florida* 27, 94; Scarry "Apalachee" 157–58; Hann *Apalachee* 5; Hann "Apalachee of the Historic Era" 328.

4. R (f12r–f12v); O (13–14).

5. R (f11v–f12r); O (13); Milanich *Florida* 122–23.

6. Biedma quotation from Clayton, Knight & Moore I: 227. Elvas quotation from Clayton, Knight & Moore I: 71–72. Garcilaso quotation from Clayton, Knight & Moore II: 197. Cabeza de Vaca quotation from R (f11r). Information from Ewen "Anhaica" 110; Hoffman "Narváez" 60; Hudson 120.

7. Diamond 267, 284–85; Hudson 107; Milanich *Florida* 93; Scarry "Apalachee" 156; Widmer 125–26.

8. Quotation from Clayton, Knight & Moore II: 185–86. Information from Scarry "Apalachee" 160, 162; Hann *Apalachee* 7; Hann "Apalachee of the Historic Era" 331; Hudson 125–26; Smith "Aboriginal" 270; Clayton, Knight & Moore II: 185n9.

9. R (f11r). Information from Scarry "Apalachee" 159; Hudson 123; Milanich *Florida* 93, 95.

10. Quotations from R (f11r–f11v). Information from Adorno & Pautz II: 137; Hudson 92; Crosby 7–8; Bishop 45.

11. R (f12r–f12v); O (13).

12. Quotations from R (f13r). The date of Narváez's withdrawal from the Apalachee village is from Adorno & Pautz I: 61n3. Other information from R (f12v); O (18). A *xeme*, or the distance between a man's thumb and his outstretched forefinger, is equivalent to about eight inches (Adorno & Pautz I: 63n1; Bishop 54). A *palmo*, according to Adorno and Pautz I: 63n4, is equivalent to the English span, or to the distance between the tips of the thumb and little finger of a man's spread hand. However, according to Hedrick and Riley (81n14), a *palmo* can denote either the width (three to four inches) or the length (eight inches) of a hand. Cabeza de Vaca says the bows of the Indians were "onze o doze palmos de largo" (R Z:f13r).

13. Quotation from Hann *Apalachee* 71. Information from Hudson 140.

14. R (f13r–f13v).

15. R (f13v, f14v); Milanich *Florida* 123; Hudson 499n17; Hoffman "Narváez" 61.

16. R (f13v); O (16); Adorno & Pautz II: 142.

17. Milanich *Florida* 94; Adorno & Pautz II: 138; Clayton, Knight & Moore I: 7.

18. R (f12v, f13v–f14r); O (16–17); Adorno & Pautz I: 65n4, II: 134.

19. R (f14r); O (17, 101); Adorno & Pautz II: 132, 135.

20. R (f13v–f14r, f16r); O (17); Adorno & Pautz I: 65n4, II: 110, 126–27, 132; Hudson 128.

21. Adorno & Pautz (II: 132) say Narváez spent fifty-nine days traveling to the Bay of Horses. Both Cabeza de Vaca (R:f15v) and Oviedo (18) estimate the distance was 280 leagues. Adorno & Pautz (II: 109) say the actual distance was much less.

22. R (f14v); Crosby 31, 39.

23. R (f14v); Adorno & Pautz II: 155.

24. R (f14v–f15r); O (17); Adorno & Pautz II: 178.

25. R (f15r–f15v, f23v); O (17–18); Adorno & Pautz II: 135; Bishop 51.

26. R (f15v, f20r); O (18, 21); Adorno & Pautz II: 144; Hedrick & Riley 81n15.

27. The figure of 640 bushels is from Adorno & Pautz I: 71n1. Other information from R (f15r–f16r, f22r); O (17–18); Bishop 180.

28. Quotation from R (f16r). Information from O (18); Adorno & Pautz II: 143. The calculation that 242 men left the Bay of Horses is from Adorno & Pautz I: 75n2.

29. R (f66v); Adorno & Pautz II: 64–65, 76–77, 79, 81, 98–104.

30. Adorno & Pautz II: 104–106.

31. Quotation from Elvas in Clayton, Knight & Moore I: 59. Information from Clayton, Knight & Moore I: 59–61, 225, 255; Adorno & Pautz II: 105.

32. Clayton, Knight & Moore II: 101–107.

33. Clayton, Knight & Moore I: 60–61, II: ix, 1, 14; Adorno & Pautz II: 105; Hudson 74–75.

34. Adorno & Pautz II: 121–23, 126–27; Clayton, Knight & Moore I: 71–72, 227, 267, II: 203; Milanich & Milbrath "Another World" 18.

35. R (f10r); Mitchem "Artifacts" 101–103; Adorno & Pautz II: 126, 145; Ewen "Anhaica" 110–17; Ewen "Soldier" 89.

36. Ewen "Soldier" 90; Marrinan, Scarry & Majors 80; Smith "Aboriginal" 257; Smith "Indian" 141; Hudson 419, 435; Hudson & Chaves Tesser 10; Richter 35; Diamond 211; Milanich *Florida's Indians* ix; Milanich *Florida* xv, 230–31, 233–34; Milanich & Milbrath "Another World" 26; Scarry "Late Prehistoric" 31–32; Scarry "Apalachee" 157–58; Hann "Apalachee of the Historic Era" 340, 346, 349.

CHAPTER 6. CASTAWAYS

1. Quotation from R (f16r). Information from R (f15r–f16v, f19v); O (18–19); Adorno & Pautz II: 134, 143–44.

2. R (f16r–f16v); Adorno & Pautz I: 75n4; Milanich *Florida* 124.

3. R (f16v); O (19); Adorno & Pautz II: 145.

4. Quotation from R (f16v). Information from R (f17r); O (19); Adorno & Pautz II: 86–87.

5. Quotation from R (f17r).

6. R (f16r); O (18); Mann 192, 198; Hudson 124.

7. Quotation from R (f17r).

8. Quotations from R (f17v). Information from R (f17r); O (20).

9. R (f17v–f18r); O (20).

10. R (f15v, f18r).

11. R (f18r–f18v); O (20).

12. R (f18v–f19r); O (21).

13. Biedma quotation from Clayton, Knight & Moore I: 232–33. Rangel quotation from Clayton, Knight & Moore I: 292.

14. R (f19r); O (21). Adorno & Pautz (I: 87n2) identify the large river as the Mississippi.

15. R (f19r–f19v); O (21). A *braza*, or 5.5 feet, was approximately the distance measured by a man's outstretched arms (Adorno & Pautz I: 87n3).

16. R (f19v); O (21–22); Adorno & Pautz II: 155.

17. Quotation from R (f20r). Information from R (f19v); O (22); Adorno & Pautz II: 156.

18. R (f20r); O (22).

19. Quotation from R (f20r). Information from R (f20v); O (22). Adorno & Pautz (I: 93n2, n6) place the landing site in the vicinity of Galveston Bay, Texas.

20. R (f20v, f24r); O (23).

21. R (f20v–f21r); Adorno & Pautz II: 188.

22. Quotation from R (f21r). Information from R (f24r–f24v, f26v); O (23); Adorno & Pautz II: 237.

23. R (f21v, f26v); O (26); Ricklis 22, 107, 114.

24. Quotation from R (f22r). Information from R (f21v); O (23); Hudson xvii.

25. Quotation from R (f22r). Information from O (27).

26. Quotation from R (f22v). Information from R (f22r); O (23–24).

27. R (f22v, f63r).

28. R (f22v).

29. R (f23r, f25v); O (27); Newcomb 363; Ricklis 4.

30. R (f20v, f23r); O (24); Chipman "In Search" 128.

31. R (f20v, f26v). In a 1987 survey of studies of Cabeza de Vaca's route across Texas, Donald E. Chipman ("In Search" 133–35, 141) notes that Brownie Ponton and Bates McFarland (1898), James N. Baskett (1907), and Cleve Hallenbeck (1940) all identified Malhado as Galveston Island, while Harbert Davenport and Joseph K. Wells (1918–19) were the first route interpreters to identify it as a combination of San Luis Island and San Luis Peninsula. Chipman ("In Search" 135) concurs with Davenport & Wells, as do Robert S. Weddle (206) and Adorno & Pautz (II: 190).

32. R (f23r–f23v, f26r–f26v); O (25); Adorno & Pautz II: 194.

33. R (f15v, f23v–f24r, f28r); O (24–25). Hickerson has computed that Malhado was some six hundred miles from Santisteban del Puerto (200).

34. R (f26r–f27r).

35. Quotation from R (f30r). Information from R (f21v, f23v–f25v, f26v); O (27); Adorno & Pautz II: 195. The term *saludadores* occurs in O (49), original Spanish in Hedrick & Riley (133); see also Hedrick & Riley 82n26. The term *físicos* occurs in R (Z:f24v, Z:f25v, Z:f35v, and elsewhere). The term *médico* occurs in R (Z:f37v and elsewhere).

36. Quotation from R (f24r). Information from R (f16r, f23v–f24r); O (18, 25); Adorno & Pautz II: 195.

37. Quotation from R (f24r). Information from R (f24v); O (25–26).

38. R (f25v–f26r).

39. R (f24v, f27r–f27v); O (26–27); Adorno & Pautz II: 284. Both Newcomb (365) and Ricklis (4) discuss men's and women's work among the sixteenth-century natives of the Texas coast.

40. R (f25r–f26v).

41. R (f38r).

42. O (49); Adorno & Pautz II: 284.

43. R (f21r, f24v); O (27).

44. R (f26v, f55v); Adorno & Pautz II: 165; Diamond 267–69, 285. The estimate of the size of the Malhado band comes from Reséndez (140n20), who extrapolates from the one hundred warriors Cabeza de Vaca saw on the beach the day he came ashore on the island (R f21r). Reséndez calculates that the ratio of adult males to the total population was likely one to four.

45. Quotation from R (f24v). Information from R (f25r, f26v).

46. R (f24v–f25r).

47. R (f22r–f22v, f26v); Adorno & Pautz II: 189.

48. R (f24v–f25v, f26v); O (26–27).

49. R (f24r, f26r–f27r); O (26, 28); Adorno & Pautz II: 196.

50. R (f17v, f27r, f29r); O (28, 39).

CHAPTER 7. TEXAS

1. R (f7r, f8r, f20v–f21r, f27r, f28r).

2. R (f22r, f23v–f24v, f25v, f27r); O (26); Ricklis 2, 4, 14–15, 22–23; Chipman *Spanish Texas* 13; Newcomb 362, 364.

3. R (f27r).

4. Quotations from R (f27v). Information from R (f28v); O (27); Adorno & Pautz II: 242; Adorno "Negotiation" 170–71; Hickerson 209, 212; Newcomb 360.

5. Ricklis 11–12, 18; Campbell 344; Chipman *Spanish Texas* 9.

6. Hickerson 202; Adorno & Pautz II: 164, 237, 239; Newcomb 359–61, 366. For studies linking the Texas natives whom Cabeza de Vaca encountered with the historical Karankawas, see Newcomb (esp. 360). Ricklis lists the five Karankawa bands known to have occupied the central Texas coast in the eighteenth century and describes their territorial ranges (4–8).

7. Newcomb 362; Ricklis 3, 9, 26, 29; Hickerson 201; Campbell 347.

8. R (f27r, f28r); Adorno & Pautz I: 123n1; Ricklis 11–12; Todorov 198–99.

9. R (f28r–f28v). Chipman ("In Search" 133) credits Ponton & McFarland (1898) with identifying the four rivers. Davenport & Wells (1918–19) accepted their identification but pointed out that, in the sixteenth century, the present Caney Creek was the main channel of Texas's Colorado River (Adorno & Pautz II: 201). Chipman ("In Search" 135) credits James N. Baskett (1907) with identifying Pass Cavallo. Davenport & Wells (1918–19) maintained that Cabeza de Vaca and Lope de Oviedo crossed from Matagorda Peninsula back to the mainland, but Adorno & Pautz argue that the two castaways are more likely to have crossed from Matagorda Peninsula to Matagorda Island (II: 215).

10. O (28); R (f42r–f43r).

11. Adorno & Pautz place the Deaguanes north of the Guadalupe River and place the Quevenes in the vicinity of Matagorda Bay (II: 218, 242).

12. R (f28r–f28v).

13. R (f28v–f29r); O (43). Chipman ("In Search" 135–36, 141) says that first Baskett (1907) and then Davenport & Wells (1918–19) identified the river of nuts as the Guadalupe, but that Hallenbeck (1940) identified it as the Colorado River of Texas. Both Campbell & Campbell (3) and Adorno & Pautz (II: 218) maintain that it was the Guadalupe. Chipman ("In Search" 134) says that Bethel Coopwood (1899–1900) was the first to deduce that the nuts were pecans.

14. Quotation from R (f29r).

15. R (f9v, f13v–f14r, f18r, f23r, f28r, f29r–f29v); O (45).

16. R f58v, f67r); Adorno & Pautz II: 408–409, 411.

17. The suggestion that Castillo was of Jewish heritage is from Schneider 29. Information from R (f66v–f67r); Adorno & Pautz II: 423; Benjamin 183.

18. R (f28r, f67r); O (62); Adorno & Pautz I: 279n1; II: 18, 414, 416, 418–19.

19. In saying that Cabeza de Vaca, Dorantes, Castillo, and Estevanico were the first men of the Old World to live for a period of years in the land that would become the United States, I am ignoring the claims of such other Narváez survivors as Juan Ortiz, Lope de Oviedo, and possibly Figueroa and the Asturian cleric.

20. Adorno & Pautz II: 205, 207.

21. For the complete list of the twenty-three Texas bands Cabeza de Vaca names, see R (f44r). For information on the territorial ranges of these bands, see Campbell & Campbell 4; Adorno & Pautz II: 238–39.

22. R (f29v–f30r); O (29); Adorno & Pautz II: 201.

23. R (f30r); O (29–30).

24. R (f30r). Chipman ("In Search" 135) credits James N. Baskett (1907) with identifying both tidal channels. Adorno & Pautz accept Baskett's identifications (II: 202–203).

25. R (f23v, f30r); O (25, 30, 32). Adorno & Pautz suggest that Figueroa was living with the Quevenes (II: 203) and that he met the two captains in April 1529 (II: 191).

26. R (f28v, f29v–f31r); O (30–31); Adorno & Pautz II: 185, 191–93.

27. R (f31r); Adorno & Pautz II: 187, 192.

28. R (f30r–f30v); O (31); Adorno & Pautz II: 185–88.

29. R (f30v); Adorno & Pautz I: 37n1.

30. R (f30v); O (31).

31. R (f30v); Adorno & Pautz II: 186.

32. Quotation from R (f31r). Information from R (f30v); O (31); Adorno & Pautz II: 194.

33. R (f28v, f30r, f31r); O (31, 42); Adorno & Pautz II: 184–88, 192–94, 202–203.

34. O (32); Adorno & Pautz II: 204.

35. O (32–33, 39); Adorno & Pautz II: 204–205.

36. O (39); Adorno & Pautz II: 206–209. Chipman ("In Search" 135) credits James N. Baskett (1907) with identifying all three tidal channels: Pass Cavallo, Cedar Bayou, and Aransas Pass.

37. R (f28r–f28v, f31r–f31v); O (39–40); Adorno & Pautz II: 209.

38. O (41); Adorno & Pautz II: 209–10.

39. O (39–42); Adorno & Pautz II: 210.

40. Quotation from R (f28r). Information from O (41–42); R (f29v, f32r); Adorno & Pautz II: 211.

41. O (30–31, 42); R (f28v, f31v); Adorno & Pautz II: 179, 192; Campbell & Campbell 13, 22.

42. O (42–43).

43. R (f29v, f34r); O (43–45); Adorno & Pautz II: 212–13, 219, 223–24; Campbell & Campbell 7, 13–14. Chipman ("In Search" 136) credits Davenport & Wells (1918) with locating the cactus thickets on the Nueces.

44. R (f29r–f29v); O (46); Adorno & Pautz I: 123n1, n8.

45. R (f28r–f28v, f29v, f34r); O (31, 40, 44–45).

46. R (f29v, f33r). The material on the blindness of the Mariames family appears in the 1555 edition of the *Relación* but not in the 1542 edition (Adorno & Pautz I: 129.e; Serrano y Sanz I: 65).

47. R (f32r–f32v); Campbell & Campbell 13. The estimate of the size of the Mariames population is from Campbell & Campbell (15) and is based on Dorantes's count of sixty males in a Mariames hunting party (O 44).

48. R (f32v).

49. Quotation from R (f31v–f32r). Information from R (f42r); Diamond 89.

50. Quotations from R ([Spanish] Z:f32v, [English] f32v). Information from R (f45r).

51. Information on the sixteenth-century range of the buffalo from Chipman "In Search" 134. Other information from O (43); R (f31v–f32r, f33r, f34r, f44r).

52. R (f32r–f32v, f33v); O (43–44).

53. First quotation from R (f32r–f32v). Second quotation from O (43). Information from R (f33r, f42r).

54. Quotation from R (f29v). Information from R (f33r, f34r–f35r); O (44–45); Adorno & Pautz II: 166, 173. In his *Relación*, Cabeza de Vaca refers to prickly-pear fruit as *tuna*, a word he had learned from the Taíno Indians of Hispaniola and Cuba (Adorno & Pautz I: 129n2).

55. R (f33r–f33v).

56. R (f29v, f33r); O (44). Adorno & Pautz place the cactus thickets at the northern limit of the territorial range of the Avavares (I: 153n1, II: 223). Campbell & Campbell infer that the castaways chose to escape to the Avavares because doing so would bring them closer to the Spanish settlement on the Río Pánuco (5–6).

57. R (f34r, f42r).

58. Quotation from R (f34v). Information from R (f34r).

CHAPTER 8. THE CHILDREN OF THE SUN

1. R (f34v); Adorno & Pautz I: 149n2, II: 225.

2. R (f34v–f35r); O (45–46); Adorno & Pautz I: 151n3, n9.

3. R (f20r, f35r); Adorno & Pautz II: 173, 183–84.

4. R (f34v–f35v); O (46); Adorno & Pautz II: 247.

5. R (f29v, f35v–f36r); Adorno & Pautz II: 248.

6. Quotation from R (f35v). Information from R (f25v–f26r, f38r); Adorno & Pautz I: 163n2.

7. O (49); Adorno & Pautz II: 284.

8. Quotation from R (f35v–f36r).

9. R (f36r, f67r); Adorno & Pautz II: 249.

10. R (f29v, f33v, f35v, f44r); O (45, 47); Adorno & Pautz II: 174, 239–40, 248, 264; Campbell & Campbell 24, 26; Chipman *Spanish Texas* 30.

11. O (47); R (f36r); Adorno & Pautz II: 249.

12. R (f36v–f37r); Adorno & Pautz I: 157n2; Campbell & Campbell 26.

13. R (f37r). The second prickly-pear area seems to have been just north of the Rio Grande in Texas's present Cameron, Hidalgo, and Starr Counties (Adorno & Pautz II: 224; Campbell & Campbell 7).

14. Quotation from R (f35r). Information from Adorno & Pautz II: 182; Campbell 344.

15. Quotation from R (f39v).

16. Quotation from R (f37v). Information from R (f37r–f37v).

17. R (f37v–f38r).

18. Quotation from R (f38v). On the term *hijos del sol*, see R ([Spanish] Z:f38v, Z:f48r–Z:f48v, [English] f38v, f48r–f48v); Adorno & Pautz I: 165n4.

19. First quotation from R (f40v). Second quotation from O (47). Information from R (f39v–f40v).

20. R (f40v–f41r); O (48).

21. R (f30r, f39v); O (39); Adorno & Pautz II: 206.

22. R (f38v–f39r); Adorno & Pautz II: 280.

23. R (f39r–f39v); Adorno & Pautz I: 167n2, II: 274.

24. O (47); R (f38v, f39v–f40r); Adorno & Pautz I: 165n3, II: xvi.

25. R (f40r); O (48); Adorno & Pautz I: 171n3.

26. R (f26r, f35v, f44r); Adorno & Pautz II: 206, 239.

27. R (f41v–f42r, f44v); Diamond 89.

28. R (f42r–f43v).

29. Quotation from R (f44v). The identification of the yaupon bush is from Newcomb 366. Other information from Adorno & Pautz I: 189n1.

30. Quotation from R (f43v–f44r).

31. R (f27r, f38v, f41r, f55v); O (49); Adorno & Pautz I: 119n8, 123n3, 129n1, 151n9, 175n4, II: 178.

32. R (f29v, f41r–f41v); O (49); Adorno & Pautz II: 170, 174, 178; Chipman "In Search" 129.

33. Quotation from O (49). Information from R (f41v); Adorno & Pautz I: 177n2; Hedrick & Riley 133.

34. R (f41v); O (49–50).

35. R (f45r–f45v); O (50); Adorno & Pautz II: 259.

36. R (f42r, f45v–f46r); O (50); Adorno & Pautz II: 261.

37. Quotations from Chipman "In Search" 129. According to Chipman ("In Search" 132) and Adorno & Pautz (II: 171), the trans-Texas theory was first put forward by Buckingham Smith in 1851. Chipman lists Hubert Howe Bancroft (1884), Adolph Bandelier (1890), Brownie Ponton and Bates McFarland (1898), Oscar W. Williams (1899), Robert T. Hill (1933–34), Carlos E. Castañeda (1936), Cleve Hallenbeck (1940), Cyclone Covey (1961), and James A. Michener (1985) as advocates of the trans-Texas theory ("In Search" 129–42). Chipman lists Bethel Coopwood (1899–1900), Harbert Davenport and Joseph K. Wells (1918–19), Morris Bishop (1933), Alex D. Krieger (1955, 2002), and T. N. Campbell and T. J. Campbell (1981) as advocates of the international-route theory ("In Search" 134–48). Adorno and Pautz supplement Chipman's list by including Roberto Ferrando Pérez (1984), Trinidad Barrera (1985), Enrique Pupo-Walker (1992), Frances M. López-Morillas (1993), and Martín A. Favata and José B. Fernández (1986, 1993) as trans-Texas advocates. Adorno and Pautz argue, however, that the Narváez survivors followed an international route and crossed the Río Grande in its lower course (II: 171, 261). In the current century, both Paul Schneider (2006, 275) and Andrés Reséndez (2007, 182) have maintained that the Narváez survivors crossed the lower Río Grande somewhere in the vicinity of the present Falcon Reservoir.

38. Quotation from R (f46r). Information from O (51).

39. O (51); R (f46r–f46v).

40. R (f46v–f47r); O (51). The observation that the men had become "catalysts to intertribal exchange" is from Adorno "Negotiation" 170.

41. R (f47r); O (51–52).

42. R (f47r); O (52); Adorno & Pautz II: 263. Reséndez suggests that Cabeza de Vaca may have refrained from claiming to have performed miracles because he did not wish to make trouble for himself with the Inquisition (7).

43. First quotation from R ([Spanish] Z:f47r, [English] f47r). Second quotation from O (52); original Spanish at Hedrick & Riley 136. Information from Adorno & Pautz II: xvi, 170–71, 264; Krieger 60.

44. The information on Cabeza de Vaca's route is from Adorno & Pautz II: 164, 170; Campbell 343–44; Krieger 58–59; Chipman "In Search" 129. According to Chipman ("In Search" 134), Bethel Coopwood (1899–1900, 1900–1901) was the first to place the mountains in Mexico, and he identified them as the Sierra de Pamoranes in Tamaulipas. According to Adorno & Pautz (II: 171), Harbert Davenport and Joseph K. Wells (1918–19) proposed that the mountains were either the Sierra de Pamoranes, the Sierra San Carlos, or the Sierra Cerralvo. Alex D. Krieger proposed in his 1955 doctoral dissertation (published in 2002) that the mountains were either the Sierra de Panorames [*sic*] or the Sierra de Cerralvos (59).

45. R (f47r–f47v); O (52).

46. First two quotations from R (f47v). Third quotation from O (53). Information from R (f47v–f48r); O (52–53). In Oviedo's account, the hosts tried to take the Narváez survivors "towards the sea" (O: 52). In Cabeza de Vaca's account, they tried to take the explorers to a friendly camp that, in the original Spanish, was *a la punta de las sierras* (Z:f47v). Adorno and Pautz translate this as "at the near end of the sierras" (f47v). Krieger translates it as "at the top of the mountains" (62).

47. Quotation from R (f47v). Other information from Adorno & Pautz I: 201n3, II: 173–74, 178. Krieger calculates that the Narváez men were some three hundred miles from the Río Pánuco when they changed course (62) and that their turn added some 2,500 miles to their journey (63).

CHAPTER 9. THE OVERLAND JOURNEY

1. R (f47v–f48r); O (53).

2. Quotation from R (f48r). Information from O (53); Adorno & Pautz I: 203n3, n4; Reséndez 185–86; Adorno "Negotiation" 178–79.

3. Quotation from R (f48r–f48v). Information from O (53–54); R (f46r); Adorno "Negotiation" 178–79.

4. Quotation from O (54). Information from R (f48v); Adorno & Pautz II: 176–77, 303; Campbell 343–44.

5. R (f48v–f49r); O (54); Adorno & Pautz I: 207n3, II: 306.

6. R (f49r); O (55); Adorno & Pautz I: 207n4, n8; Krieger 67–68.

7. R (f49v); Adorno & Pautz II: 288, 306, 308–309.

8. First quotation from R (f49v–f50r). Second quotation from R (f50v). Information from O (54–55); Adorno & Pautz I: 213n2, n3; Krieger 76–78.

9. R (f50r–f50v); O (55).

10. Adorno & Pautz I: 213n1, 217n2; Adorno "Negotiation" 181; Reséndez 7.

11. R (f50v–f51r); O (55–56); Adorno "Negotiation" 179–81.

12. R (f51r); O (55–56). Adorno and Pautz propose that the mountains were the Sierra Madre Oriental, the river was the Rio Grande, and the Narváez survivors crossed it in the vicinity of the present town of Boquillas del Carmen (I: 215n2, n3). Krieger proposes that the river was the Río Conchos and that the Narváez survivors crossed it above its confluence with the Rio Grande (79).

13. R (f51r); O (56); Diamond 78.

14. First quotation from R (f51r). Second quotation from R (f51v). Information from R (f52r); O (56–57); Adorno "Negotiation" 181–82.

15. R (f52r); O (57).

16. Quotations from R (f52v). Information from R (f53r); O (57–58, 60); Adorno & Pautz I: 221n5, II: 319.

17. Mann 181; Diamond 30.

18. Quotation from R ([Spanish] Z:f53r, [English] f53r). Information from R (f53v); O (58–59).

19. Quotation from R (f34r). Information from R (f53r); O (60–61); Adorno & Pautz II: 231, 236; Chipman *Spanish Texas* 37.

20. Quotation from Krieger 90. Information from R (f52v–f53r); O (57–58, 60); Adorno & Pautz I: 223n2, II: 318–19; Krieger 84–85, 89–90, 96; Chipman "In Search" 146.

21. Quotation from R (f53r). Information from R (f53v).

22. Quotation from R (f54r). Information from Adorno & Pautz II: 320.

23. Quotation from R (f53v). Information from R (f54r); O (58, 60–61).

24. Quotation from R (f54r–f54v). Information from R (f49r–f49v, f53v); O (54, 60); Adorno & Pautz II: 178, 325.

25. R (f54v); O (60); Adorno & Pautz I: 229n1, n4, II: 327; Krieger 99, 103, 107.

26. Quotation from R (f54v). Information from O (61); Adorno & Pautz I: 229n7, II: 328–29; Krieger 108.

27. R (f54v–f55r); Lekson 85–87; Schaafsma & Riley 8, 237, 242, 244; Riley 194, 198.

28. Adorno & Pautz II: 330–31, 336; Krieger 108; Riley 196, 198.

29. Quotations from R (f55r). Information from O (61, 63); Adorno & Pautz II: 307; Diamond 127, 180.

30. Quotation from R (f55v). Information from R (f55r); O (61–62, 64); Adorno & Pautz II: 336.

31. Quotation from R (f56r). Information from R (f55v); O (62); Adorno & Pautz II: 280.

32. R (f55v, f60r); Adorno & Pautz II: 368.

33. R (f28r, f55v); Adorno & Pautz II: 416–17.

34. O (62–64); R (f54v, f56r, f58r); Adorno & Pautz II: 335–36. Many route interpreters have placed Corazones on the Río Sonora near the modern town of Ures (Krieger 109). However, Krieger proposes that Corazones was closer to the Gulf of California and on an arroyo rather than a river (119). Adorno and Pautz place Corazones on the Río Yaqui, upstream from its confluence with the Río Chico (II: 341).

35. R (f56r–f56v); Adorno & Pautz II: 343; Hammond & Rey 232, 297.

36. Quotations from R (f55r). Information from O (63); Adorno & Pautz I: 231n1, II: 325; Krieger 108; Schaafsma & Riley 7; Riley 197.

37. R (f56r, f58r); O (62–63); Adorno & Pautz II: 323.

38. Quotations from R (f56r). Information from R (f49r–f49v, f54v–f55r); O (63); Adorno & Pautz II: 338–39.

39. R (f56v, f58r); O (64); Adorno & Pautz I: 237n3, II: 337, 342; Krieger 125.

40. R (f56r); O (63–65); Adorno & Pautz II: 338.

41. R (f55v, f56v–f57r); O (64).

42. Quotation from R (f58r). Information from Adorno & Pautz II: 325, 335, 337, 347, III: 357.

43. Quotations from R (f56r, f57r). Information from R (f57v); O (64–65); Adorno & Pautz II: 339–40.

44. Quotations from R (f57r–f57v). Information from Adorno & Pautz II: 347.

45. R (f57r–f57v); O (65).

46. R (f57v–f58r); O (65–66); Adorno & Pautz II: 348.

47. R (f58r); Adorno & Pautz I: 243n3, II: 337, 347, 362.

48. Quotations from R (f58v). Information from O (66); Adorno & Pautz II: 363.

49. Cabeza de Vaca says there were four horsemen (f58v), but Oviedo gives the number as twenty (67). The information about the harquebuses is from a manuscript fragment cited by Carl Sauer (*Road* 20). Other information from R (f60r); Adorno & Pautz II: 361–62.

CHAPTER 10. NEW SPAIN

1. Quotation from R (f58v–f59r). Information from O (66).

2. R (f59r); O (66–67); Adorno & Pautz II: 361, 363.

3. R (f59r); Adorno & Pautz II: 325, 371, 385, 387, III: 323, 354, 368; Chipman *Spanish Texas* 45. The distance from Culiacán to México (today's Mexico City) is given by Krieger 43. The Narváez survivors can have had no knowledge of explorations conducted in the 1530s by Hernán Cortés in Baja California and by Nuño Beltrán de Guzmán in northern Mexico (Adorno & Pautz II: 323, 325).

4. R (f38v, f63r); Adorno & Pautz I: 263n7, III: 107. The itinerary of the men's journey is from Krieger 2. Adorno and Pautz calculate that the distance from where the Narváez survivors started their overland journey to where they encountered other Spaniards is at least nine hundred miles (II: 384). Both Cabeza de Vaca (f63r) and Oviedo (50) say that the four men spent ten months on their overland journey, from the time of their departure from the Avavares (in midsummer of 1535) until their encounter with Alcaraz. Eighteen to nineteen months had elapsed since the four men escaped from the Mariames and the Yguases (Adorno "Negotiation" 165).

5. R (f59r); Adorno & Pautz I: 247n3, 325, II: 365. The only statements that mention dates in either of the primary accounts of the Narváez expedition are that it was around Christmastime when they came to Corazones (O: 64), that it was hot in Sonora in January (R:f58r), and that they left Culiacán on 15 May (R:f63v).

6. O (67).

7. R (f57r–f57v, f59v, f60v); O (65); Adorno & Pautz I: 328–29. Adorno and Pautz cite a sixteenth-century document that both names Diego de Alcaraz as the boldest of several slave-hunters operating on the frontiers of Nueva Galicia and indicates that trafficking in Indian slaves was lucrative (II: 362).

8. R (f55v, f59r); Adorno & Pautz II: 419.

9. O (66); R (f55v, f58r, f59r–f59v); Adorno & Pautz II: 363, 365–66.

10. R (f59r–f59v, f61v); O (67).

11. First two quotations from R (f59v). Third quotation from R (f60r).

12. Quotation from R (f59v). Information from R (f59r–f59v, f60v); O (68); Adorno & Pautz II: 363, 366–67, 371.

13. Quotation from R (f59v). Information from O (68). The conflict between Cabeza de Vaca and the slavers does not appear in Oviedo's account, but Oviedo asks rhetorically: "Do you not believe, Christian reader, that one should ponder on the difference between the ways and practices of the Spaniards that were in that land and that of the four pilgrims: the former making slaves and attacking, as told above, and the latter curing the sick and working miracles?" (67).

14. Quotation from R (f60v). Information from R (f61v); O (68); Adorno & Pautz II: 374.

15. R (f60v–f61r); O (69); Hammond & Rey 158.

16. R (f61r); O (69); Adorno & Pautz II: 377.

17. R (f61r–f61v); O (69); Adorno & Pautz II: 395.

18. Quotation from R (f61v). Information from R (f57v, f60r, f61v–f62v); Adorno & Pautz I: 265n10, II: 12–13, 368, 378.

19. R (f62r–f62v); O (69).

20. R (f62v–f63r).

21. R (f57v, f62r); Adorno & Pautz II: 395, III: 53–54, 115; Adorno "Discursive" 228. We know from the Gentleman of Elvas that Cabeza de Vaca wished to return to La Florida as its governor (Clayton, Knight & Moore 48). Cabeza de Vaca's account (f61v–f62v) of his peaceful resettlement of Indians in San Miguel de Culiacán is, according to Adorno and Pautz, "virtually the only account in print of peaceful Spanish conquest anywhere" (III: 115).

22. Adorno & Pautz III: 336; Bishop 149.

23. Adorno & Pautz III: 279, 323, 327, 333–34.

24. Quotation from Adorno & Pautz III: 368. Information from Adorno & Pautz I: 255n2, II: 325, 371, III: 316–17, 325, 340, 343, 356, 364; Elliott "Cortés" xxxvi.

25. Quotation from Todorov 134. The figure of 5,800 Indian slaves is from Chipman *Nuño* 212, 217. Other information from Adorno & Pautz III: 334, 336; Chipman *Nuño* 200–201, 208–209.

26. First quotation from Adorno & Pautz III: 326. Other quotations from Casas 65. The exchange rate of a maximum of fifteen slaves for a horse is from Chipman *Nuño* 203.

27. Adorno & Pautz III: 115, 308–309, 333, 340–41, 349; Elliott "Cortés" xxxiv; Chipman *Spanish Texas* 27.

28. Quotation from Casas 66–67. Information from Adorno & Pautz III: 344–49; Todorov 97.

29. Quotations from Casas 67–68.

30. Adorno & Pautz III: 354, 357, 359–65, 368–69; Sauer *Road* 7; Casas 66.

31. Adorno & Pautz I: 247n1, II: 348–49, III: 312, 374.

32. R (f63v); Adorno & Pautz I: 265n1; Krieger 43.

33. R (f63v); Adorno & Pautz III: 107.

34. R (f63v); Adorno & Pautz II: 385–86.

35. R (f57r–f58r, f60v, f63v); O (65); Adorno & Pautz II: 346, III: 326–27.

36. R (f63v); Adorno & Pautz II: 387, III: 326, 376–77.

37. First quotation from R (f63v). Second quotation from R (f63r). Information from Adorno & Pautz I: 265n7, II: 387–88. Both Adorno and Pautz (II: 387) and Krieger (43) say that the distance from Compostela to México/Tenochtitlán was 120 leagues. Krieger estimates that the Narváez survivors walked at least 700 miles from San Miguel de Culiacán, via Compostela, to México/Tenochtitlán (43). Adorno and Pautz estimate that their entire odyssey comprised between 2,500 and 2,800 miles (II: 389). Krieger says the four men covered a distance of between 2,300 and 2,640 miles in the fourteen months between their leaving the Avavares and their arrival in the city of México (138). He calculates that to reach that city from where they escaped from the Mariames and the Yguases, they walked 2,800 miles (144).

38. Adorno & Pautz I: 265n4, II: 392, III: 309; Clendinnen 15, 273; Mann 114; Cortés 322, 495n89, 507n56.

39. R (f63v); Adorno & Pautz III: 307–309, 311, 322–23, 333; Elliott *Imperial* 175; Elliott "Cortés" xxxiv, xxxvi.

40. Adorno & Pautz I: 385, II: 393–94.

41. R (f63v); Adorno & Pautz I: 265n7, II: 391–92, 410, 420, III: 318.

42. R (f65v, f66v); Adorno & Pautz I: 277n3, II: 392, 425.

43. Adorno & Pautz III: 314, 318, 320.

44. Quotation from Adorno & Pautz III: 126. The declaration about the absence of human sacrifice and idolatry appears both in R (f63r) and in O (70). Other information from Adorno & Pautz II: 392, III: 122, 127; Adorno "Discursive" 222.

45. Adorno & Pautz II: 393–94, III: 12.

46. Quotation from Hammond & Rey 197. Information from Chipman *Spanish Texas* 34.

47. First quotation from R (f58r). Second quotation from R (f60r). Information from R (f49r–f49v, f54v–f55r, f58v, f59v, f63r–f63v); Adorno & Pautz III: 124. Oviedo (79) challenges Cabeza de Vaca's statement in his *Relación* that he had seen "signs of gold and galena, iron, copper, and other metals," and Oviedo's challenge suggests that the information was not in the *Joint Report*.

48. Quotation from R (f56r). Information from Adorno & Pautz II: 306, 334, 338–39, III: 123–24, 127; Weddle 209.

49. Adorno & Pautz III: 23.

50. O (70); Adorno & Pautz II: 234, 394, III: 12–15, 17–18, 46; Hedrick & Riley vi.

51. First quotation from O (6). Second quotation from O (72). Information from Adorno & Pautz III: 16–17, 23.

52. Quotation from Hammond & Rey 51–52. Information from Adorno & Pautz II: 395, 421, III: 55; Chipman *Spanish Texas* 34.

Chapter 11. Further Explorations

1. Quotation from Adorno & Pautz III: 4. Information from R (f63v); Adorno & Pautz II: 395; Clayton, Knight & Moore I: 48.

2. Adorno & Pautz II: 393, 396, 425, III: 46; Reséndez 222.

3. R (f64r); Adorno & Pautz II: 396–97; Benjamin 231.

4. R (f64r, f65r); Adorno & Pautz II: 396–97; Schneider 60.

5. O (70); Adorno & Pautz II: 394, III: 13–15.

6. R (f64r–f65r); Adorno & Pautz II: 398, III: 48.

7. D. A. Howard 39; Adorno & Pautz II: 399–400.

8. R (f65r–f65v); C (95).

9. R (f57v); Adorno & Pautz II: 72, III: 4, 46, 55, 64.

10. R (f2v); Adorno & Pautz I: 295, 379, II: 402.

11. Quotation from Clayton, Knight & Moore I: 360. Information from R (f64r); Adorno & Pautz III: 54; Clayton, Knight & Moore I: 365.

12. Clayton, Knight & Moore I: 5, 47, 176n6, 251, 251n6, 256–57, 360, II: 71; Hudson 39–42, 44; Mitchem "Initial" 51; Diamond 68–70; Sauer *Sixteenth Century* 126.

13. Quotation from Adorno & Pautz II: 402. Information from Adorno & Pautz I: 380, III: 50.

14. Most of the quotations are from Clayton, Knight & Moore I: 48–49. However, "he had found cotton cloth . . ." is from Clayton, Knight & Moore I: 148. Information from Adorno & Pautz III: 47, 50; Adorno "Negotiation" 163. Two men who sailed with

De Soto, Baltasar de Gallegos and Cristóbal de Espindola, were kinsmen to Cabeza de Vaca (Clayton, Knight & Moore I: 48).

15. Quotation from Clayton, Knight & Moore I: 48. Information from D. A. Howard 30.

16. Clayton, Knight & Moore I: 5–7, 77, 115, 134; R (f38v, f48r).

17. Hudson 50; Clayton, Knight & Moore I: 50–51.

18. Clayton, Knight & Moore I: 50, 57, 81, 225, 251n7, 254, II: 72–73, 90.

19. Quotation from Hammond & Rey 51–52. Information from Adorno & Pautz II: 410–11, III: 48; Reséndez 223.

20. Adorno & Pautz II: 407–408, 411–12, 428, III: 115.

21. Adorno & Pautz II: 422–23, 426–28; Reséndez 223.

22. First quotation from Hammond & Rey 52. Second quotation from Adorno & Pautz II: 421. Coronado's version of the viceroy's acquisition of Estevanico is from Hammond & Rey 45. The alternative version is reported in Reséndez 225, 302n16.

23. Quotations from Hammond & Rey 59, 61. Information from Hammond & Rey 52–53, 59, 63; Sauer *Road* 8–9; Reid & Whittlesey 261; Casas 110–14.

24. Quotations from Hammond & Rey 64, 75, 145. Information from Hammond & Rey 65–66, 69–70, 77.

25. Hammond & Rey 66. Adorno and Pautz note that two accounts of Nuño de Guzmán's 1530–31 conquest of Nueva Galicia refer to a place called Cíbola (III: 371).

26. Hammond & Rey 67–70.

27. Hammond & Rey 70–72.

28. Hammond & Rey 73–75.

29. Quotation from Hammond & Rey 76. Information from Hammond & Rey 75–77.

30. Quotations from Hammond & Rey 78–80.

31. Sauer *Road* 24, 28, 32n37; Hammond and Rey 58, 78–79, 81, 199; Adorno & Pautz II: 422, III: 126.

32. Quotation from Adorno & Pautz II: 420.

33. Quotations from Hammond & Rey 177–78. Information from Hammond & Rey 170n11.

34. Quotation from Hammond & Rey 199. Information from Hammond & Rey 198, 298.

35. Quotation and information from Hammond & Rey 145.

36. Quotation from Cushing 174. Information from Cushing 5, 12; Hammond & Rey 56.

37. Clayton, Knight & Moore I: 56–60, 225, 252–55; Chipman *Spanish Texas* 36; Hudson 64, 85.

38. Clayton, Knight & Moore I: 71–72, 227, 267; Hudson 119–20.

39. Mann 97; Clayton, Knight & Moore I: 104, 113, 130, 137–38, 233, 243, 292, 294; Hudson 234, 284, 286, 349–50, 418.

40. Quotations from Clayton, Knight & Moore I: 146–47. Information from Clayton, Knight & Moore I: 139; Hudson 351–52, 364, 373.

41. Quotation from Clayton, Knight & Moore I: 147. Information from Clayton, Knight & Moore I: 150, 153–54, 164–65, 245–46; Hudson 380, 385, 388.

42. Hammond & Rey 83–85; Adorno & Pautz II: 428, III: 141.

43. Quotations from Hammond & Rey 243, 302. Information from Milanich & Milbrath "Another World" 21; Chipman *Spanish Texas* 40–41; Clayton, Knight & Moore I: 146–47, 244.

44. Hammond & Rey 94, 96.

45. Hammond & Rey 21, 87, 104, 106, 200, 232, 269, 364, 394–95; Adorno & Pautz III: 127; Reid & Whittlesey 263.

46. Quotation from Hammond & Rey 162–63. Information from Hammond & Rey 169, 169n9, 179, 286; Chipman *Spanish Texas* 36; Sauer *Road* 8–9; Reid & Whittlesey 261, 263.

47. Quotations from Hammond & Rey 170, 200, 208, 210. Information from Hammond & Rey 162.

48. Information from Hammond & Rey 24, 209–10, 219, 221–31, 234, 330–35; Reid & Whittlesey 264–65.

49. Quotations from Hammond & Rey 186. Information from Hammond & Rey 187, 242, 246; Reid & Whittlesey 259, 265; Milanich & Milbrath 21.

50. Hammond & Rey 264, 266–68, 270, 275, 293–94, 365, 371.

51. Quotation from Hammond & Rey 313. Information from Hammond & Rey 29, 221n2, 242n1, 314–19, 398; Adorno & Pautz III: 142.

52. Quotation from Hammond & Rey 355. Information from Hammond & Rey 30, 337–39, 340–41n2, 367. Although the captain should properly be known as López, he changed his name upon his return to Spain from García López de Cárdenas to García Ramírez de Cárdenas (Hammond & Rey 341), and therefore I have chosen to call him Cárdenas.

53. Hammond & Rey 365; Chipman *Spanish Texas* 39; Chaney & Deagan 166; Ivey.

54. Hudson et al. "De Soto's Expedition" 132, 134; Smith "Indian" 135; Mann 98; Riley 194.

55. Quotation from R (f67r). Information from Adorno & Pautz III: 46.

56. First quotation from R (Z:f1v). Other quotations from R (f2r–f2v). Information from Adorno & Pautz II: 394, III: 55.

57. First two quotations from R (f63r). Third quotation from R (f57v).

58. R (f65v); Adorno & Pautz I: 381, III: 4, 54–55, 102; D. A. Howard 39.

Chapter 12. Río de la Plata

1. C (95–96); O23 (377); Adorno & Pautz I: 381, 387, III: 102–103; D. A. Howard 40; Domínguez 32n4. Today Santa Catalina Island belongs to Brazil and is known in Portuguese as Ilha Santa Catarina.

2. D. A. Howard 40, 91, 195; Bishop 186.

3. Bishop 186; Adorno & Pautz I: 387.

4. Adorno & Pautz I: 382, 385; D. A. Howard 40; Morison *European* 298; Domínguez xv.

5. Gimlette 276, 278; "South America" 27: 587, 625, 627.

6. Gimlette xvii; "South America" 27: 625.

7. The distance in leagues between Asunción and Buenos Aires is from C (103); RG (91). Other information from Morison *European* 548–49, 568.

8. Gimlette xviii, 299; Miller 1, 3; "South America" 27: 611–12, 628–29.

9. "South America" 27: 586–87, 625–26, 628.

10. S (19); C (114); O23 (373); D. A. Howard 45–46, 54; Métraux 69, 80; Mann 10; Ganson 17–18, 22. The term "Guaraní," although used by most of the authors of my secondary sources, did not come into widespread use until the seventeenth century.

In the sixteenth century, the Guaraníes spoke of themselves as the Mbiazás, and Europeans generally spoke of them as the Carios or called them by various locally specific subtribal names (Métraux 69–70; D. A. Howard 45–46).

11. D. A. Howard 11, 38, 46, 66; Métraux 76; Gimlette 122.

12. O23 (352); Morison *European* 300–302; Domínguez xxvi.

13. C (190); Métraux 75–76; Adorno & Pautz I: 382–84, 387; Morison *European* 544–46; Gimlette 115, 117–18; Miller 9.

14. O23 (353, 356); Morison *European* 537, 539, 542, 544–47; Adorno & Pautz I: 384; Métraux 76.

15. O23 (357); Morison *European* 548–50, 552, 555.

16. Morison *European* 552–54.

17. O23 (360); Morison *European* 537, 541, 554–55.

18. Adorno & Pautz I: 380, 385; Diamond 68; Métraux 76; Morison *European* 562–63.

19. First quotation from S (5). Second quotation from O23 (364). One of the women who went with Mendoza was Doña Isabel de Guevara, who wrote a 1556 letter "To the Princess Juana" (in Parry & Keith V: 264–65). Other information from S (2, 6–7, 14, 29, 32); H (310); O23 (363); Morison *European* 563–64, 583; Adorno & Pautz I: 380, 386, III: 100; D. A. Howard 92.

20. S (5); Domínguez xv–xvi; Morison *European* 564.

21. S (4–6, 8–11); Morison *European* 565–67; D. A. Howard 38; Adorno & Pautz (I: 386); Domínguez (xxvi).

22. S (12); C (102, 243–44); O23 (368–69); D. A. Howard 58; Métraux 76; Adorno & Pautz I: 385–86; Morison *European* 567.

23. The number of 170 men is from Irala to the Emperor 265. Other information from Irala to the Emperor 265–66; O23 (371–72); H (309); S (14); Bishop 182; Adorno & Pautz I: 386, III: 98; Morison *European* 567; Métraux 76.

24. The information that 130 men went with Ayolas and 33 men stayed with Irala is from Irala to the Emperor 266. Adorno and Pautz (I: 386–87) report the number of Ayolas's men in two ways, saying first that Ayolas took 130 men in his exploring party, and then that Ayolas and all 136 of his men were lost in the Chaco. Other information from Irala to the Emperor 266; S (25–26); O23 (374); Morison *European* 568; Adorno & Pautz I: 381, 386.

25. S (13); Irala to the Emperor 266; O23 (375); Morison *European* 567; Adorno & Pautz I: 386, III: 113.

26. Adorno & Pautz I: 380–81, 386, II: 399–400; Bishop 184; D. A. Howard 59.

27. Quotation from S (20). Information from S (21); Gimlette xvi, 114, 121, 126.

28. Quotation from S (20). Information from S (22); Bishop 183; D. A. Howard 67, 69; Métraux 77; Morison *European* 569.

29. Quotation from S (20). Information from S (19–20); Métraux 80, 82–85, 88–89; Bishop 206; Bakewell & Holler 62; Ganson 18–19, 22.

30. Quotations from S (21, 19). Information from D. A. Howard 11, 66; Métraux 76; Gimlette 122.

31. Morison *European* 568; Adorno & Pautz I: 386.

32. The latitude of Asunción is from Domínguez 74n2. The distances from Asunción to Buenos Aires and to Candelaria are from C (102–103). Other information from S (22); C (125, 167); Irala to the Emperor 266; O23 (375); D. A. Howard 59, 62; Bishop 184; Métraux 77.

33. S (14); C (95); O23 (377); Serrano y Sanz II: 110; Bishop 184–85; Adorno & Pautz I: 381; D. A. Howard 92.

34. Quotation from S (28). Information from Irala to the Emperor 266; O23 (377); Adorno & Pautz I: 381, III: 103; Morison *European* 569; D. A. Howard 60, 77.

35. Quotations from O23 (380). The probable date of the massacre of the Ayolas party is from D. A. Howard 77. Other information from Irala to the Emperor 266–67; C (102–103); S (28); RG (5–7); H (314); O23 (369, 376, 379); Métraux 75; Adorno & Pautz I: 382, 386.

36. C (95); O23 (377); Adorno & Pautz I: 381; Bishop 184–85.

37. Quotations from Adorno & Pautz III: 103. Information from Adorno & Pautz I: 381, III: 102–104.

38. RG (98); Adorno & Pautz I: 388, III: 97; Domínguez xli; Morison *European* 579; D. A. Howard 181, 238.

39. C (95–96); RG (3); Serrano y Sanz II: 111–12; D. A. Howard 39, 42; Bishop 189–90; Morison *European* 570.

40. Adorno & Pautz I: xvi, 279, III: 68, 70, 326.

41. C (96); RG (3); Adorno & Pautz I: 391, III: 46, 75; D. A. Howard 45; Morison *European* 571.

42. RG (3, 7); C (104); Bishop 188–89; D. A. Howard 42–43, 92.

43. Orúe's claim is from O23 (381). Other information from C (96–97); Adorno & Pautz I: 391.

44. The latitude of Santa Catalina is from Morison *European* 544. Other information from C (98–100); RG (3); O23 (381); Domínguez xxvi; Adorno & Pautz I: 383; Morison *European* 302, 545–46; D. A. Howard 40, 45–46.

45. The estimate of the number of Guaraníes in Santa Catalina is from D. A. Howard 46. Other information from D. A. Howard 45–46; Gimlette 115.

46. RG (4); C (100); Irala to the Emperor 267; O23 (382); D. A. Howard 46, 96; Adorno & Pautz I: 382, 391.

47. RG (5); C (101); O23 (382); Adorno & Pautz I: 381, 391; D. A. Howard 50.

48. C (101–104); RG (5–7); O23 (382); D. A. Howard 48, 50, 62.

49. RG (5–6); C (101–102); H (321–22); O23 (382); D. A. Howard 112; Adorno & Pautz III: 105.

50. RG (8); C (104); D. A. Howard 49–50.

51. Quotation from Adorno & Pautz III: 104. Information from C (104–105); RG (7–8); O23 (382); D. A. Howard 143; Adorno & Pautz I: 391.

52. O23 (382); RG (9–10); C (106–107); Bishop 197; D. A. Howard 63.

53. Quotation from D. A. Howard 143. Information from RG (30); Bishop 197.

54. Quotation from RG 15. Information from RG (9–10); C (106–108, 118); Adorno & Pautz I: 391; D. A. Howard 160.

55. Quotations from RG (15–16). Information from C (108–11, 113); Domínguez 108n2; "South America" 27: 625; D. A. Howard 54.

56. Quotation and information from C (109–10).

57. Quotation from Adorno & Pautz III: 117. Information from C (109–10); RG (12); D. A. Howard 52; Adorno & Pautz I: 396.

58. C (110–11).

59. RG (11, 14); C (109); Irala to the Emperor 267.

60. C (111, 116); Benjamin 70.

61. Quotation from C (115). Other information from C (111–16).

62. C (115–16); RG (13); O23 (383).

63. C (117–18, 122); RG (11, 14); O23 (383). By Cabeza de Vaca's account, he wrote to the royal officials twice, the first time on 5 December 1541 and the second time in January 1542 (RG: 11, 14).

64. The latitude of Iguazú Falls is from C (120); Morison *European* 573. Other information from C (108, 119–20); RG (16); Domínguez 120n2.

65. Quotation from C (120). Information from Halliburton 51, 146.

66. C (120); RG (16); Adorno & Pautz I: 391.

67. C (120–21); RG (16). The width of the Paraná is from Morison *European* 574.

68. C (123). The distance from the river confluence to Asunción is from Morison *European* 574.

69. RG (17); C (122); O23 (383).

70. C (123–24); RG (12).

71. C (101, 103, 123–24); RG (5, 17, 19–20); Irala to the Emperor 267–68; D. A. Howard 60; Adorno & Pautz I: 391.

72. Quotation from RG (27). The distance in leagues of Cabeza de Vaca's overland march is from RG (15). Other information from RG (18, 22); C (125); D. A. Howard 56–57, 63; Adorno & Pautz I: 390.

CHAPTER 13. ASUNCIÓN

1. Irala says there were 400 Europeans then living in Asunción ("Memorial" 274), but both Adorno & Pautz (III: 102) and D. A. Howard (63) say there were 300. Other information from C (125); Bishop 205.

2. C (125); RG (19, 21, 30); Irala to the Emperor 268; Adorno & Pautz II: 22; Bishop 222.

3. Adorno & Pautz III: 100; Serrano y Sanz II: 245.

4. C (125); RG (18–19); O23 (383).

5. Quotation from Irala to the Emperor 269. Information from RG (19); Adorno & Pautz I: 387, III: 103–106.

6. Adorno & Pautz I: 381, III: 102; D. A. Howard 98.

7. Quotation from C (175). The illustration concerning the barter system is from Bishop 210. Other information from C (95, 134, 175); RG (28, 31–32); D. A. Howard 93–95; Adorno & Pautz III: 114.

8. Quotation from C (134). Information from D. A. Howard 92, 96, 100, 178.

9. C (170–71); D. A. Howard 100, 141.

10. RG (22); D. A. Howard 166–67. There were two men named Juan de Salazar in Río de la Plata. One was a priest of the Order of Mercy, and the other, Captain Juan de Salazar de Espinosa, was the principal founder of Asunción.

11. C (126–27); RG (22); Irala to the Emperor 268.

12. C (127–28); RG (20); D. A. Howard 64.

13. First quotation from C (144). Second quotation from RG (28–29). Information from C (129); D. A. Howard 68.

14. RG (23); C (128–29); D. A. Howard 66, 96.

15. Quotations from H (319). The number of Guaraní women given to the Spaniards is from D. A. Howard 67, and the numbers of mestizo children are from D. A. Howard 70. Other information from RG (29–30); Irala "Memorial" 274; D. A. Howard 65–68, 180; Métraux 77.

16. Quotations from RG (29). Information from D. A. Howard 68–69, 71–73; Métraux 87.

17. Quotation and information from C (129–30).

18. Quotation from RG (23–24). Information from C (129); D. A. Howard 65, 74, 76.

19. RG (24); C (135, 148); D. A. Howard 76.

20. C (131–33); RG (35); D. A. Howard 76–77; Miller 6.

21. C (136–37); RG (24).

22. Quotation from C (138). Information from C (137–38, 141, 149); RG (24); D. A. Howard 103.

23. C (138, 140).

24. Quotation from C (141).

25. Quotations and information from C (142–43).

26. C (145–46).

27. Quotation from C (147). Information from C (145–48).

28. Quotation from C (153). Information from C (152–54); D. A. Howard 80.

29. Quotation from C (155). Information from C (154–55); D. A. Howard 188; Bishop 277.

30. C (149–51, 158); RG (36); D. A. Howard 82.

31. C (150, 156–57); D. A. Howard 82.

32. RG (36); C (151, 158); Bishop 213.

33. First quotation from RG (33). Second quotation from O23 (383). Information from C (241); D. A. Howard 92; Adorno & Pautz I: 388, 391.

34. C (128, 159); RG (26).

35. RG (32); C (159, 162).

36. RG (31–32); D. A. Howard 93, 95, 100, 108–109.

37. C (159–60); RG (32); Irala to the Emperor 269; D. A. Howard 38, 49, 58, 88.

38. RG (32); C (160–61, 167); Irala to the Emperor 269.

39. C (161, 163).

40. C (163–64).

41. First quotation from RG (35). Second quotation from C (164). Information from C (163–64); S (37); D. A. Howard 86–87.

42. C (164–65); RG (30); Bishop 222.

43. Quotation from C (165). The date of the second founding of Buenos Aires is from Morison *European* 580. Other information from C (164–65); Irala "Memorial" 274, 276; D. A. Howard 64.

44. RG (34, 42); C (166–67, 177); Bishop 214, 222.

45. C (167–68); RG (32); Irala to the Emperor 269; Bishop 222; D. A. Howard 87.

46. C (168); RG (38); D. A. Howard 102–106, 122.

47. C (169–70); RG (37–39); S (38); D. A. Howard 89.

48. C (170–72); D. A. Howard 106.

49. Quotations from Irala to the Emperor 269. Information from C (173–74); S (39).

50. Quotation from C (175). Information from RG (40); C (134, 175–76); O23 (385); D. A. Howard 96, 98, 136; Adorno & Pautz I: 392.

51. C (176–77, 181); RG (42–43); D. A. Howard 98, 110; Adorno & Pautz I: 392.

52. RG (38, 43); C (177–78); D. A. Howard 110.

CHAPTER 14. THE SEARCH FOR GOLD AND SILVER

1. Quotation from C (178). Information from RG (42–43); C (125, 177); O23 (385); D. A. Howard 103, 110, 155–56.

2. C (179–84, 187, 189); Gimlette 247; Miller 9.

3. C (185–86); Irala to the Emperor 266.

4. C (186–87); D. A. Howard 112–13.

5. C (188–90); RG (45); O23 (385); D. A. Howard 114.

6. C (189–90, 192–94); D. A. Howard 119.

7. C (190, 195–97).

8. C (197); RG (38, 45); Irala to the Emperor 269; D. A. Howard 115.

9. C (197–98, 201); RG (45).

10. Quotation from D. A. Howard 116. Information from RG (45, 53, 55); C (198, 237).

11. Quotations from S (40). Information from C (168, 199–201).

12. I have adopted D. A. Howard's spelling of "Arrianicosies" (134), but alternatives are "Arianicosies" (C 271), "Arianeçoçies" (RG 49), and "Ariosicosies" (Adorno & Pautz III: 111). Information from RG (5–6, 46); C (102, 187, 197, 201–203, 205, 225); D. A. Howard 115, 138; Métraux 75.

13. C (205–206); RG (47); D. A. Howard 118.

14. C (192, 206–207); RG (44, 46); O23 (385); D. A. Howard 119–20.

15. C (207–12); S (43); RG (47).

16. C (209, 211–14).

17. C (215); RG (47–48).

18. RG (47–48); C (215–18); H (330); Morison *European* 576; D. A. Howard 121–22.

19. C (218–19).

20. Quotations from S (41). Information from RG (48); D. A. Howard 182.

21. I have followed D. A. Howard (125) in using "Ytapoa Guazú" as the name of the high hill. Information from C (218–20); RG (47–48); D. A. Howard 122.

22. First quotation from D. A. Howard 123. Second quotation from C (261). Information from RG (49); C (220); H (335); D. A. Howard 109, 143.

23. Quotation from O23 (385). Information from C (220–21); RG (49); D. A. Howard 122, 126; Adorno & Pautz I: 392.

24. Quotation from C (221). Information from RG (49); S (41); D. A. Howard 126.

25. RG (49); C (222); D. A. Howard 126.

26. C (223); RG (49); D. A. Howard 128, 138.

27. Quotation from C (224–25). Information from C (223–26); RG (50); D. A. Howard 128.

28. RG (52); C (225–27); D. A. Howard 133.

29. Serrano y Sanz II: 122–24; D. A. Howard 133–34.

30. C (193–94, 236).

31. C (207, 211, 225–26); RG (50); S (41); D. A. Howard 129–30.

32. C (228–31); RG (50–51); D. A. Howard 131.

33. C (230–32); RG (51).

34. RG (51); C (194, 231–33, 236); Irala to the Emperor 270; D. A. Howard 132.

35. RG (51–52); C (233, 236); D. A. Howard 132, 135, 149–50.

36. RG (51–52); C (236, 263–68); S (47).

37. C (45); Adorno & Pautz I: 387; Morison *European* 577.

38. Quotations respectively from S (45, 43, 49). Information from S (41–50); D. A. Howard 136.

39. RG (53); C (234–35); Domínguez 41n5.

40. RG (54); C (235); D. A. Howard 139–40.

41. Quotations from S (50–51). Information from RG (54); O23 (385); D. A. Howard 133, 140, 188; Adorno & Pautz I: 392, III: 108, 111.

42. First two quotations from Serrano y Sanz II: 132. Third quotation from Serrano y Sanz II: 123.

43. RG (57); Adorno & Pautz III: 117.

44. C (236–37); Irala to the Emperor 270; D. A. Howard 133, 141–43; Adorno & Pautz III: 114.

45. First quotation from RG (56–57). Second quotation from D. A. Howard 149. Information from RG (55–56); D. A. Howard 124, 143, 149–50.

46. First quotation from C (236). Second quotation from D. A. Howard 144. Information from RG (57); C (237); D. A. Howard 143–44.

47. Quotation from C (238). Information from RG (55); C (237); D. A. Howard 145; Adorno & Pautz I: 388.

48. Quotation from RG (58). Information from D. A. Howard 145.

49. RG (58); C (238).

50. RG (58–59); C (238–39).

Chapter 15. Mutiny

1. First quotation from C (239). Second quotation from D. A. Howard 150. Information from C (239–41); RG (18, 60); D. A. Howard 147; López-Castilla 124.

2. Quotation from Serrano y Sanz I: 340. Information from C (239–40); O23 (385); D. A. Howard 147–49.

3. RG (61); C (240–41).

4. Quotation from C (241). Instances of Cabeza de Vaca's using the terms "Comuneros" and "servants of His Majesty" are in RG (62, 67). Other information from RG (66); D. A. Howard 162.

5. Quotation from RG (62). Information from RG (64–65); C (241, 244, 247); D. A. Howard 181.

6. Quotations from C (241). Information from RG (62–63); D. A. Howard 148.

7. RG (63–64); C (242, 256); D. A. Howard 161.

8. First two quotations from C (243, 244). Third quotation from S (53). Information from RG (65); O23 (386); Irala to the Emperor 270.

9. Quotation from C (244). Information from RG (73–74, 81, 88); C (249); D. A. Howard 169.

10. C (244–47, 251–52); RG (64–67, 70, 79); H (345); D. A. Howard 153, 180.

11. First two quotations from RG (87). Third quotation from RG (73). Information from RG (74, 77–78); D. A. Howard 169–70.

12. C (245, 247); RG (66, 70); D. A. Howard 153–54.

13. Quotation from C (248). Information from C (247–48); RG (66, 70–71); D. A. Howard 169–70.

14. RG (78); D. A. Howard 148, 164–65.

15. RG (71).

16. RG (66, 68); D. A. Howard 155.

17. Quotations from D. A. Howard 156, 173. Information from RG (68–69, 83); H (346); D. A. Howard 155–56, 160.

18. First quotation from RG (72). Second quotation from D. A. Howard 166. Information from H (318, 352).

19. First quotation from C (249). Second quotation from D. A. Howard 163. Information from RG (66–68); D. A. Howard 161, 166.

20. Quotation from Serrano y Sanz II: 133. Information from RG (78); C (254); Serrano y Sanz II: 146.

21. Quotation from S (54). Information from RG (81); C (249); S (61); D. A. Howard 163, 166.

22. D. A. Howard 70, 163; Ganson 26; Gimlette 125.

23. Quotation from D. A. Howard 134. Information from RG (40, 69, 79–80); C (175–76, 250–51, 262); D. A. Howard 167–68.

24. C (244, 263); H (358); D. A. Howard 161, 185; Adorno & Pautz III: 97, 113.

25. Quotation from RG (85–86). Information from C (254–55); D. A. Howard 39, 171.

26. Quotation from D. A. Howard 173. Information from RG (96); C (256); D. A. Howard 172–73.

27. C (226, 236, 263–64, 269–70); D. A. Howard 135, 172.

28. First quotation from C (256). Second quotation from D. A. Howard 133. Third quotation from Irala to the Emperor 270. Information from Irala to the Emperor 268–70; D. A. Howard 72, 123, 181; Adorno & Pautz III: 104.

29. Adorno & Pautz III: 75; Bishop 253; D. A. Howard 154.

30. Cabeza de Vaca (RG: 85) and Schmidt (S: 53) say that the vessel was a caravel, but Hernández (C: 257) and Oviedo (O23: 386) say it was a brigantine. Other information from RG (84, 88); C (256–57); D. A. Howard 184.

31. Quotations from RG (84–85). Information from RG (88); C (257); Adorno & Pautz I: 380, 388, 393.

32. By some accounts, Luis de Miranda stayed in Asunción (D. A. Howard 185). Other information from RG (88, 90–91); C (259–60).

33. C (257); RG (91).

34. First quotation from C (258). Other quotations from D. A. Howard 148. Information from RG (92); D. A. Howard 149, 164, 185.

35. S (54).

36. Quotation from C (259). Information from RG (88–89); D. A. Howard 186.

37. RG (91–92); C (260); D. A. Howard 185.

38. RG (91, 93, 95–96); Bishop 279.

39. Quotation from C (261).

40. Quotations from C (260–61). Information from RG (93–95).

41. C (261); RG (96); O23 (386).

42. RG (96–97). Oviedo says that Cabeza de Vaca went ashore on Terceira to seek medical attention (O23: 386).

43. First quotation from C (261). Other quotations from López-Castilla 228. Information from RG (96).

44. Quotation from Adorno & Pautz I: 393–94. Information from C (262). Prince Philip served as regent of Spain from 1543 to 1556 (Adorno & Pautz I: 283n4).

45. First quotation from Adorno and Pautz I: 394. Second quotation from C (262). Information from C (261); Bishop 274; D. A. Howard 187.

1. C (262); RG (68–69, 83); D. A. Howard 187; Bishop 276; Elliott *Imperial* 171.

2. Bishop 280–81; Adorno & Pautz I: 396.

3. Cohen 262–64; Elliott "Cortés" xxxvi; Adorno & Pautz II: 387, III: 142, 307, 311, 326, 376–77; Hammond & Rey 340–41n, 398.

4. Quotation from Hammond & Rey 366–67. Information from Hammond & Rey 24, 226–27, 337, 340–41n, 367–68; Reid & Whittlesey 264.

5. Adorno and Pautz (III: 98) identify the prosecutor as Juan de Villalobos; Bishop (276) and D. A. Howard (187) identify him as Marcelo de Villalobos; and Serrano y Sanz (II: 156) identifies him as the "licenciado Antonio Villalobos." A *licenciado* is a university graduate with an advanced degree. Other information from Adorno & Pautz III: 98–99, 336; Hammond & Rey 340–41n; Bishop 276, 276n; D. A. Howard 187; Hanke 91.

6. Bishop 10, 287; Adorno & Pautz I: 393–94.

7. Quotation from RG (98). Information from RG (1); D. A. Howard 43; Adorno & Pautz III: 105.

8. Adorno & Pautz III: 104–105; Bishop 281; D. A. Howard 39.

9. The date of Cabeza de Vaca's indictment was either 20 January (Bishop; D. A. Howard) or 20 February 1546 (Adorno & Pautz). Information from Adorno & Pautz III: 97–99; Bishop 276; D. A. Howard 187.

10. First two quotations from Adorno & Pautz III: 108. Third quotation found in both Bishop 277 and Adorno & Pautz I: 396. Information from Bishop 276–77; D. A. Howard 188.

11. Bishop (280) says that Cabeza de Vaca lodged his complaint on 12 April 1546; D. A. Howard (188) says that he did so in July. Other information from RG (68–69, 83); Bishop 279; Adorno & Pautz I: 395–96.

12. Quotation from Serrano y Sanz II: 105. Information from Serrano y Sanz II: 105–107; Adorno & Pautz I: 396–97, III: 99.

13. The *interrogatorio* is in Serrano y Sanz II: 109–36. Quotations from Serrano y Sanz II: 132–33. Information from Adorno & Pautz I: 397–98, III: 99, 105–107, 111; D. A. Howard 133–34, 139–40, 188.

14. Adorno & Pautz I: 398, III: 97; D. A. Howard 134, 188; Bishop 279.

15. Quotation from Bishop 281. Information from D. A. Howard 156; Bishop 279.

16. Quotation from D. A. Howard 189. Information from O23 (386); Bishop 282.

17. Quotation from O23 (364). Information from S (62, 73–76); Domínguez 65n, 66n; Adorno & Pautz I: 387; D. A. Howard 121; Bishop 283; Morison *European* 571, 580.

18. Quotation from Parry and Keith V: 265. Information from Serrano y Sanz I: xxvi; D. A. Howard 189; Morison *European* 579; Bishop 289; Gimlette 122.

19. Quotations respectively from Adorno & Pautz I: 395, 403, 389. Information from Adorno & Pautz I: 394–95.

20. The terms *primera relación* and *segunda relación* appear in English translation in O (73, 76–77); the Spanish original is in Hedrick & Riley 156, 159–60. Quotations

respectively from O (72, 73, 79). Information from Adorno & Pautz I: 389, III: 3, 12, 18; Hedrick & Riley v.

21. In Oviedo's original textual divisions, the sections of the *Historia* relating to Cabeza de Vaca were not designated as Book 23 and Book 35. Quotations respectively from O23 (383, 386, 386, 371, 371). Information from 023 (383–86); Adorno & Pautz I: 388–90, III: 6–7, 130; D. A. Howard 189–90.

22. Quotation from C (262). Information from Bishop 281–82.

23. Quotation from Bishop 285. Information from Adorno & Pautz I: 363, 398, III: 99, 117.

24. Quotations from Bishop 286–87. Information from Adorno & Pautz I: 398–400, III: 99; D. A. Howard 180, 190.

25. Quotation from Adorno & Pautz I: 400. Information from Adorno & Pautz I: 399–401, III: 117–18; Bishop 287; Morison *European* 579.

26. Quotation from C (262).

27. Quotation from Adorno & Pautz I: 411. Information from Adorno & Pautz I: 401–402; Bishop 288.

28. Adorno & Pautz I: 406, III: 84, 87, 101, 118; D. A. Howard 199.

29. Quotation from Serrano y Sanz I: 148. Information from Adorno & Pautz III: 97, 100; D. A. Howard 161; López-Castilla 132.

30. C (266–67); Adorno & Pautz III: 101, 111–13.

31. H (318–19, 321–22, 352); Adorno & Pautz III: 113.

32. First quotation from C (120). Second quotation from R (185, 187). Information from C (115, 130, 138, 147, 155, 177–78, 194); Adorno & Pautz III: 89.

33. Quotation from Adorno & Pautz I: 209.c. Information from Adorno & Pautz I: 231.a, III: 90, 93, 95; Serrano y Sanz I: 379.

34. Quotations from Adorno & Pautz I: 283. Information from Serrano y Sanz I: 1–2; Adorno & Pautz III: 73, 87, 155.

35. Adorno & Pautz III: 112, 115, 117.

36. Serrano y Sanz I: xxviii–xxix; Adorno & Pautz III: 87–90, 100.

37. First two quotations from Serrano y Sanz I: 147–48. Third quotation from R (17). Information from Adorno & Pautz I: 402–403.

38. Second quotation from Serrano y Sanz I: 149. Other quotations from Serrano y Sanz I: 152. Information from Adorno & Pautz I: 405–406.

39. Quotations from Serrano y Sanz I: 150–51. Information from Adorno & Pautz I: 403–404.

40. Quotation from Adorno & Pautz III: 138. Information from Adorno "Discursive" 221–22, 224, 226; R (f63r).

41. Schmidt's book, originally published in German, is available in English translation in Domínguez. Quotation from S (43). Information from S (91); Domínguez xxii, xxviii, xxxii, xli–xliii, xlvii; Morison *European* 579, 583; Adorno & Pautz I: 383.

42. Quotation from D. A. Howard 190. Information from Adorno & Pautz I: 283n4; Bishop 290; Morison *European* 579.

43. Quotation from D. A. Howard 190. Information from Adorno & Pautz I: 411, II: 404; Bishop 290.

44. Quotations from Bishop 290. Information from Adorno & Pautz I: 403.

45. Adorno & Pautz I: 283, 407, 411.

46. Quotation from Adorno & Pautz I: 326. Information from Adorno & Pautz I: 331, 340, 407, 412, II: 404.

Works Cited

Seven frequently cited primary sources are identified by the following abbreviations:

C   Hernández, Pero. *The Commentaries of Álvar Núñez Cabeza de Vaca.* Published originally in Valladolid, Spain, in 1555. Domínguez 95–270.

H   Hernández, Pero. *Relación de las cosas sucedidas en el Río de la Plata.* Serrano y Sanz II: 307–58.

O   Oviedo y Valdés, Gonzalo Fernández de. Prologue and chapters I–VII of libro XXXV of *Historia general y natural de las Indias.* Hedrick & Riley 1–80.

O23   Oviedo y Valdés, Gonzalo Fernández de. Libro XXIII of *Historia general y natural de las Indias.* Edición y estudio preliminar de Juan Perez de Tudela Bueso. Biblioteca de autores Españoles desde la formacion del lenguaje hasta nuestros dias. Vol. 118. Madrid: Ediciones Atlas, 1959. 351–86.

R   Cabeza de Vaca, Álvar Núñez. *La Relación que dio Álvar Núñez Cabeza de Vaca de lo acaescido en las Indias en la armada donde iva por governador Pánphilo de Narbáez, desde el año de veinte y siete hasta el año de treinta y seis que bolvió a Sevilla con tres de su compañía.* Published originally in Zamora, Spain, in 1542. Adorno & Pautz I: 13–279. (In a dual numbering system, pages are also headed with notations preserving the foliation of the original 1542 Zamora edition of the *Relación.* Pages transcribed from the original Spanish are published face-to-face with Adorno & Pautz's English translation. The Spanish transcriptions are headed with notations, such as Z:f3r, identifying the Zamora edition, folio number, and side of the leaf [*r* for recto or *v* for verso]. The facing English translation is simply headed f3r. I have retained this numbering system in my notes.)

RG   Cabeza de Vaca, Álvar Núñez. *Relación general que yo, Álvar Núñez Cabeça de Baca, Adelantado y Gobernador y Capitan general de la probincia del rrio de la Plata, por merced de Su Magestad, hago para le ymformar, y á los señores de su rreal Consejo de Indias, de las cosas subcedidas en la dicha probincia dende que por su mandado partí destos reynos á socorrer y conquistar la dicha probincia.* Serrano y Sanz II: 1–98.

S   Schmidt, Ulrich. *A true and agreeable description of some principal Indian lands and islands, which have not been recorded in former chronicles, but have now been first explored amid great danger during the voyage of Ulrich Schmidt of Straubing, and most carefully described by him.* Published originally in 1567. Domínguez 1–91.

Adorno, Rolena. "The Discursive Encounter of Spain and America: The Authority of Eyewitness Testimony in the Writing of History." *William and Mary Quarterly* 49 (1992): 210–28.

———. "The Negotiation of Fear in Cabeza de Vaca's *Naufragios*." *Representations* (University of California Press, Winter, 1991): 163–99.

Adorno, Rolena, and Patrick Charles Pautz, eds. *Álvar Núñez Cabeza de Vaca: His Account, His Life, and the Expedition of Pánfilo de Narváez.* 3 vols. Lincoln: University of Nebraska Press, 1999.

Bainton, Roland H. *The Reformation of the Sixteenth Century.* Boston: Beacon, 1952.

Bakewell, Peter, and Jacqueline Holler. *A History of Latin America to 1825.* 3rd ed. Chichester, UK: Wiley-Blackwell, 2010.

"Bartolomé de las Casas." *The Norton Anthology of American Literature.* Gen. ed. Nina Baym. 7th ed. Vol. A: *Literature to 1820.* New York: W. W. Norton, 2007. 35–36.

Benjamin, Thomas. *The Atlantic World: Europeans, Africans, Indians and Their Shared History, 1400–1900.* Cambridge: Cambridge University Press, 2009.

Biedma, Luys Hernández de. *Relation of the Island of Florida.* Trans. John E. Worth. Clayton, Knight & Moore I: 225–46.

Bishop, Morris. *The Odyssey of Cabeza de Vaca.* New York: Century, 1933.

Burkholder, Mark A., and Lyman L. Johnson. *Colonial Latin America.* 7th ed. New York: Oxford University Press, 2010.

Cabeza de Vaca, Álvar Núñez. *Carta de las Azores.* Ed. Pablo Pastrana-Pérez. López-Castilla 221–28.

———. *Relación general que yo, Álvar Núñez Cabeça de Baca, Adelantado y Gobernador y Capitan general de la probincia del rio de la Plata, por merced de Su Magestad, hago para le ymformar, y á los señores de su rreal Consejo de Indias, de las cosas subcedidas en la dicha probincia dende que por su mandado partí destos reynos á socorrer y conquistar la dicha probincia.* Serrano y Sanz II: 1–98.

———. *La Relación que dio Álvar Núñez Cabeza de Vaca de lo acaescido en las Indias en la armada donde iva por governador Pánphilo de Narbáez, desde el año de veinte y siete hasta el año de treinta y seis que bolvió a Sevilla con tres de su compañía.* Published originally in Zamora, Spain, in 1542. Adorno & Pautz I: 13–279.

———. "Prohemio al serenissimo, muy alto y muy poderoso señor, el infante Don Carlos, N.S." Serrano y Sanz I: 147–55.

Call, James, and Frank Stephenson. "Spring Time in Florida." *Florida State University: Research in Review* 13.3 (Fall 2003): 12+.

Calvert, Albert F. *Spain: An Historical and Descriptive Account of Its Architecture, Landscape, and Arts.* 2 vols. New York: William Helburn, 1924.

Campbell, T. N. "Coahuiltecans and Their Neighbors." *Handbook of North American Indians: Southwest.* Vol. 10. Ed. Alfonso Ortiz. Gen. ed. William C. Sturtevant. Washington, D.C.: Smithsonian Institution Press, 1983. 343–53.

Campbell, T. N., and T. J. Campbell. *Historic Indian Groups of the Choke Canyon Reservoir and Surrounding Area, Southern Texas.* Choke Canyon Series 1. San Antonio: Center for Archaeological Research, University of Texas at San Antonio, 1981.

Casas, Bartolomé de las. *A Short Account of the Destruction of the Indies.* Ed. and trans. Nigel Griffin. London: Penguin, 1992.

Castañeda Nájera, Pedro de. *Narrative of the Expedition to Cíbola, Undertaken in 1540, in Which Are Described All Those Settlements, Ceremonies, and Customs; Written by Pedro de Castañeda of Náxera.* Hammond & Rey 191–283.

Chaney, Edward, and Kathleen Deagan. "St. Augustine and the La Florida Colony: New Life-styles in a New Land." Milanich & Milbrath *Encounters* 166–82.

Chipman, Donald E. "In Search of Cabeza de Vaca's Route across Texas: An Historiographical Survey." *Southwestern Historical Quarterly* (October 1987): 127–48.

———. *Nuño de Guzmán and the Province of Pánuco in New Spain, 1518–1533*. Glendale, Calif.: Arthur H. Clark, 1967.

———. *Spanish Texas, 1519–1821*. Austin: University of Texas Press, 1992.

Clayton, Lawrence A., Vernon James Knight, Jr., and Edward C. Moore, eds. *The De Soto Chronicles: The Expedition of Hernando de Soto to North America in 1539–1543*. 2 vols. Tuscaloosa: University of Alabama Press, 1993.

Clendinnen, Inga. *Aztecs: An Interpretation*. Cambridge: Cambridge University Press, 1991.

Cohen, J. M., ed. and trans. *The Four Voyages of Christopher Columbus*. London: Penguin, 1969.

Cortés, Hernán. *Letters from Mexico*. Ed. and trans. Anthony Pagden. New Haven, Conn.: Yale University Press, 1986.

Covey, Cyclone, ed. and trans. *Cabeza de Vaca's Adventures in the Unknown Interior of America*. Albuquerque: University of New Mexico Press, 1961.

Crosby, Alfred W., Jr. *The Columbian Exchange: Biological and Cultural Consequences of 1492*. Contributions in American Studies, Number 2. Westport, Conn.: Greenwood Press, 1972.

Cushing, Frank Hamilton. *Zuñi: Selected Writings of Frank Hamilton Cushing*. Ed. Jesse Green. Lincoln: University of Nebraska Press, 1979.

Deagan, Kathleen A. "The Search for La Navidad, Columbus's 1492 Settlement." Milanich & Milbrath *Encounters* 41–54.

Debo, Angie. *A History of the Indians of the United States*. The Civilization of the American Indian Series. Norman: University of Oklahoma Press, 1970.

Diamond, Jared. *Guns, Germs, and Steel: The Fates of Human Societies*. New York: W. W. Norton, 1999.

Díaz del Castillo, Bernal. *The Discovery and Conquest of Mexico, 1517–1521*. Ed. Genaro García. Trans. A. P. Maudslay. New York: Da Capo Press, 1996.

Domínguez, Luis L., ed. and trans. *The Conquest of the River Plate (1535–1555)*. London: Hakluyt Society, 1891.

Elliott, John Huxtable. "Cortés, Velázquez and Charles V." Cortés xi–xxxvii.

———. *Imperial Spain, 1469–1716*. London: Penguin, 1963, 2002.

Elvas, Gentleman of. *True Relation of the Hardships Suffered by Governor Hernando de Soto & Certain Portuguese Gentlemen during the Discovery of the Province of Florida; Now Newly Set forth by a Gentleman of Elvas*. Trans. James Alexander Robertson. Clayton, Knight & Moore I: 25–219.

Espinosa, Aurelio. *The Empire of the Cities: Emperor Charles V, the Comunero Revolt, and the Transformation of the Spanish System*. Studies in Medieval and Reformation Traditions. Vol. 137. Leiden: Brill, 2009.

Ewen, Charles R. "Anhaica: Discovery of Hernando de Soto's 1539–1540 Winter Camp." Milanich & Milbrath *Encounters* 110–18.

———. "Soldier of Fortune." Thomas 83–91.

Ewen, Charles R., and Maurice W. Williams. "Puerto Real: Archaeology of an Early Spanish Town." Milanich & Milbrath *Encounters* 66–76.

Ganson, Barbara. *The Guaraní under Spanish Rule in the Río de la Plata*. Stanford, Calif.: Stanford University Press, 2003.

Garcilaso de la Vega, the Inca. *La Florida*. Trans. Charmion Shelby. Clayton, Knight & Moore II: 25–559.

Gimlette, John. *At the Tomb of the Inflatable Pig: Travels through Paraguay*. New York: Knopf, 2003.

Goodwyn, Frank. "Pánfilo de Narváez, A Character Study of the First Spanish Leader to Land an Expedition to Texas." *Hispanic American Historical Review* 29 (1949): 150–56.

Griffith, Jim. *Saints of the Southwest*. Tucson, Ariz.: Rio Nuevo, 2000.

Guillermo, Jorge. *Cuba: Five Hundred Years of Images*. New York: Abaris, 1992.

Halliburton, Richard. *Complete Book of Marvels*. Indianapolis: Bobbs-Merrill, 1937.

Hammond, George P., and Agapito Rey, eds. and trans. *Narratives of the Coronado Expedition, 1540–1542*. Vol. 2 of Coronado Cuarto Centennial Publications, 1540–1940. 12 vols. Albuquerque: University of New Mexico Press, 1940.

Hanke, Lewis. *The Spanish Struggle for Justice in the Conquest of America*. Philadelphia: University of Pennsylvania Press, 1949.

Hann, John H. *Apalachee: The Land between the Rivers*. Gainesville: University of Florida Press, 1988.

———. "The Apalachee of the Historic Era." Hudson & Chaves Tesser 327–54.

Hedrick, Basil C., and Carroll L. Riley, eds. and trans. *The Journey of the Vaca Party: The Account of the Narváez Expedition, 1528–1536, as Related by Gonzalo Fernández de Oviedo y Valdés*. University Museum Studies, Number 2. Carbondale, Ill.: University Museum, Southern Illinois University, 1974.

Hernández, Pero. *The Commentaries of Álvar Núñez Cabeza de Vaca*. Published originally in Valladolid, Spain, in 1555. Domínguez 95–270.

———. *Relación de las cosas sucedidas en el Río de la Plata*. Serrano y Sanz II: 307–58.

Hickerson, Nancy P. "How Cabeza de Vaca Lived with, Worked among, and Finally Left the Indians of Texas." *Journal of Anthropological Research* 54 (1998): 199–218.

Hoffman, Paul E. "Lucas Vázquez de Ayllón's Discovery and Colony." Hudson & Chaves Tesser 36–49.

———. "Narváez and Cabeza de Vaca in Florida." Hudson & Chaves Tesser 50–73.

Howard, David A. *Conquistador in Chains: Cabeza de Vaca and the Indians of the Americas*. Tuscaloosa: University of Alabama Press, 1997.

Howard, Kathleen, ed. *The Metropolitan Museum of Art Guide*. New York: Metropolitan Museum of Art, 1983.

Hudson, Charles. *Knights of Spain, Warriors of the Sun: Hernando de Soto and the South's Ancient Chiefdoms*. Athens: University of Georgia Press, 1997.

Hudson, Charles, and Carmen Chaves Tesser, eds. *The Forgotten Centuries: Indians and Europeans in the American South, 1521–1704*. Athens: University of Georgia Press, 1994.

Hudson, Charles, Chester B. DePratter, and Marvin T. Smith. "Hernando de Soto's Expedition through the Southern United States." Milanich & Milbrath *Encounters* 77–98.

Hudson, Charles, Marvin T. Smith, Chester B. DePratter, and Emilia Kelley. "The Tristán de Luna Expedition, 1559–1561." Milanich & Milbrath *Encounters* 119–34.

Irala, Domingo Martínez de. Letter to the Emperor. 1 March 1545. Parry & Keith V: 265–70.

———. Memorial left at Buenos Aires. 1541. Parry & Keith V: 274–76.

Ivey, James. "An Uncertain Founding: Santa Fe." *Common-Place* 3.4 (July 2003). Web. 31 Aug. 2009.

Johnson, Willis Fletcher. *The History of Cuba*. Vol. I. 5 vols. New York: B. F. Buck, 1920.

Krieger, Alex D. *We Came Naked and Barefoot: The Journey of Cabeza de Vaca across North America*. Ed. Margery H. Krieger. Texas Archaeology and Ethnohistory Series. Austin: University of Texas Press, 2002.

Las Casas, Bartolomé de. *See* Casas, Bartolomé de las.

Lekson, Stephen H. "Was Casas a Pueblo?" Schaafsma & Riley 84–92.

León-Portilla, Miguel, ed. *The Broken Spears: The Aztec Account of the Conquest of Mexico*. Boston: Beacon Press, 1962.

López-Castilla, María del Pilar. "Alvar Núñez Cabeza de Vaca and His Narratives about the Exploration of the Río de la Plata (1540–1545)." Diss. Western Michigan University, 2010.

Lyon, Eugene. "Niña, Ship of Discovery." Milanich & Milbrath *Encounters* 55–65.

———. "Pedro Menéndez's Plan for Settling La Florida." Milanich & Milbrath *Encounters* 150–65.

Machiavelli, Niccolò. *The Prince*. Ed. and trans. David Wootton. Indianapolis: Hackett, 1995.

Mann, Charles C. *1491: New Revelations of the Americas before Columbus*. New York: Knopf, 2005.

Marrinan, Rochelle A., John F. Scarry, and Rhonda L. Majors. "Prelude to de Soto: The Expedition of Pánfilo de Narváez." Thomas 71–82.

Métraux, Alfred. "The Guarani." *Handbook of South American Indians*. Ed. Julian H. Steward. Smithsonian Institution Bureau of American Ethnology Bulletin 143. 3 vols. New York: Cooper Square, 1963. III: 69–94.

Milanich, Jerald T. *Florida Indians and the Invasion from Europe*. Gainesville: University Press of Florida, 1995.

———. *Florida's Indians: From Ancient Times to the Present*. Gainesville: University Press of Florida, 1998.

Milanich, Jerald T., and Susan Milbrath. "Another World." Milanich & Milbrath *Encounters* 1–26.

———, eds. *First Encounters: Spanish Explorations in the Caribbean and the United States, 1492–1570*. Gainesville: University of Florida Press, 1989.

Milbrath, Susan. "Old World Meets New: Views across the Atlantic." Milanich & Milbrath *Encounters* 183–210.

Miller, Elmer S., ed. *Peoples of the Gran Chaco*. Native Peoples of the Americas. Gen. ed. Laurie Weinstein. Westport, Conn.: Bergin & Garvey, 1999.

Mitchem, Jeffrey M. "Artifacts of Exploration: Archaeological Evidence from Florida." Milanich & Milbrath *Encounters* 99–109.

———. "Initial Spanish-Indian Contact in West Peninsular Florida: The Archaeological Evidence." Thomas 49–59.

Morison, Samuel Eliot. *Admiral of the Ocean Sea: A Life of Christopher Columbus*. Vol. 1. New York: Time Inc., 1962.

———. *Admiral of the Ocean Sea: A Life of Christopher Columbus*. Vol. 2. Boston: Northeastern University Press, 1983.

———. *The European Discovery of America: The Southern Voyages*, A.D. *1492–1616*. New York: Oxford, 1974.

Morison, Samuel Eliot, and Mauricio Obregón. *The Caribbean as Columbus Saw It*. Boston: Little, Brown, 1964.

Newcomb, W. W., Jr. "Karankawa." *Handbook of North American Indians: Southwest.* Vol. 10. Ed. Alfonso Ortiz. Gen. ed. William C. Sturtevant. Washington, D.C.: Smithsonian Institution Press, 1983. 359–67.

Niza, Marcos de. Report of 2 September 1539. Hammond & Rey 63–82.

Núñez Cabeza de Vaca, Álvar. *See* Cabeza de Vaca, Álvar Núñez.

Olsen, Fred. *On the Trail of the Arawaks.* Norman: University of Oklahoma Press, 1974.

Oviedo y Valdés, Gonzalo Fernández de. Libro XXIII of *Historia general y natural de las Indias.* Edición y estudio preliminar de Juan Perez de Tudela Bueso. Biblioteca de autores Españoles desde la formacion del lenguaje hasta nuestros dias. Vol. 118. Madrid: Ediciones Atlas, 1959. 351–86.

———. Prologue and chapters I–VII of libro XXXV of *Historia general y natural de las Indias.* Hedrick & Riley 1–80 (English translation), 85–163 (original Spanish).

Pagden, Anthony. "Introduction." Casas xiii–xli.

———. "Translator's Introduction." Cortés xxxix–lx.

Paniagua, Eduardo. Liner notes. *La conquista de Granada: Isabel la Católica, siglos XV y XVI.* Pneuma, 2004.

Parry, John H., and Robert G. Keith, eds. *New Iberian World: A Documentary History of the Discovery and Settlement of Latin America to the Early 17th Century.* 5 vols. New York: Times Books, 1984.

Perry, I. Mac. *Indian Mounds You Can Visit: 165 Aboriginal Sites on Florida's West Coast.* St. Petersburg, Fla.: Great Outdoors, 1993.

Pupo-Walker, Enrique, ed. *Castaways.* Trans. Frances M. López-Morillas. Berkeley: University of California Press, 1993.

Rangel, Rodrigo. *Account of the Northern Conquest and Discovery of Hernando de Soto.* Trans. John E. Worth. Clayton, Knight & Moore I: 251–306.

Reid, Jefferson, and Stephanie Whittlesey. *The Archaeology of Ancient Arizona.* Tucson: University of Arizona Press, 1997.

Reséndez, Andrés. *A Land So Strange: The Epic Journey of Cabeza de Vaca.* New York: Basic Books, 2007.

Richter, Daniel K. *Facing East from Indian Country: A Native History of Early America.* Cambridge, Mass.: Harvard University Press, 2001.

Ricklis, Robert A. *The Karankawa Indians of Texas: An Ecological Study of Cultural Tradition and Change.* Austin: University of Texas Press, 1996.

Riley, Carroll L. "The Sonoran Statelets and Casas Grandes." Schaafsma and Riley 193–200.

Rosenblat, Ángel. "The Population of Hispaniola at the Time of Columbus." *The Native Population of the Americas in 1492.* Ed. William M. Denevan. Madison: University of Wisconsin Press, 1976. 43–66.

Rosenthal, Earl. "Plus Ultra, Non Plus Ultra, and the Columnar Device of Emperor Charles V." *Journal of the Warburg and Courtauld Institutes* 34 (1971): 204–28.

Sauer, Carl Ortwin. *The Road to Cíbola.* Ibero-Americana: 3. Berkeley: University of California Press, 1932.

———. *Sixteenth Century North America: The Land and the People as Seen by the Europeans.* Berkeley: University of California Press, 1971.

Scarry, John F. "The Apalachee Chiefdom: A Mississippian Society on the Fringe of the Mississippian World." Hudson & Chaves Tesser 156–78.

———. "The Late Prehistoric Southeast." Hudson & Chaves Tesser 17–35.

Schaafsma, Curtis F., and Carroll L. Riley, eds. *The Casas Grandes World.* Salt Lake City: University of Utah Press, 1999.

Schmidt, Ulrich. *A true and agreeable description of some principal Indian lands and islands, which have not been recorded in former chronicles, but have now been first explored amid great danger during the voyage of Ulrich Schmidt of Straubing, and most carefully described by him.* Published originally in 1567. Domínguez 1–91.

Schneider, Paul. *Brutal Journey: The Epic Story of the First Crossing of North America.* New York: Holt, 2006.

Serrano y Sanz, Manuel, ed. *Relación de los naufragios y comentarios de Álvar Núñez Cabeza de Vaca.* 2 vols. Colección de libros y documentos referentes a la historia de América 5, 6. Madrid: Victoriano Suárez, 1906.

Simpson, Terrance L. "Introduction and Summary." *The Narvaez/Anderson Site (8Pi54): A Safety Harbor Culture Shell Mound and Midden,* A.D. *1000–1600.* Central Gulf Coast Archaeological Society. Sept. 1998. Web. 27 Dec. 2004.

Smith, Marvin T. "Aboriginal Depopulation in the Postcontact Southeast." Hudson & Chaves Tesser 257–75.

———. "Indian Responses to European Contact: The Coosa Example." Milanich & Milbrath *Encounters* 135–49.

"South America." *The New Encyclopedia Britannica.* 15th ed. Vol. 27. 2007.

Tarassuk, Leonid, and Claude Blair, eds. *The Complete Encyclopedia of Arms & Weapons.* New York: Bonanza, 1979.

Thomas, David Hurst, ed. *Columbian Consequences: Archaeological and Historical Perspectives on the Spanish Borderlands East.* Washington, D.C.: Smithsonian Institution Press, 1990.

Todorov, Tzvetan. *The Conquest of America: The Question of the Other.* Trans. Richard Howard. 1984. Norman: University of Oklahoma Press, 1999.

Weddle, Robert S. *Spanish Sea: The Gulf of Mexico in North American Discovery, 1500–1685.* College Station: Texas A&M University Press, 1985.

Widmer, Randolph J. "The Structure of Southeastern Chiefdoms." Hudson & Chaves Tesser 125–55.

Wilson, Samuel M. *Hispaniola: Caribbean Chiefdoms in the Age of Columbus.* Tuscaloosa: University of Alabama Press, 1990.

Yeager, Timothy J. "The Spanish Crown's Choice of Labor Organization in Sixteenth-Century Spanish America." *Journal of Economic History* 55.4 (Dec. 1995): 842–59.

Index

Cabeza de Vaca's unfitness to govern, 269; and demand by Cáceres to return to Asunción (mid-March), 269–70; *entrada* planned into land of Tarapecosies, 265; *entrada* up Río Paraguay (8 Sept. 1543), 252; excessive cruelty by Cabeza de Vaca charged by detractors, 268; formal possession taken of area, 255; Francisco de Ribera's report on Ytapoa Guazú search, 263–64; and Guajarapos country, 254; and Guaraníes, 257; and Guaraní interpreter, 258–59; hostile Indians placated with gifts, 261; and illness of many, including Cabeza de Vaca, 265, 269, 270, 271; instructions to Mendoza in approaching Arrianicosies, 262; Irala appointed *maestre de campo,* 255; and march into unchartered country to west, 259; and Mendoza's trouble with Guajarapos, 257; and Orejones Indians, 255–56; and Payaguás country, 253–54; and plots against Cabeza de Vaca by Irala and Cáceres, 259–60, 271, 272; and rainy season, 263; and return journey to Asunción, 271; return to Puerto de los Reyes demanded by men, 261; and Sacocis, Xaqueses, and Chanés, 254, 256; and Schmidt's account of mission with H. de Ribera, 266–67; skirmish with Arrianicosies resulted in chaos, 262–63; terror campaign of Sacocis, Xaqueses, and Guajarapos, 267–68; war declared by Cabeza de Vaca on Sacocis, Xaqueses, and Guajarapos, 268; and warning of rainy season onset by Cabeza de Vaca, 260–61; warrior women reported to H. Ribera, 266, 267, 301; and women offered to captains by Indians, 255; and Xarayes, 257, 263; and Yguatú channel, 254–55; and Ytapoa Guazú as goal, 260
Gómez de Santoya, Alonso, 306–307
Gonzalo (Chané Indian youth), 220
Gourd rattles, 150–51, 177

Granada, 3
Guaçani (Guaraní chief), 249
Guadalupe River, 113
Guajarapos (Indians of South America), 254, 257
Guaraníes (Indians of South America): Cabeza de Vaca's generosity to, 227; description of in sixteenth century, 212–13, 331n10; fearful of horses, 228; Guaycurúes complained about by, 240; information provided to Cabeza de Vaca, 228; lifeways of, 218–19; natives of Santa Catalina, 223–24; and relationship with Europeans, 238; and search for gold and silver, 257
Guaycones (Indian band), 139
Guaycurúes (Indians of South America), 240–43
Guzmán, Alonso Riquelme de. *See* Riquelme de Guzmán, Alonso
Guzmán, Juan Alonso de, 17–18
Guzmán, Juan de, 15, 17
Guzmán, Nuño Beltrán de: appointed governor of province of Pánuco (1525), 34, 180; arrest of in 1537 and deportation to Spain, 290; and conquest of Nueva Galicia, 182–83; Cortés on, 182; critics of, 180–81; European clothing given to Cabeza de Vaca and others, 183; as governor of Nueva Galicia (1528), 176, 290; and last days of power before arrest, 184; and mistreatment of Indians, 180; power of in New Spain, 180; war declared on Jalisco by, 181, 182

Hans (Indians on Malhado), 99, 100, 103, 109, 110, 116, 138
Hatuey (Taíno leader), 27
Havana, Cuba, 56, 186
Henry VIII (king of England), 20
Heredia, Pedro de, 294
Hernández de Córdoba, Francisco, 53
Hernández, Pero, 269; on armada launched by governor, 252; arrest of by Comuneros, 273; background of, 234; on "bad spirit" toward Cabeza de Vaca, 236; on Cabeza de Vaca's

Las Casas, Bartolomé de (*continued*)
26–27; on *encomienda* system, 14; on
Narváez, 25–26; on what Columbus
brought back, 12
Las Navas de Tolosa, battle of, 7
Las Piedras (Río de la Plata), 246–47
Laws, changes in Spanish, 179–80. *See
also* Laws of Burgos; New Laws (Leyes
Nuevas, 1542)
Laws of Burgos, 14
League, defined, 47–48, 315n25
Lebrón, Fray Alonso: adversary of
Cabeza de Vaca, 224; and friction
with Cabeza de Vaca, 229, 236; Irala
backed in coup against governor, 280;
and letters discovered, 250
Le Moyne de Morgues, Jacques, 70–71
López de Gómara, Francisco, 6
Luna, Tristán de, 207
Luther, Martin, 20

Machiavelli, Niccolò, 13
Madrid, 289
Magellan, Ferdinand, 23
Maize: in Apalachee, 73, 75, 76;
cultivation of and permanent villages,
163; in Florida, 60–61, 62, 68–69;
indigestibility of, 90; and maize
villages, 163; on overland journey,
163; in search of, 161; and seven years
without seeing cultivation of, 89; theft
of in Aute, 79–80, 87, 88
Mala Cosa (evil being), 137–38
Malaria, 265
Malhado, Isla de: Cabeza de Vaca
abandoned in, 106, 107; Cabeza de
Vaca as healer, 102–103; castaways
stranded on, 98–101; and deaths of
castaways on, 104, 106; discovery of,
94; disputed exact location, 98–99;
and funeral customs on, 104; and
Indian community structure, 103–
104, 320n44; languages of, 104; living
conditions on, 100; and marriage
customs of Indians, 105; naming of,
101; survivors fit to travel, 106. *See also*
Castaways
Maliacones (Indian band), 134–35, 139;
Christians join, 138

Mariames (Indian band), 115, 139; acting
on dreams, 122–23; cruel games
played on Dorantes by, 122–23;
Dorantes moved with, 123, 129;
Esquivel killed by, 120; and harsh
treatment of Cabeza de Vaca, 128; as
hosts to castaways, 112; lifeways of,
124–27; on mainland shore of Texas,
116; migratory range of, 123; and nut
gathering, 113
Marmolejo, María (wife of Cabeza de
Vaca), 21–22
Marriage customs, Indian, 105, 125–26
Martin archaeological site, 87
Martin skins, 90
Matagorda Island, 118, 119
Matagorda Peninsula, 118
Maximilian I (of Hapsburg), 19
Medina del Campo, 20
Medina Sidonia, house of, 15, 17, 18, 21
Méndez, 100, 117
Mendicas (Indian band), 116, 139
Mendoza, Antonio de (viceroy), 189,
215; questioning of Cabeza de Vaca
by, 186; and resolve to explore country
described by Cabeza de Vaca, 188–89;
welcoming Cabeza de Vaca party to
México, 185
Mendoza, Gonzalo de (captain), 215,
236, 241, 247, 262; on Arrianicosies,
265
Mendoza, Pedro de (governor of Río de
la Plata), 215–16, 291. *See also* Ayolas,
Juan de
Menéndez de Avilés, Pedro, 61
Mesoamerica, long-distance trade route,
166
Mesquite, 132–33, 138, 143, 144, 145
México (capital of New Spain), 184–85.
See also Tenochtitlán (Aztec capital)
Miranda, Louis, de, 284
Miruelo: assigned to find port, 59–60;
hired as pilot by Narváez, 49–50;
miscalculations of, 51, 52; and Ortiz,
85; in search of Río de las Palmas, 63;
and Tampa Bay discovered by, 84
Miruelo Bay, 60
Montalbán, Alonso de, 294
Montejo, Francisco de, 38, 39, 41, 42

CPSIA information can be obtained
at www.ICGtesting.com
Printed in the USA
LVHW030240091221
705720LV00006B/719